EAN

ISBN-13: 978-0-87687-500-1
ISBN-10: 0-87687-500-2

9 780876 875001

50895

THE BOOK OF THE
NAVAJO

RAYMOND FRIDAY LOCKE

THE BOOK OF THE
NAVAJO

RAYMOND FRIDAY LOCKE

HOLLOWAY HOUSE CLASSICS are published by

Kensington Publishing Corp.
119 West 40th Street
New York, NY 10018

The Book of the Navajo, 6th Edition
Copyright © 1976, 1979, 1986, 1989, 1992, 2001 by Raymond Friday Locke

Originally published by Mankind Publishing Company, an imprint of Holloway House Publishing

This Holloway House Classics mass market edition: July 2010

Cover: Detail of a painting by Glen Tarnowski
Based on the drawings and field notes of
Dr. Washington Matthews (c. 1882)
Cover design by Jesse Dena

International Standard Book Number 978-0-87687-500-1
Printed in the United States of America

10 9 8 7 6 5 4 3

www.kensingtonbooks.com

Raymond Friday Locke brings Navajo history and legends to life in a book that is fascinating, informative and vital to our understanding. It is the Navajo's own history taken from the authentic Navajo "Singer" tales. It is tribal history extended through two hundred years of bitter conflict with Spain, the Civil War internment by the USA in a futile search for gold on Navajo land (to finance the Union army), the evolution of the relations between the tribe and the Bureau of Indian Affairs, right up to the still on-going Navajo-Hopi land dispute and the (Tribal Council Chairman) Peter MacDonald scandal. The Book of the Navajo is a work that shows us why the Navajos face a uncertain future that demands America's attention.

"Many books have been written about one or more aspects of the Navajo Indians. Many touch on their history or culture or legends. This work covers all these areas and more. The book first appeared in 1976. In this new (revised third) edition the author makes it clear in his introduction that the work is not a rehash of other books on the Navajo. In fact, much of the material found between this work's two covers came from the Navajo people themselves."
 — *The American Book Collector*

"Locke writes splendidly; (*The Book of the Navajo*) is history laced with data, you-are-there commentary and poetic symbolism. He rarely minces words."
 — *The Boston Globe*

"*The Book of the Navajo* is beautifully written and gives a much needed view unfettered by anthropological conjecture."

 — *Dr. Ray Brandes Chairman,*
 Department of History
 University of San Diego

THE BOOK OF
THE NAVAJO

ABOUT THE AUTHOR

Raymond Friday Locke was the founding editor of Mankind, the internationally acclaimed magazine of popular history. He edited the Mankind/Hawthorn Great Adventures of History series. He has published extensively in the fields of the American West and Native American history and has guest lectured on American Indian culture and history at several schools and universities. He recently completed and extensive research project on the Indians of Southern California.

Mr. Locke lives in Studio City, California. He is a member of several historical associations and foundations and has served on the advisory boards of such organizations as the Urban Indian Development Association and the American Indian Scholarship Fund. He was a member of a Navajo Tribal ad hoc committee (Chaired by Dr. Edgar Kahn of the London School of Economics) to study the social, economic and cultural results of the recent relocation of Navajos from their ancient homelands.

His book on Navajo mythology and folk tales, Sweet Salt, first published in 1990 will be reissued in paperback in the fall of 2001 by Mankind.

•CONTENTS•

PART FIVE: The Long Walk

PART SIX: The Way Back

Maps

INTRODUCTION
The Navajos and American Indian History

In the introduction to the first edition of this book, published in 1976, I complained, rather strongly, that the Navajos had not been given a fair shake by historians and cited "army, missionary, and Indian Bureau reports" and lumped in Spanish colonists and priests as sharing the blame. Now, twenty-five years later I don't see any reason to revise that complaint; as a matter of fact a few more culprits could be added to that list, including a few Navajos, themselves.

In the 1976 edition I also quoted the western historian and journalist Charles Fletcher Lummis who, among other accomplishments, founded the Los Angeles City Library system and can rightly be called the father of the wonderful but presently troubled Southwest Museum of Los Angeles. In his book *The Land of Poco Tiempo*, Lummis called the Navajo "sullen, nomad, horse-loving, horse-stealing vagrants of the saddle: pagans first, last and all the time, and inventors of the mother-in-law joke gray centuries before the civilized world awoke to it."

Well *certainly* no one is writing that sort of thing anymore. Are they? Lummis originally voiced his opinion in one of a series of dispatches to the *Los Angeles Times* while supposedly walking to California from his home in the east to take a job with that publication. What he was really doing was gathering a lot of publicity for himself and his new employer but that is another story.

I single out Lummis because he held his opinion of Navajos (and Indians) in common with many writers who were just as vitriolic--and just as ignorant--before and since. My point was (and is) that very often people, and especially when writing about Indians, come equipped with preconceived ideas and prejudices. They tend to either like Indians too much or not at all. They (and a good example of this "they"was film maker John Ford) tend to look on Indians, both past and present, as "dirty Indians" or "noble savages" and form their impressions after the most cursory exposure, as did Lummis. John Ford and John Wayne had plenty of time to review first impressions while making all those films with Navajos up in Monument Valley. The Navajos played tit for tat and got them (and a couple of other film makers) pay back. See "The Searchers" or "Cheyenne Autumn" with an audience of Navajos who will hoop and holler much the same as a"Rocky Horror Film" audience. When Ford (or whomever) told the Navajo players to "speak Indian" they did, commenting on the stars, producers, directors (especially if it was Ford), the script and whatever else came to mind, none of it favorable. So much for the *Bilagaana*.

White Americans, referred to by the Navajo as *Bilagaana*, from the beginning, found it difficult to deal with the Navajo, primarily, because, like Lummis, they made little effort. The culture and spiritual beliefs are in direct opposition to "western culture" and the Bilagaana find this disconcerting, to say the least, and always have. (To keep the record straight here, a Bilagaana can, in the larger meaning of the word, be any white person, although there is another word for Mexicans). Sometimes the word is used, with tongue in cheek, for "city Navajos."

The Spaniards came in the 1500s offering the Dine new gods and a new way of life. The only thing the Navajo wanted from them were their sheep and horses. Those descendants of Spain, for the most part, still hadn't caught on when the United States took claim of Dinetah--the Navajos name for their homeland--from Mexico in 1846. The Bilagaana still have not caught on.

I've watched them over the years. Do Gooders, social workers, missionaries, government employees, tourists and just plain meddlers. At Chinle, Window Rock, Kayenta, Ganado, wherever they get out of their cars, buses, "rolling homes" (as the Navajo sometimes call RVs) and trucks, with the expectation of being welcomed with open arms in exchange for sympathy, religion, "white culture" or some such nonsense.

A haughty look and quick withdrawal from a too eager handshake often results in bitterness on the part of the Bilagaana. It has always been so and Navajos (who would, instead, welcome respect for their way of life, their religion and culture and, perhaps, a decent price for what they have to sell) have always been misunderstood, and almost always paid for the cultural clash in the end. It has been that way throughout recorded history. In the summer of 1992 I heard an Anglo tourist in Window Rock refer to Navajo religion as "devil worship." Of course it is no such thing. The devil belongs to Jews and Christians. In Navajo belief Coyote is a "devil" but no comparison between that rascal and the Christian devil can be made.

There was a time when historians and anthropologists almost always wrote about the Navajos within the context of Anglo-American history. However, I am glad to say that has changed somewhat within the last thirty or so years, although far too many journalists are still guilty of the practice. For example, there was an article published by an Associated Press writer in 1998 in the Los Angeles Times on the infamous division of Hopi/Navajo joint use land. The writer had not a clue that the land was originally set aside as "joint use land for the use of Hopi, Navajo and other Indians" by the federal government.

This sort of thing was actually started by the early Spanish chroniclers who somehow arrived at the conclusion that the Navajo were recently arrivals in the Southwest and, therefore, had far less business being there than they did. After all they were bringing the gift of Christianity to the Navajo and to show their appreciation, the Navajo in turn were stealing their horses and sheep.

Can we really believe 17th century writers when they state that the Navajos incessantly made war on the Pueblo Indians before the Europeans entered the American Southwest and conquered and made allies of those "town Indians"? It was not until the 1960s that American historians such as Jack D. Forbes began to re-examine the spectrum of Navajo-Spanish and Navajo-Pueblo relations and came to the conclusion, as I have, that the Navajos were more often the victims of Spanish aggression than viceversa. Of course, a people who puts up a fight against an enemy who controls the writing of history is hardly ever given praise or credit.

Actually there is no real evidence that the Navajos made war on the Pueblos to any extent before Onate marched up the Rio Grande to settle his Spanish Colonists in New Mexico in hope of gaining riches for himself and the king of Spain. Only a few years before his arrival the Navajos joined the people of Acoma in an attack on a Spanish expedition. The evidence indicates that the Navajos and Pueblos generally enjoyed a live-and-let live relationship prior to the entry of the Spaniards into the arena of the Southwest. At times the Navajos--or a group of Navajos--would be at war with one group (or village) of Pueblos while remaining on trade terms with others. For instance, the Navajo often quarreled with the Hopi, but there is very little history of them fighting with the nearby Zuni.

Once the Spaniards came to the Southwest to stay, and made vassals of the Pueblos--with the notable exception of the Zuni and Hopi--the entire spectrum of Indian relations underwent a change just as it had in Mexico when those Europeans conquered the Aztecs. The Navajos categorically rejected Spanish culture and religion--but not their horses and sheep. They incessantly warred on the invaders from Europe and, by extension, often their Indian allies. On the other hand, Pueblos (and especially the Tiwas of Jemez) often, either covertly or openly, joined the Navajos in raids on Spanish livestock. At any rate, Spanish chroniclers conveniently (for their view of history) decided the Navajo had always been enemies of the Pueblos, ignoring the fact that they, themselves, were the real enemy.

And an American military commander, during the American Civil War, was so convinced that "fields of gold and other precious metals" lay under the Navajo homeland, that he turned loose a war of genocide on the Dine. At the time the United States was engaged in a war that was, to great extent, over black slavery, Commander James H. Carleton and Christopher "Kit" Carson were criss-crossing Dinetah in a war of extermination. Ute allies were told they could take any Navajos they captured as slaves. Others were allowed to be sold into Mexico. Eight thousand people--men, women and children--were marched over three hundred miles across New Mexico, where they were kept without sufficient food, water or shelter for four years.

The Navajos were told they were being punished because they'd made war, not on Americans, but on the Spaniards and the Mexicans whom the Americans had, so recently, engaged in war themselves. That was entirely beside the point; it was those "fields of gold and other precious metals" that Carleton was after and he'd convinced his superiors in Washington that once the Navajo were out of the way, those fields could be harvested to help pay for the "war against slavery." What it came down to was that Carleton had convinced Abraham Lincoln to exterminate and make slaves of an entire nation of Native Americans to support a war to free black slaves imported from Africa.

As it turned out there was no gold or other precious metals and the military department found itself having to beg and borrow funds to try to feed, clothe and guard eight thousand starving Navajos for four years. There was no work for them to do--except to dig roots for firewood as far as twenty miles away--nor a way of making a living in that piece of desert next to the Pecos River to which they'd been exiled.

Eventually the Navajo were allowed to go home and occupy a small portion of their old homeland. If they'd learned anything from that bitter experience they still refer to as "the long walk" they'd learned that letting the Bilagaana get too close could be painful and costly. A recent and costly--for everyone--Hopi and Navajo land dispute which was orchestrated by latter day Bilagaana brought that point home again. And, and again, some eight thousand Navajo have been removed from their homes and, once again, they are the victims of a very tragic blunder on the part of the Bilagaana government that will, it is estimated, end up spending more than five hundred million dollars as a result.

Yes, indeed, the Navajo people welcome you as a visitor but only as long as you remember that you are a visitor and act accordingly. Would you go into the home of friends and ask them to show you "how they dance" or shove a camera in their faces over and over while they're going about their daily chores? Or suggest, as I heard a group of tourists do in the winter of 1987—as Lummis had done nearly a hundred years before—they have "no culture, religion or history of their own." The complexity of Navajo "religion" is overwhelming, still, to me, and I've been studying it for more than thirty years.

Well into the twentieth century historians were convinced that the first Native Americans arrived in the Americas about the time of Christ. However, in 1926, the prescribed doctrine of a recent peopling of the New World was subjected to a new look when an African-American cowboy named George McJunkin came upon some gigantic bones along with stone spear points near Folsom, New Mexico. In the scientific investigation that followed it was learned that the bones belonged to Taylor's bison, an animal that had been extinct for at least ten thousand years. The bison had been killed by the spears. Subsequent investigations revealed that ancient man, of what came to be called the Folsom culture, had hunted Taylor's bison from Canada to Texas ten thousand years ago.

The discovery of Folsom man eventually led to the discovery of the Llano or Clovis culture. Clovis man used d distinctive spear point and the Clovis points as well as other artifacts associated with the culture have been found from Alaska to Mexico and in every one of the contiguous states. Clovis preceded Folsom man by at least two thousand years.

Finally, in 1936, archaeologists discovered evidence of a still earlier man in a cave in the Sandia mountain range just east of Albuquerque. From bones left beside ancient campfires, people of the Sandia culture were hunting horses twenty-five thousand years before the Spaniards reintroduced a later version of that animal to New Mexico.

Ten millennia before Christ, ancestors of the American Indian developed the facility for killing mammoths. Twelve thousand years ago he hunted caribou in what is now New York. inhabited a cave in southern Illinois, lived on the shores of a long forgotten lake in California's Mohave Desert and hunted in the woodlands of Alabama. If we subscribe to the prevailing theory that he crossed over the Bering Strait from Asia, then he followed his prey down through the Isthmus of Panama to the southernmost tip of the New World where, in Fels Cave at Tierra Del Fuego, Chile, he roasted the flesh of camels and horses over his campfire ten thousand, seven hundred years ago and left the bones to be dated by carbon fourteen in the twentieth century.

Indians were cultivating corn in central Mexico six thousand years ago—three millennia before the bow and arrow made its appearance in the New World.

At about the time, or shortly after, Roman Emperor Octavius Augustus charged architect Marcus Vitruvius Pollio with rebuilding Rome, the Tiwanaku (also written as Tiahuanacu) embarked on a building program that would have staggered the imagination of those proud Romans who found Rome a city of clay and left it a city of marble. South of Titicaca, thirteen thousand feet above sea level in the Andes, they mined massive blocks of stone that weighed as much as one hundred tons, transported them several miles over mountainous terrain and, without the use of mortar, fitted them with a precision and exactness in cutting, squaring, dressing and notching that amazes architects even today. The monumental capital city of the Tiwanakans boasted a complex underground sewer system built with finely fitted stone to carry waste water away at precisely calibrated grades.

The tale of dozens of other Indian civilizations such as the Maya, Toltecs, Incas, the Anasazi, and even the Aztecs, whose capital, Tenochtitlan, was said by Cortes to rival the splendor and size of Venice, could be related here. The evidence that the people we call "Indians" have been here a very long time and produced societies that have rivaled those of the Old World in "civilzation" cannot be denied. But this book deals with a people who, in light of evidence to the contrary, arrived in America comparatively late and reached a zenith of power only after and, to an extent, because of contact with Europeans.

It is not possible to trace the arrival of the Navajos and their linguistic cousins, the Apaches, to the American Southwest, although there have been numerous attempts to do so. In Part One of this book I discuss the prevailing theory that they recently migrated from Northwest Canada, Alaska and the Pacific Coast where other Athapascan speaking people are to be found, but dating the arrival of the Athapascans in the Southwest is not the purpose of this book.

No need really exists to account for such. What is important is that some time in the distant past the Navajos did arrive in the American Southwest, they did confront three overwhelmingly stronger cultures from which they borrowed what they could use and, in spite of the fact that two of the dominant cultures tried by every means possible to destroy them, they survived.

The Navajos are still resisting a dominant culture. The great majority have chosen not to become carbon copies of white Americans and are successfully retaining their unique culture, their ceremonies, legends and, to a great extent, their way of life. It is no longer unusual to encounter young Navajo college graduates who have returned to Dinetah to live and who still practice the ancient Navajo Way (there is no word for religion in the Navajo language. therefore it cannot be said a Navajo practices "religion" unless he is a Christian).

Much of the material in this book was derived from the Navajo themselves. The remainder is based on published and unpublished works, from reports of agents and workers in the field, from Department of the Army and Department of the Interior and other government files. Direct quotes are credited within the text with the name of the author and the date of the work.

I have departed from the usual format for this sort of study. Navajo society is very complex, and I must admit that, for the sake of clarity and a consideration of space limitations, I have but skimmed the surface in many instances. I have preceded the history of Navajo-Spanish and Navajo-American relations with an introduction to The People and their way and also a shortened version of their Creation and Emergence Story (in 2001 I am updating my book, *Sweet Salt* which contains a much longer and more detailed version of the "main stalk" story of the Navajo. I have drawn heavily on Navajo versions of the history of the Dine (the Navajo name for themselves).

It is not possible to single out each and every individual] who gave help in the preparation of a book of this size and scope. Various individuals helped with requests for research materials at the Southwest Museum Library, The University of California Library at both Los Angeles and Berkeley, The University of Arizona and Arizona State University libraries, The Heard Museum in Phoenix, The Museum of Navajo Ceremonial Art in Santa Pe, Navajo Tribal Museum and Library, and in supplying me Materials and information from the Round Rock Demonstration School at Round Rock, Arizona, Navajo College library and collections at Tsalie, Arizona, and elsewhere, and to them I owe a deep debt of gratitude.

Among those who assisted with in-the-field research on the reservation and to whom I owe a special note of appreciation are Larry Issacs, Jr. LL.D., now of Leupp, Arizona, John Cook, Cliff Gorman, and Charlie Vail of Canyon de Chelly, Harold Drake and his lovely family of Navajo Mountain, the late Harry Goulding of Monument Valley, Mary Shepardson of Palo Alto, California, and, in particular, the Cato Sells family of Window Rock. The Navajo artist, R. C. Gorman, gave his encouragement to the project as did the late Navajo historian, educator, and former tribal council chairman, Paul Jones.

Dozens of Navajos, some of whom prefer to remain nameless, willingly gave their aid in many ways and by just extending friendship and hospitality. The aid of Elizabeth Sells of Window Rock and the late Shirley Sells Teller of Fort Defiance in securing rare research materials and giving constant support to this project over a period of many years was invaluable, as was the friendship of the entire Sells family. The late Singer Manuelito Begay, a descendant of the famous headman, Manuelito, can be credited for the inspiration for this project and whatever else I may do on the Navajo.

Lastly, I would like to take this opportunity to express my sincere appreciation to Dr. Ray Brandes, Chairman, Department of History, University of San Diego, for reading the manuscript and making valuable margin notes, most of which were incorporated in the final draft, to Ronald J. Schnell who helped with the library research and to Marianne Greenwood for serving as my in-the-field research assistant. I wish to thank Edith Bornstein Shakell who spent many long hours typing and retyping the manuscript. A note of thanks is due Dr. Edgar Kahn, the late Ninabah Kahn and the late Ruth Green for their friendship and help in research done after the first edition of this book was written. Too, I would like to express my joy is having known, however briefly, those great Navajo leaders who have left us since the last edition of this book was published. Certainly included among their number are Annie Dodge Wauneka, and Carl Gorman.

Raymond Friday Locke
Studio City, California
July 20, 2001

PART ONE
Dine: "The People"

One
The Navajos: An Introduction to The People

]

Virtually all that most white Americans know about the largest Indian tribe in the United States is that they are called the Navajo; the women weave beautiful blankets, often dress in long full skirts and loose blouses of bright-colored velveteen and the men (and some women) design and make beautiful silver jewelry and often wear their hair long and tied in a "knot" at the base of the neck or banded with colorful silk scarves; they live in funny-looking little round houses called hogans and the smiling children herd the family sheep.

And of their history little more is taught in secondary schools than this definition from John Stoutenburgh Jr.'s *Dictionary of the American Indian:* (Navajo) This was a strong athapascan tribe that lived in Arizona and New Mexico The Navajos were visited by Onate in 1597. The Navajos were very warlike and usually won their battles against the whites. They were beaten by Colonel "Kit" Carson, who attacked them in 1863 and killed most of their sheep and so more or less starved them into submission. In 1867 there were seven thousand three hundred Navajos held in prisons. In 1906 there were over twenty-eight thousand Navajos, spilling out of the boundaries of their allotted reservation. In a treaty with the United States signed at Canyon de Chelly in Arizona on September 9, 1849, the

Navajo made peace and acknowledged the rule of the United States."

Between those few stilted sentences of "Navajo history" is concealed one of the epic tales of mankind; the history of a people who brought a halt to the Spanish advance in the American Southwest and fought, often against overwhelming odds, to keep their homeland. They succeeded in not only retaining their tribal identity but also much of their culture even after a crushing defeat administered by the Americans.

The Navajos successfully resisted the Spanish and their Indian allies for almost three hundred years in what amounted to a continuing war, and they most often held the upper hand. Their war with the United States lasted for two decades and in the end they were not just defeated; they were a beaten people, starved into submission and eight thousand of their number, men, women and children, were marched three hundred miles across New Mexico and imprisoned for four long years. During their imprisonment those that survived subsisted on the most meager rations imaginable . . . rations that often consisted of rancid bacon and weevily flour deemed unfit to be eaten by their soldier guards. Taken from their burning hogans—a shelter that is warm in the winter and cool in the summer—by Kit Carson's soldiers, they were given no shelter in return at their Bosque Redondo prison. Almost overnight a people with a culture far in advance of that of any of their neighbors was turned into a nation of beggars, living in the open and eating coffee beans and raw flour to stay alive. Their gods, they said, had deserted them.

Finally the Navajos were returned to their beloved homeland because the United States government was tired of feeding them and simply didn't know what else to do with eight thousand prisoners of war. They returned to the land they called *Dinehtah* pitifully poor, ill of body and ill of soul. They had signed a treaty promising to remain at peace forever for which, in return, they were to receive token replacements for their sheep and other livestock that had been systematically killed by Carson's soldiers, and an American teacher for every thirty of their children. They kept their part of the treaty in spite of the great temptation to raid the New Mexican neighbors who had caused most of their problems. From that low point in their history, just a little over a hundred years ago, the Navajos have, primarily through their own efforts, become the largest and one of the richest tribes of Indians in the United States. There were no miracles to account for their recovery . . . and certainly none performed on the part of the United States government that failed to honor its treaty with the Navajos. The Navajos survived through an innate sense of "oneness" that compels them to help each other both in times of wealth and in times of poverty.

But that oversimplified explanation of the recovery of the Navajo Nation is far from complete. The true story of their survival can only be found in studying their culture, a culture so strong that it remains almost completely unaltered in spite of the extreme effort made to obliterate it first by the Spaniards and later by American government officials and Christian missionaries. Theirs is a cultural concept that is as foreign to most white American as is that of the Afghans of Afghanistan. Their concept of family relationships, of man's relation to the world around him and his place in the order of things, is directly opposed to that of Anglo-American society. The Navajo's concept of religion is so total that it can be said that there is no such thing as religion in Navajo culture because everything is religious. Everything a Navajo knows—his shelter, his fields, his livestock, the sky above him and the ground upon which he walks—is holy. The Navajos for the most part, have long resisted Christianity. They look upon it as a "part-time" religion where a man's god is available to him for only a few hours on Sunday and then has to be sought out in a special house where his spirit dwells. From the beginning, the Navajos were repulsed by the European's disrespect for and misuse of the land, for the land is the Earth Mother, she who gives life to humanity. A society that would destroy the source of life and worship an abstract god in a place set aside for that purpose has, historically, had little to offer the Navajo. For there is nothing more revered nor more loved by the Navajos than the land they call *Dinehtah.*

Today about one hundred thirty thousand Navajos live on their reservation which encompasses about twenty-four thousand square miles of rugged, semi-arid land in the states of Arizona, New Mexico and Utah. The reservation, which is about the size of the state of West Virginia, is crowded and several thousand Navajos spill over into adjacent lands, some of which are owned by individuals and others by the Navajo tribe.

It is a land of flat alluvial valleys where stretches of sagebrush are interspersed with groves of pinyon and juniper trees; of rolling upland plains and high pine-clad mountains and brightly colored mesas. In this land deep mysterious gorges and towering cliffs of spectacular beauty abound. But it is also a hard land and farmers still depend upon irrigation to grow crops of corn, beans, pumpkins and melons much as they did in the time of Christ.

Here and in adjacent lands have been found evidence of the earliest known habitation of man in the Western Hemisphere. Here too, about two thousand years ago evolved the first known civilized American Indian culture in what is now the continental United States, that of the Anasazi as they are called after a Navajo word meaning the "ancient ones." It was to this land that a wandering tribe of mysterious origins came about a thousand years ago. And once these people reached this land they settled down and became tillers of the soil, and as much a part of this beautiful land as the deep red canyons and tall pine trees of its mountains. Little wonder that strong men cried when told they could leave their prison camp in 1868 and return to their beloved *Dinehtah*. For many centuries their ancestors had loved, respected and lived in harmony with the land. This was their land of the rainbow.

> "This is your home, my grandchild!"
> He says to me as he sits down beside me;
> "My grandchild!
> "I have returned with you to your home,"
> He says to me as he sits down beside me;
> "Upon the pollen figure I have returned
> to sit with you, my grandchild!"
> He says to me as he sits down beside me;
> "Your homes are yours again—
> "Your fire is yours again—
> "Your food is yours again—
> "Your mountains ranges are yours again,
> my grandchild,"
> He ways to me as he sits down beside me.
> —*Navajo song*

TWO

Athapascan Ancestors

First there was the beautiful and rugged land. And then came the people to the land and they called themselves *Dineh.* But they, the descendants of those Athapascan-speaking people, would come to be known by many names. *Dineh* (or *Diné*), their name for themselves, cannot be translated exactly into English as there are no articles in the Navajo language. The translation, "The People," is formally permissible and accepted by most linguists and anthropologists, but *Dineh* can also be translated as "men," or "people" or even "earth people."

They became known by many names in other languages, not a few of which meant "enemy" and not all of them as flattering as that. For example, the Hopi called them the Tasavuh which, loosely translated, meant "head pounders" because of their habit of killing their enemies by pounding them on the head with a stone axe. Finally they became universally known by the name which the Spanish called them—the Navajo.

According to Navajo tradition their ancestors, after many generations of wandering through inhospitable lands, came together and settled in a new land in this, the fifth world of their mythology. This land was called *Dinehtah*—the land of The People. *Dinehtah,* or Old Navajoland, was bounded on the North by the La Plata mountains of Colorado, on the East by the Sierra Blanca in Colorado and the Pelado Peak, twenty miles east of Jemez, New Mexico, on the South by Mount Taylor and the Zuni mountains in central New Mexico and on the West by the San Francisco Peaks near Flagstaff, Arizona, which is roughly the area of extended Navajo occupation today. The tradition of an early Navajo occupation, centered in the eastern half of this area, is borne out by the fact that archaic Navajo place names abound within these boundaries, and especially that portion in the region of Governador Canyon, New Mexico. This area also figures prominently in the ancient legends of the Navajos which are discussed in detail in Part Two of this book.

It was supposed until recently that the ancestors of the Navajos did not arrive in *Dinehtah* until about the time or shortly before the Spanish penetration of the American Southwest, or about 1540. In the opinion of anthropologists Frederick Webb Hodge and Albert H. Schroeder the Navajos and other Athapascan-speaking tribes were still in the process of migrating south as late as 1600. But with the twentieth-century development of the science of dendrochronology, or tree-ring dating, by Dr. Andrew E. Douglass, it has been determined that the ruins of hogan-type dwellings such as those used by the Navajos, and only by the Navajo in the Southwest, were constructed in what is now western Colorado about 1000 A.D. Too, a Navajo homesite, dated by dendrochronology at approximately 1380 A.D., has been found south of Gallup, New Mexico. This finding, incidentally, places Navajos in the area of the first contact between the Indians of the American Southwest and the Spanish conquistadores searching for their fabled Seven Cities of Cibola. This also gives credibility to the Navajo oral tradition that has their ancestors arriving in the area of Chaco Canyon, just northeast of Gallup at the time the great Anasazi pueblo there was being constructed—between the years of 900 A.D. and 1130 A.D. And, too, pottery of a kind made by Athapascan-speaking tribes has been found in Governador Canyon in association with tree-ring dates of 710-875 A.D.

Spanish chroniclers and, by extension, the early Anglo historians who authored the first English-language Southwest histories assumed that the "nomadic" Athapascans arrived in the Southwest in one great wave by traveling down the eastern slopes of the Rocky Mountains and displaced the Anasazi from their magnificent cliff dwellings in the Four Corners area, causing the latter to disperse and some of their number to migrate to the Rio Grande valley and build the pueblos there. We now know that the Anasazi abandoned their large settlements primarily because of drought and the arrival of the wandering ancestors of the Navajos and Apaches had little, if anything, to do with the dispersal of the Anasazi. According to Navajo tradition their ancestors arrived in *Dinehtah* not in one large group of fierce migrants but in small poverty-stricken groups, some of which came from the West, probably from the coast of California and Oregon where there were pockets of Athapascan-speaking peoples.

The diffusion of the Athapascan language family, or *Tinneh*, has been equated—specifically by the historian Hubert Howe Bancroft—with that of the Aryan or Semitic nations of the Old World. The Tinneh exists in three major divisions, the Southwestern Apacheans (Navajo and the various Apache groups), the aforementioned Pacific Coast group and the Canadian-Alaskan group. This last group has long been regarded as the largest, most important and, therefore, the root stock of the southern Athapascans. But the importance of the Canadian-Alaskan group has been questioned in recent years by such Athapascan history scholars as Grenville Goodwin and Jack D. Forbes who said: "In all probability . . . the southern division was as large as the northern in pre-European contact times and cannot be considered an offshoot of the northerners . . . future studies may, in fact, indicate that the southern division was the largest of the three." (Forbes, Oklahoma, 1960: xiv.)

Forbes and others have pointed out that the three divisions of Athapascans have very little in common culturally while closely culturally resembling their immediate neighbors, indicating a separation of many centuries.

At any rate it is unreasonable to presume, as did the Spanish and early American historians, that a poor, wandering but fierce group of nomads, seed gatherers and hunters, dressed in skins and woven plant fibers, could have possibly dislodged a much stronger and far more culturally advanced people such as the Anasazi from their stone and mortar pueblos. The presumption was, of course, based on the theory of a very recent migration of all Indians from Asia, one wave coming on the heels of another and displacing the first, pushing it farther south and being pushed in turn. In light of the fact that the native Americans have been in the New World for at least twenty-five thousand years and possibly twice that long, migrations of people not only from north to south but from south to north were not only possible but highly probable.

Interestingly, this theory adheres to a Navajo tradition. It is said that while a group of their ancestors were in the process of migrating *east* to *Dinehtah* in search of a "like people" they had heard about who lived in that land, a group of their kin grew disheartened and wandered off far to the North where they still live today. The Navajos refer to these people as the Break-Away or Live-Again people. In one version of the story of these people who went north, twelve Navajos were sent to find them two years after they had departed. It took six months for the Navajos to travel far to the North where the Break-Away people lived and when they saw them they said: "Here are the *Dineh*, living again." They had already concluded that these Break-Away people had died or had been killed by enemies so they named them the Live-Again Dineh.

The Navajos invited these kinsmen to return to *Dinehtah* with them but they refused, whereupon the Navajos became angry and told them, "You will not be our people anymore!" and returned home. The Navajos say this happened a very, very long time ago. But in 1893 when a Navajo agent named E. H. Plummer took a party of Navajos to the Chicago World's Fair the Live-Again *Dineh*—also called *Dineh Nahotloni,* or Navajos of Another Place—were again encountered. While some of the Navajo visitors were walking about the Indian villages at the Fair they saw a totem pole and stopped to admire it. A man from that village came out and much to the surprise of the Navajos they learned that these people of Canada who had carved the totem pole—as they had adopted the culture of their northern neighbors—spoke their language. Upon discovering who they were the Canadian became very angry and told them to go away and never come back. "We split up a long time ago," he said, "and it is said that if we ever saw each other again the world would be destroyed." The Navajos went away and for the three weeks that they were in Chicago they avoided the Live-Again *Dineh* from the North.

The Navajos also say that the Jicarilla Apaches left them and became a separate tribe at the same time. There is no tradition of other Apache groups having once "belonged" to the *Dineh* in Navajo mythology. Apaches are always recognized as being related although they are often cast as the Navajos' cultural inferiors which, indeed, they were.

There is no archaeological evidence that the Athapascans, arriving in the American Southwest in one great wave of invasion, caused the abandonment of such Anasazi strongholds as Chaco Canyon in New Mexico and Mesa Verde in Southwestern Colorado. There is evidence of Athapascan raids on some of the smaller Anasazi pueblos but there were much more pertinent reasons for the Anasazi's desertion of the cliff dwellings and large pueblos in the Four Corners area.

There were two periods of severe drought in the Four Corners area, one in the latter part of the eleventh century and another two hundred years later. Crops failed year after year, springs dried up and game went elsewhere to seek foliage. Then, when the rains finally did come, they came in torrents and cut deep into the fertile canyons, washing away the topsoil and destroying the irrigation systems on which the Anasazi depended for their crops. With the irrigation systems and the fields ruined and the game gone, the area could no longer support so many people. Gradually the Anasazi dispersed. The ancestors of the Hopis moved to their mesas where there were springs and where they stayed. Others moved to the Río Grande valley and established themselves there.

Some Pueblo groups of the Río Grande valley have a tradition that when their Anasazi ancestors moved into that area which would have been, of course, soon after they abandoned their homes in the Four Corners area, they displaced an original people living there and that these original people were the ancestors of the Apaches and the Navajos. This legend is mentioned by two early Spanish chroniclers: Fray Alonso de Benavides, who lived in New Mexico from 1626 to 1630, was told the story by the Pueblos, and Juan de Villagutierre y Sotomayor who, writing in 1690, said: "The Apaches have burned some of their pueblos many times, because they (the Apaches) say that they are the natives of that settled land, or at least that they went to it first before those others (the Pueblos) populated it, and as a result they always go about in pretension of throwing them out of it." The early Spanish writers seldom differentiated between Apaches and Navajos. Presuming that this legend is based on fact then the Anasazi, or Pueblos, and that branch of Athapascans who would come to be known as the Navajos exchanged places of residence sometime between the end of the eleventh and the end of the thirteenth centuries. Other Athapascans, dislodged from the Río Grande area, moved into what is now Southern Arizona and became the Western Apaches. When the ancestors of the *Dineh* arrived in what is now the American Southwest and from what direction they came is still a matter of conjecture.

They probably already knew the rudiments of agriculture before their arrival and possibly they knew how to weave. While it is generally believed that the Navajos learned weaving from the Pueblos, no less an authority than Gladys Reichard has pointed out very specific similarities between Navajo weaving and that of the Salish people of the Puget Sound region. On the other hand, as Miss Reichard has also pointed out, there are significant differences between Navajo weaving and that of the Pueblos.

The Navajos, in particular, were greatly influenced by the town-dwelling Indians with whom they came into contact. In Navajo folk tales the Pueblos always appear as wealthy, sophisticated people and are credited with introducing the *Dineh* to the cultivation of corn. The Athapascans brought some ceremonials to the Southwest with them but they were greatly awed by those of the Pueblos, some of which they adopted wholly. Others were changed and incorporated into Navajo culture while still others were rejected.

It is not unreasonable to presume that the Navajos began arriving in the Southwest along with some of their Apache kinsmen at least a thousand years ago and possibly long before that. The Navajos settled down near the Pueblos and began borrowing from their culture, and shaping what they borrowed to fit their particular needs. Yet, while borrowing from what was an overwhelmingly superior culture and adapting to a new physical environment, the Navajos managed to retain their identity as *Dineh*—The People—and developed a way of life uniquely their own.

12

THREE

The Beautiful Rainbow of the Navajo

The Navajos do not refer to their mode of living as a way of life; it is *the* way of life . . . the Beautiful Rainbow of the Navajo. At the center of the Navajo world is their shelter, the hogan. The ancient hogan, known as the "forked stick hogan" was a conical hut constructed of three forked poles covered with logs, brush and mud. Called the "male" hogan by the Navajos, examples of this dwelling can still occasionally be found in the western part of the reservation. More common today is the "female" hogan, a circular or six-sided dwelling constructed of logs or stone, with a doorway facing east and a smoke hole in the center of the roof. The dome-shaped roof is formed of cribbed logs covered with dirt. The fire is placed on the hard-packed dirt floor beneath the smoke hole and a flap or hinged door covers the doorway. Traditionally the hogan lacked windows and was ventilated by the smoke hole in the roof and the east-facing doorway. Nowadays not only do most hogans have windows but they may also contain stoves, chimneys, beds and even a refrigerator and a television set. Too, white prototype houses of wood or stone and even mobile homes are common on the reservation now, but families that live in such dwellings also often construct a hogan nearby. Many of The People have retained their native religion and Navajo ceremonies can be conducted only in a hogan.

Most Navajo families own two, three or several hogans and more than one permanent establishment if they own sheep. A family that owns several hundred sheep and other livestock might have as many as five or six separate clusters of buildings scattered over a large area as the animals must be moved from place to place at various seasons of the year. Too, variations in the weather and the water supply may require that a family live in one place during the summer and another during the winter. Usually, however, each family has one location which is its main residence at which there are more or less permanent corrals, storage dugouts, several hogans and temporary shades or bush hogans for summer use. Nearby, but out of sight, will be at least one sweat hogan. The sweat hogan is a small-scale replica of the old-style forked stick hogan but without the smoke hole. It is constructed of three sticks with forked ends which are fastened together in a tripod. Two straight sticks are leaned against the apex from the east to make the sides of the door. Then sticks and boughs are placed against the low framework and the whole is covered with cedar bark and mud until it is practically airtight. It is heated by placing hot rocks within, the door being closed with several blankets. The sweat hogan provides excellent bathing and purifying facilities for the Navajos in their land of scarce water. As in virtually everything a Navajo does, there are prescribed rituals that must be followed in taking a sweat bath. Four verses of the Sweat Bath Song must be sung before a Navajo can leave the sweat hogan, which the Navajos call the Son of the She Dark, to plunge into cold water or dry himself in the sand.

> He put it down. He put it down.
> First Man put down the sweat house.
> On the edge of the hole where they came up,
> He put down the Son of the She Dark.
> He built it of valuable soft materials.
> Everlasting and peaceful, he put it there.
> He put it there.
> —*A Verse of the Navajo Sweat Bath Song*

The bather then reenters the sweat hogan and sings four

more verses of the song. He repeats the ritual until the entire song has been sung.

The Navajo hogan is more than just a place to eat and sleep and the concept of it as a "home" bears little resemblance to a white person's attitude toward his dwelling place. The hogan is a gift of the gods and as such it occupies a place in the sacred world. The first hogans were built by the Holy People of turquoise, white shell, jet, and abalone shell. The round hogan is symbolic of the sun and its door faces east so that the first thing that a Navajo family sees in the morning is the rising sun . . . Father Sun, one of the most revered of the Navajo deities. The construction of a new hogan is almost always a community affair. Once completed, the new hogan is consecrated with a Blessing Way rite whereby the Holy People are asked to "let this place be happy."

The positions of persons and objects within the hogan are prescribed in the legends: the south side of the hogan "belongs" to the women, the north to the men. The male head of the family, and any distinguished visitors, sits on the west side facing the doorway. The placement of all persons and seating arrangements during ceremonials or other important events are prescribed in considerable detail.

If a hogan is struck by lightning it is considered *chindi*—bewitched—and is deserted. It is also deserted if a death occurs within and the body is removed through a hole broken in the north wall—the direction of evil.

Whites from a society where each family dwells in one house automatically presume the same is true of the Navajos and are amazed that an entire Navajo family can exist in a single hogan that might measure twenty-five square feet. Actually most Navajo families don't live in a single hogan. Within the main hogan goods have a fixed disposal which utilizes all available space to the maximum extent. Seldom-used goods, such as spices, herbs, off-season clothing and guns are stored away in the rafters or suspended against a wall by thongs or nails. Bedding, reserve clothing, jewelry and other personal items are stored away in trunks which are stacked against the walls where the roof is lowest. Pots, pans and other utensils are stacked near the central fire or put into boxes attached to the walls as are foodstuffs such as flour, sugar and coffee. Nowadays families that own white-type dwellings use them for beds, tables, stoves and other accouterments of white society but still utilize the hogan which is warmer in the winter and cooler in the summer than the white prototype dwelling. The hogan is also easier to keep clean in the desert climate.

Supplementary hogans are used for storage, and as a place where the women may weave undisturbed or sew when the weather prohibits such activity from being done outside. Older children and visitors are usually housed in secondary hogans near the main shelter. When weather permits the area around the hogan, usually swept clean and shaded by a brush roof, is used as a summer living room. Then most cooking and other chores are done outside, including weaving. In the summer most if not all the family eats and sleeps outdoors.

Just as in white society, cleanliness varies from family to family, although most Navajo women are good housekeepers. Household and family chores are sex-typed to a degree but in a way that the average middle-class white American family might find hard to comprehend. The males do most of the work in the fields, look after his horses, sheep and cattle, the wagons and saddles, and haul wood and water. But Navajo men also often cook, even when their wives are present, and attach no stigma to assuming responsibilities for children, even small babies, which most white men commonly evade. Where the Pueblo men and the males of some Mexican tribes are excellent weavers, Navajo men seldom weave. But formerly almost all Navajo girls were taught to weave. Navajo women weavers, as has often been said, are among the best in the world. In the past only Navajo men were silversmiths but in recent times a few women have begun to participate in that art.

The Navajos are matriarchal and descent is traced through the mother. While the basic unit of social cooperation is the biological family, the term "family" is considerably broader in its application to Navajo society than it is in the white American world. A biological family, historically, lived in a cluster of hogans and nearby, usually within shouting distance, lived the "extended family." An extended family would consist of an older woman, her husband and unmarried children, and her married daughters together with their husbands and unmarried children. Probably not even a majority of Navajo families live in extended family groups now as they once did. Matriarchal practices are not as widespread as they once were and it is no longer unusual for a bride to go to live with her husband's family or, for that matter, move to another part of the reservation entirely where the husband might find employment. The influence of white customs and especially of white interpretations of inheritance laws has caused a noticeable decrease in the strict practice of the matriarchal system in recent times.

An extended family might also consist of unmarried, widowed or other relatives of the older woman of the household. Historically an extended family lived together in a designated vicinity and changed the place of residence as a group as the weather or foliage for the livestock dictated. Within the extended family labor is pooled to a great extent in herding and other productive activities. A man living with his wife's family may also participate in the work activities of his own extended family. He often visits the homes of his mother and sisters and lends a helping hand in harvesting and other group activities. A man will sometimes pasture his livestock with that of his mother or sister rather than with the property of his wife and children.

Until recently there was no conception of joint property ownership between husband and wife. As a result Navajo women have always enjoyed a favored and somewhat more "liberated" position in their society than have their white counterparts. A woman controls the hogan, built on land that was set aside for her by her family; she owns the children, which belong to her clan, her sheep, the product of her sheep and other livestock, her jewelry and all blankets she might weave and the income from the sale of any of her property. A husband owns what he has inherited from his own family and all goods which he has bought out of his own earnings which, nowadays, often includes a pickup truck. Either partner may sell or trade what he owns, though one usually consults with the other about any major transaction.

The Navajo's concept of property ownership is confusing to many people of European descent and, in the past, caused much misunderstanding in their relations with whites, as we shall see. Certain things are communal property in which no individual or family has vested or exclusive rights. Timber areas, water resources and patches

17

of salt bush which serve the livestock in lieu of mineral salt belong to everyone, but certain restrictions are observed in using communal property. It is an unwritten law that no Navajo will use a water hole that has been, historically, used by members of another family. A stand of timber near the hogan cluster of a family is reserved for the use of that family and no one else would cut wood there without permission. Farm and range lands are said to "belong" to the family that has traditionally used it. Such ownership is, of course, passed through the lineage of the mother. A man never inherits the use-ownership of his wife's property but he might, conceivably, inherit that of his mother or sisters. In recent times, and especially in the case where land allotments were made to families living off the reservation, many Navajos have begun to practice the white concept of range and home ownership.

Livestock is always privately owned. Even young children own their own animals, given to them at birth and at other times, which are branded with their private earmark. The children are expected to care for their animals and resume responsibility at a very young age. Too, a child is expected to contribute from his private flock in supplying meat for the family and also his share when animals are slaughtered to feed guests at a ceremonial. The produce of animals belongs, primarily, to their individual owners, but a portion is taken for the general use of the family. In times of financial trouble all the livestock is entirely for general use. Clothing, jewelry, saddles, ceremonial equipment, blankets and intangibles such as songs and prayers—the teaching of which is purchased from an older person—are indisputably the property of the individual and may be disposed of in any way he sees fit.

As stated before, many Navajos now adhere to white inheritance laws but many others still practice the ancient laws of the Navajos whereby all of a woman's property was passed on to her children and/or to the children of her sisters who are also considered her children. Navajos always refer to the children of their mother's sisters as "my brother" and "my sister." The paternal cousins are thought of as cousins much as they are in white society as they cannot belong to one's own clan. The offspring of a father's sisters belong to his clan while the offspring of his brothers belong, of course, to the clan of their mother.

In the case of a divorce the children always remain with their mother or, in the case of the death of the mother, they most often remain with the maternal grandmother or with a maternal aunt—their "second mother." It is rare, even today, to find children residing with their paternal grandparents as members of their own clan have a prior claim and obligation to rear them.

The Navajo language differentiates many categories of relatives, making distinctions which are unfamiliar to whites. There are prescribed ways of behaving toward relatives of different classes. Younger and older brothers are always distinguished. The children of a mother's sister, as stated before, are addressed in the same manner as actual biological brothers and sisters just as her sisters are called "mother." The relationship between adult brothers and sisters is marked with great reserve in physical contact and by restrictions in speech. Even Navajos who have received a higher education and have been exposed to white relationships still usually avoid physical contact with their adult brothers and sisters. For example, a male Navajo would never dance with his biological sister and more conservative Navajos still consider all female members of their clan as "sisters."

The "outfit" is a term Navajos use to designate a group of relatives who regularly cooperate for work purposes. An outfit may consist of two or more extended families who are always related but who may live widely scattered over an area. Usually one biological or extended family is a nucleus for the outfit and the size of the group tends to depend on the wealth of its leader, or of the leader and his wife and, of course, her family. The wealthy Navajo headmen of the nineteenth century who were considered by the whites to be "chiefs" were usually heads of large outfits, and with but few notable exceptions their influence did not extend beyond the outfits. As the Navajos have turned more and more away from a pastoral economy since World War II the outfit now exists only on a social level except in the more isolated parts of the reservation.

Each Navajo belongs to the clan of his mother but he was "born for" his father's clan. Clan membership is, as Kluckhorn and Leighton said: " . . . important in establishing the larger circle of one's relatives. Clans may be thought of as threads of sentimental linkage which bind together

Navajos who are not biologically related, who have not grown up in the same locality, who may indeed never see each other, or may do so but once in a lifetime. This sentimental bond gives rise to occasional economic and other reciprocities. Sometimes clansmen who discover each other accidentally at a large gathering will exchange gifts. A Navajo will always go out of his way to do a favor or show preference for a clan relative, even if the individual in question has not been previously known." (Kluckhorn and Leighton, American Museum of National History, 1962: 112.)

Historically the Navajo clans, of which there were about sixty, were an important agency in social control. All clansmen were responsible for the crimes and debts of other members of the clan. Therefore it was in their own interest to prevent other members of their clan from committing crimes for which they might be held financially responsible. This loyalty was also misinterpreted by the white Americans of the nineteenth century. A rich Navajo might—and often did—turn over stock to Americans because a clansman of his had been accused of stealing a like number of stock. To the American's way of thinking, the man turning over the stock must have either participated in or at least have had prior knowledge of the theft.

Nowadays the principal importance of clan is that of limiting marriage choices: one may never marry within one's own clan nor that of one's father, although the latter is not considered as incestuous as it once was. The Navajos still look upon incest and the practice of witchcraft as the most repulsive of crimes and marriage within your own clan is thought of as incest.

The traditional Navajo wedding ceremony is a complicated and colorful affair. To a great extent marriages are still arranged by a prescribed order of events. Once a boy becomes of marriageable age—usually in his late teens—his father begins to survey the local families in search of a suitable girl. Of course, nowadays the son has often already found the girl of his choice and, in any event, he is consulted on the choice of his father as are the rest of the adult members of the biological and sometimes the extended family. If the father knows of no family that has a suitable daughter of marriageable age, he might consult his relatives. Sometimes the entire matter is handled by the potential groom's maternal uncle. A maternal uncle is honored as a second father and traditionally he disciplined and taught his nephews.

When the father or uncle has decided upon a girl to which there are no objections within the family group, a member of the boy's family is appointed to go to the prospective bride's family and ask for her hand in marriage. Once it has been decided who will act as the boy's emissary, the matter of dowry is discussed. In the old days a boy's family would offer up to twelve horses and several sheep, contributed by various members of the family and even by the boy himself.

Nowadays it is more usual for jewelry or other goods, which may include livestock, to be offered. It is still not unusual for the prospective groom and bride to be strangers; in rare cases they may not have ever seen each other. When the emissary from the boy's family arrives at the girl's home he states his business to her mother, her father and perhaps to a maternal uncle. It is the duty of the emissary to overcome all objections to the boy that might crop up and to make the dowry offer. The mother of the girl usually has the final word as to whether the offer is accepted. She may, however, leave the decision up to the father or any other respected member of the family. The prospective bride is usually consulted in the matter today but she seldom was in the past.

Once the bride's family decides to accept the marriage offer, a date is selected which is always an odd number of days—five, seven, twenty-one or more—away. Once the offer has been accepted and the date of the ceremony selected, the boy's representative thanks the family and returns home to make his report. The bride's family notifies friends and relatives of the coming wedding. They in turn, give them gifts of food to help feed the expected guests. Then they usually build a separate hogan for the wedding and in which the bride and groom will reside.

On the morning of the wedding the girl is bathed and dressed in her best clothing. The wedding feast is prepared and all is put in readiness for the guests. Meanwhile, the bridegroom is likewise undergoing a ritual cleansing and is dressed in his best clothing. His party leaves home so as to arrive at the bride's home at sundown. When they arrive they place the dowry livestock in the corral and/or give the bride's maternal uncle the dowry previously agreed upon. The bride's family inspects the dowry to see if it is as promised. In a rare case they might find the dowry wanting; then the wedding is immediately called off.

The groom's party retires to the wedding hogan. When he enters the hogan, carrying his saddle, he proceeds "sunwise" south around the fire and takes his place in the rear opposite the entrance. The remainder of his party follows him in and they take their prescribed places to the north of the groom. Meanwhile the bride's mother is preparing unseasoned corn mush which she must cook in a clay pot. When it is ready she places it in a ceremonial woven basket. The other women of her family are getting the feast ready. A wicker jug is filled with water and a gourd ladle is placed beside it. A special dish of meat is prepared for the bridal couple also. Once the repast is ready, a master of ceremonies who may be a respected Singer or some favored member of the bride's family, carrying a bag of corn pollen and the jug of water, leads the bride's procession to the marriage hogan. The bride walks behind him, carrying the corn mush. Other members of her party follow her, carrying the food for the feast.

The mother still usually remains behind. Mothers-in-law are not supposed to look upon their sons-in-law. This taboo—what Lummis called the "mother-in-law joke"— intrigues white people who have searched for a hidden significance that really doesn't exist. Navajo children, playing outside the hogan, will still warn a visiting grandmother that their father is approaching and she will take her leave. It would be considered bad manners for her to remain, just as it would be considered such if her son-in-law visited her hogan unannounced. Perhaps the only explanation for this custom is that given me by a Navajo friend who said, "It avoids a lot of trouble in the family."

The bride's party enters the hogan and they take their prescribed places on the south. The bride places the basket of corn mush in front of the bridegroom and takes a seat to his right. The master of ceremonies puts the wicker jug in front of the bridal couple and gives the gourd ladle to the bride. He pours water into it and tells her to pour the water onto the groom's hands. After he has washed his hands, the bride gives him the ladle and he in turn pours water on her hands while she washes them.

The master of ceremonies then takes out his bag of corn pollen. The basket of mush is placed so that the termination of the weaving faces the east and the fire. He takes a pinch of pollen and sprinkles it from east to west over the mush, then from north to south. Next he makes a clockwise pollen circle around the basket.

Turning to the guests, he asks if there are any objections to his turning the basket halfway around, which is symbolic of turning the minds of the bride and groom toward each other. After turning the basket, he tells the groom to take a pinch of the corn mush at the edge where the pollen ends at the East. The groom places the mush in his mouth and the bride then does the same. Next, with the groom preceding, they take pollen from the South, the West and the North and finally from the center where the two lines of pollen cross, and eat it. When they have finished, the master of ceremonies tells everyone to start eating the wedding feast. The woven basket used in the ceremony is usually given to the groom's mother.

When the feast has been consumed one of the visiting party makes a speech, thanking the bride's people for the food and for their reception and also for the gift of the fine daughter.

Then the master of ceremonies or some other respected member of one of the families selected for that purpose instructs the bride and groom as to their required future conduct toward each other and their connubial duties. The latter is frank and uninhibited and of a nature that would prove most embarrassing to a white bridal couple were it given to them in the presence of friends and relatives. It is then suggested that the bride and groom stay in the hogan for four nights and four days, and the wedding party leaves.

The birth of a Navajo child is a matter for celebration as The People are inordinately fond of their children. Of course a large percentage of Navajo children are now born in hospitals, but once the infant is taken home the family most often holds a blessing rite, called a *hozoniji*, which is attended by relatives and friends. Historically the child was laced in a cradle, made for it by its father with a great deal of pride and care, and it still is not too unusual to see a baby in a cradle on the reservation today. Navajo women are certain that a child who spends his infancy in a cradle will have a strong back and will be flat-shouldered. Too, the cradle is extraordinarily safe and convenient. It can be set down within sight of the mother; it can be carried on her back when she rides horseback and in her lap when she is traveling in a pickup truck or wagon. The baby is taken out of its cradle and made comfortable every three or four hours and is bathed thoroughly every day. The husband-and-wife writing team known as T. D. Allen tell, in their book *Navajos Have Five Fingers* (Oklahoma, 1963), of being repulsed by finding shredded cedar bark beneath the skirts of an ill Navajo child they removed from its cradle board: " . . . the sort of nest one might expect for a bird or wild animal." Some time later they learned from medical journals that such sawdust, used consistently by Navajo mothers instead of diapers until recent times, was not only more absorbent than cotton but the resins and turpentine in the wood are astringent, antiseptic, and act as a deodorant.

Navajo children never lack company. There are usually older family members around to care for them in addition to the mother. As soon as they are old enough to resume responsibility, often by the age of two or three, they are required to do so. Perhaps it is because they are surrounded by love, growing up in the extended family, and required at such an early age to take part in family affairs that Navajo children—as commented on by virtually everyone who has had the opportunity to observe them—seem so much better behaved than their counterparts in other societies. One seldom hears a Navajo child scream or cry and severe punishment that is common in other societies is virtually unheard of among the Navajos. A short word is usually enough to stop a misbehaving Navajo child.

Soon after birth a Navajo child is given a secret or "war" name. This name is considered a person's personal property and is not—or was not formerly—used, even by members of his family. In fact a man's war name might conceivably never be revealed to his wife. The entire Navajo system of names was—and continues to be to some extent—most baffling to whites and especially to governmental agents and missionaries. Children are given "war" names by their parents, but bound in by the family, they actually have very little need for names. Kinship terms were, and still are, enough for a child to address or refer to every member

24

of the family and they, in turn, designate him adequately by such terms. "My brother who is the son of my mother's youngest sister" is much easier to say in Navajo than it is in English and exactly describes the person referred to.

During the course of his life a Navajo was in the past called by one or more nicknames by which he was known outside his family. Often he was referred to by his family and friends by one or more different nicknames—but never in his presence. A Navajo girl might be given the "war" name of Zhiltnapah and be referred to by her family and eventually by others as Running Girl for being lively. Later she might be given another nickname such as Daughter of Red Weaver. The great Navajo headman who came to be known to the Americans by his Spanish nickname, Manuelito, was given a war name by his parents, possibly Holy Boy. Later he was called Son-in-Law of Late Texan because he was the son-in-law of a man called Late Texan. Later still, he was called Bullet Hole as the result of a wound received in battle with the Utes. He was also nicknamed Man of Black Weeds because he lived at a place called Black Weeds and Warrior Grabbed Enemy for the obvious reason. While prominent Navajos such as Manuelito and Ganado Mucho (Many Cattle) who were well known to the Mexicans were given Spanish nicknames, the *Dineh* generally never accepted nor employed the Spanish names themselves.

And it was not until the 1940's and World War II that the English binomial system found widespread favor among The People. Since the majority were never missionized, there was no systematic introduction of the binomial system. Traders gave names to people with whom they did business for the purpose of identifying individuals. Missionaries and government school teachers gave Navajos with whom they came in contact Anglo names which were often accepted and became fixed designations. Often Navajos were, and for that matter still are, known by one name in a white relationship and by another name in a Navajo relationship.

Many older Navajos still consider it bad manners to address a person by his name in his presence. Only Navajos who have had considerable contact with whites do not find this practice offensive. In a social gathering a Navajo will refer to someone who is present by a kinship term or by "this one" or "my friend" or even "you" but not by name, even a nickname. Names are used generally only as terms of reference. But since World War II almost all Navajo children have been given some sort of an English name and it is now common for parents to summon children by their English names. As schools require a family name, children are forced to use the binomial system, but they do not always adhere to the white practice. A child still might take his mother's name as soon as that of his father or, for that matter, even a clan name might be adopted. Navajo parents are now aware of the importance of their children having "white" names if, for no other reason, than to save them embarrassment when they go out into the major culture. During World War II Navajo men had to answer army roll calls to all sorts of horrible names, bestowed on them by teachers and traders, such as Mumbo Jumbo, Lady, Pop-sickle and Angel Face. The Navajo language is so precise that it is not necessary that The People "use" such designations in addressing each other.

Navajo is a language of the subgroup of the Athapascan branch of the Nadene language family. Linguistic research seems to indicate that the Nadene-speaking people arrived in the Americas about three thousand years ago but so far there has been no conclusive evidence dating their arrival. There has been an effort made to establish a relationship between the Nadene language and Sino-Tibetan, the ancestral form of the Chinese and Tibetan languages but, again, no conclusive evidence establishing such a relationship has been presented. At least two thousand years ago the language split into the Tlingit and Athapascan branches. Other splits came later.

Of the approximately twelve hundred Indian dialects found in the Americas, none were spoken over as wide an area as were the many dialects of the Nadene. In 1910 Franciscan Father A.G. Morice said: "No other aboriginal stock in North America, perhaps not even excepting the Algohquian, covers so great an extent of territory as the Dene. The British Isles, France and Spain, Italy, and two or three of the minor European Commonwealths, taken together, would hardly represent the area or the region occupied by this large family." *(Ethnologic Dictionary of the Navajo Language,* Franciscan Fathers, 1910: 27.)

There is a misconception prevalent among whites that

all American Indian languages were basically the same and consisted of only a few hundred vocabulary words. Nothing could be further from the truth. Linguistics have pointed out that there is as much difference between Keres, a language spoken by some Pueblos, and Navajo as there is between English and Russian. As for a vocabulary of only a few hundred words, there are over thirty ways to say "wind" in Navajo. A Navajo dictionary compiled by Father Berard Haile and the Franciscan priests of St. Michaels is comparable in size to the average English dictionary.

Navajo is a highly complex language that is full of movement, of subtle meaning, of verbs the action of which may be modified by a wide variety of prefixes. Like Chinese, Navajo is a tonal language and the meaning of a word is distinguished by the pitch of the voice. As the sound system of Navajo exhibits many features foreign to English and other Indo-European languages, most English-speaking persons find it very difficult to learn Navajo. Navajo is the court language of the Southwestern Indian tribes and while many of their Indian neighbors speak Navajo, very few of The People learn other Indian languages. English is still a second language on the reservation.

Robert Young, one of the few whites who has gained exceptional proficiency in Navajo, has pointed out that there are very few borrowed words in Navajo: "Somewhat after the fashion of German, Navajo tends to devise its own designations for new things, rather than borrow such names from other languages. Nouns like gohwei, coffee (from Spanish café); 'aloos, rice (from Spanish arroz); and nóomba (from English number) are borrowed." *(Navajo Yearbook*, 1961: 451.) The Navajos, like all peoples, think with words. Because of their language, their pattern of thought varies so greatly from the English pattern that, in retrospect, it is quite understandable that there was no meeting of the Navajo and English minds during the early treaty contacts.

The nature of the Navajo language, as well as its subtle beauty, permits a startlingly humorous rendering of a great variety of situations. Navajos are masters of the pun, and utilize their language, which will permit a tri-dimensional pun, for wit and repartee in conversation. Navajo humor is often subtle. Kluckhorn and Leighton give this example: "If a fat person is seated in a hogan, someone may use the verb form which means 'the round object is in position' instead of the correct form, meaning 'the living object is in position.' " (Kluckhorn and Leighton, 1962, ibid: 98.)

Kluckhorn and Leighton have pointed out that the greatest contrast between Navajo and European humor lies in the degree of participation. As Navajo culture possesses no system of social stratification, it is possible for every individual in the culture to participate wholly in all aspects of humorous expression. It is possible for the Navajo equivalent of the European savant to indulge in a sophisticated play on words one minute and participate in some simple-minded practical joke the next without transgressing the bounds of the established cultural pattern, and a respected Navajo elder can act the fool without losing his dignity. Too, children can tease their parents or even their grandparents unmercifully and to a degree that would never be accepted in white society. Navajos appreciate practical jokes and are willing to go to a great deal of trouble to pull one off.

Typical is the tale of the white school teacher who wanted to learn some Navajo songs. She badgered her Navajo acquaintances until they finally taught her one song. But every time she sang the song she was greeted with gales of laughter. She finally became suspicious and had the song translated by Navajos other than the ones who had taught it to her and discovered that the verses were of a very sexual nature.

While The People have a keen sense of humor and are fond of jokes, their humor is seldom obscene for the simple reason that there are hardly any words in the language that are considered "obscene." One can say that a man does not look good or that he is uglier than his horse but the language does not allow a duplication of the vulgarities encountered in spoken English. But some Navajos, who speak no other English, have picked up a sizable vocabulary of American swear words. One of the most humorous monologues I ever heard was that of an old Navajo man who, very angry, was telling off a Navajo forest ranger in his native tongue and frequently utilizing a very blunt and very understandable four-letter English swear word to get his point across.

The Navajos' innate sense of humor also manifests itself in their games, and particularly in gambling. The People love to gamble but they do not put the emphasis on winning that white Americans do. They have adopted American card games and are particularly fond of poker. The Navajos deal from the bottom of the deck and double-dealing, or hiding or marking cards, are not considered cheating—as long as one doesn't get caught. If a player is caught doing tricks with the cards he merely loses the pot and everyone has a good laugh at his expense. Navajos still play their ancient games, stick dice, the arrow game and the moccasin game, and informal foot and horse races are very popular. Children amuse themselves with cat's-cradles and their versions of the adult games.

As with all rural people, the Navajos delight in occasions which bring crowds together such as a ceremonial or a "squaw dance" and particularly, in recent years, the rodeo. The Navajos have been great horsemen for centuries and are very good at the cowboy sports. Hardly a weekend goes by in the summer when there is not at least one rodeo being held someplace on the reservation. What is now known as the squaw dance was once an important ceremony, the Nda, or Enemy Way. It was held for warriors returning from contact with an enemy people. Nowadays the squaw dance, held in the summer, is a three-night affair, held at a different location each night, that functions as a coming-out affair for young Navajo girls. The squaw dance and other summer festivals give Navajos an opportunity to see old friends, exchange news and gossip, to look over prospective mates for their children and to trade livestock and equipment and buy and sell jewelry and other articles. Navajos from all over the reservation get together at the Gallup Inter-Tribal Ceremonial in August, at the Navajo Tribal Fair at Window Rock in September and again the next month at the Shiprock Fair.

Puberty rites are still held and are an occasion for family reunions, but unlike white Americans, Navajos—with the exception of those who have been converted to Christianity—do not come together when a member of the family dics. Death and everything connected with it is repulsive to the *Dineh* and dead humans are buried as quickly as possible. Traditional Navajos have no belief in a glorious afterlife. The afterworld is a place similar to the earth and is said, by some Navajos, to be the world from whence the Navajos came before they entered this world. Therefore it is located in the North, the direction of evil, and is beneath the surface of the earth. The spirit of the dead travels down a mountain trail after the shell, or body, is deserted and left behind on earth. At the bottom of the trail the deceased is met by relatives who appear as they did in life. The deceased relatives then guide the spirit to the underworld on a journey that takes four days.

The shell, or body, of the deceased is buried with elaborate precautions by relatives. Formerly slaves were given this abhorrent duty, and later white traders were often asked to bury the dead. The dead, if proper precautions are not taken, are believed to be capable of returning to earth as ghosts to plague the living. The ghosts of an Earth Surface People might return if they have not been interred properly or to avenge some neglect or offense. The ghost is thought to come back in many of several forms but only at night and while their appearance and actions are frightening, they are also believed to be an omen of disaster.

The belief in witchcraft is still widespread among the Navajo but it is a subject that is seldom discussed with whites. The Navajos called their witches "human wolves" or "Navajo wolves" and believe that they become witches to obtain riches. Witches can be either men or women and are capable of causing the illness or death of those whom they dislike. Like ghosts, they go about at night dressed in the skins of wolves or coyotes; it is also said that they can turn themselves into wolves. To become a *chindi*—a witch—one goes through an elaborate ceremony and pays for the privilege by designating a relative, usually either a brother or a sister, as a sacrifice. Two days later the relative dies.

The belief in witchcraft was, in the past, a form of social control. If a man was stingy and grew too rich he was in danger of being accused of being a witch. Such a man, unlike most Navajos, would refuse to share his food with hungry passers-by and his riches with relatives. He might also take the water supply and grazing grounds used by others without their permission. Navajos suspected of being witches were tried and executed. A few years after the *Dineh* were returned from their Fort Sumner imprisonment some of the young men started raiding their neighbors and caused the threat of another outbreak of hostilities between the Navajos and the American army. The respected headmen, Manuelito and Ganado Mucho, went on a "witch hunt," caught, tried and executed forty men, including Ganado Mucho's own uncle and, thereby, put an end to the troubles.

While extensive studies have been made of Navajo religious ceremonies, particularly by Washington Matthews, Father Berard Haile, Sheila Moon and others, very little study has been done in regard to extrasensory perception and mental telepathy as practiced by the Navajos. Many whites who have lived among The People are convinced that some, particularly older, Navajos are capable of accurately predicting future events and particularly their own deaths. Franc Johnson Newcomb, who lived on the reservation for many years and wrote of her experiences in her book, *Navaho Neighbors,* (Oklahoma, 1966) tells the story of Hosteen Beaal, who convinced her with several vivid demonstrations that he could not only find lost articles, but could trace exactly the movements of thieves and murderers several days after their crimes had been committed. He once described a gruesome murder in detail and told Gallup law officers exactly where they could find the culprits. Others, among them Laura Gilpin, have written of similar experiences.

The attitude of traditional Navajos toward the supernatural and nature is directly opposed to that of most white Americans. In the Navajo view, nature can be controlled to an extent—a man may divert the water of a stream to irrigate his crops—but those who would attempt to master the forces of nature are looked upon with suspect. Man is not and can never be the master of nature; nature is the master of man, a weak creature who is but one entity within the overall plan of the master forces. Even today traditional Navajos are suspicious of their younger, progressive tribesmen who have allowed whites on the reservation to take coal from Black Mesa (and not without justification, say the ecologists). Where whites would, and have attempted to, shear the malignant forces of nature, lightning, floods, storms, of their power, the Navajo has long since accepted such as forces over which he has no control. The Navajo attitude toward the destructive aspects of nature are not unlike the Christian who says, "The Lord giveth and the Lord taketh away." If a sudden winter storm freezes some of a Navajo's sheep he might very well say, "He who has given us the sheep to use has taken them back."

It is the belief of the Navajo that the gifts of nature are just that, gifts, and a man must be industrious to receive those gifts for his own use. But he could never be so selfish as to accumulate nature's riches for the sake of having them, or more than he and his relatives could use. Riches, like food, are to be shared with a man's family and, by extension, his clan and related clans. A Navajo leader once said: "You can't get riches if you treat your relatives right. You can't get rich without cheating people. Cheating people is the wrong way. That way gets you into trouble. Men should be honest to get along."

Work for the sake of accumulating possessions, therefore, is a foreign concept, one introduced to the Navajos by white Americans. Even today a Navajo will most often stop working when he feels he has enough and that his relatives are taken care of, although several Navajos in this century have built up considerable fortunes even by white standards. But people who have acquired personal wealth are not generally admired nor held up as models to be emulated by children. In fact they are still sometimes suspected of being witches, especially if they are stingy with their wealth and are not inclined to share some of it with poorer relatives.

Certain skills, the ability to weave a fine blanket or to work jewelry, to "talk easy," and to make a fine appearance, which includes the ability to dress well, are valued much more highly than personal wealth. A display of jewelry and other trappings of wealth is not as much a personal matter as it is a family matter. As John Adair says: "It is not 'see how much money I have!' but 'see how much money we have in our family.'"

The first Americans to visit the Navajos in the nineteenth century commented, almost without exception, on the industrious nature of the Navajos, their hospitality, praising them for their knowledge of animal husbandry, their ability to raise substantial crops on land that would have been shunned by a white farmer. Next in order of comment was the exceptional weaving or their "heathen ways," all of which have stood the test of a century and a quarter of contact with white America.

FOUR

Navajo Art: "Handiwork of the Gods"

A European lady, visiting America for the first time, stood among a group of tourists near Kayenta watching a Navajo woman weaving. The visitor was completely engrossed. Invited to come closer, she touched the rug with her hands, then turned to her companions and said so matter-of-factly that there could be no disputing her, "It is the handiwork of the gods." Perhaps she was right, for the Navajo believe that weaving was taught them by one of the Holy People and, like any activity that has religious connotations, weaving has its own songs, prayers and even taboos.

According to the legends, the *Dineh* were taught weaving by Spider Woman who, it is said by some, lives atop Spider Rock in Canyon de Chelly. When and from whom the Navajos actually learned weaving is a matter of conjecture but they were weaving cloth from the wild cotton, which grew like tall grass with a single long head on the prairies of northern Arizona, before the Spanish entered the Southwest from Mexico. Perhaps, as is usually presumed, they were taught weaving by the Pueblos and perhaps, as Gladys A. Reichard has made a case for, they already knew how to weave when they wandered into the American Southwest a thousand or more years ago. Folktales relate that the two Navajo women who were stolen by the Great Gambler of Kintyel, the legendary builder of Chaco Canyon's Pueblo Bonito (between 919 and 1127, A.D.), were weavers of Beautiful Design: embroidery in colors on a background of white cotton cloth much as the Hopis still make. Too, in the ancient Night Chant cotton cloth was used to receive the sacrifices, but that rite could have been borrowed from the Pueblos, or based on a Pueblo legend.

The first Navajos encountered by the Spanish were observed trading wild animal skins to the people of Acoma for woven cloth and, as a result, at least one historian has written that the Navajos were not weaving before the Spanish entered New Mexico. Applying the same logic, he could just as well have said that the people of Acoma did not hunt animals before the coming of the Spanish because they traded woven cloth to the Navajos for skins.

Spider Woman, in some Navajo legends, is a Kisani (Pueblo) woman who was taught the craft by a spider. In acknowledgment of their debt to Spider Woman, one of the Holy People of Navajo mythology, Navajo weavers always left a hole in the center of each blanket, like that of a spider's web, until the traders in the early part of this century refused to buy such blankets. Most Navajo weavers still acknowledge the debt by leaving a "spirit outlet" in the design. The spirit outlet usually takes the form of a thin line made from the center of the blanket to the edge, and also serves, Navajo weavers believe, to prevent "blanket sickness." The People have a phrase similar to "cobwebs in the brain" and believe that Spider Woman, to whom the tribute of a spider hole has been denied, will spin webs in the head of the weaver if the spirit outlet is omitted. Since the weaver carries the pattern of the blanket in her head from beginning to ending, perhaps blanket sickness is more real than imagined.

It is not known when Navajo women started weaving with wool on their crude, upright looms. It is not unlikely that they used the fine underhair of the wild mountain goat before the Spanish introduced the little *churro* sheep to the Americas in the sixteenth century. As we shall see, Navajos acquired sheep very soon after the Spanish colonists arrived in New Mexico in 1598. Not long after Don Roque de Madrid's July, 1705, campaign against the Navajos, New Mexican governor Cuero y Valdes wrote: "They (the Navajos) make their clothes of wool and cotton, sowing the latter and obtaining the former from the flocks which they raise." Four decades later another New Mexican governor, Codallos y Rabal, mentions "black wool" woven by the Navajos. Then, on February 23, 1780, Theodore de Croix, Commander-General of the Interior Provinces of New Spain, wrote: "The Navajos, who although of Apache kinship have a fixed home, sow, raise herds, and weave their blankets and clothes of wool . . ."

Then, in a letter written by Governor Fernando de Chacon on July 15, 1795, to Pedro de Nava, military commander in Chihuahua, not only is Navajo weaving mentioned, but so is the ownership of silver jewelry: "The Navajos," wrote Chacon, "whom you suspect may have aided the Apaches in their incursions, have since the death of their general Antonio been irreconcilable enemies, to such a degree that with us they have observed an invariable and sincere peace. These Gentiles are not in a state of coveting herds (of sheep), as their own are innumerable. They have increased their horse herds considerably; they sow much and on good fields; they work their wool with more delicacy and taste than the Spaniards. Men as well as women go decently clothed; and their Captains are rarely seen without silver jewelry; they are more adept in speaking Castilian than any other Gentile nation; so that they really seem 'town' Indians much more than those who have been reduced . . ."

Four years later Don José Cortez established that the Navajos were already using the produce of their weaving as a trade item. Don José wrote: "The Navajos have manufactures of serge, blankets, and other coarse cloths, which more than suffice for the consumption of their own people; and they go to the province of New Mexico with the surplus, and there exchange their goods for such others as they have not, or for the implements they need." The earliest known specimens of Navajo weaving were found in Massacre Cave in Canyon del Muerto where the Spaniards killed over one hundred Navajos, mostly women and children, in 1805. Several fragments worn by these unfortunates were found much later, including half of a woman's dress, and inferentially dated prior to the massacre as no Navajo dared venture into the cave after so many people were killed there.

By the beginning of the nineteenth century Navajo weavers were working almost exclusively in wool (their sheep and goats had destroyed most of the wild cotton) and were rapidly developing new techniques and designs. Unlike the Pueblos who never departed from their original, simple, banded designs, the Navajos from the beginning gave vent to their lively imagination to produce elaborate patterns and each succeeding generation seems to have contributed to the refinement of the craft as well as producing new designs and patterns. Contact with the Spanish invaders affected Navajo weaving patterns and designs very little, if at all. Of course the introduction of the domestic sheep changed Navajo weaving as well as lifestyles considerably. Once the Navajo blankets became an important trade item, certainly by the end of the 1700s, the Spanish realized that Navajo women were far better weavers than either their own women or the subjected Pueblo men. As a result Navajo women became the primary objective of Spanish slave raids.

The earliest examples of Navajo weaving still in existence are closely woven of native hand-spun wool, the prevailing patterns being of white with transverse stripes of either dark brown or black. The wool for the latter was obtained from the brown-black sheep common in every herd. Later the black was strengthened by a dye composed of ocher burned in piñon gum and then boiled in a decoction of alder bark. Experiments with color led to the use of a dull red dye from the roots of native shrubs; a yellow obtained from a plant closely related to the goldenrod; a deep yellow and an orange from the root of the dock weed; and blue which was obtained by boiling sumac with a pulverized blue clay. The blue native dye was soon superseded by indigo obtained from Spanish colonists.

Colors of blue, brown, a native red and black were found in the Massacre Cave fragments and half a dress, found there by Mrs. Sam Day II, was black with figures in indigo blue and with bayeta red strips and end panels. Baise, called bayeta by the Spanish, was a loosely woven red flannel, originally manufactured in Manchester, England, and shipped to Mexico by way of Spain. At the time the Massa-

36

cre Cave dress was woven, very little of this cloth had found its way into New Mexico, but later bolts of it were shipped up the trade trails. Its brilliant red color, obtained from cochineal dye, soon found great favor with Navajo weavers. The Navajos unraveled and retwisted the bayeta but its weaving led to a marked refinement of the craft, for it made necessary the finer spinning of their own yarn to match the fineness of the bayeta. Once bayeta became reasonably plentiful, probably during the Mexican period, it led to what has come to be known as the Classic Period of Navajo weaving, a period that lasted from the 1846 American conquest until after the Navajos returned from Fort Sumner in 1868. The oldest bayeta blankets still in existence consist of narrow strips of the red cloth interspersed with wider strips of natural-colored wool. These blankets are very rare. Later geometrical designs were developed, and beautiful blankets called "Chief Blankets" were produced in combinations of red, white, blue and yellow. The Chief Blankets had developed into a distinctive trade item for the Navajos by the middle of the nineteenth century. They were deliberately woven for trade or sale to other Indians in the Southwest and some of them were traded as far east as Kansas. They were worn by "chiefs" of other tribes because it was said that they were the only ones who could afford to obtain them.

Just when Navajo women had perfected their weaving and were producing a truly remarkable blanket, the tribe was defeated by an American force under the command of Christopher Carson, in 1863-64, and imprisoned at Fort Sumner for four long years. Very little weaving was done there as there was virtually no wool available. When they were returned to *Dinehtah* from Fort Sumner the weavers began to experiment with native and commercial yarns and dyes in new color combinations and in much more varied designs. With the introduction of aniline dyes in the late 1880s, the use of native dyes declined, not to be revived except in a few areas until the 1930s. Navajo weaving went into a sharp decline with the introduction of the aniline dyes by the traders on the reservation. The traders, who found a ready market for the heavier Navajo rugs in the East, paid the Navajo weavers for their work by the pound. As a result the women worked quickly; yarn was poorly cleaned and the spinning and dyeing was carelessly done.

37

Soon Navajo women quit washing the wool to remove grease and dirt and some went so far as to pound sand into the yarn to make the blankets heavier. The fine weavers were also paid by the pound—at the same rate—for their product. This decline and revival of Navajo weaving is discussed in detail later in this narrative as it was an important economic factor.

Fortunately Navajo weaving was revived and, beginning in the 1930s, Navajo women gradually returned to the old techniques and designs and began using native dyes again. Today many of the good weavers refuse to use any dyes that they, or a member of their family, have not prepared themselves. No two Navajo rugs are exactly alike and, just as an expert can identify the section of Persia where a Persian rug was woven, Navajo rugs have similar geographic identity. Most experts consider the black, white, gray and brown geometrically designed rugs woven in the Two Gray Hills area the finest examples of the craft since the classic period. The Two Gray Hills rugs, and particularly those woven by Daisy Togelchee, considered by many to be the finest Navajo weaver of modern times, are avidly collected by museums and important private collectors. Actually there are thirteen weaving regions on the reservation, each producing a characteristic rug. Runners are produced chiefly in the Coyote Canyon area northwest of Gallup. Other areas where distinctive rugs are produced are Teec Nos Pos, Lukachukai, Red Mesa, Crystal, Chinle, Wide Ruins, Ganado, Keams Canyon, Coal Mine, West Reservation and Shiprock where the colorful Yei Blanket is produced. The Yei is a religious figure taken from the highly stylized sandpaintings and while the rug itself has no religious significance, at first old Navajos vehemently objected to the depicting of this holy figure in yarn.

The novice often thinks that the designs of Navajo rugs has some religious symbolism, but they never do. The design comes from the imagination of the weaver. A few years ago Navajo weaving seemed to be a disappearing art and even today there are very few really good weavers on the reservation, but the few that remain are turning out a product that is comparable to the best of the classic period. And for the first time, at Navajo Community College, young Navajo women who did not learn to weave as children are being taught the art.

Until the turn of the last century Navajo women also wove their clothing. The velvet blouses and full cotton skirts that are now considered the traditional dresss of Navajo women were not copies, as has often been written, of the clothing of soldiers' wives at Fort Sumner but came into popularity soon after the arrival of a large number of white women, teachers, wives of agents and missionaries on the reservation beginning in the 1880s. The old-style dress was a simple wool blanket, woven in two pieces of identical size and pattern. As described by Charles Avery Amsden, these were "sewn together after weaving, the sides being joined except for a gap of several inches at both top and bottom. The bottom gap formed a slit in either side of the skirt, designed to give freedom in movement to the wearer, while that at the top provided neck and arm room, the garment being sleeveless. The upper edges were joined for a few inches on each side to form straps over the shoulders, the middle portion remaining open to allow passage for the woman's head. The style of the dress was thus roughly that of the Pueblo woman's (except for the one bare shoulder in the latter), of which it was almost certainly an adaptation." (Amsden, New Mexico, 1949: 96.)

As Amsden also pointed out, "There is no doubt that the woman's dress is among the oldest of all" of the early products of the Navajo loom. This dress, girded at the waist with a chonco belt, is still occasionally worn by Navajo women to important functions. It was given up for the most part when traders introduced calico on the reservation. The calico was cheap and it took weeks to weave the old-style dress. The Navajo women adapted the dress of the white women to suit their needs, later fashioning the top of it of velvet, and never found a reason to change.

Navajo women also wove a shirt for their men. This straight tunic, to which sleeves were later added, closely resembled a modern football jersey. Before Navajo women turned their attention almost exclusively to weaving the commercial blankets, they also produced shoulder blankets, serapes and ponchos. Saddle blankets are still produced but not in quality, as are saddle throws and girths. Sashes and hair cords are still woven.

While weaving was, and is, almost the exclusive domain of the women of the tribe, Navajo men knitted—although very few do today. According to the *Ethnologic Dictionary:*

"Knitting is practiced by the Navajo to quite an extent . . . At present only steel needles are used in knitting, which are either purchased at the trading post, or made of wire or the ribs of an umbrella. These are broken to the proper length and slightly rubbed upon a stone to obtain a smooth blunt point.

"Before steel and iron was available, knitting needles were made of wood, for which the slender twigs of . . . *Findlera rupicola,* or of . . . black greasewood, were used. Both are very hard and susceptible of a smooth, slick polish.

"For knitting, blue, white and black yarns are used, and the present output of the knitting industry is limited to leggings and gloves. The latter is made with a separate thumb, although in late years some have also been knitted with all five fingers separate.

"Leggings consist of long footless stockings, encasing the leg from the kneecap to instep. At the top end a raised rim, about one-half to one inch wide, is knitted by using *left* stitches, that is, the yarn is passed from left to right instead of the usual way. This rim affords a hand grip, and also adds to the wear and tear in pulling on the legging. To distinguish the right from the left legging, and the inside from the outside, a line or ridge is knitted down along the outside of the leggings in relief, like a raised seam, by using *left* stitches at this point. At the lower end of the leggings a knitted or plaited wool cord is fastened, which passes under the foot below the instep, and to keep the legging from working upward. The foot and lower legging is covered by the moccasin . . .

"Since leggings were always considered a part of the male attire (women have begun to wear them only in recent years) knitting was and still is mostly done by the men. The yarn leggings were not made or worn for riding purposes, for which they made leggings of leather or buckskin, and both were worn at the same time." W.W.H. Davis observed that Navajo men were wearing the knitted leggings in 1855.

John Adair, whose book *The Navajo and Pueblo Silver-smiths* is considered the authoritative work on Navajo silver-work says: "Silversmithing is not an ancient art among the Navajo. They did not learn the craft until after the middle of the nineteenth century, although they had been wearing silver for many years. They acquired knowledge of the art from the Mexican *plateros* (silversmiths) who lived in villages in the upper Rio Grande valley and at the southeastern edge of the present Navajo reservation. It is not surprising that they did not learn to make silver earlier, for they were continually at war with the Mexicans and made frequent raids into their villages. Hostility such as this was not conductive to the learning of an art which requires instruction over a period of time. Furthermore, the Navajo had no tools. Even if a man had wanted to learn the craft and had watched one of the *plateros* at work, he would not have been able to produce any work of his own without a hammer, an anvil, and files." (Adair, Oklahoma, 1944: 3.)

Perhaps the Navajos did not begin working silver until after their return from Fort Sumner, as is Adair's thesis, but his conclusions are suspect. Adair used neither Chacon, who mentioned the silver jewelry of the Navajo "captains" in 1795, nor W.W.H. Davis, who observed that the Navajos were wearing "*many* valuable belts of silver" in 1855, as sources. It is true that the Navajos, as Adair says, were "continually at war with the Mexicans" but they managed to obtain, and were using, bayeta soon after that cloth was introduced into the Americas. As for tools, if the Navajos could obtain the silver belts from the Mexicans, they certainly could obtain the tools to make them. All the earlier observers tell us that the Navajos were very quick to adopt the crafts of other societies that appealed to them. Therefore, it is not illogical to presume that since the Navajos were wearing silver belts in 1795 they were either already making them or doing so soon afterwards. Adair and others have assumed that since the Navajos evidenced no ownership of silver jewelry at Fort Sumner, they had not yet started working in silver. But since we know from Chacon and Davis that they owned silver ornaments long before that, the question of what happened to them arises. The answer is very simple: people do not take valuables, such as silver jewelry, to prison with them.

It is my theory that when Henry Linn Dodge arrived on the reservation as agent in 1853 he learned that the Navajos were working in silver and, as a result, he imported blacksmithing equipment to teach them that trade also, although history tells us that the Navajos learned blacksmithing first. During the protracted wars with the Americans after Dodge's death which reduced the Navajos to virtually paupers, they disposed of their silver, exchanging it for food and other necessities. The little they owned when Christopher Carson rounded them up in 1863-64 would have been secreted. Carson's soldiers and Ute allies killed Navajos solely for amusement and they certainly would not have hesitated to kill for silver. The Navajos would have had no trouble obtaining silver ore. If they did not have mines of their own, as contemporary Americans suspected, they could have easily obtained it from the Apaches and other Indians.

As for learning the craft from *plateros,* it has been established that prior to the mid-1800s it was the custom of Mexican silversmiths, in times of peace, to roam through the Navajo country producing silver ornaments in exchange for horses. The early silver jewelry of the Navajos was exclusively hammered work made with crude homemade tools and copied from the ornaments of the Spanish and trade items of English manufacture. In the beginning the Navajos fashioned domed buttons, hollow spherical beads, powder chargers, silver-mounted bridles and a small pomegranate, the forerunner of the well-known squash blossom necklace. Bracelets, rings and conchos were copied from similar pieces used by the Plains Indians that were obtained from the Utes. These were made of brass, copper and German silver which the Plains tribes obtained from traders.

Arthur Woodward says: "The ancestry of Navajo silver ornament forms has its roots in the silver trade jewelry distributed to the tribes east of the Mississippi River after 1750, and in the Mexican-Spanish costume ornaments and bridle trappings of the late eighteenth and early nineteenth centuries." (Woodward, Museum of Northern Arizona, 1938: 47.)

The earlier Navajo smiths often worked in copper and brass. In fact the only jewelry made during the Fort Sumner imprisonment was fashioned of these metals.

The first Navajo silversmith of note that we know by name was Atsidi Sani or Old Smith. He is credited by most historians as being the first member of the tribe to learn the art. Navajo informants say that Atsidi Sani learned to work silver from a Mexican after he returned from Fort Sumner and taught the art to his sons. In 1872, only four years after the Navajos returned to *Dinehtah,* a smith named Atsidi Chon (Ugly Smith), who is credited with being the first to fashion the concho belt, moved to Zuñi and taught Lanyade, the first Zuñi smith. Lanyade, in turn, taught the art to Sikyatala, the first Hopi smith, twenty-six years later.

Until 1890 when such use was prohibited by government authorities, the Navajo smiths melted American silver coins to fashion their silver ornaments. After that they used Mexican pesos, which contained more silver, and were softer and more easily worked. Since 1930, when Mexico forbade the export of its coin, Navajo smiths have used sterling silver in both slug and sheet form purchased from silver refineries. The jewelry made from the old American coins, because of the high copper content, is slightly more yellowish than that made from the Mexican and sterling silver.

The Navajos started using metal stamps during the 1880s and were quick to develop new techniques after that date. Shortly after that the design of the best known of all Navajo silver, the bracelet, began to take new and complicated forms. The squash blossom necklace is said to have come into existence in the 1880s also. Generally thought of as typically Navajo, the individual parts of the squash blossom necklace can be traced to outside sources. The squash blossom is an elongated version of the silver pomegranate once worn by Spanish men on their trousers and capes. The origins of the crescent-shaped pendant, called the *naja*, was in the Middle East and North Africa where it was used as an amulet to ward off the evil eye. The Spanish copied it from the Moors and used it as a bridle ornament and the Navajos borrowed it from the Spanish.

By the late 1800s Navajo silversmiths were fashioning tobacco canteens, buckles, blouse ornaments, buttons, pins, headstalls, rings, earrings, and even a small silver bell which was worn by older Navajo women to warn their son-in-laws of their approach. Fred Harvey and others began encouraging Navajo smiths to make souvenirs for tourists in the early 1900s. This demand, as with the blankets, led to a deterioration of the art when Navajo smiths began turning out shoddy pieces of poor design. Hitherto unknown pieces such as salad sets, spoons, cuff links and tie bars were produced exclusively for the tourist trade. They were poorly crafted and decorated with crossed arrows, thunderbirds and other objects that the tourists thought were typically Indian.

Fortunately Navajos continued to value their personal silver jewelry more than money and Navajo smiths continued to copy the old pieces and do quality work for themselves and to sell to other Navajos. Traditional jewelry of fine craftsmanship is being made in quantity again. Today the seven or eight hundred Navajo silversmiths working on and near the reservation—quite a few of whom are women—may turn out a few light flimsy key chains for the tourist trade one day and a fine sandcast bracelet for both the Navajo and the discerning white trade the next. Because more quality Navajo silver is being produced today than at any single time in the past and is bringing higher prices than ever before, there is little danger of the art disappearing. On the other hand much jewelry of inferior quality is also being mass-produced off the reservation and palmed off to white buyers as "Navajo" jewelry.

As Washington Matthews astutely observed in 1880: "The Navajos are not good potters . . . their crucibles are not durable. After being put in the fire two or three times they swell and become very porous, and when used for a longer time they crack and fall to pieces." Navajo pottery was a crude cooking ware. Following 1680 when they took in the Pueblo refugees, the Navajos made a painted pottery but these decorated pots were inferior imitations of the Pueblo product. Basketry and beadwork were never developed to an art among The People. The Navajos trade rugs and silver to the Pueblos for pottery and to the Utes for the baskets used in the Navajo marriage and some other ceremonies, although important ceremonial articles are made by The People themselves.

FIVE

The World is Holy

The Navajos have no collective center for worship, no calendrical worship, and no word or phrase in their language which could possibly be translated as "religion." Religion is not a separate entity to be believed in or subscribed to, it is ever present. It could no more be separated from the traditional Navajo's daily life than eating, breathing, sleeping, or the ground he walks on which gives him substance, the sun which gives him warmth or the summer lightning which gives him fear. Religious rites and practices are an essential element in nearly every aspect of traditional Navajo culture, pervading it to such an extent that, paradoxical as it may seem, it was several decades before white Americans living among the Navajo realized they possessed any form of worship at all.

Dr. Jonathon Letterman, Post Surgeon at Fort Defiance in the 1850s, reported to the Smithsonian Institution in 1855: "Of their religion little or nothing is known as, indeed, all inquiries tend to show they have none; and even have not, we are informed, any word to express the idea of Supreme Being. We have not been able to learn that any perseverances of a religious character exist among them; and the general impression of those who have had means of knowing them is that, in this respect, they are steeped in the deepest degradation . . . It is impossible to learn anything from the people themselves, as they have no traditions. A volume of no mean size might be written, were all the stories of interpreters taken for truth; but it would be found a mass of contradictions, and of no value whatever."

We have no way of knowing what stories the interpreters told Dr. Letterman, but since his time several substantial volumes of no mean size have been written on Navajo ceremonials. What the Spanish called "the great dances of the Navajos" a hundred years before Dr. Letterman's time were religious ceremonials, as Dr. Washington Matthews, who arrived on the reservation in the 1880s, learned. Dr. Matthews, after several years of concentrated study of Navajo ceremonials and rites, began the publication of what eventually amounted to nearly a dozen papers and books on Navajo "religion." Father Berard Haile, who devised the first Navajo-English dictionary, wrote several substantial books each of which is devoted to one of the dozens of Navajo ceremonials, as has Leland C. Wyman and others.

Because a volume the size of this one can be written about just one of the complex Navajo ceremonials, and there are fifty-eight of them, plus the variations, this dissertation will, of necessity, be cursory.

In the Navajo pantheon there is no distinguished deity who can be described as a supreme being. The most important deities include Changing Woman (Estsánatlehi), who created human beings and is associated with the earth, Sun, First Man, First Woman, and the Hero Twins, Monster Slayer and Born of Water, sons of Changing Woman and her sister White Shell Woman (Yolkaí Estsán). Changing Woman and White Shell Woman are one entity in some tales. Other entities, or Holy People, occupy less dominant or minor positions without, however, the clear-cut divine hierarchy which characterized the Greek or Roman pantheons.

The Universe, as viewed by the Navajo, is an orderly system of interrelated elements, an all-inclusive unity that contains both good and evil. Therefore the universe is good, benevolent and dangerous and, with the exception of Changing Woman, who is always benevolent, so are the

Holy People. Some entities which are described by Gladys Reichard as "persuadable deities" are predominantly good. These include figures who played an important role in the creation legend and in the proper development of the universe for the ultimate benefit of man. Among these are Sun, the Racing Gods, First Man, First Woman, Salt Woman, Talking God and House God. While First Man and First Woman are sometimes motivated for good, they control witchcraft and through sorcery are sometimes responsible for disease and misery.

They and other deities, including the *Yeis*, representing forces of nature, and a group called the Helpers that bridge the gap between the Holy People and the Earth Surface People (humans) figure prominently in the Navajo legends and in various ceremonials as do the Monsters, called the Fearful or Dreadful Ones.

Navajo belief is not formalized in the familiar Asiatic-European pattern, therefore the legends and ceremonials are not embodied in a creed or formalized doctrine by the Navajos. With the Navajo concept of the universe being a state in which good and evil are maintained in interrelated harmony, the problem, therefore, is maintaining that harmony. The primary purpose of the ceremonials, called "sings" after Matthews' translation of the word *hatal* to holy chant or song, is to keep man in harmony with the universe. Father Berard Haile concluded that *way* was a more accurate English rendering of the word hatal and the English names for most of the ceremonials are now suffixed with the word *way*.

The ceremonials are conducted by a "Singer" or "Chanter," called a *Hataali* by the Navajos and a "medicine man" by most whites. Most Singers know two or three complete ceremonials and specialize in those. It would be impossible for one man to learn all the complicated rituals for more than a few ceremonials. In the Night Way alone, Matthews recorded five hundred seventy-six songs and each song must be uttered word and intonation perfect to accomplish its purpose. The Singer must also, besides remembering all the songs for a ceremonial that might last nine days, hold in mind clearly the details of the symbols and their positions, the equipment, the elaborate rituals and the dances, and direct the creation of the drypainting.

An apprentice Singer studies the rite that he wishes to

learn by observing, and finally aiding, an older, respected Singer—an honor for which he pays. To master some of the more complicated ceremonials might take up to six or seven years of study.

Disease, misfortune, distress and other evils caused by failure to observe taboos and ceremonial regulations, by spirits, by natural elements or phenomena such as whirlwinds, lightning, water or, worst of all, witchcraft, are reasons for a ceremonial. Each rite is especially adapted to a particular set of uses, to combat or thwart one or another disease or misfortune. The specific ceremony required is determined by divination, itself a ceremony, and one carried out by a process of hand trembling, star gazing or listening. A diviner interprets the involuntary motions of his hand, or the thing he sees or hears while in a trancelike state, and discovers the cause of the trouble. He determines the proper ritual for a cure and may recommend a Singer.

The Singer is contacted and a date is set for the beginning of the ceremonial, usually four days ahead unless there is an urgency. Meanwhile the family of the patient must prepare for the sing; the hogan is emptied and swept; firewood, medicinal plants, sand, sandstone and other materials for the drypainting are gathered; grinding stones, baskets, buckskins and calico must be provided and much food must be prepared for the visitors. Some members of the family and the extended family and possibly others visit throughout the ceremonial but on the final day and night of a chant a hundred or more people may attend. The family and the visitors also receive benefits from the sing. The Singer is always paid in advance. The cost of a one- or two-night sing may be the equivalent of fifty dollars or under but a great nine-night chant such as the Mountain Top Way may cost a thousand dollars or more. A lengthy curing rite might tax the finances of the entire extended family.

The patient is purified through the rituals and eventually becomes identified with the deities whose help is sought to restore him to harmony with the universe. It has been pointed out that the sense of security the patient derives from the host of relatives and friends who surround him during the ceremony is also conducive to his recovery. Not only are the herbs and native medicines administered during many of the ceremonials to the patient beneficial to his physical condition but many white doctors at hospitals and health centers on the reservation have recognized the psychological benefits of the ceremonies in recent years. It is no longer unusual for a Singer to visit a patient in one of the modern hospitals on the reservation either at the invitation of the administrators or with their permission.

The curing chantways are always concerned with some specific disease. Hailway and Waterway treat illness resulting from cold or rain. The Shooting Chant is used to cure injuries received from lightning—which are not all that uncommon in the Navajo's part of the world—and from arrows or snakes, which are cognate to lightning or arrows. Snakes are also an important etiological factor, associated with Navajo Windway and Beautyway. Beautyway is also used against aching feet, legs, arms, back and waist, swollen ankles, itching skin and mental confusion. Insanity, very rare among the Navajos, and paralysis require the Night Chant.

The Night Chant, commonly referred to as the *Yeibichai*, is a major ceremony that may be given only between the first frost and the first thunderstorm, when the snakes are in hibernation and there is no danger from lightning. Of all the chants, this nine-day ceremonial is the most frequently given, but it must be carried out in a minute detail and in exactly prescribed order.

The Navajos believe that a mistake either by the Singer or the patient during its performance can result in crippling, paralysis or a loss of sight or hearing. Both boys and girls, at some time between the ages of seven and thirteen, are initiated into participation in the ceremonial life of the adults on the last night of a Night Way. Two masked figures appear, representing *Yei*, Grandfather of the Monsters and Female Divinity. Each of the boys to be initiated, naked to the waist, is in turn led out into the firelight, where one of the masked figures places sacred corn pollen on his shoulders, while another impersonator of the gods strikes him with a bundle of reeds. The girls, in turn, are marked with sacred yellow corn pollen. Finally these awesome creatures remove their masks, revealing to the initiates that they are not the gods themselves but human impersonators, known to the children. The masks are then placed on the face of each child in turn. It is said that the child then sees the world as it is seen through the eyes of the gods.

After the initiation ceremony, the long Yeibichai dance begins, usually with twelve dancers taking part, and continues for the remainder of the night. When dawn breaks everyone, visitors and performers alike, stand, face the East and repeat the Prayer of Dawn. When the prayer is finished, the Bluebird Song is heard. The bluebird is the symbol of happiness and heralds the break of day:

> Just at daylight Bluebird calls.
> The Bluebird has a voice
> His voice is melodious that flows in gladness
> Bluebird calls, Bluebird calls.
> — *Verse of the Navajo Bluebird Song*

The creation of drypaintings, often incorrectly called "sandpaintings," are an integral part of almost all ceremonies. There are five required during the Night Way. Among almost all the Indians of the Southwest, the drypainting is an important part of curing ceremonies. But no other people have developed this art to the degree that the Navajo have. The People recognize between six hundred and one thousand separate designs of drypaintings. There are thirty-five different drypaintings for the Red Antway ceremony alone. Most often the Singer directs the "painters" but does not directly participate in the creation of the drypainting. The painting is created on sand or sometimes on cloth or buckskin with, of course, sand, corn meal, flower pollen, powdered roots, stone and bark. Because of the sacred nature of the ceremony, the paintings are begun, finished, used and destroyed within a twelve-hour period. The purpose of the painting is curative and it is believed that the patient, by sitting upon the representations of the Holy People represented in the drypainting, will become identified with them and absorb some of their power.

At the ceremonies' conclusion the sands of the drypainting are carefully gathered upon the buckskin or a blanket. The Singer then walks east, then south, then west and north. With symbolic gestures up to the sky and down to the earth, he scatters the sands to the six directions from whence they came. Sometimes those present are given a small amount of the sacred sand. In some ceremonies all the sand is buried.

A drypainting may be a simple affair of three or so feet wide or it may be as large as twenty feet long and almost as wide and require several assistants to execute. The paintings that are executed during a sacred ceremonial follow a prescribed sequence and outsiders are very seldom allowed to photograph it. On the other hand, because of the desire of so many whites to see a "sandpainting," they are executed for exhibition purposes. In the latter color and direction are usually reversed and many variations brought into effect. Navajo singers considered the creation of an authentic drypainting for exhibition purposes a profanity.

For the same reason a complete relating of the Navajo legends to an outsider is taboo. There is no such thing as an "official" version of the all-important Navajo story of Creation, or the legend of the emergence as it is often called even among the Navajos. Details of the story, as told by a Singer from the Kayenta area will vary a great deal from those told by a Singer, say, from Shiprock. And in relating the story to a white recorder both Singers will change some parts of the story and leave out still others. The story of the *Dineh's* emergence into this world and the events that followed are told in the Navajo ceremony, the Blessingway which has been called "the backbone of Navajo religion." This legend—actually a series of legends—was said by Dr. Washington Matthews to be the Navajo's version of his history before the Europeans came to the Southwest. This epic tale comprises the next part of this book.

PART TWO

Navajo Legends

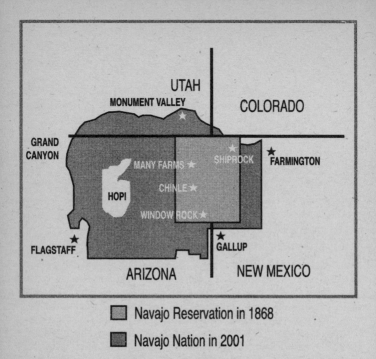

Navajo Reservation in 1868

Navajo Nation in 2001

After the peace treaty of 1868, at the end of the Navajos four years of imprisonment at Fort Sumner in eastern New Mexico, the Navajos were allowed to return to a small portion of the land they'd occupied for centuries. Since then large portions of traditional Dinetah has been returned to them. The Hopi reservation was created in 1872 in what was Navajo-Hopi joint use land (JUL).

ONE

The Fifth World of the Navajo

The Navajo legends are not only the basis of the complex ceremonials, they are also the history of the Navajos, much as the Old Testament is both the Judaic religious base and the history of the ancient Jews. The New Testament is not only the history of the first Christians, it is the foundation of Christianity. Hence, the Legends are, in fact, the Navajo's version of his own history. The all-important Story of Creation, also called the Story of Emergence, is retold in its entirety in the most sacred of all Navajo ceremonials, the nine-day Blessing Way, much as a rabbi might instruct a Jewish child in the Books of Moses or a priest might read the story of Christ to his congregation.

The first part of the Navajo Story of Creation parallels the Biblical book of Genesis in that it tells of the creation of the world. In fact the Navajo concept of the world is not unlike the early Judaic-Christian concept which described the earth as a land area floating in an immense ocean overspread by a solid domed heaven which fit like a great lid with its edges on the horizon, resting on supports in the water. Above the sky was still another similarly domed world. The Navajo Story of Creation traces the evolution of life through four such underworlds until The People emerged in this, the fifth and present world. As The People passed through each of the four first worlds, they went through a process of evolution, starting out as insects and finally becoming people as we know them today in the fourth world—with the explicit aid of the gods. Above this fifth world there is yet another world where all things blend into one with the cosmos.

Subsequent events in the Navajo Story of Creation and other legends also parallel Biblical stories. The expulsion of the Insect People from the first world for committing adultery parallels Adam and Eve's expulsion from the Garden of Eden; the destruction of both the First World and the Fourth World by flood might, of course, be compared to the story of Noah, and the slaying of the monsters of the fifth world by the Hero Twins can, with a stretch of the imagination, be compared to David slaying Goliath, but such parallels are coincidental and should not be used, as has been attempted, to find a common root for the Navajo Story of Creation and the Old Testament.

The Navajo legends are an oral history of the tribe that has been passed down from father to son, from generation to generation. There are variations in various versions of the legends as there must be in any oral history, but the variations are slight and the characters are always the same, though they are, as in the case of Estsánatlehi (Changing Woman, also called Turquoise Woman) and her sister, Yolkaí Estsán (White Shell Woman), sometimes interchangeable. But this is an abstraction that is perfectly clear to the Navajo although perhaps difficult for whites to comprehend.

I have drawn heavily on the work of Dr. Washington Matthews for the simple reason that the versions of the legends he recorded in the 1880s were composite versions told him by several different Singers.

More important, Matthews conducted his study of the Navajo legends before The People were overly exposed to the influence of white teachers and missionaries who often altered the legends and taught them to Navajo children to fit within quasi-Christian concept. Too, some white students of Navajo history and anthropologists have made changes in some of the legends which caused them to conform to a personal thesis.

For example, it was not until recent years that the theory of the Navajo's recent migration from the North was questioned in spite of the fact that the Navajos—those who chose not to believe the "migration" theory taught them by white teachers—have maintained the legend of an early migration from the West. Therefore most writers who have bothered to tell the "origin myth" at all have expediently left out the Navajo's version of an eastward migration.

Both Dr. Washington Matthews and Frederick Webb Hodge stated that, omitting a few obvious mythical elements, "the Story of Creation and subsequent Navajo legends can be substantiated by recorded history" long before we had archaeological proof that at least parts of the story are credible. For example, a Navajo Singer told Matthews in the 1880s that traditionally his people believed their ancestors arrived in the area around Chaco Canyon, New Mexico, when the Anasazi were in the process of building the pueblos there. It wasn't until Dr. Andrew E. Douglass developed the dating process known as dendrochronology (tree-ring dating) in 1929 that we were able to attach dates to the massive ruins in Chaco Canyon. Thanks to Douglass's work, we now know that the oldest section of the ruins dates from about A.D. 900. Building continued in Chaco Canyon until about 1130.

While drawing heavily on Matthews and consulting the work of others who have studied Navajo legends, I have been told two slightly varying versions of the Story of Creation by Navajo Singers. What follows is an abbreviation of the Navajo's version of his own "bible."

TWO

The Navajo Story of Creation

The First World was an island, surrounded by oceans, and there lived the first beings who started out in life. Although these beings are referred to as people, they were not people as we now know them but were insects and, therefore, they are called the Insect People.

The Insect People were twelve in number: Dragon Flies, Red Ants, Black Ants, Red Beetles, Black Beetles, White-Faced Beetles, Yellow Beetles, Hard Beetles, Dung Beetles, Bats, Locusts and White Locusts.

These Insect People lived in dwelling places on the borders of three streams in the middle of the first world, all of which emerged from a central place. Two flowed to the South and one flowed to the North.

In this First World, the surface of which was red in color (some versions give the color as black), white arose in the East and the Insect People regarded it as day there; blue arose in the South and they still regarded it as day, but when yellow arose in the West they knew that evening had come; then black arose in the North and the Insect People lay down to sleep.

In the oceans that surrounded this First World dwelt the

four chiefs (Gods) of the Insect People. These chiefs were Tieholtsodi (Water Monster) who dwelled in the ocean to the East, Tgaltl'a Gallé (Blue Heron) who lived in the ocean to the South, Ch' al (Frog) who lived in the ocean to the West and Adini dzil (White Mountain Thunder) who lived in the northern ocean.

The four chiefs soon became angry with The People and this is the way it happened. They committed adultery, one sort of Insect People with the other, and as a result, were constantly quarrelling among themselves. Tieholtsodi, chief of the East, observed the Insect People and said: "What shall we do with them? They do not like the land in which they dwell."

In the South Tgaltl'a Gallé warned them of the consequences of their conduct as did the other chiefs but still the people continued to sin and quarrel among themselves until it came to pass that none of the chiefs would speak to them.

Again they sinned and more they quarrelled until Ch' al lost all patience with them and said: "Go elsewhere at once. Leave here!"

Then Adini dzil said: "Go elsewhere and keep on going," as he, too, was through with them. But the Insect People paid no attention to the warnings of their Gods and continued to do the same things until finally the Gods held a council that lasted all night to decide what they must do with these people. At dawn Tieholtsodi called to The People and said: "You pay no attention to our words. Constantly you disobey, therefore you must go to some other place. Not in this world shall you remain."

For four nights the women of the Insect People talked about what the chiefs had said but as they knew of no other place but this one they came to no decision and did nothing. At the end of the fourth night, as morning broke, The People saw something white appear in the East. Then it also appeared in the South, the West and the North. It looked like a wall of white, as high as mountains and without a break, surrounding them. And soon, as it came closer, they saw what the white was. It was water, impassable and insurmountable, flowing all around them.

The Insect People had no choice but to leave the First World. They flew around in circles until they reached the sky, which was smooth and hard. When they looked down they saw that water had risen and covered the First World. While they were flying around, wondering where they could go now, a creature having a blue head thrust out his head from the sky—and called to them: "In here, to the East, there is a hole." They entered the hole and emerged on the surface of the Second World, which was blue in color.

The blue creature who had brought them there was a (cliff) swallow and belonged to the Tgashji'zhidine (Swallow People) who inhabited this world. About the surface of this world were scattered their houses which were rough and lumpy and tapered toward the top where there was a hole for entrance. A great many of the Swallow People gathered around the strangers but said nothing.

Now the Insect People wondered what was in this strange Second World so they sent out two couriers, a Locust and a White Locust, to find out. The couriers went to to the East first and at the end of two days they returned and said that after one day's travel they had reached the edge of the world which was the top of a great cliff that arose from an abyss the bottom of which they could not see. They had seen no people like themselves; nothing had they seen in fact but bare, level ground.

Then the Locust and the White Locust were sent to the South, to the West and to the North but each time they returned at the end of the second day and told the people that they had again reached the edge of the earth and, again, had seen nothing but flat, level ground. Then the Insect People knew that they were in the center of a vast barren wasteland where there was no food, nor kindred people.

It was after the couriers had returned from their last journey that the Swallow People visited the camp of the Insect People and asked them why they had sent out the couriers.

"We sent them out," was the reply, "to see what was in this land, and to see if any people like ourselves dwelt in it."

"And what did your couriers tell you?" the Swallow People asked.

"They told us that four times they had come to the edge of this world and four times they returned, yet saw no plant or other living thing in all the land."

"They spoke the truth," the Swallow People said. "Had

you asked us in the beginning what this land contained we would have told you and saved you all your trouble. Until you came, no one has ever dwelt in all this land but ourselves."

The Insect People then said to the Swallows: "You understand our language and are somewhat like us. You have legs, feet, bodies, heads and wings, as we have. Why cannot your people and our people become friends?"

"Let it be as you wish," replied the Swallows, and both people began at once to treat each other as members of one tribe; they mingled one among the other, and addressed one another by the terms of relationship, as my brother, my sister, my father, my mother, my daughter, and my son.

The Insect People and the Swallow People lived together in the Second World in harmony for twenty-three days. But on the night of the twenty-fourth day one of the Insect People made too free with the wife of the chief of the Swallow People. The next morning, when the chief found out what had transpired in the night, he said to the strangers: "We have treated you as friends as you requested and look how you have returned our kindness. We doubt not that for such crimes you were driven out of the lower world, and now you must leave this world. This is our land and we will have you here no longer. Besides this is a bad land, barren and without substance, and even if we spare you you will soon perish here."

When the Swallow chief had finished speaking, the Locusts took the lead and soared upwards; the others followed, and all soared and circled until they again reached the sky.

But they found the sky of the second world like that of the first, smooth, hard, and with no opening. They circled around under it, looking for a way to get through until they saw a white face peering out at them. It was the face of Nilch'i', the Wind. He told them that if they would fly to the South they would find a slit in the sky through which they might enter the Third World. They did as they were told and found the slit in the sky, which slanted up toward the South. They flew through the slit into the Third World, the color of which was yellow.

Now, inhabiting this Third World were the Grasshopper People who, like the Swallow People, gathered around the strangers but said nothing. The Grasshoppers lived in holes in the ground along the banks of a great river which flowed through their land to the East. Again the Insect People sent out the Locust couriers to see what was in this third world. The Locusts explored the land to the East, to the South, to the West and to the North, but returned from each journey after two days, saying they reached the edge of the world and found no kindred people in it, nor anything else but a barren land in which no people lived except the Grasshoppers.

When the Locust couriers returned from their fourth and last journey, the two great chiefs of the Grasshoppers visited the strangers and asked them why they had sent out explorers. Again the strangers answered that they had sent out the Locusts to see what was in the land and if there were any people like themselves living in it.

"And what did your couriers find?" the Grasshopper chiefs asked.

"They found nothing but a barren land in which there is a river and peopled by none save yourselves."

"There is nothing else in this land," said the Grasshopper chiefs. "Long we have lived here, but we have seen no other people but ourselves until you came here."

As the strangers had spoken to the Swallows in the second world, they now spoke to the Grasshoppers, pointing out that they spoke the same language and were alike in many ways and begged that they might remain and become one people with them. The Grasshoppers consented to allow the strangers to stay and at once the two peoples mingled among one another and embraced one another, and called each other by the endearing terms of relationship, as if they all belonged to the same tribe.

As before the strangers were treated with great kindness and lived happily among the Grasshoppers for twenty-three days, but on the night of the twenty-fourth day one of them served a chief of the Grasshoppers as the chief of the Swallows had been served in the Second World. In the morning, when the wrong was discovered, the Grasshopper chief called the strangers around him and said: "I suppose you were chased from the world below for such sins. You shall drink no more of our water, you shall breathe no more of our air. Begone!"

Again the Insect People flew upwards and circled around and around until they came to the sky but, as before, they found it hard, smooth, and impenetrable. When they had circled around for some time, looking for an opening in the sky of the Third World, they saw a red head appear out of the sky. It was the head of Red Wind and he told them that if they would fly to the West they would find an opening.

The passage which they found in the West was twisted round like the tendril of a vine as it had been made by the wind. They flew in circles through it and came out into the Fourth World. Four of the Grasshoppers came with them: one white, one blue, one yellow and one black and that is why there are grasshoppers of those four colors.

The surface of the Fourth World was mixed black and white. The colors in the sky of this world were the same as in the lower worlds but there was little of the white and yellow; the blue and the black lasted most of the time. But still, in the Fourth World, there was neither sun, moon nor stars.

The strangers saw no living beings in the Fourth World when they arrived but they could see four great snow-covered peaks sticking up at the horizon—one to the East, one to the South, one to the West and one to the North.

Again the Locust couriers were sent out to see what this world contained. Journeying to the East first, they returned after two days to report that they had travelled far but had been unable to reach the eastern mountain—and that they had seen no sign of life. Next they journeyed south and again returned after two days. The couriers related that they had reached a low range of mountains but had been unable to reach the great peak. And while they had seen no living creatures, they had seen two different kinds of tracks, such as they had never seen before. The tracks they saw and described were those made by the deer and the turkey.

Again two couriers were sent to the West but they returned after two days, having failed to reach the western peak, nor had they seen any living creature or sign of life. Then the couriers were sent to the North. When they returned from their journey of two days they related that they had failed to reach the northern peak but that they had found living creatures. The creatures were a race of strange men who cut their hair square in front, who lived in houses and cultivated fields. These people were engaged in gathering the harvest of their fields, the couriers said, and treated them most kindly, giving them food to eat.

The day after the return of the couriers from the North, two of the newly discovered race visited the camp of the exiles. This strange race of men were the Kisani (Pueblos) and the two visitors guided the strangers to a stream of water. The water was red and the Kisani told the wanderers that they must not walk through the stream, for if they did they would injure their feet. Then the Kisani showed them a square raft made of four logs—a white pine, a blue spruce, a yellow pine and a black spruce—on which they might cross the stream to visit the homes of the Kisani on the other side of the stream, which they immediately did.

Now this land of the Kisani had neither rain nor snow but the people who lived in it raised crops of corn, squash and pumpkins by irrigation and shared their harvest with the strangers. The wanderers held a council among themselves and decided that since the Kisani had treated them kindly and fed them, they would mend their ways and do nothing to make their newfound friends angry. They lived on the food the Kisani gave them daily and all was well in this Fourth World.

Late in autumn, after the exiles had been in the new world for some time, they heard the distant sound of a great voice calling in the East. They listened and waited, and soon the voice called again, this time nearer and louder. The third time the voice called it was louder than before and closer still, and the fourth time it called the voice was louder still and clear, like the voice of one near at hand. A moment later four strange, mysterious beings appeared before them.

These four beings were Sits'is Lagai', or White Body, a being similar to the god of this world whom the Navajos call Hastseyalti; Sits'is' Dotl'ish', or Blue Body, who was like the present Navajo god Tonenili, or Water Sprinkler; Sits'is' Li'tso, or Yellow Body, and Sits'is' Lizhin, or Black Body, who was the same as the present Navajo god of fire, Hastsezhini.

Now these beings did not speak to the wanderers but made many signs, as if instructing them, none of which the people understood, then left. When these gods had gone, the people long discussed the mysterious visit, and tried to determine what the gods meant by the signs they had made. In the same manner the four gods appeared for four days in succession and made signs to the people which they were unable to understand. But on the fourth day, when the other three had departed, Black Body remained behind and spoke to the people in their own language and this is what he said:

"You do not seem to understand the signs that these gods make to you, so I must tell you what they mean. They want to make more people, but in form like themselves. You have bodies like theirs, but you have the teeth, the feet, and the claws of beasts and insects. The new creatures are to have hands and feet like ours. But you are unclean and you smell badly. Have yourselves well cleansed when we return; we will come back in twelve days."

On the morning of the twelfth day The People washed themselves well. The women dried themselves with yellow corn meal, the men with white corn meal (Yellow corn belongs to the female, white corn to the male. This rule is observed in all Navajo ceremonies). Soon after the ablutions were completed, they heard the distant call of the approaching gods. It was shouted as before, four times, nearer and louder with each repetition—and after the fourth call, the gods appeared. Blue Body and Black Body each carried a sacred buckskin. White Body carried two ears of corn, one yellow, one white, each of which were completely covered with kernals.

The gods placed one of the sacred buckskins on the ground with the head to the West, on which they placed the two ears of corn, with their tips to the East. Under the white ear they placed the feather of a white eagle and under the yellow ear they placed the feather of a yellow eagle. Then they spread the second buckskin, with its head to the East, over the corn and told the people to stand at a distance and allow the wind to enter. The white wind blew from the East and the yellow wind blew from the West, between the skins. While the wind was blowing the Mirage People (supernatural beings) came and walked around the objects on the ground four times, and as they walked the eagle feathers, whose tips protruded from between the buckskins, were seen to move. When the Mirage People had finished their walk the upper buckskin was lifted; the ears of corn had disappeared. The white ear of corn had been changed into a man, the yellow ear into a woman. It was the wind, the Navajos say, that gave them life. When the mouth wind ceases to blow we die. In the skin at the tips of our fingers we see the trail of the wind; it shows where the wind blew when our ancestors were created.

The pair created from the corn were First Man (Atse Hastiin) and First Woman (Atse Asdzan). The gods directed The People to build an enclosure of brushwood for the pair. When the enclosure was finished, First Man and First Woman entered it, and the gods said to them: "Live together now as husband and wife."

At the end of four days hermaphrodite twins were born, and at the end of four more days a boy and girl were born, who in four days grew to maturity and lived with one another as husband and wife. First Man and First Woman had in all five pairs of twins, the first of which only were barren, being hermaphrodites.

Four days after the last pair of twins were born, the gods came again and took First Man and First Woman away to the East where the gods dwelt, and kept them there for four days. And when they returned all their children were taken to the same place and kept there for four days. First Man, First Woman and their children were taught many things in the eastern mountains. Soon after they returned they were seen occasionally to wear masks such as Hastéyalti (Talking God) and Hastéhogan (House God) wear now, and when they wore these masks they prayed for all good things, such as abundant rain and good crops. It is thought, too, that during their visit among the gods they learned the awful secrets of witchcraft for the witches always keep such masks with them and marry those too closely related to themselves.

When they returned from the eastern mountains the brothers and sisters separated; and, keeping the fact of their former unlawful marriages to each other secret, the brothers married women of the Mirage People and the sisters married men of the Mirage People. They kept secret, too, all the mysteries they had learned in the eastern mountains. The women thus married bore children every four days, and the children grew to maturity in four days, were married, and in their turn had children every four days. This numerous offspring married among those who had come from the lower worlds, as well as among the Kisani, and soon there was a multitude of people in the land.

These descendants of First Man and First Woman made a great farm, the seed for which were given to them by the

Kisani. (In other versions they stole the seeds from the Pueblos.) They built a dam and dug a wide irrigation ditch. But they feared the Kisani might injure their dam or their crops. So they put one of the hermaphrodite twins to watch the dam and the other one to watch the lower end of the field. The hermaphrodite who watched at the dam invented pottery. He made first a plate, a bowl, and a dipper, which were greatly admired by the people. The hermaphrodite who lived at the lower end of the farm invented the wicker water bottle. Others made tools for farming, such as hoes from the shoulder blades of deer, axes of stone and implements from thin split boards of the cottonwood tree which they shoved before them to clear the weeds out of the land.

Still others, hunters among them, killed deer and one among them thought that perhaps they might make a mask from the skin of the head of the deer, by which means they could approach other deer and kill them. But they were unable to make the mask fit until the gods returned and showed them how it should be made, how the motions of the deer were to be imitated, and explained to them all the mysteries of the deer hunt. Making use of the knowledge the gods had taught them, the hunters went out the next day and killed several deer, from which more masks were made and more men were able to join the hunt. After that time The People had an abundance of meat and dressed themselves in garments made from the deerskins.

When The People from the Third World had been in the Fourth World eight years—and had married among the descendents of First Man and First Woman and no longer resembled their former selves—a strange thing happened. One day they saw the sky stooping down and the earth rising up to meet it. For a moment the sky and the earth came into contact, and then there sprang out of the earth, at the point of contact, the Coyote and the Badger. The Coyote rose first, and for this reason he is the elder brother of the Badger and they both are children of the sky. At once the Coyote came over to the farm and skulked around among the people, while the Badger went down into the hole that led to the lower world.

First Man was the chief of all these people who lived in the Fourth World, except the Kisani, who had their own chief. He was a great hunter and a wise man. He told The

People the names of the four mountains that rose in the distance. They were named the same as the four mountains that now bound Navajo land. There was Tsisnaajini (Mount Blanca), Sacred Mountain of the East, Tsoodzil (Mount Taylor), Sacred Mountain of the South, Doko'oosliid (San Francisco Peaks), Sacred Mountain of the West, and Dibentsaa (Mount Hesperus), Sacred Mountain of the North. He also told them of the different race of people that lived in each mountain.

While First Woman had given birth to The People, she was obese and untidy and prone to argue with First Man. One day he brought home a fine fat deer from the hunt. First Woman boiled some of it and had a hearty meal. When they had done the woman wiped her greasy hands on her dress and said, "E'yehe sitsod" (Thanks, my vagina).

"What is that you said?" asked First Man.

She repeated what she had said.

"Why do you speak thus?" he asked. "Was it not I who killed the deer whose flesh you have eaten? Why do you not thank me? Was it your vagina that killed the deer?"

"Yes," she replied. "If it were not for that, you would not have killed the deer. If it were not for that you lazy men would do nothing. It is (for) that which (you do) does all the work."

"Then, perhaps you women think you can live without men," he said.

"Certainly we can. It is we women who till the fields and gather food. We can live on the produce of our fields, and the seeds and fruits we collect. We have no need of you men." Thus they argued. First Man became more and more angry with each reply that his wife made, until at length he jumped across the fire and spent the rest of the night by himself in silence.

The next morning First Man went out early and called aloud to the people: "Come hither, all you men," he said. "I wish to speak to you, but let all the women stay behind. I do not wish to see them."

Soon all the males gathered and he told them what his wife had said the night before. "They believe," he said, "that they can live without us. Let us see if they can hunt game and till the fields without our help. Let us see what sort of a living they can make by themselves. Let us leave them and persuade the Kisani to come with us. We will cross the river and when we are on the other side we will keep the raft there with us."

Then he sent for the hermaphrodites and they came, covered with meal, for they had been grinding corn.

"What have you made yourselves?" he asked.

"We have made two mealing-stones, and we have cups and bowls and baskets and many other things," they answered.

"Then take these along with you," he ordered, "and join us to cross the river."

Then all the men and the hermaphrodites assembled at the river and crossed to the north side on the raft. With them they took their stone axes, their farm implements and everything else they had made. When they had all crossed the river they sent the raft down to the Kisani for them to cross. The men left the women everything the latter had helped to make or raise, but the Kisani took their women with them.

As soon as they had crossed the river the men began working. Some of them went out hunting—for the young boys needed food—while others set to work chopping down willows and building huts. By the end of four days they had shelters in which to live.

That winter the women had an abundance of food, and they feasted, sang and had a good time. Often they came down to the edge of the river and called across to taunt the men.

The next year the men prepared a few small fields and raised some corn, but they did not have enough corn to eat and still had to live mostly by hunting. The women planted all the old farm, but they did not work it very well and when the second winter came they had much less and did not sing and make merry as they had done the first year. In the second spring the women planted even less, while the men increased the size of their fields by clearing more land and planting more. Thereafter each year the fields and crops of the men increased, while those of the women diminished and they began to suffer for want of food. In the autumn of the third year of separation many women jumped into the river and tried to swim over, but they were carried under the surface and never seen again. In the fourth year the men had more than they could eat; corn and pumpkins lay untouched in the fields, while the women were starving.

At length, First Man began to think what the effect of his course might be. He saw that if he continued to keep the men and the women apart the race would die out, so he called the men together and spoke his thoughts to them. Some said, "Surely our race will perish," and others said, "What good is our abundance to us? We think so much of our poor women starving in our sight that we cannot eat."

First Man then sent one of the men to the river bank to call across to find if First Woman was still there, and to bid her come down to the river if she were. She came to the bank, and First Man called to her and asked if she still thought she could live alone.

"No," she replied. "We cannot live without our husbands."

The women were then told to assemble at the shores of the stream. The raft was sent over and the women were ferried across. But before the women were allowed to mingle with the men they were made to bathe their bodies and dry them with corn meal. Then they were put in a corral and kept there until night, when they were let out to join the men in their feasts.

Now during the separation of the sexes, both men and women were guilty of unnatural sex acts. Through the transgressions of the women the Naye'i (alien gods or monsters) who afterwards nearly annihilated the human race, came into existence, but no evil consequences followed the transgressions of the men.

When the women were let out of the corral that first night, it was found that three of them were missing. After dark, voices were heard calling from the other side of the river. They were the voices of the missing ones—a mother and her two daughters. They begged to be ferried over, but the men told them it was too dark, that they must wait until morning. Upon hearing this reply, they jumped into the river and tried to swim across. The mother succeeded in reaching the opposite bank and finding her husband. The daughters were seized by Tieholtsodi, the water monster, and dragged down under the water.

For three days and three nights nothing was heard of the young women and The People supposed them lost forever. But on the morning of the fourth day the call of the gods was heard—four times as usual—and after the fourth call White Body made his appearance, holding up two fingers and pointing at the river. The people supposed that these signs had reference to the lost girls. Some of the men crossed the stream on the raft and found the tracks of the lost ones, which they traced to the edge of the water. White Body went away, but soon returned, accompanied by Blue Body. White Body carried a large bowl of white shell, and Blue Body a large bowl of blue shell. They asked for a man and a woman to accompany them, and they went down to the river. They put both the bowls on the surface of the water and caused them to spin around. Beneath the spinning bowls the water opened, for it was hollow, and gave entrance to a large house of four rooms.

The man and the woman descended and Coyote followed them. In the room in the East, which was made of dark waters, they found nothing. In the room in the South, which was made of blue waters, they found nothing. And in the room in the West, which was made of yellow waters, they again found nothing. But when they went into the room in the North, which was made of waters of all colors, they found the water monster Tieholtsodi, with the two girls he had stolen, and two children of his own. The man and the woman demanded the girls he had stolen, and as he said nothing in reply, they took them and walked away. But as they went out, Coyote, unperceived by all, took the two children of Tieholtsodi and carried them off under his robe. Now Coyote always wore his robe folded close around his body and always slept with it folded in this manner, so no one was surprised to see that he still wore his robe in this way when he came up from the waters of the river—and of course no one suspected that he had stolen the children of Tieholtsodi.

The next day The People were surprised to see deer, turkey, and antelope running past from east to west, and to see animals of six different kinds (two kinds of Hawks, two kinds of Squirrels, the Hummingbird, and the Bat) come into the camp of The People for refuge. The concern of The People grew as the game animals ran past in increasing numbers for three days. On the morning of the fourth day, when the white light rose, The People observed in the East a strange white gleam along the horizon, and they sent out the Locust couriers to see what caused this unusual white light. The Locusts returned at sunset and told The People that a vast flood of waters was fast approaching from the

East. On hearing this, The People all assembled together, the Kisani along with the others, in a great multitude, and they wailed and pulled at their hair over the approaching catastrophe. The People wept and moaned all night. The next morning, when the white light arose in the East, the waters were seen high as mountains encircling the whole horizon, except in the West, and rolling on rapidly. The People packed up all their goods as fast as they could, and ran up on a high hill nearby, for temporary safety. Here they held a council. Some one suggested that perhaps the two Squirrels (Hazaitso and Hazai) might help them.

"We will see what we can do," said the Squirrels. One planted a piñon seed, the other a juniper seed, and they grew so very fast that The People hoped that they would soon grow so tall that the flood could not reach their tops, and that they all might find shelter there. But after the trees had grown but a little way they began to branch out and grew no higher. Then The People, more frightened than ever, called on the Weasels (Dlu'ilgai and Dlu'ilitso). One of these planted a spruce seed and the other a pine seed. The trees sprouted at once and grew fast, and again The People began to hope. But soon the trees began to branch, and they dwindled to slender points at the top and ceased to grow higher. Now The People were in the depths of despair, for the waters were coming nearer with each moment. It was then that they saw two men approaching the hill on which they were gathered. One of the men was very old and gray of hair while the other, who walked in advance, was young. They ascended the hill and passed through the crowd, speaking to no one. The young man sat down on the summit, the old man sat down behind him, and the Locust sat down behind the old man—all facing East.

The old man took seven bags from beneath his robe and opened them. Each contained a small quantity of earth. He told The People that the earth was from the seven sacred mountains. (There were in the Fourth World seven sacred mountains, named and placed like the sacred mountains of the present Navajo land.)

"Ah, perhaps our father can do something for us," said The People.

"I cannot, but my son may be able to help you," said the old man.

Then they begged the son to help them and he said that

he would if they would all move away from where he stood, face to the West and not look around until he called them; for no one should see him at his work. They did as he asked and in a few moments he called and told them to come to him. When they came they saw that he had spread the sacred earth on the ground and planted thirty-two reeds in it, each of which had thirty-two joints. As they gazed they saw the roots of the reeds striking out into the soil and growing rapidly downward. A moment later all the reeds joined together and became one reed of great size, with a hole in its eastern side. He then told them to enter the hollow of the reed through this hole. When they were all safely inside, the opening closed. Scarcely had it closed when they heard the loud noise of the waters surging outside.

The waters rose fast but the reed grew faster, and soon it grew so high that it began to sway. The People inside, of course, were in great fear that their weight would cause the reed to break and topple over into the water. White Body, Blue Body, Yellow Body and Black Body were along. Black Body blew a great breath out through a hole in the top of the reed; a heavy dark cloud formed around the reed and kept it steady. But as the reed grew higher and higher, again it began to sway, and again The People within were in great fear, whereupon Black Body blew and made another cloud to steady the reed.

By darkness it had grown up close to the sky, but it swayed and waved so much that they could not secure it to the sky until Black Body, who was uppermost, took the plume out of his headband and stuck it out through the top of the cane against the sky, and this is why the reed (*Phragmites communis*) always carries a plume on its head now.

Still the water continued to rise. As the Turkey was the last to enter the reed, he was at the bottom. When the waters rose high enough to wet the Turkey he began to gobble and the people knew that danger was near. Often did the waves wash the end of the Turkey's tail and it is for this reason that the tips of the turkey's tail feathers are, to this day, lighter in color than the rest of his plumage.

Seeing no hole in the sky, The People sent up the Great Hawk, to see what he could do. He flew up and began to scratch in the sky with his claws, and he scratched and scratched until he was lost to sight. After a while he came back and said that he had scratched to where he could see light, but he could not get through the sky. Next they sent up all the digging animals, each in turn, to try to dig through the sky to the Fifth World. The Bear tried first and he grew tired, then the Wolf, the Coyote and the Lynx, each trying to dig through and each growing tired in turn. The Badger was the last to try and while he was digging water began to drip down from above. The people knew they had struck the waters of the upper world but Badger was too tired to dig any more. Next Locust was sent up. He made a shaft in the soft mud, such as locusts make to this day, and managed to reach the Fifth World.

Locust was gone a long time and when he returned he had this story to tell: He had gotten through to the upper world and came out on a little island in the center of a lake. When he got out he was approached from the East by a White Grebe (Swan in other versions), from the South by a Blue Grebe, from the West by a Yellow Grebe and from the North by a Black Grebe. The Grebes told the Locust that they owned this upper world and offered him a challenge. "If you can do as we do," they said, "we shall give you this world. If you cannot, you must die."

Each of the Grebes had an arrow made of the black wind. Each in turn passed the arrow from side to side through his heart and flung it down to Wonistisidi, the Locust. The Locust picked up the arrows and ran them from side to side through his heart as he had seen the Grebes do, and threw them down. The Grebes departed, leaving the land to the Locust. To this day we see in every Locust's sides the holes made by the arrows.

But the hole the Locust made in ascending to the Fifth World was too small for many of the people, so they sent Badger up to make it larger. When Badger came back his legs were stained black with mud, and the legs of all badgers have been black ever since. Then First Man and First Woman led the way and all the others followed them, and climbed up through the hole to the surface of this—the Fifth World.

The lake in which they emerged was surrounded by high cliffs, from the top of which stretched a great plain. Finding no way out of the lake, they called on Blue Body to help them. Blue Body had brought four stones with him from the lower world, and he threw one of each toward the four cardinal points against the cliffs, breaking holes through the cliffs through which the waters flowed away in four directions. While the lake did not altogether drain out through the holes Blue Body had made, the bottom did become bare in one place—in the East—connecting the island with the mainland. But the mud was so deep in this place that The People still hesitated to cross so they prayed to Smooth Wind to come to their aid. The wind came and in one day dried up the mud so that the people could easily walk over. While they were waiting for the ground to dry, the Kisani camped on the east side of the island and built a wall of mud and stone to shelter them from the wind, and the others (the Navajo) built a shelter of brushwood for protection against the wind. That is why the Pueblos build houses of stone and adobe now and the Navajo built brushwood shelters for protection against the summer wind.

The next day, when they reached the mainland, they sought to divine their fate. To do this one of The People threw a hide-scraper into the water, saying: "If it sinks we perish, if it floats we live." It floated and all rejoiced.

But Coyote said, "Let me divine your fate." He picked up a stone and said, "If it sinks we perish, if it floats we live," as he threw it into the water. The stone sank and all The People were angry with him, but he answered them, sayiing, "If we all live, and continue to increase as we have done, the earth will soon become too small to hold all of us, and there will be no more room for cornfields. It is better that each of us should live but a time on this earth and then leave and make room for our children." The People saw the wisdom of his words and were silent.

On the fourth day after the emergence someone went to look at the hole through which they had come from the underworld and saw water welling up there; already it was nearly to the top of the hole and each moment it grew higher. Quickly he ran back to his people and told them what he had seen. A council was called at once to consider the new danger that threatened them. First Man, who rose to speak, pointed at Coyote who had pointed knowingly with his protruded lips at the rising water. "Yonder is a rascal, and there is something wrong about him. He never takes off his robe, even when he lies down to sleep. I have watched him for a long time, and have suspected that he carries some stolen property under his robe. Let us search him."

They tore the robe from Coyote's shoulders and two strange little objects that resembled buffalo calves, but were spotted all over in various colors, dropped out. These were the children of Tieholtsodi. At once the people threw them into the hole through which the waters were pouring and in an instant the waters subsided and rushed back into the lower world with a deafening noise.

On the fifth night one of the twin hermaphrodites ceased to breathe. They left him alone all that night and, when morning came, Coyote proposed to lay him at rest among the rocks. This they did, but they all wondered what had become of his breath. They went in various directions to seek its trail, but could find it nowhere. While they were hunting, two men went over to the hole from which they had emerged from the lower world. It occurred to one of them to look down into the hole. He did so, and saw the dead one seated by the side of the river in the Fourth World, combing his hair. Then he returned to The People and told them what he had seen, but in four days he died. Ever since the Navajos feared to look upon the dead or to behold a ghost, lest they die themselves.

Soon after this it was learned that the Kisani, who had made their camp a little distance away from the others, had brought an ear of corn for seed from the lower world. Some of the people proposed that they go to the camp of the Kisani and take the corn away from them. But others, of better counsel, said that this would be wrong as the Kisani had suffered as much as the rest, and if they had the foresight to bring corn with them from the lower world they should profit by it. In spite of these words, some of the young men went to the Kisani and demanded the corn.

After some angry talk on both sides, the Kisani said, "We will break the ear in two and give you whichever half you choose." The young men agreed to this proposition and the woman who owned the ear of corn broke it in the middle and laid the pieces down for the others to choose. The young men looked at the pieces considering which they should choose, when Coyote impatiently picked up the tip end of the ear and made off with it. The Kisani kept the butt, and this is the reason the Pueblos have always had better crops than the Navajos. But the Pueblos had become alarmed at the threats and angry language of their neighbors and moved away from them to the East, and this is why the Navajos and the Pueblos now live apart from one another.

After the Kisani had moved away, First Man and First Woman, Black Body and Blue body left the people and set out to build the seven sacred mountains of the present Navajo land. They made them all of earth which they had brought from similar mountains in the Fourth World. The mountains they made were Tsisnaajini in the East, Tsoodzil in the South, Doko'oosliid in the West and Dibentsaa in the North. They also made Ch'oolii, Dzil'na'oodilii, and Naatsis'aan in the middle of the land.

Through Tsisnaajini (Mount Blanca) in the East, they ran a bolt of lightning to fasten it to earth and decorated it with white shells, white lightning, white corn, dark clouds and male rain. (The Navajos refer to a heavy downpour as a "male rain." A light shower or drizzle is called a "female rain.") Then they set a large bowl of shell on its summit in which they placed two eggs of the Pigeon to make feathers for the mountain. They covered the eggs with a sacred buckskin to make them hatch and all these things they covered with a sheet of daylight. Then they put Rock Crystal Boy and Rock Crystal Girl, the deities of Tsisnaajini, into the mountain to dwell. The deities were brought up from the lower world as small images of stone, but as soon as they were placed in the mountain they came to life.

Next they made the sacred mountain of the south, Tsoodzil, (Mount Taylor), and fastened it to the earth with a great stone knife, thrust through from top to bottom. They adorned Tsoodzil with turquoise, with dark mist, female rain and different kinds of game animals. On its summit they placed a dish of turquoise in which they put two eggs of the Bluebird, which they covered with the sacred buckskin to make them hatch, and over all these things they spread a covering of blue sky. Into this mountain to dwell they placed the Boy Who Carries One Turquoise and the Girl Who Carries One Grain of Corn.

They fastened Doko'oosliid (San Francisco Peaks), the sacred mountain of the West, to the earth with a sunbeam and adorned it with haliotis shell, with black clouds, male rain, yellow corn and all sorts of wild animals. Upon the top of Doko'oosliid they placed a dish made of haliotis shell and placed in it two eggs of the Yellow Warbler, covering them with the sacred buckskin. Over all this they spread a yellow cloud and placed White Corn Boy and Yellow Corn Girl to dwell.

They fastened Dibentsaa (Mount Hesperus), the sacred mountain of the North, to the earth with a rainbow and adorned it with black beads, dark mist, with many kinds of plants and many different wild animals. On its top they placed a dish of paszini (black beads) in which they placed two eggs of the Blackbird, over which they laid a sacred buckskin. Over all this they spread a covering of darkness. Then they put Pollen Boy and Grasshopper Girl in the mountain to dwell.

Dzil'na'oodilii was fastened with a sunbeam, and was decorated with goods of all kinds, with dark cloud and male rain. On top of it they put nothing, leaving its summit free in order that warriors might fight there, but they did put Boy Who Produces Goods and Girl Who Produces Goods in the mountain to dwell.

Ch'oolii was fastened to the earth with a cord of rain. They decorated it with pollen, the dark mist and female rain. On top of Tsolihi they placed a yellow bird called Tsozgali (species undetermined), and they put Boy Who Produces Jewels and Girl Who Produces Jewels in the mountain to live.

They fastened the mountain of Naatsis'aan to the earth with a mirage stone (silicate of magnesia) and decorated it with black clouds, male rain and all sorts of plants. They placed a live Grasshopper to live on its summit and inside they put Mirage Stone Boy and Carnelian Girl to dwell.

Now as The People only had the three lights and the darkness from the lower worlds in the Fifth World, First Man and First Woman thought they might form some lights which would make the world brighter. After much discussion, they decided to make the Sun and the Moon. For the sun they made a round flat object, like a dish, out of a clear stone. They set turquoises around the edge and outside of these they put rays of red rain, lightning and snakes of many kinds. For a while they debated putting four points on it, as they afterwards did to the stars, but finally they decided to leave it round. They made the Moon of crystal and bordered it with white shells. Upon its face they put sheet lightning and all kinds of water.

Then they held a council to decide what to do with the Sun and the Moon. The East Wind begged that they might belong to his land, so the people dragged them off to the edge of the world where he dwelt. There they gave the Sun to the young man who had planted the great reed in the lower world and appointed him to carry it. To his father, the old gray-haired man, they gave the Moon to carry. These men had had no names before this, but now the young man was given the name of Tsohanoai (or Tsinhanoai) and the old one was named Klehanoai. When they were about to depart, in order to begin their labors, a great sorrow came upon the people, for they were loved by all. But First Man said, "Mourn not for them, for you will see them in the heavens."

On the fifth day after The People entered the Fifth World, the Sun climbed to the zenith and stopped. The day grew hot and the people all longed for the night to come but the Sun did not move. Then the Coyote, who had invented death by tossing a stone in the water, said: "The Sun has stopped because he has not been paid for his work. He demands a human life for every day that he labors and he will not move again until someone dies."

Soon a woman, the wife of a great chief, ceased to breathe and grew cold, and while they all drew around her in wonder, the Sun was observed to move again, and he travelled down the sky and passed behind the western mountains. That night the Moon stopped in the zenith, as the Sun had done during the day, and the Coyote told the people that the Moon also demanded payment and would not move until it was given. He had scarcely spoken when the man who had seen the departed hermaphrodite in the lower world died and the Moon, satisfied, continued his journey to the West. And thus it is that someone must die each day and each night or the Sun and the Moon would not continue to journey across the sky. And that was what First Man meant when he told the people not to mourn for the old man and his son, for all that die will join them in the heavens and become theirs in return for their labors.

THREE

How the Mexicans Came to Be

After First Man and First Woman had made the stars because they thought it would be better if the heavens had some lights as the Moon did not always shine at night (as the old gray-haired man was often too tired from his labors to make the journey across the night sky), The People began to travel toward the East. At a place called White Spot on the Earth they camped for the night and it was here that a woman gave birth, but her offspring was not like a child. It was round and had no head. The people had a council and decided to throw it in a gully, which they did. But the monster lived and grew up to be Teelget, who afterwards destroyed so many of The People.

The next day they continued to travel east, but when they stopped at a place to camp called Rock Bending Back, another woman gave birth to a misshappen creature. It had something like feathers on both its shoulders and looked like nothing that had ever been seen before so the people took it to an alkali bed nearby and cast it away. But it lived and grew and became the terrible Tse'nahale.

Still travelling east, they camped the third night near a broad high cliff that was like a wall and here a woman bore another strange creature. It had no head, but had a long, pointed end where the head should be. The People placed this monster in a hole in the cliff and sealed it up with stone. They left it there to die but it grew up and became the destroyer Tse'tahotsiltali.

The fourth night they stopped at a place called Rock with Black Hole and twins were born to a woman. The twins were round with one end tapering to a point. There were no signs of limbs or head, but there were depressions which had somewhat the appearance of eyes. The People lay them on the ground and the next day they moved on, abandoning them. The twins grew up, however, and became the Binaye Ahani, who slew with their eyes.

All of these monsters were the consequence of the transgressions of the women in the Fourth World which took place when they were separated from the men. Still other monsters were born on the march east and still others sprang from the blood which had been shed during the birth of the first monsters and they all grew up to become enemies and destroyers of The People.

Next The People journeyed until they came to a place called Water in a Narrow Gully, and here they remained for thirteen years, making farms and planting corn, beans and pumpkins every spring.

From that place The People moved to a place called Standing White Rock and lived for thirteen more years; then they moved to White on Face of Cliff and here, once more, they remained for thirteen years. It was during this time that the monsters began to devour the people.

From White on Face of Cliff they moved to the neighborhood of Kintyel in the Chaco Canyon (New Mexico), where the ruins of the great pueblo still stand. When the Navajos arrived in the Chaco Canyon area, the Kisani (Pueblos) had already arrived and were in the process of building the great pueblo, but had not yet finished it. The reason the Pueblos were building Kintyel was to release some of their people from bondage.

A short time before a divine gambler named Nohoilpi (He Who Wins Men) had descended among the Pueblos from the heavens. Nohoilpi's talisman was a great piece of turquoise. When he came he challenged the Pueblos to all sorts of games of chance and contests and in all of these he was successful. Not only did he win their property but he also won their women, their children, and finally some of the men themselves. After he had accumulated much of their property and many of the Pueblos as slaves, he told them he would give everything back if they would build a great house for him. So when the Navajos came into that country the Pueblos were busy building Kintyel in order that they might release their relatives and their property from He Who Wins Men. They were also busy making a racetrack and preparing for all kinds of games of chance and skill.

But in spite of their losses, the Pueblos continued to gamble with Nohoilpi. People came from other pueblos and gambled away not only their valuables, but also their women, children and finally themselves. The Navajos, observing all this, tried to keep count of Nohoilpi's winnings but people came in such numbers to Chaco that it became impossible. Of course with the labor of all the slaves who had lost themselves to Nohoilpi, it was not long until the great Kintyel was finished.

Now the Navajos had been merely spectators of the games and had never taken part. But one day the voice of the beneficial god, Hastéyalti (Talking God) was heard faintly in the distance crying his usual call—*Wu'hu'hu'hu'*, similar to the coo-coo of the dove. His voice was heard, as it is always heard, four times, each time nearer and nearer, and immediately after the last call, which was loud and clear, Hastéyalti appeared at the door of the hut of a young childless couple.

Hastéyalti told the young couple that the people of Ki'ndotliz (Blue House Pueblo) had gambled with Nohoilpi and lost two great shells, the greatest treasures of the pueblo. He went on to say that the Sun coveted these shells and had asked the gambler for them but had been refused and now the Sun was angry. Because of this, Hastéyalti said, twelve days after his visit certain gods would meet in the mountains, in a place he designated, to hold a great council. He then invited the young man to be present at the council and disappeared.

The young Navajo man kept count of the passing days, and on the twelfth day he travelled to the appointed place where he found a great assemblage of the gods. Besides Hastéyalti, there were Hastéhogan and his son, Nlch'i (Wind), Chahalqel (Darkness), Beeka'li (Bat) Tl'ish (Snake),

Tsilkali (Little Bird), Naazi'si (Gopher) and many others. Besides the gods there were also many pets belonging to the gambler who were dissatisfied with their lot and longed to be freed. Nlch'i had spoken to them and they had come to enter the plot against their master. All that night the gods danced and sang and performed mystic rites for the purpose of giving the young Navajo man powers, as a gambler, equal to those of Nohoilpi. When morning came they washed him with yucca suds, dried him with corn meal, dressed him in clothes exactly like those of the gambler and in every way made him look as much like Nohoilpi as possible. Then the Navajo set out to best the gambler, with the help of the various gods. They arrived at the brow of Chaco Canyon at sunrise the next morning.

Nohoilpi had two wives, who were the prettiest women in the whole land. Wherever they went each of them carried a stick in her hand on which something was tied as a sign that she was the wife of the great gambler.

It was the custom of Nohoilpi's wives to go to a nearby spring each morning at sunrise to fetch water. That morning the young Navajo followed one of the wives to the spring and, as he was dressed and adorned to represent her husband, she let him approach her. When she discovered her error, she deemed it prudent to say nothing and let him follow her into the house. As he entered he observed that many of the slaves had assembled, having heard that trouble was brewing for Nohoilpi. When the gambler saw the stranger, who looked so much like himself, follow his wife into the house, his face became clouded with anger. "Have you come to gamble with me?" he asked the young intruder. He repeated the question four times and each time the Navajo answered, "No."

In the meantime the party of gods, who had been watching from above, came down among the people and dressed two young boys in costumes similar to those worn by the wives of the gambler. When these two mock-women entered the gambler's house along with a great many people from the neighboring pueblos, the Navajo pointed at them and said: "I will bet my wives against your wives."

Nohoilpi accepted the wager and they played the game of thirteen chips. (The game is played with thirteen flat pieces of wood, colored red on one side and white on the other. Success depends on the number of chips which, when thrown upwards, fall with the white sides up.) The gambler tossed the chips first and turned up many white chips and a few red ones. When the Navajo tossed the chips into the air, Bat, who had hidden himself in the ceiling, grasped them and tossed down thirteen chips that were white on both sides, and so the Navajo won the wives of Nohoilpi.

Next they went outside and wagered on the game nanzoz (a game where a hoop is rolled along the ground and long poles are thrown after it to make it fall). Great Snake had hidden himself in the hoop and caused it to fall on the Navajo's pole and again the gambler was defeated.

Very angry now, the gambler pointed to two small trees and challenged the Navajo to the game of tsinbetsil (or push-on-the-wood, a contest in which the opponents find trees of equal size and push against them, the first to cause the tree to be torn from its roots and fall being the winner). But the Navajo insisted that larger trees be found and they finally agreed on two of good size that grew close together. Wind told the Navajo which tree to select. The gambler strained with all his might at his tree but he could not move it. When the Navajo's turn came he shoved his tree prostrate with little effort for its roots had been severed by Gopher.

Then followed a variety of games, on one of which Nohoilpi staked his wealth in shells and precious stones, his houses and his slaves—and lost all. The victor ordered all the shells, beads and precious stones and the great shells brought forth. He gave the beads and shells to Hastéyalti for distribution among the gods, and the two great shells were given to the sun, who desired them for his house.

After losing all he had, Nohoilpi was very angry and bemoaned his fate and cursed his enemies. "I will kill you all with lightning. I will send war and disease among you. May the cold freeze you! May the fire burn you! May the waters drown you!" he cried.

Wind decided that Nohoilpi had cursed enough and told the Navajo to put an end to his angry words. So the young Navajo called the gambler to him and said: "You have bet yourself and lost; you are now my slave and must do my bidding. You are not a god, for my power has prevailed against yours." The young Navajo owned a magic bow, the Bow of Darkness, which he bent upwards and placing the string on the ground bade the gambler stand on the string; then he shot Nohoilpi up into the sky.

Up and up Nohoilpi flew like an arrow, growing smaller and smaller until he disappeared altogether. He flew up in the sky until he came to the home of Klehanoai, the god who carries the Moon and is thought by the Navajos to be identical with the Christian god of the Americans, a very old man who dwells in a long row of stone houses. When Nohoilpi arrived at the house of Klehanoai he told him what had happened in the lower world, saying, "Now I am poor and this is why I have come to see you."

"You need be poor no longer," said Klehanoai, "for I will provide for you."

Then the moon god made all sorts of new kinds of animals for Nohoilpi: sheep, asses, horses, swine, goats and fowls. He also gave him *bayeta* (Spanish for baize which the Navajos obtained from the Mexicans.) and other cloths of bright colors, more beautiful than those woven by his slaves at Kintyel. Then he made a new people for the gambler to rule over, the Mexicans, and sent him back to this world again. But he descended far to the South of his former home and reached the earth in Mexico, where the moon god had placed the new people.

Nohoilpi's people increased greatly in Mexico and after a while they began to move toward the North and build towns along the Rio Grande and soon enslaved the Pueblos who lived there. That is how the Mexicans and their domestic animals came about and why they were always enemies of the Navajo.

FOUR

The Tale of Coyote, the Troublemaker

Soon after the young Navajo shot Nohoilpi into the sky they moved away from Chaco, to the North and West, and it was while the wanderers were at this new place that Coyote again caused a lot of trouble. Coyote sulked about the new camp for nine days, then he went to visit Dasani, the Porcupine. Coyote did not treat Porcupine well and they soon parted. Then he visited Maitso, the Wolf, and the same thing happened.

Next he visited the camp of the Chicken Hawks and the Hummingbirds, who were friendly to one another in those days. Now Coyote was a dandy; he was always beautifully dressed,—he had a nice otter-skin quiver and his face was painted in spots—so when he arrived at the camp of the Chicken Hawks and the Hummingbirds two Hummingbird maidens, who were alone in the camp as everyone else was out hunting, mistook him for someone of importance. He spent the day gossiping with the maidens and telling them tales of great deeds he pretended he had done. He told them that he was a god and that he could will the death of animals and that, with his help, it would no longer be necessary for the people to hunt.

When the hunters returned at nightfall, the maidens told them about the visitor and what he had said. The chief directed one of the young men to spy on the stranger. He did so and reported to the chief that he was, indeed, fine-looking and beautifully dressed, whereupon the chief decided that what Coyote had told the maidens might be true. The chief then sent one of the maidens back to the hut to serve Coyote.

The next morning Coyote went out with the hunters and had them conceal themselves at the edge of a field while he went out and drove the game toward them. This he did by tying a fagot of shredded cedar bark to his tail, which he set on fire. He then ran over the country in a wide circle as fast as he could go. Everywhere the fagot touched, it set fire to the grass, and raised a long line of flame and smoke which drove the antelope up to where the hunters were concealed. A great quantity of game was killed by the hunters, and their faith in the power of Coyote knew no bounds.

The next morning Coyote again accompanied the men out to hunt and again he proceeded to drive the game to them in the same manner. But the night before the maiden who had been designated to serve Coyote had told him of certain neighbors of theirs who were considered bad by the Chicken Hawks and Hummingbirds and, instead of returning to the hunters as he had done the day before, Coyote went off to seek these neighbors.

After a while he came to two great trees, a spruce and a pine, growing close together, each filled with birds of a different kind. The birds were chattering and playing a game which Coyote had never seen before. They would pull out their eyes, toss them up to the top of the tree and cry, "Drop back, my eyes! Drop back!" and catch their eyes as they descended in their proper sockets. Coyote watched this game for a long time, fascinated. Then he cried out to the birds in the pine tree, "Pull out my eyes for me. I want to play too."

"No," they replied. "We will have nothing to do with you."

Again and again he begged to be allowed to join in the game and again they refused him. But when he had pleaded for the fourth time, they flew down to where Coyote sat, and, taking up sharp sticks, gouged his eyes out. They tossed his eyes up to the top of the pine tree, and when they fell down Coyote caught them in his sockets and could see again as well as ever. Coyote was so delighted that he begged them to pull his eyes out again, but they said angrily: "We do not want to play with you. We have done enough for you. Go and leave us now." But he continued to whine and beg until they again pulled his eyes out, and tossed them up with the same result as before. Four times he implored them to pull out his eyes and four times they did so, tossed them up in the tree and he caught them again in his head.

But when he continued to beg them to pull out his eyes, the birds held a council among themselves. Then they pulled out his eyes once more but this time they took pains to pull out the optic nerves at the same time. These they tied together, and when they flung the eyes up into the tree they caught on one of the branches and there they stayed. "Drop back, my eyes! Drop back!" Coyote cried but back they never came. Coyote sat there with his nose pointed up toward the top of the tree, howling, praying and weeping until at last the birds took pity on him and decided to make other eyes for him. They took a couple of partly dried pieces of pine gum and rolled them into two balls which were stuck into the empty eye sockets, and although they were not good eyes, they gave him enough sight to see his way home. The gum was yellow and for this reason coyotes have had yellow eyes ever since.

Coyote crept back, as best he could, to where the hunters were cooking the game he had driven to them earlier. The hunters handed him a piece of raw liver, supposing he could cook it for himself. But he did not dare look at the fire, as he knew his new eyes would surely melt, so he threw the liver on the coals without looking at it, and when he tried to fetch it he thrust his hand at random into the fire and caught nothing but hot coals that burned him. Fearing that he was being observed, he tried to pass his strange actions off as a joke by crying "Don't burn me, liver! Don't burn me, liver!" each time he picked up a hot coal. After a while one of the hunters noticed his strange actions and said to another: "He does not act as usual. Go and see what is the matter with him."

The hunter who was thus bidden went over in front of Coyote, looked at him closely, and saw melted gum pouring from between his eyelids. They had already heard, from a messenger who had come among them, of an individual named Coyote who was said to be an idler and a trickster, so when they saw what was happening to Coyote's eyes they said: "This must be the Coyote of whom we have heard. He has been playing with the birds and has lost his eyes."

They decided to get rid of him and did so by tricking him into following the dress of the maiden who had served him. The dress was decorated with rattles which a Chicken Hawk took in his beak and shook. Coyote, thinking the maiden was nearby, but unable to see well any more, followed the sound of the dress as the Chicken Hawk led him away to the brink of a deep canyon. Here the hawk shook the dress beyond the edge of the precipice, causing Coyote to jump toward the sound and into the bottom of the canyon where he was dashed to pieces.

But Coyote did not die. He did not, like other beings, keep his vital principle in his chest where it might easily be destroyed but, instead, kept it in the tip of his nose and in the end of his tail, where no one would expect to find it. Therefore he soon came back to life again and went back to the camp of the birds and asked for the maiden who had served him. He was told that she had gone away and was ordered to leave as they now knew who he was and that he was worthless.

Coyote left the camp of the birds and wandered about until he came to the house of one of the Naye'i (the monsters or alien gods) named Yelapahi (Brown Giant), one of those who had sprung from the blood of those monsters the women had given birth to for their transgressions in the lower world. Yelapahi was half as tall as the tallest pine tree, evil and cruel. Coyote said to the Brown Giant, "Yelapahi, I want to be your servant as I can be of great help to you. The reason that you often fail to catch your enemies is that you cannot run fast enough. I can run fast and jump far; I can jump over four bushes at one bound. I can run after your enemies and help you catch them."

"My cousin," responded Brown Giant, "you can do me service if you will." Coyote then directed the giant to build a sweat house for himself, and, while the latter was building it, he went out on another errand.

In those days there was a maiden of renowned beauty

in the land. She was the sister of eleven divine brothers. She had been sought in marriage by the sun and by many other gods, but she had refused them all because they could not comply with certain conditions she had imposed on all suitors. It was to visit her that Coyote went when he left Brown Giant at work on the sweat house.

"Why have you refused so many beautiful gods who want you for a wife?" asked Coyote of the maiden after he had greeted her. She replied that it would profit him nothing to know as he would not be able to comply with even one of her demands. Four times he asked and three times he got the same reply. When he asked the fourth time she answered, "In the first place I will not marry anyone who has not killed one of the Naye'i." When he heard this Coyote arose and returned to the domain of Brown Giant.

On his way back he found the thigh bone of some great animal which he concealed under his shirt. When he got back Brown Giant had finished the sweat house, which they entered.

"Now," Coyote said, "if you want to become a fast runner I will show you what to do. You must cut the flesh of your thigh down to the bone and then break the bone. It will heal again in a moment and when it heals you will be stronger and swifter than ever. I often do this myself and each time I do it I am fleeter of foot than I was ever before. I will do it now, so that you may observe how it is done." Coyote then produced a great stone knife and pretended to cut his own thigh, wailing and crying and acting as if he suffered great pain. After a while he put the old femur on top of his thigh, held it by both ends and said to the giant, "I have now reached the bone. Feel it."

When the giant had put forth his hand, in the absolute darkness of the sweat house, and felt the bare bone, Coyote shoved the hand away and struck the bone hard with the edge of the knife several times until he broke the bone. Then he made the Giant feel the fractured ends. Then he threw away the old bone, rubbed spittle on his thigh, prayed and sang, and in a little while presented his sound thigh to the giant for his examination, saying: "See! my limb is healed again. It is as well as ever."

Then he handed the knife to Brown Giant and the latter, with many tears and loud howls, slowly amputated his own thigh. When the work was done he put the two severed ends together, spat upon them, sang and prayed as Coyote had done. "Stick! Stick! Stick!" he cried. "Heal together! Grow together!" he commanded, but the severed ends would not unite. "Cousin," he called to Coyote, "help me heal this leg." But Coyote did not help him. Instead he ran from the sweat house, seized his bow and discharged his arrows into the helpless Yelapahi, who soon expired of many wounds.

Coyote scalped his victim, took the quiver and weapons of the slain and set out for the lodge of the maiden. He knew she could not mistake the scalp, for the Yei (gods), both friendly and alien, in those days had yellow hair such as no other people had.

When he reached the lodge he said to the maiden: "Here is the scalp and here are the weapons of one of the Naye'i. Now you must marry me."

"No," said the maiden, "not yet; I have not told you all that one must do in order to win me. He must be killed four times and come to life again four times."

"Do you speak the truth? Have you told me all?" asked Coyote.

"Yes, I speak only the truth," she replied four times, as Coyote asked the question of her four times. Whereupon Coyote said: "Here I am. Do with me as you will." The maiden then took Coyote a little distance from the lodge, laid him on the ground, beat him with a great club until she thought she had smashed every bone in his body, and left him for dead. But she had not smashed the point of his nose nor the tip of his tail.

She returned to the lodge and went about her work, of which she had much to do, but she had hardly begun her work when she looked up and saw Coyote standing in the door. "Here I am," he said. "I have won one game; there are only three more to win."

This time she took him farther away from the lodge and pounded him to pieces with her club. She threw the pieces away in different directions and again returned to her work.

She had taken but a few stitches in a basket she was making when Coyote again appeared in the doorway, saying: "I have won two games; there are only two more to win."

Again she led him forth, taking him even farther away

from the lodge, and with a heavier club she pounded him into a shapeless mass, until she thought he must certainly be dead. Then she took the mass to a great rock and there she beat it into still finer pieces which she scattered in all directions as she had done before and went back to the lodge. But she had still failed to injure the two vital spots. It took Coyote a longer time to pull himself together but she still had not wrought much on her basket when he again presented himself and said: "I have won three games; there is but one more game to win."

The fourth time she led him farther away than ever. She not only mashed him to pieces, but she mixed the pieces with earth, ground the mixture like corn between two stones until it was but a fine powder and scattered the powder far and wide. But again she had neglected to crush the point of the nose or the tip of the tail. She went back to the lodge and worked for a long time undisturbed. She had just begun to entertain hopes that she had seen the last of her unwelcome suitor when he again entered the door.

Now she could not refuse him. He had fulfilled all her conditions and she consented to become his wife. He remained all afternoon. At sunset they heard the sound of approaching footsteps and she said: "My brothers are coming. Some of them are evil of mind and may do you harm. You must hide yourself." Then she hid him behind a pile of skins and told him to be quiet.

When the brothers entered the lodge they told their sister: "Here is some fat young venison which we bring you. Put it down to boil and put some of the fat into the pot, for our faces are burned by the wind and we want to grease them."

The pot was put on and the fire replenished but when it began to burn well an odor denoting the presence of some beast filled the lodge. One of the brothers said: "It smells as if some animal has been in the wood pile. Let us throw out this wood and get fresh sticks from the bottom of the pile." They did as he desired, but the unpleasant odor continued to annoy them, and again the wood was taken from the fire and thrown away. Deciding that the whole pile of wood was tainted with the smell, they went out, broke fresh branches from trees and built the fire up again, but this did not abate the rank odor in the least. Then one said: "Perhaps the smell is in the water. Tell us, little sister, where did you get the water in this pot?"

"I got it from the spring where I always get it," she replied. But they told her to throw out the water and fill the pot with snow, and to put the meat down to boil again. In spite of all their pains the stench was as strong as ever.

At length one of the brothers turned to his sister and said: "What is the cause of this odor? It is not in the wood. It is not in the water. Where does it come from?" She was silent. He repeated the question four times, yet she made no answer. But when the question had been asked the fourth time, Coyote jumped out of his hiding place into the middle of the lodge and cried: "It is I, my brothers-in-law!"

"Run out of here!" the brothers commanded, and turning to their sister, they said: "Run out you with him!"

As Coyote ran from the lodge, with his wife following him, he took a brand from the fire and with it he lighted a new fire. Then he broke boughs from the neighboring trees and built a shelter for himself and his wife to live in. When this was completed she went back to the lodge of her brothers, took out her pots, skins, four awls, baskets, and all her property and carried them to her new home.

One of the elder brothers said to the youngest: "Go out tonight and watch the couple and see what sort of a man this is that we have for a brother-in-law. Do not enter that shelter, but lie hidden outside and observe them." This he did, and while he watched Coyote killed his wife four times and each time she was resurrected. After the fourth time she lay down and Coyote followed her to the couch. From time to time during the night they held long, low conversations which the youngest brother of the woman could not hear. At dawn, when he returned to the lodge, he said: "I cannot tell you all that I saw and heard, and they said much that I could not hear, but what I did hear and behold was evil."

The next morning when the eleven divine brothers started out to hunt, Coyote came and asked if he might join them, but they told him to stay home with his wife as she might get lonely and need someone to talk to. Then they chased him away and left. But they had not gone far when he overtook them. Three times they chased him back, but on the fourth try they consented to take Coyote along. At the edge of a canyon they made a bridge of rainbow, on which they proceeded to cross the chasm. Before the brothers reached the opposite bluff, Coyote jumped on it from the bridge of rainbow, with a great bound, and began to frolic around, saying: "This is a nice place to play."

They left him there and travelled farther on. After a while they came to a mesa where they observed the tracks of four Rocky Mountain sheep. Coyote came and they sent him out of the mesa to drive the sheep to them, which he did. The sheep were all killed and presently Coyote returned to them and lay down on the sand.

In those days the horns of the Rocky Mountain sheep were flat and fleshy and could be eaten. The eldest brother said: "I will take the horns for my share."

"No," said Coyote, "the horns shall be mine. Give them to me." Three times each repeated the same declaration. When both had spoken for the fourth time, the eldest brother, to end the controversy, drew out his knife and began to cut one of the horns. As he did so Coyote cried out, "Turn to bone! Turn to bone! Turn to bone!" Each time he cried the horn grew harder and harder and the knife slipped as it cut, hacking but not severing the horn. That is why the horns of the Rocky Mountain sheep are now hard, not fleshy, and to this day they bear the marks of the hunter's knife.

The hunters gathered the meat all into one pile and by means of the mystic powers which they possessed they reduced it to a very small mound which they tied into a small bundle such as one person might carry and gave it to Coyote to take home. They warned him to travel back home the way they had come and not cross through the canyon they had avoided as an evil people dwelt there. They also told him not to open the bundle until he got home.

Of course Coyote promised to heed all that he had been told, but as soon as he was well out of sight of the hunters he slipped the bundle off his back and opened it. At once the meat expanded and became a heap of formidable size, such that he could not bind it up again and carry it; so he tied up as much of it as he could carry and left the remainder scattered on the ground, then continued on his journey.

When he came to the edge of the forbidden canyon he looked down and saw some birds playing a game he had never witnessed before. They rolled great stones down the slope, which extended from the foot of the cliff to the bottom of the valley, and stood on the stones as they were rolling; yet the birds were not upset or crushed or hurt in the least by this diversion. The sight so pleased Coyote that he descended into the canyon and begged to be allowed to join the game. The birds rolled a stone gently for him, and he got on it and handled himself so nimbly that he reached the bottom of the slope without injury. Again and again he begged them to give him a trial, and for three times they let him descend without injuring himself; but on the fourth time, tiring of him, they hurled the stone with such force that Coyote lost his footing and he and the stone rolled over one another to the bottom of the slope, with him screaming and yelping all the way down.

After this experience he prudently left the birds and travelled on until he observed some otters at play by the stream at the bottom of the canyon. They were playing the Navajo game of nanzoz and betting their skins against one another on the results of the game. But when one lost his skin at play he jumped into the water and came out with a new skin. Coyote approached the otters and asked to be allowed to take part in the game, but the otters had heard about him and knew what a rascal he was. They told him to begone but still he remained and pleaded. After a while they went apart and held a council, and when they returned they invited Coyote to join them in the game. Coyote bet his skin and lost it. The moment he lost, the otters all rushed at him, and, despite his piteous cries, they tore the hide from his back, beginning at the root of his tail and tearing forward. When they came to the vital spot at the end of his nose his wails were terrible. When he found himself denuded of his skin he jumped into the water, as he had seen the otters do, but, alas! his skin did not come back to him. He jumped in again and again but came out each time as bare as when he went in. At length he became thoroughly exhausted, and lay down in the water until the otters took pity on him and pulled him out. They dragged him to a badger hole, threw him in there, and covered him up with earth. Previous to this adventure

Coyote had a beautiful smooth fur like that of the otter. But when he dug his way out of the badger hole he was again covered with hair but it was no longer the glossy fur he once wore. It was coarse and rough, much like that of the badger, and such a pelt the coyotes have worn ever since.

The loss of his beautiful coat of fur did not cause Coyote to mend his ways in the least. He challenged the otters to a new game but they told him to begone as his new fur was of no value and no one would play for it. Becoming angry, Coyote retired to a safe distance and began to revile the otters shamefully. "You are braggarts," he cried. "You pretend to be brave, but you are cowards. Your women are like yourselves: their heads are flat, their eyes are little, their teeth stick out and they are ugly while I have a bride as beautiful as the sun."

He would approach them, and when they made motions as if to pursue him, he would take a big jump and soon place himself beyond their reach. When they quieted down he would again approach them and continue to taunt and revile them. After a while he went to the cliff, to a place of safety, and from there he shouted his words of derision. The otters decided they would suffer his abuse no longer, so they sent word to the spiders who lived farther down the stream, telling them what had occurred and asking for their aid.

The spiders crept up the bluff, went around behind where Coyote sat cursing and scolding, and wove strong webs in the trees and bushes. When their work was finished the otters came up the bluff to attack Coyote. Conscious of his superior swiftness, he acted as if indifferent to them and allowed them to come quite close before he turned to run, but he did not get far. He became trapped in the webs of the spiders, was seized by the otters, dragged to the bottom of the hill and was killed. At least the otters thought they had killed him. The cliff swallows flew down from the walls of the canyons and tore him to pieces and carried the fragments of his body off to their nests, leaving only a few drops of blood on the ground. They tore his skin into strips and made of these bands which they put around their heads, and this is why the cliff swallow wears a band upon his brow today.

When her brothers returned home without Coyote his

bride came to them and looked about inquiringly. The eldest brother told her: "Go back to sleep and don't worry about that worthless man of yours. He is not with us and we know not what has become of him. We suppose he has gone into the canyon where we warned him not to go and has been killed." She was angry and returned to her lodge.

Before the brothers lay down to sleep they again sent the youngest brother to hide and watch their sister, and this is what he saw that night: At first she pretended to go to sleep. After a while she rose and sat facing the East. Then she faced in turn the South, the West, and the North. When she had done this, she pulled out her right eyetooth, broke a large piece from one of her four bone awls and inserted it into the place of the tooth, making a great tusk where the little tooth had once been. As she did this she said aloud: "He who shall hereafter dream of losing a right eyetooth shall lose a brother." After this she opened her mouth to the four points of the compass in the order in which she had faced them before, tore out her left eyetooth and inserted in its place the pointed end of another awl. As she made this tusk she said: "He who dreams of losing a left eyetooth shall lose a sister."

Then she made, in the same manner, two tusks in her lower jaw. When she had made the one on the right she said: "He who dreams of losing this tooth (right lower canine) shall lose a child." And when she had made the one on the left she said: "He who dreams of losing this tooth (left lower canine) shall lose a parent."

When she first began to pull out her teeth hair began to grow on her hands, and as she went about her mystic work the hair spread up her arms and her legs, leaving only her breasts bare. Finally the hair grew over her breasts and she was covered with a coat of shaggy hair like that of a bear. She continued to move around in the direction of the sun's course, pausing and opening her mouth at the East, the South, the West, and the North as she went. After a while her ears began to wag, her snout grew long, her teeth were heard to gnash and her nails turned to claws. The youngest brother watched her until dawn; then, fearing he might be discovered, he returned to his lodge and told his brothers all that had happened. They said: "These must be the mysteries that Coyote explained to her the first night."

A moment after the young man finished telling his story

they heard the whistling of a bear and soon a great female bear rushed past the door of the lodge, cracking the branches as she went. She followed the trail which Coyote had taken the day before and disappeared in the woods.

That night she returned, groaning. She had been in the fatal canyon all day fighting the slayers of Coyote and she had been wounded in many places. Her brothers saw a light in her hut and, from time to time, one of them would go and peep through an aperture to observe what was happening within. All night she walked around the fire and, at intervals, by means of her magic, drew arrowheads out of her body and healed the wounds.

Next morning the bear-woman again rushed past the lodge of her brothers and again went off toward the fatal canyon. At night she returned as before, groaning and bleeding, and again spent the long night in drawing forth missiles from her body and healing her wounds by means of her magic.

Thus she continued for four days and four nights, but at the end of the fourth day she had conquered all her enemies. She had slain many and those she had not killed she had dispersed. The swallows flew up into the high cliffs to escape her vengeance; the otters hid themselves in the water; the spiders retreated into holes in the ground, and in such places these creatures have been obliged to dwell ever since.

During the four days the bear-woman had journeyed to the fatal canyon and slain her enemies, the brothers remained at home, but at the end of that time ten of them left. They divided themselves into four parties, one of which travelled to the East, another to the South, another to the West and the last to the North. They left the youngest brother at home to watch the lodge.

When they were gone, the Whirlwind and the Knife Boy came to the lodge to help the youngest brother. They dug a hole for him in the center of the hogan, and from this they dug four branching tunnels, running east, south, west and north, and over the end of each tunnel they put a window of gypsum to let in light from above. They gave him four weapons, the chain-lightning arrow, a stone knife as big as the open hand, the rainbow arrow and the sheet-lightning arrow. They roofed his hiding place with four flat stones, one white, one blue, one yellow and one black. They put earth over all of these, smoothing the dirt and tramping it down so that it looked like the natural floor of the lodge. Then they gave him two monitors, Nlch'i, the Wind, at his right ear to warn him by day of the approach of danger, and Chahalgel, Darkness, at his left ear, to warn him by night.

When morning came and the bear-woman, having healed herself for the fourth night in a row, discovered that her brothers were gone she was very angry for she still blamed them for the death of her husband. She poured water on the ground to see which way they had gone. The water flowed to the East; she rushed in that direction and soon overtook three of her brothers, whom she killed. Then she returned and again poured water on the floor. It flowed off south so she followed in that direction and overtook and killed three more of her brothers. The next time it flowed to the West and following in that direction she overtook and killed three more of her brethen. The fourth time the water flowed to the North, and going in that direction, she overtook and killed the tenth of her brothers. She returned to the lodge and poured water on the ground to see what had become of her youngest brother. The water sank directly into the earth.

She scratched all around the deserted hut, working her way toward the center. Here she found that the earth was soft, as if recently disturbed. She dug rapidly downward with her paws until she came to the stones and, removing these, saw her remaining brother hidden beneath them. "I greet you, my younger brother! Come up, I want to see you," she said in a coaxing voice. Then she held out one finger to him and said: "Grasp my finger and I will help you up."

But Wind told him not to grasp her finger as she would throw him upward, he would fall at her feet and be at her mercy. "Get up without her help," whispered Wind.

He climbed out of the hole on the east side and walked toward the East. She ran toward him in a threatening manner, but he looked at her calmly and said: "It is I, your younger brother." Then she approached him in a coaxing way, as a dog approaches one with whom he wishes to make friends, and she led him back toward the deserted hogan. But as he approached it Wind whispered: "We have had sorrow there, let us not enter," so he would not go in.

This is the origin of the custom the Navajos have of never entering a house in which a death has occurred or where a great misfortune has taken place.

"Come," the bear-woman said, "and sit with your face to the West and let me comb your hair."

"Heed her not," whispered Wind. "Sit facing the North so that you watch her shadow and see what she does. It is thus that she has killed your brothers." They both sat down, she behind him, and she untied his queue and proceeded to arrange his hair while he watched her out of the corner of his eye.

Soon he observed her snout growing longer and approaching his head, and he noticed that her ears were wagging. "What does it mean that your snout grows longer and that your ears move so?" he asked. She did not reply but drew her snout in and kept her ears still. When these occurrences had taken place four times, Wind whispered in his ear: "Let not this happen again. If she puts out her snout the fifth time she will bite your head off. Yonder, where you see that chattering squirrel, are her vital parts. He guards them for her. Now run and destroy them."

He rose and ran toward her vital parts and she ran after him. Suddenly, between them, a large yucca sprang up to retard her steps, and then another cactus of a different kind. She ran faster than he, but was so delayed in running around the plants that he reached the vitals before her and heard her lungs breathing under the weeds that covered them. He drew forth his chain-lightning arrow, shot it into the weeds, and saw a bright stream of blood spurting up. At the same instant the bear-woman fell with blood streaming from her side.

"See!" whispered Wind, "the stream of blood from her body and the stream from her vitals flow fast and approach one another. If they meet she will revive and then your danger will be greater than ever. Draw, with your stone knife, a mark on the ground between the approaching streams." The young man did as he was told, and the blood instantly coagulated and ceased to flow.

Then he turned to his sister and said: "You shall live again but no longer as the mischievous bear-woman. You shall live in other forms, where you may be of service to your kind and not a thing of evil." He cut off the head and said to it: "Let us see if in another life you will do better.

When you come to life again, act well, or I will slay you again." He threw the head at the foot of a piñon tree and it changed into a bear, which at once started to walk off. But presently it stopped, shaded its eyes with one paw and looked back at the man, saying: "You have bidden me to act well but what shall I do if others attack me?"

"Then you may defend yourself," said the young man, "but begin no quarrel and be ever a friend to your people, the *Dineh*. Go yonder to Black Mountain and dwell there."

Next the hero cut off the nipples and said to them: "Had you belonged to a good woman and not to a foolish witch, it might have been your luck to suckle men. You were of no use to your kind but now I shall make you of use in another form." He threw the nipples up into a pinon tree, heretofore fruitless, and they became edible pine nuts.

Next with the help of his friends, Whirlwind and Knife Boy, he found the corpses of his brothers and brought them back to life. They went back to the place where the brothers had dwelt before and built a new house. They could not return to the old hogan for it was now accursed.

The holy ones then gave the young hero the name of Leyaneyani, or Reared Under the Ground, because they had hidden him in the earth when his brethren fled for the wrath of his sister. They bade him go and dwell at a place called Big Point on the edge which is in the shape of a hogan where he still dwells as a god.

FIVE

The Hero Twins

Meanwhile the Navajos had scattered because the monsters (Naye'i, alien gods) had been actively pursuing and devouring The People. Of the group still living at White Standing Rock, the camp where Coyote had taken his leave of them, there were only four left. But the people there found, a few days after they arrived, a small turquoise image of a woman, which they preserved.

One day Hastéyalti appeared before the people left there, an old man and an old woman and their two children, and told them to come up to the top of a certain holy mountain after twelve nights had passed and bring the turquoise image they had found with them.

On the morning of the appointed day they ascended the mountain by a holy trail, and on a level spot near the summit they met a party that awaited them there. In the party of gods were Hastéyalti, Hastéhogan, White Body (who came from the lower world with The People), the eleven brothers of bear-woman, the Mirage Stone People, the Daylight People standing in the East, the Blue Sky People standing in the West and the Darkness People standing in the North. White Body stood in the East among the

Daylight People, bearing in his hand a small image of a woman wrought in white shell, about the same size and shape as the blue image which the Navajos brought with them.

Hastéyalti laid down a sacred buckskin with its head toward the West. The Mirage Stone People laid on the buckskin, heads west, the two little images, of turquoise and white shell, a white and a yellow ear of corn, the Pollen Boy and the Grasshopper Girl. On top of these Hastéyalti laid another sacred buckskin with its head to the East and under this they put Nlch'i (Wind).

Then the gods and the Navajos formed a circle, leaving an opening in the East through which Hastéyalti and Hastéhogan went in and out as they sang a sacred song. Four times the gods entered and raised the cover. When they raised it for the fourth time, the images and the ears of corn were found changed to living beings. The turquoise image had become Estsánatlehi, Changing Woman, and the white shell image had become Yolkaí Estsán, the White Shell Woman. Then the assembly departed, and the two divine sisters Estsánatlehi and Yolkaí Estsán were left on the mountain alone.

For four nights they remained there but on the fourth morning Estsánatlehi said: "Younger sister, why should we remain here? Let us go to yonder high point and look around us." They went then to the highest point of the mountain. When they had been there several days Estsánatlehi said: "It is lonely here; we have no one to speak to but ourselves; we see nothing but that which rolls over our heads (the sun) and that which drops below us (a small dripping waterfall). I wonder if they can be people? I shall stay here and wait for the one in the morning, while you go down among the rocks and seek the other."

In the morning Estsánatlehi found a bare, flat rock and lay on it with her feet to the East, and the rising sun shone upon her. Yolkaí Estsán went down where the dripping waters descended and allowed them to fall on her. At noon the women met on the mountain top and Estsánatlehi said to her sister: "It is sad to be so lonesome. How can we make people so that we may have others of our kind to talk to?"

Yolkaí Estsán answered: "Think, elder sister, and perhaps after some days you may plan how this is to be done."

Four days after this conversation Yolkaí Estsán said: "Elder sister, I feel something strange moving within me. What can it be?"

Estsánatlehi answered: "It is a child. It was for this that you lay under the waterfall. I feel, too, the motions of a child within me. It was for this that I let the sun shine upon me." Soon afterwards the voice of Hastéyalti was heard to call four times, as usual, and after the last call he and Tonenili (Water Sprinkler), appeared before them. They came to prepare the women for their approaching delivery.

In four more days they felt the commencing of labor, and one said to the other: "I think my child is coming." She had scarcely spoken when the voices of Hastéyalti and Tonenili were heard and the gods appeared. The former was the accoucheur of Estsánatlehi and the latter of Yolkaí Estsán. To one woman a drag rope of rainbow was given; to the other a drag rope of sunbeam, and on these they pulled when in pain, as the Navajo woman now pulls on the rope. Estsánatlehi's child was born first and he, therefore was the elder brother of Yolkaí Estsán's son and they were to become the Hero Twins.

When the gods returned after four days the boys had grown to the size of ordinary boys of twelve years of age. The gods challenged them to a race around a neighboring mountain. Before the race was half done the boys, who ran fast, began to flag; and the gods, who were still fresh, got behind them and scourged the lads with twigs of mountain mahogany. Hastéyalti won the race and the boys came home rubbing their sore backs. When the gods left they promised to return at the end of another four days for another race.

As soon as they had gone Wind whispered to the boys and told them that the old gods were not all that fast and if the boys would practice during the next four days they might win the coming race. So for four days they ran hard around the mountain, and when the gods returned the boys had grown to the full stature of manhood. In the second race the gods began to flag and fall behind, and the boys got behind their elders and scourged them to increase their speed. The elder of the boys won the race, and when it was over the gods laughed and clapped their hands for they were pleased with the prowess they had witnessed.

The night after they had won the race the boys approached their mothers and asked who their fathers were. "You have no fathers," they were told. "You are illegitimate."

Again the boys demanded: "Who are our fathers?"

The women answered: "The cactus are your fathers."

The next day the women made rude bows of juniper wood and arrows, such as children play with, and said to the boys, "Go and play with these but do not go out of sight of our hut and do not go to the East." Of course the boys were curious and went to the East the first day. When they had travelled a great distance they saw an animal with brownish hair and a sharp nose. They drew their arrows and pointed them toward the strange animal, but before they could shoot he jumped down into a canyon and disappeared. When they returned home they told the women what they had seen. The women said: "That is Coyote which you saw and he is a spy for the alien god, Teelget."

The next day, in spite of warnings not to go out of sight of the lodge, the boys wandered far to the South and there they saw a great black bird seated on a tree. They again aimed their arrows at the strange creature, but again, before they could shoot, the creature disappeared by spreading its wings and flying away. The boys returned to their hogan and said to the women: "Mothers, we have been to the South today and there we saw a great black bird which we tried to shoot, but before we could let loose our arrows it flew off."

"Alas!" said the women. "It was the Raven you saw. He is the spy of Tsenahale, the great winged creature that devours men."

On the third day the boys slipped off and walked toward the West, where they saw a dark bird with a skinny red head that had no feathers on it. This bird they tried to shoot also, but before they could do so it spread its wings and flew away. When they returned home that night they learned that the creature was the Buzzard, the spy for the alien god Tsetahotsiltali (He Who Kicks Men Down the Cliffs.).

On the fourth day the boys stole off as usual and went toward the North, where they saw a bird of black plumage perched on a tree on the edge of a canyon. They aimed at this creature, but it also spread its wings and flew away down the canyon. As it flew the boys noticed that its plumes were edged with white. When they returned home they told their mothers, as before, what they had seen. "The bird you saw," said the women, "is the Magpie. He is the spy for the Binaye Ahani, who slay people with their eyes. Alas, our children? What shall we do to make you hear us? What shall we do to save you? You would not listen to us. Now the spies of the alien gods in all quarters of the world have seen you. They will tell their masters and soon the monsters will come here to devour you, as they have devoured all your kind before you."

The next morning the women made a corncake and laid it on the ashes to bake. Then Yolkaí Estsán went out of the hogan and, as she did so, she saw Yeitso, the greatest and fiercest of all the alien gods, approaching. She quickly returned to the hogan and the women hid the boys under bundles and sticks. Yeitso came and sat down at the door, just as the women were taking the cake out of the ashes. "That cake is for me," said Yeitso. "How nice it smells."

"No," said Estsánatlehi, "it was not meant for your great mouth."

"I don't care," said Yeitso. "I would rather eat boys. Where are your boys? I have been told you have some here and I have come to eat them."

"We have none," said Estsánatlehi. "All the boys have gone into the paunches of your people long ago."

"No boys?" said the giant. "What, then, made all the tracks around here?"

"Oh, these tracks I have made for fun," replied the woman. "I am lonely here and I make tracks so that I may fancy there are many people around me." Then she showed Yeitso how she could make tracks with her fist. He compared these tracks with the ones he had noticed before, seemed to be satisfied and went away.

When he was gone, Yolkaí Estsán, the White Shell Woman, went up to the top of a neighboring hill to look around and from there she saw many of the alien gods approaching in the direction of their hogan. She quickly returned to the lodge and told her sister what she had seen. Estsánatlehi took four colored hoops and threw one toward each of the cardinal points—a white one to the East, a blue one to the South, a yellow one to the West and a black one to the North. At once a great gale arose, blowing so fiercely in all directions from the hogan that none of the monsters could advance against it.

The next morning the boys got up before daybreak and stole away. The women soon missed them but could not trace their tracks in the dark. When it was light enough to examine the ground the women found only four footprints of each boy and these were pointed in the direction of Dzil'na'oodilii (Huerfano Mesa), but more than eight tracks they could not find. They came to the conclusion that the boys had taken a holy trail, so they gave up the search and returned to the lodge.

The boys travelled rapidly on the holy trail. (In Navajo mythology the gods and such men as they favor are represented in the tales as making a rapid and easy journey on rainbows, sunbeams and streaks of lightning. Such miraculous paths are called holy trails.) Soon after sunrise, they came to a place where they saw smoke arising from a hole in the ground. They entered the hole by means of a ladder which projected through it and were welcomed by an old woman, the Spider Woman. When they reached the floor of Spider Woman's subterranean chamber, she asked, "Whither do you two go walking together?"

"Nowhere in particular," they replied. "We came here because we have nowhere else to go."

She asked this question four times and each time she received a similar answer. Then she said: "Perhaps you seek your father?"

"Yes," they answered, "if we only knew the way to his dwelling."

"Ah," said the woman, "it is a long and dangerous way to the house of your father, the Sun. There are many of the Naye'i dwelling between here and there and perhaps, when you get there, your father may not be glad to see you, and may punish you for coming. You must pass four places of danger: the rocks that crush the traveller, the reeds that cut him to pieces, the cane cactuses that tear him to pieces and the boiling sands that overwhelm him. But I shall give you something to subdue your enemies and preserve your lives."

Then she gave them a charm which consisted of a hoop with two life-feathers (feathers plucked from a living eagle) attached and another life-feather to preserve

107

their existence. She also taught them a magic formula, which, if repeated to their enemies, would subdue their anger: "Put your feet down with pollen. (Pollen is the Navajo emblem of peace and this is the equivalent to saying: Put your feet down in peace, etc.) Put your hands down with pollen. Put your head down with pollen. Then your feet are pollen; your hands are pollen; your body is pollen; your mind is pollen; your voice is pollen. The trail is beautiful. Be still."

Soon after leaving the house of Spider Woman the boys came to a narrow chasm between two high cliffs that were covered with rocks. When a traveller approached, the rocks would open wide, apparently to give him easy passage and invite him to enter. But as soon as he was within the cleft, the rocks would close like hands and crush him to death. These rocks were the Tseyeintili (the rocks that crush) and were alien gods that thought like men. When the boys reached these rocks they lifted their feet as if about to enter the chasm, and the rocks opened to let them in. Then the boys put down their feet, but withdrew them quickly. The rocks closed with a snap but the boys remained safe on the outside. Thus four times did they deceive the rocks. When they had closed for the fourth time, the rocks asked, "Who are you, whence come you two together and whither go you?"

"We are children of the sun," answered the boys. "We come from Dzil'na'oodilii and we go to seek the house of our father." Then they repeated the words the Spider Woman taught them, and the rocks said: "Pass on to the house of your father, the Sun." When next they stepped into a chasm the rocks did not close and they passed safely on.

They continued on their way until they came to a great plain covered with reeds that had great leaves on them as sharp as knives. When they came to the edge of the field of reeds, the latter opened, showing a clear passage to the other side. They pretended to enter, but quickly retreated, and as they did so the walls of reeds rushed together to kill them. Thus four times did they deceive the reeds. Then the reeds spoke to them, as the rocks had done; they answered and repeated the sacred words. "Pass on to the house of your father, the Sun," said the reeds, and the boys passed on in safety.

108

Next they came to a country covered with cane cactuses. These cactuses rushed at, and tore to pieces, whomever attempted to pass through them. When the boys came the cactuses opened their ranks to let them pass as the reeds had done. But the boys deceived them as they had the reeds and passed safely on.

After they had passed the country of the cactus they reached, in time, the land of the rising sands. Here was a great desert of sands that rose and whirled and boiled like water in a pot, and overwhelmed the traveler that ventured among them. As the boys approached the sands became still more agitated and the boys did not dare venture among them. "Who are you?" asked the sands, "and where do you come from?"

"We are the children of the Sun, we came from Dzil'na'-oodilii and we go to see the house of our father, the Sun," they answered.

Four times the sands asked and four times the boys answered; then the elder of the boys repeated his sacred formula and the sands subsided, saying, "Pass on to the house of your father, the Sun," and the boys continued on their journey.

Other monsters were encountered and appeased in a like manner before they reached the house of their father. Near Ojo Gallina (the hot springs near San Rafael) they encountered Tieholtsodi, the water monster, whom they appeased with the prayer. Next they came upon Old Age People who treated them kindly but warned them not to follow the trail that leads to the house of Old Age.

They came to Nandza'gai (Daylight) which rose from the ground and let them pass under and then to Chahalgel (Darkness) which also rose and let them pass under. Next they came to Water, which they were able to walk over. They met two bears that growled angrily as if to attack them, a pair of sentinel serpents, a pair of sentinel winds and a pair of sentinel lightnings, all guardians of the dwelling place of the Sun but to all of these the boys repeated the words of the magic formula and were allowed to pass. Finally they met their sister, the daughter of the Sun. She did not speak, but turned silently around and they followed her to the hogan of their father.

The house of the Sun God was built of turquoise, was square like a pueblo house and stood on the shore of a great water. When the boys entered they saw, sitting in the West, a woman; in the South, two handsome young men (named Black Thunder and Blue Thunder in some versions of the legend); and in the North, two handsome young women. The women gave a glance at the strangers and then looked away. The young men gazed at them more closely and then, without speaking, the women arose, wrapped the strangers in four coverings of the sky and laid them on a shelf.

The boys had lain there quietly for some time when a rattle that hung over the door shook and one of the young women said: "Our father is coming." The rattle shook four times and soon after it had shaken the fourth time, Tsohanoai, the bearer of the sun, entered his house. He took the sun off his back and hung it up on a peg on the west wall of the room, where it shook and clanged for some time, going "tla, tla, tla, tla," until at last it hung still.

Then Tsohanoai turned to the women and said in an angry voice: "Who are these two who entered here today?"

The women made no answer and the young people did not look at one another, each fearing to speak. Four times he asked the question and at length the woman said: "It would be well for you not to say too much. Two young men came here today seeking their father. When you go abroad, you always tell me that you visit nowhere, and that you have met no woman but me. Whose sons, then, are these?" she asked, and pointed to the bundle on the shelf. The children smiled significantly at one another.

Tsohanoai took the bundle from the shelf. He first unrolled the robe of dawn with which they were covered, then the robe of blue sky, next the robe of yellow evening light and lastly the robe of darkness. When he unrolled this the boys fell out on the floor. He seized them and threw them first upon great sharp spikes of white shell that stood in the East, but they bounded back, unhurt, from these spikes as they were holding their life-feathers tightly all the while. Next he threw them on spikes of turquoise in the South, on spikes of haliotis in the West and on spikes of black rock in the North, but each time they came back uninjured. Tsohanoai said: "I wish it were indeed true that they were my children."

He said then to the elder children who lived with him: "Go and prepare the sweat house and heat for it four of the hardest boulders you can find. Heat a white, a blue, a yellow and a black boulder." But the Winds heard what he said and knew that he planned to kill his twin sons from earth and made plans to avert their danger.

The sweat house was built against a bank. Wind dug a hole into the bank and concealed the opening with a flat stone. Then he whispered into the ears of the boys and told them about the hole but added that they should not hide in it until they had answered their father's questions. The boys went into the sweat house, the great hot stones were put in, and the opening of tl. lodge was covered with the four sky-blankets. Then Tsohanoai called out to the boys: "Are you hot?" and they answered: "Yes, very hot." Then they crept into the hole Wind had made and hid there. After a while Tsohanoai came and poured water through the top of the sweat house on the stones, making them burst with a loud noise, and raising a great heat and steam. But in time the stones cooled and the boys crept out of their hiding place into the sweat house. Tsohanoai came and asked again: "Are you hot?" expecting to get no reply, but the boys still answered: "Yes, very hot." Then he took the coverings off the sweat house and let the boys come out. He greeted them in a friendly way and said: "Yes, these are my children," but he was not yet certain and was thinking of other ways in which he might destroy them if they were not.

The four sky-blankets were spread on the ground one over another, and the four young men were told to sit on them, one behind another, facing east. "My daughters, make these boys to look like my other sons," ordered Tsohanoai. The young women went to the strangers, pulled their hair out long, and moulded their faces and forms so that they looked just like their brothers. Then Sun bade them all rise and enter his house. They arose and went, in a procession, the two strangers last.

As they were about to enter the door they heard a voice whispering in their ears: "Psst! Look at the ground." They looked down and saw a spiny caterpillar, who, as they watched, spat out two blue spits on the ground. "Take each of you one of these," whispered Wind, "and put it in your mouth, but do not swallow it. There is one more trial for you, a trial by smoking."

When they entered the house Tsohanoai took down a

pipe of turquoise that hung on the eastern wall and filled it with tobacco. "This is the tobacco he kills with," whispered Niltsi to the boys. Tsohanoai held the pipe up to the sun that hung on the wall, lit it, and gave it to the boys to smoke. They smoked it, and passed it from one to another until it was finished. They said it tasted sweet, but it did them no harm.

When Tsohanoai saw that the boys had smoked all of the tobacco and had not been killed by it, he was satisfied and asked: "Now my children, what do you want of me? Why do you seek me?"

"Father," they replied, "the land where we dwell is filled with the Naye'i, who devour the people. There are Yeitso and Teelget, the Tsenahale, the Binaye Ahani and many others. They have eaten nearly all of our kind; there are few left; already they have sought our lives, and we have run away to escape them. Give us, we beg, the weapons with which we may slay our enemies. Help us to destroy them."

"Know," said Tsohanoai, "that Yeitso is also my son, yet I will help you kill him. I shall hurl the first bolt at him and I will give you those things that will help you in war." He took from pegs where they hung around the room and gave to each a hat, a shirt, leggings, moccasins, all made of flint, a chain-lightning arrow, a sheet lightning arrow, a sunbeam arrow, a rainbow arrow and a great stone knife. "These are what we want," said the boys and put on the clothes of flint and were now dressed exactly like their brothers who dwelt in the house of the Sun.

The next morning Tsohanoai led the boys out to the edge of the world, where the sky and the earth came close together in those times and beyond which there was no world. Here sixteen wands or poles leaned from the earth to the sky, four of which were of white shell, four of which were of turquoise, four of haliotis shell and four of which were of red stone.

"On which wands will you ascend?" Tsohanoai asked his sons. Wind whispered that the red wands were for war, the others for peace, so the boys told their father they wished to ascend on the red ones, for they sought war with their enemies. Along with their father, the boys ascended to the sky on the wands of red stone and they travelled about until Tsohanoai pointed down and asked: "Where do you belong in the world below? Show me your home."

The brothers looked down and scanned the land but they could distinguish nothing as all the land seemed flat; the wooded mountains looked like dark spots on the surface; the lakes gleamed like stars and the rivers like streaks of lightning. The elder brother said: "I do not recognize the land. I do not know where our home is." At this time Wind prompted the younger brother and showed him which were the sacred mountains and which the great rivers and the younger brother exclaimed, pointing downwards: "There is the Male Water (San Juan River) and there is the Female Water (Rio Grande), yonder is the mountain of Tsisnaajini (Mount Blanca, San Luis Valley, Colorado); below us is Tsoodzil (Mount Taylor, New Mexico) and there in the West is Doko'oosiliid (the San Francisco Peaks, near Flagstaff, Arizona); that white spot beyond the Male Water is Dibentsaa (Mount Hesperus, Colorado) and between these mountains is Dzilna'oodilii near which our home is."

"You are right, my child, it is thus that the land lies," said Tsohanoai. Then, renewing his promises, he spread a streak of lightning and made his children stand on it, one on each end, and shot them down to the top of Tsoodzil (Mount Taylor). They descended the mountain on its south side and walked toward the warm spring at Tosato (Warm Spring, about three miles south of Grants, New Mexico) where in ancient days there was a much larger lake than there is now. There was a high, rocky wall in the narrow part of the valley and the lake stretched back to where Blue Water is today.

When they came to the edge of the lake, one brother said to the other: "Let us try one of our father's weapons and see what it can do." They shot one of the lightning arrows at Tsoodzil (Warm Spring is about five miles from the base and eighteen miles from the summit of Mount Taylor) and it made a great cleft in the mountain, which remains to this day, and one said to the other: "We cannot suffer in combat while we have such weapons as these."

Soon they heard the sound of thunderous footsteps, for the feet of the monster Yeitso, who lived nearby, stretched as far away as a man could walk between sunrise and noon, and soon they beheld the head of the monster peering over a hill in the East. In a moment he withdrew, and soon afterwards the monster raised his head and chest over a hill in the South, and remained a little longer in sight than when he had in the East. Later he displayed his body to the waist over a hill in the West; and lastly he showed himself, down to the knees, over Tsoodzil. Then he descended the mountain, came to the edge of the lake and put down the basket which he always carried.

Yeitso stooped four times to the lake to drink, and each time he drank the waters perceptibly diminished. When he had done drinking, the lake had nearly drained. As he took his last drink the brothers advanced to the edge of the lake and the monster saw their reflection in the water. He raised his head, and, looking at them, roared: "What a pretty pair have come in sight! Where have I been hunting that I never saw them before?"

"Throw his words back into his mouth," said the younger to the elder brother.

"What a great thing has come in sight! Where have we been hunting that we never saw it before?" shouted the elder brother to the giant.

Four times the taunts were repeated by each party, whereupon the brothers were warned by Wind to take care. They were standing on a bent rainbow just then, which they straightened out. They descended to the ground just as a lightning bolt, hurled by Yeitso, passed thundering over their head. He hurled four bolts rapidly. As he hurled the second, they bent the rainbow and rose, and it passed under their feet; as he hurled the third they descended and the bolt passed over them, and as he hurled the fourth they again bent the rainbow very high and it passed under their feet and did them no harm. He drew a fifth bolt to throw at them but at this moment the lightning descended from the sky on the head of the giant, causing him to reel. Then the elder brother sped a chain-lightning arrow causing the monster to reel toward the East. The second arrow caused him to stumble toward the South, falling lower. The third lightning arrow made him topple toward the West and the fourth to the North. Then he fell to his knees, raised himself partly again, fell flat on his face, stretched out his limbs and moved no more.

When the arrows struck him, his armor was shivered in pieces and the scales flew in every direction. The elder brother said, "They may be useful to the people in the future."

The brothers then approached their fallen enemy and the younger scalped him. Heretofore the young brother bore only the name of To'badzistsini, or Child of Water, but now his brother gave him also the warrior name of Naidikisi (He Who Cuts Around). Thereafter the elder brother was called Nayenizgani (Slayer of the Alien Gods), or Monster Slayer.

They cut off his head and threw it away to the other side of Tsoodzil, where it still may be seen on the eastern side of the mountain. The blood from the body now flowed in a great stream down the valley, so great that it broke down the rocky wall that bounded the old lake and flowed on. Wind whispered to the brothers that if the blood reached the dwelling of Binaye Ahani, toward which it was flowing, Yeitso would come to life again, so the elder brother took his great knife and drew a line across the valley with it. When the blood reached the line he'd made, it stopped flowing and piled itself up in a high wall. But now it began to flow off in the direction of the dwelling place of the alien god, Bear that Pursues, so again the elder hero drew a line with his knife and again the blood piled up and stopped flowing. The blood of the monster Yeitso fills all the valley today, and the high cliffs of black rock that are there now are the places where Nayenezgani stopped the flow with his knife.

Then the Hero Twins put the broken arrows of Yeitso and his scalp into the basket and set out for their home near Dzil'na'oodilii. When they neared the house, they took off their suits of flint armor and hid them, along with the basket and its contents, in the bushes. The mothers were rejoiced to see them and asked where they had been.

"We have been to the house of our father, the Sun," they replied. "And we have been to Tsoodzil and we have slain Yeitso."

"Ah, my child," said Estsánatlehi, "do not speak thus. It is wrong to make fun of such an awful subject."

Then the Hero Twins led their mothers to where they had hidden the basket and showed them the trophies of Yeitso. Changing Woman and White Shell Woman rejoiced and had a dance to celebrate the victory.

"Now," the elder brother asked, "where does Teelget

dwell?"

"Seek not to know," his mother replied, "for you have done enough. Rest contented. The land of the alien gods is a dangerous place. They will kill you."

"Yes," the son replied, "and it was hard for you to bear your child, yet you prevailed."

Then Changing Woman told her son where the monster lived, and the next morning he set off to kill him. He came, in time, to a great plain, and from one of the small hills that bordered it he saw the monster lying down a long way off. He paused to think how he could approach the monster without attracting its attention, and while he was doing this, Gopher came up to him and said: "I greet you, my friend! Why do you come here?"

"Oh, I am just wandering around," replied the boy.

Four times the question was asked and four times the answer was given, then Gopher said: "I wonder why you came here. No one but I ever ventures in these parts, for all fear Teelget. There he lies yonder on the plain."

"It is him I seek, but I do not know how to approach him."

"Ah, if that is all you want, I can help you," said Gopher. "And if you slay him, all I ask is his hide. I often go up to him and I will go now to show you." Having said this, Gopher disappeared in a hole in the ground.

While Gopher was gone the Hero Twin watched Teelget. After a while he saw the great creature rise, walk from the center in four directions, as if watching, and lie down again in the spot where he was first seen. He was a great four-footed beast, with horns like an antelope, as his father was an antelope horn.

Soon Gopher returned and said, "I have dug a tunnel up to Teelget and I have made a hole upward from the tunnel to his heart and four more tunnels in the cardinal directions in which you may hide. I have gnawed the hair off near his heart. When I was gnawing the hair he spoke to me and asked why I was taking his hair, and I replied that I was taking it to make a nest for my children. Then he rose and walked around, but then he came back and lay down where he lay before, over the hole that leads to his heart."

The Hero Twin entered the tunnel and crawled to the end. When he looked up through the ascending shaft of which Gopher had told him, he saw the great heart of Teelget beating there. He sped his arrow of chain-lightning and fled into the eastern tunnel. The monster rose, stuck his horns into the tunnel and ripped it open. The Hero fled to the South, the West and the North as the monster followed, but when he had uncovered but half the north tunnel he fell and lay still. Monster Slayer, not knowing that his enemy was dead, and still fearing him, crept back through the long tunnel to the place where he first met Gopher and there he stood gazing at the distant form of Teelget.

While he was standing there, he saw a little old man dressed in tight leggings and a tight shirt, with a cap and feather on his head, approaching him. This was Ground Squirrel. "Do you not fear the Naye'i that dwells on yonder plain?"

"I don't know," replied Nayenezgani. "I think I have killed him, but I am not certain."

"Then I shall find out for you," said Ground Squirrel, "for he never minds me. I can approach him any time without danger. If he is dead I will climb upon his horns and dance and sing."

The Hero Twin watched, and before long he saw Ground Squirrel climbing one of the great horns of the monster, dancing and singing.

When Monster Slayer approached his dead enemy he found that Ground Squirrel had streaked his own face with the blood of the slain (and the streaks remain on the ground squirrel's face to this day) and that Gopher had already begun to remove the skin by gnawing on the insides of the forelegs. When Gopher had removed the skin, he put it on his back and said: "I shall wear this in order that, in the days to come when The People increase, they may know what sort of skin Teelget wore." Then Ground Squirrel cut out a piece of the bowel, filled it with the monster's blood, cut off a piece of his liver and gave these to Monster Slayer for his trophies.

He took his trophies home and again there was much rejoicing for another of the alien gods had been destroyed. The Hero Twin tarried at home only one day; then he set off to destroy Tsenahale, that monster whose father was a bunch of eagle feathers. He travelled far until he came to a great black rock which looks like a bird, and while he was walking along there, he heard a tremendous rushing sound overhead, like the sound of a whirlwind. Looking up, he saw a creature of great size, something like an eagle in form, flying toward him from the East. This creature was the male Tsenahale.

The warrior had barely time to cast himself prone on the ground when Tsenahale swooped over him. Thus four times did the monster swoop at him, coming each time from a different direction. Three times the Hero Twin escaped but the fourth time, flying from the North, the monster seized him in his talons and bore him off to a broad level ledge on the side of a mountain where Tsenahale reared his young. He dropped the Hero Twin on this ledge, as was his custom with all his victims, and perched on a pinnacle above. The fall had killed all the others but the Hero Twin was saved by the life-feather given him by Spider Woman. Then two young of the Naye'i approached to devour the body of the new victim, but he said, "Sh!" at them.

They stopped and cried up to their father: "This thing is not dead! It says 'Sh!' at us."

"That is only air escaping from the body," said the father. "Never mind that. Eat it." then he flew away in search of other prey.

When the old bird was gone, Monster Slayer hid himself behind the young ones and asked them, "When shall your father return and where will he sit?"

They answered: "He will return when we have a he-rain and he will perch on yonder point," indicating a rock close by on the right. Then he asked: "When shall your mother return and where shall she sit?"

They answered: "She will return when we have a she-rain and will sit on yonder point," indicating a rock on the left.

He had not waited long when drops of rain began to fall, thunder rolled, lightning flashed, and the male Tsenahale returned and perched on the rock to which the young had pointed. Whereupon Monster Slayer hurled a lightning arrow and the monster tumbled to the foot of Winged Rock, dead.

After a while rain fell again but there was neither thunder nor lightning with it. Then there fell upon the ledge the body of a Pueblo woman, covered with fine clothes and ornamented with ear pendants and necklaces of beautiful shells and turquoise. Monster Slayer looked up and saw the female Tsenahale soaring overhead. A moment later she glided down and was just about to light on her favorite crag when Monster Slayer hurled another lightning arrow and sent her body down to the plain to join that of her mate.

The young ones now began to cry and asked the warrior if he would slay them too. "Cease your wailing," he said. "Had you grown up here you would have been things of evil; you would have lived only to destroy my people, but I shall now make of you something that will be of use in days to come when men increase in the land."

He seized the elder and said: "You shall furnish plumes for men to use in their rites, and bones for whistles." He flung the fledgling back and forth four times; as he did so it began to change into a beautiful bird with strong wings, and it said "suk, suk, suk, suk." Then he threw it high in the air. It spread its pinions and soared out of sight, an eagle. To the younger he said: "In the days to come men will listen to your voice to know what will be their future; sometimes you will tell the truth; sometimes you will lie." He swung it back and forth and as he did so its head grew large and round, its eyes grew big and it began to say, "uwu, uwu, uwu, uwu," and it became an owl. Then he threw it into a hole in the side of the cliff and said, "This shall be your home."

Now that his work was done at this place, Monster Slayer decided to return home, but soon discovered there was no way to get down off the ledge. He waited until the sun was about halfway down to the horizon when he observed Bat Woman walking along near the base of the cliff. "Grandmother," he called, "come here and take me down." But she made a sound denoting impatience and contempt and hid behind a rock. Three times she appeared and was asked to take him down and three times she answered in the same way, but when she appeared the fourth time and the Hero Twin asked to be taken down, he added: "I will give you the feathers of the Tsenahale if you will take me off this rock." When she heard this she approached and, after much trouble, took him down in the large carrying-basket which she bore on her back.

Together they plucked the two Tsenahale, put the feathers in her basket, and got it on her back. He kept only the largest feather from one wing of each bird for his trophies. As she was starting to leave he warned her not to pass through either of two neighboring localities, which were the dry beds of temporary lakes, one of which was overgrown with weeds, the other with sunflowers. Despite his warning she walked toward the sunflowers. He called after her and begged her not to enter, but she heeded him not and went on.

She had not taken many steps among the sunflowers when she heard a fluttering sound behind her and a little bird of strange appearance flew past close to her ear. At each step she took she heard more fluttering and saw more birds of varying plumage, such as had never been seen before, flying over her shoulders and going off in every direction. She looked around and was astonished to behold that the birds were swarming out of her own basket. She tried to hold them in, to catch them as they flew out, but all in vain. She put down her basket and watched, helplessly, her feathers changing into little birds of all kinds—wrens, warblers, titmice, and the like—and flying away until her basket was empty. Thus it was that the little birds were created.

Monster Slayer returned home with his trophies and the very next day started off to find the alien god known as He Who Kicks People Down the Cliff (Tsetahotsiltali). This Naye'i lived on the side of a high cliff. A trail passed at his feet, and when travellers went that way he kicked them down to the bottom of the precipice. Monster Slayer had not travelled long when he found a well-beaten trail. Following this, he found it led him along the face of a high precipice, and soon he came in sight of his enemy, who had a form much like that of a man. The monster reclined quietly against the rock, as if he meditated no harm, and Monster Slayer advanced as if he feared no danger, yet closely watched his adversary. As he passed, the monster kicked at him, but he dodged the kick and asked: "Why do you kick at me?"

"Oh, my grandchild," said the Naye'i, "I was weary lying thus, and I only stretched out my leg to rest myself." Four times did Nayenezgani pass him and four times did the monster kick at him in vain. Then the hero struck his enemy with his great stone knife over the eyes, and struck him again and again until he was sure he had slain him, but he was surprised to find that the body did not fall down the cliff. He cut with his knife under the corpse in different places, but found nothing that held it to the rock until he came to the head, and then he discovered that the long hair grew, like the roots of a cedar, into a cleft in the rock. When he cut the hair, the body tumbled out of sight.

The moment it fell, a great clamor of voices came up from below. "I want the eyes," screamed one. "Give me an arm," cried another. "I want the liver," said a third. "No, the liver shall be mine," yelled a fourth, and thus the quarrelling went on.

"Ah," thought Monster Slayer, "these are the children quarrelling over the father's corpse. Thus, perhaps, they would have been quarrelling over mine had I not dodged his kicks."

Finding a trail that led to the bottom of the cliff, the Hero Twin followed it and soon came upon the young of the Naye'i, twelve in number, who had just devoured their father's corpse. He ran among them, hacking at them in every direction with his stone knife, until he had killed all but one. This one ran faster than the rest and climbed among some high rocks, but Nayenezgani followed and caught him. He saw that the child was disgustingly ugly and filthy. "You ugly thing," said Monster Slayer, "when you ran from me so fleetly I thought you might be something handsome and worth killing, but now that I behold your face I shall let you live. Go to yonder mountain of Naatsis'aan (Navajo Mountain in southeastern Utah) and dwell there. It is a barren land, where you will have to work hard for your living, and will wander ever naked and hungry."

The boy went to Naatsis'aan as he was told, and there he became the progenitor of the Paiutes, a people ugly, starved and ragged, who never wash themselves and live on the vermin of the desert.

The Hero Twin returned home with his trophy, a piece of hair from the Naye'i, and again there was much rejoicing. And, again, the next day he started off in search of others of his enemies, the Binaye Ahani, the people who slay with their eyes. This time, in addition to his other weapons, he carried with him a bag of salt. When he came to the lodge where the alien monsters lived, he entered and sat down on the north side. In other parts of the hogan sat the old couple of the Binaye Ahani and many of their children. They all stared with their great eyes at the intruder, and flashes of lightning streamed from their eyes toward him, but glanced harmlessly off his armor. Seeing that they did not kill him, they stared harder and harder at him, until their eyes protruded far from their sockets. Then he threw the salt into the fire in the center of the lodge, which spluttered and flew in all directions, striking the eyes of the monsters and blinding them. When they held down their heads in pain, he struck with his great stone knife and killed all except the two youngest.

Thus he spoke to the two which he spared: "Had you grown up here, you would have lived only to be things of evil and to destroy men, but now I shall make you of use to my kind in the days to come when men increase on the earth." To the elder he said: "You will ever speak to men and tell them what happens beyond their sight; you will warn them of the approach of enemies," and he changed him into a bird called Tsidildoni (the Screech Owl). Of the younger he made a bird whose duty it was to make the earth happy and the bird is called Hoshdo'il (the Whippoor-will), which is sleepy in the daytime and comes out at night.

When he reached home with the trophies, the eyes of the first Binaye Ahani he had killed, and told what he had done, his mother sang a song about his trophies which would cause the people to be restored.

Next the Hero Twin went out and found Bear that Pursues and killed him. When he had cut off the monster's head, he addressed it, saying: "You were a bad thing in your old life, and tried only to do mischief, but in new shapes I shall make you useful to the people. In the future, when they increase on earth, you will furnish them with sweet food to eat, with foam to cleanse their bodies and with threads for their clothing." He cut the head into three pieces. He threw one piece to the East, where it became Tsa'zi (*Yucca baccata*); he threw another to the West, where it became tsasitsos (*Yucca angustifolia*); and he threw the third to the South, where it became the mescal. He cut off the forepaw and took it home for a trophy.

Next the Hero Twin went off in search of Traveling Stone, an alien god who hurled himself at his victims, and found it in the lake which was his home. Traveling Stone hurled itself at Monster Slayer, as if propelled by a giant

122

hand, but the hero raised his lightning arrow, held it in the course of the stone and knocked a piece off the latter. When the stone fell he struck off another piece with his knife.

Traveling Stone now saw it had a powerful foe to contend with, so instead of hurling itself at him again, it fled, and Monster Slayer went in pursuit. He chased it all over the present Navajo land, knocking pieces off it in many places, and at each place where a piece fell there is a constant spring today. Finally he chased it to the San Juan river. Traveling Stone sped down with the current and Monster Slayer ran along the bank after it. Four times he got ahead of the stone, but three times it escaped him by dipping deep into the river. When he headed it off the fourth time, he saw it gleaming like fire under the water and he stopped to gaze at it. Then the stone spoke and said: "Sawe (my baby, my darling), take pity on me, and I shall no longer harm your people, but will do good to them instead. I shall keep the springs in the mountains open and cause your rivers to flow; kill me and your lands will become barren."

The Hero Twin answered: "If you keep this promise I shall spare you, but if you evermore do evil as you have done in the past, I shall seek you again and then I shall not spare you." Traveling Stone kept his promise ever since and has become the Tieholtsodi (Water God) of the upper world.

Now Monster Slayer returned home to rest for four days and give his relatives a full account of his journeys and his adventures from the first to the last.

But still there were many of the Naye'i to be killed. There was White Under the Rock, Blue Under the Rock, Yellow Under the Rock, Black Under the Rock, and many, many brown giants. Besides these there were a number of stone pueblos, now in ruins, which were inhabited by various animals. During the four days of rest, the brothers talked about how they might slay all of these enemies who filled the land and left no room for the people, and determined to again visit the house of the sun.

On the morning of the fourth night they started out toward the East. They encountered no enemies on the way and had a pleasant journey. When they entered the house of the sun, no one greeted them. They sat down on the floor, and as soon as they were seated lightning began to shoot into the lodge. It struck the ground near them four times. Immediately after the last flash Bat and Water Sprinkler entered. "Do not be angry with us," they said. "We flung the lightning only because we feel happy and wanted to play with you."

Still the brothers kept wrathful looks on their faces, until Wind whispered into their ears: "Do not be angry with the strangers. They were once friends of the Naye'i and did not wish them to die, but now they are friends of yours, since you have conquered the greatest of the monsters."

Then, at last, Sun spoke to his children, telling them to be seated, and offered the brothers a seat of shell and a seat of turquoise. But Niltsi whispered in their ears again and told them not to take the seats as they were seats of peace but to take the seats of red stone—the warrior's seats—instead.

Sun then asked his children why they had come to see him again. Three times he asked the question and three times he was told that his sons had come for no special reason, only to pass away the time. But when he asked them the question the fourth time he demanded that they speak the truth. The elder brother replied: "Father, there are still many of the monsters left, and they are increasing. We wish to destroy them all."

"My children," said Sun, "when I helped you before, I asked you for nothing in return. I am willing to help you again, but I wish to know first if you are willing to do something for me. I have a long way to travel every day, and often, in the long summer days, I do not get through in time, and then I have no place to rest or eat till I get back to my home in the East. I wish you to send your mother to the West that she may make a new home for me there."

"I will do it," said the younger brother. "I will send her there."

But the elder brother said, "No. Changing Woman is under the power of no one. We cannot make promises for her, as she is her own mistress and must speak for herself, but I will tell her of your wishes and plead for you." Then Sun gave his sons five hoops, one black, one blue, one yellow, one white and a fifth of many colors and shining, and bade them goodbye. "Your mother will know what to do with these things," he said.

As they made their way homeward they beheld a beautiful vision. The gods spread out before them the country of the Navajos as it was to be in the future when men increased in the land and became rich and happy.

When the brothers reached home they gave Changing Woman the hoops and told her that their father had said that she'd know what to do with them. She replied that she had no knowledge of these talismans of the Sun God as she had never seen him except from afar. But finally she took up the hoops, saying she would see what she could do with them. She took the black hoop, and after spitting the black hail through it, rolled it off to the East. She spat the blue hail through the blue hoop and rolled it off to the South, spat the yellow hail through the yellow hoop and rolled it off to the West, and spat the white hail through the white hoop and sped it to the North until it, like the others, was seen no more. Then she threw the hoop of many colors up toward the zenith, and blew a powerful breath after it. Up it went until it was lost to sight in the sky.

For four days nothing happened, but at the end of the fourth day they heard thunder high up in the sky, after which there were four more days of good weather. Then the sky grew dark and a great white cloud descended from above. The cloud was followed by great whirlwinds which uprooted tall trees as if they were weeds and tossed great rocks around as if they were pebbles. For four days and nights a storm of wind and hail prevailed, such as had never been seen before. When the storm subsided and they came out of their lodge, the air was yet dark and full of dust raised by the high wind, but soon a gentle rain came, laying the dust, and all was clear again.

They marvelled at the sight of the changes the great storm had wrought. Near their house a great canyon had been formed; the bluffs around had been changed and solitary pillars of rock, as one often sees now in Navajoland, had been shaped by the winds.

"Surely this storm killed all the Naye'i," said Changing Woman. But Wind whispered in Monster Slayer's ear, "Sa (Old Age) still lives."

The next morning he set out northward, and travelled until he came to a place where he saw an old woman who came slowly toward him leaning on a staff. Her back was bent, her hair was white and her face was deeply wrinkled. He knew this must be Old Age. When they met he said:

"Grandmother, I have come on a cruel errand. I have come to slay you."

"Why would you slay me?" she asked in a feeble voice. "I have never harmed anyone. I hear that you have done great deeds in order that men might increase on earth, but if you kill me there will be no increase of men. The boys will not grow up to become fathers, the worthless old men will not die and the people will stand still. It is well that people should grow old and pass away and give their places to the young. Let me live and I shall help increase the people."

"Grandmother, if you keep your promise I shall spare your life," said the Hero Twin, and he returned home without a trophy.

When he reached home Wind whispered: "Hakaz Estsan (Cold Woman) still lives." Again he set out for the North for Cold Woman also lived there, high on the summits where the snow never melts. He travelled to where no trees grew and where the snow lies white all through the summer, and here he found a lean old woman, sitting on the bare snow, without clothing, food, fire, or shelter. She shivered from head to foot, her teeth chattered, and her eyes streamed water. "Grandmother," he said, "a cruel man I shall be. I am going to kill you so that men may no more suffer and die by your hand."

"You may kill me or let me live, as you will. I care not," she said to the hero. "But if you kill me it will always be hot, the land will dry up, the springs will cease to flow, the people will perish. You will do well to let me live. It will be better for your people."

He paused and thought upon her words and decided to let her live.

Again, when he reached home, Wind whispered in his ears saying, "Tgaei (Poverty) still lives."

The next morning he went out and walked until he came upon an old man and an old woman who were filthy, clad in tattered garments, and had no goods in their house. "Grandmother, grandfather," he said, "a cruel man I shall be. I have come to kill you."

"Do not kill us, my grandchild," said the old man. "It would not be well for the people, in the days to come, if we were dead. Then they would always wear the same clothes and never get anything new. If we live the clothing will wear out and the people will make new and beautiful garments and they will gather goods and look handsome. Let us live and we will pull their old clothes to pieces for them." So he spared them and went home.

The next journey was to seek out Dichin (Hunger). He journeyed until he came upon twelve of the Hunger people. Their chief was a big, fat man, although he had no food to eat but the little brown cactus. "I am going to be cruel," the hero said, "so that men may suffer no more the pangs of hunger and die no more of it."

"Do not kill us," said the chief, "if you wish your people to increase and be happy in the days to come. We are your friends. If we die people will not care for food and they will never know the pleasure of cooking and eating nice things, and they will never care for the pleasures of the chase." So he spared Hunger and went home.

When the Hero Twin reached home Wind spoke to him no more of enemies that lived. The Slayer of the Alien Gods said to his mother, "I think all the Naye'i must be dead, for every one I meet now speaks to me as a relation; they say to me, 'my grandson,' 'my son,' 'my brother.' " Then he took off his armor and put it away with the weapons the Sun had given him, and sang a song.

When he had finished the song, his father visited him and took away the armor and trophies, saying, "These I shall carry back to my house in the East and keep them safe. If you ever need them again, come and get them." Then he promised to return in four days and meet Changing Woman on the top of Ch'oolii (Gobermador Knob) and left.

At the end of four days Changing Woman went to the top of Ch'oolii and met the Sun, who asked her to come away and make a home for him in the West. She agreed on the condition that he would build her a house as beautiful as the one he had in the East, which her sons had told her about. "I want it built floating on the western water," she said, "away from the shore so that in the future, when people increase, they will not annoy me with too many visits. I want all sorts of gems—white shell, turquoise, haliotis, jet, soapstone, agate, and redstone—planted around my house, so that they will grow and increase. Then I shall be lonely over there and shall want something to do, for my sons and my sister will not go with me. Give me animals to take along. Do all this for me and I shall go with you to

the West." He promised all these things to her, and he made
elk, buffalo, deer, long-tail deer, mountain sheep, jackrabbits
and prairie dogs to go with her.

When she started for her new home some of the divine
people went with her to help her drive her animals, which
were already numerous and increasing daily. At Black Mountain the buffaloes broke from the herd and ran to the East;
they never returned and are in the East still. Sometime later
the elks went to the East and they never returned. From
time to time a few of the antelope, deer and other animals
of the herd left and wandered East. After a while Changing
Woman arrived at the great water in the West and went to
dwell in her floating house beyond the shore. Here she still
lives, and here the Sun visits her, when his journey is done,
every day that he crosses the sky.

When Changing Woman had departed, her sons went, as
their father had bidden them, to the valley of the San Juan
River where they made their dwelling. They are there to
this day and the Navajos still go there to pray for success in
war, but only warriors go.

SIX

How The People Came *Dinetah*

Changing Woman's younger sister, White Shell Woman, went with the two brothers but when they stopped to build their dwelling she went on, alone, to the San Juan Mountains as that was where The People had come from long before. There, on the shores of the Place of Emergence, she built a good hogan for herself. She swept the floor clean and made a comfortable bed of soft grass and leaves for herself but she was terribly lonely.

Four days after she had constructed her hut, she was visited by all the gods, including Hastséyalti, Talking God, and Hastséhogan, the House God, the divine ones of the sacred mountains, and also her sister, who said to her, "Go stand in the East. My place is in the West," and thus they stood during the ceremony that followed, which was the same as the corn ceremony by which First Man and First Woman were created, and again the white ear of corn was changed into a man and the yellow ear of corn was changed into a woman and these were given the breath of life by Wind. When Hastséyalti threw the sacred top buckskin off the new pair, a dark cloud descended and covered their forms like a blanket. White Shell Woman led them into her hogan and the assembled gods dispersed, but before he left, Hastséyalti promised to return in four days.

When Hastséyalti returned to White Shell Woman's hogan he brought another couple with him. Then he gave her two ears of corn saying, "Grind only one grain at a time," and departed. White Shell Woman said to the newly arrived couple: "This boy and girl of corn cannot marry one another for they are brother and sister; neither can you marry one another, for you also are brother and sister, yet I must do something for you all."

So she married the boy made of corn to the new girl and the girl made of corn to the boy that Hastséyalti had brought, and soon each couple had two children, a boy and a girl. From these people descended the clan called House of Dark Cliffs.

Thirteen years passed and they saw no sign of existence of any people but themselves until one night they saw the gleam of a distant fire. For four days and four nights they sought out the fire but could not find it until Wind whispered, "The fire shines through a crack in the mountain at night. Cross the ridge and you will find the fire." They had not gone far over the ridge when they saw the footprints of men, then the footprints of children, and soon they came to a camp. One party was as much rejoiced as the other to find people like themselves in the wilderness. They embraced one another and shouted mutual greetings and questions. The new people said they had come from a poor land where they had lived on ducks and snakes. The new party consisted of twelve persons, five men, three women, one grown girl, one grown boy and two small children. The place where the strangers were encamped was called Bend in a Canyon, and so they were given that name and from them are descended that clan.

Soon afterwards White Shell Woman left The People and went to dwell forever in the San Juan Mountains in a house of White Shell which had been prepared for her. But she still comes to visit the Navajos in the she-rain for she is ever present in the soft rains.

Fourteen years later The People were joined by another people who had come from Huerfano Mesa and seven years later a fourth clan joined them. The new arrivals said they had been seeking The People all over the land for many years. Sometimes they would come upon the dead bushes of old camps and again they would find deserted brush shelters, partly green or, again, quite green and fresh. Occasionally they would observe faint footprints and think they were just about to meet another people like themselves in the desolate land, but again all traces of humanity would be lost. They were rejoiced to meet at last The People they had so long sought. The new people camped close to the people from Huerfano Mesa and discovered that they and the latter carried similar red arrow-holders, such as the other clans did not have, and this led them to believe they were related.

Fourteen years after the accession of the fourth clan, the Navajos moved to Chaco Canyon. They camped at night in a scattered fashion and made so many fires that they attracted the attention of some strangers camped on a distant mountain, and these strangers came down next day and they too were a similar people and joined the tribe. It was autumn when the fifth clan arrived. Then the whole tribe moved to the banks of the San Juan River, where they built warm huts for winter. All the fall and winter, when the days were fair, they worked in the bottom lands grubbing up roots and getting the soil ready for gardens to be planted in the spring.

When the tribe had been living on the banks of the San Juan for six years a new band joined them. As yet The People had no horses, domestic sheep or goats. They rarely succeeded in killing deer or Rocky Mountain sheep. When they secured deer it was sometimes by still-hunting them, sometimes by surrounding one and making it run until it was exhausted, and sometimes by driving them over precipices. When a man got two skins of these larger animals he made a garment of them by tying the forelegs together over his shoulders. The women, in those days, wore a garment consisting of two webs of woven cedar bark, one hanging in front and one behind. Everyone wore sandals of yucca fiber or cedar bark. Their blankets were made of cedar bark, of yucca fiber, or of skins sewed together. Each house had, in front of the door, a long passageway in which hung two curtains, one at the outer, the other at the inner end, usually made of woven cedar bark. In winter they brought in plenty of wood at night, closed both curtains, and made the house warm before they went to sleep. Their bows were of plain wood as the Navajos had not yet learned to put

131

animal fiber on the backs of the bows. Their arrows were mostly of reeds tipped with wood. The land which they farmed was surrounded by high bluffs.

After a time The People became too numerous for all of them to dwell where they were, so some went up on the bluffs to live and built stone storehouses in the cliffs, and others moved across the San Juan and raised crops on the other side of the stream.

In the next two decades The People were joined by three other bands of Navajos, the third of which was very numerous and came from the White Valley among the Waters, which is near where the city of Santa Fe now stands. These people had long viewed in the western distance the mountains where The People dwelt, wondering if anyone lived there and, at length, set out to see. They journeyed westward twelve days till they reached the mountains and spent eight days travelling among them before they encountered The People. The people of this new clan were good hunters and very skilled in making weapons and beautiful buckskin shirts and they taught their arts to the other clans. The chief of these people was named Góntso, or Big Knee.

Now at this time The People still lived about the valley of the San Juan, remaining in one place both summer and winter as the Navajos did not become wanderers until they got the sheep. But The People became so numerous that the men had to go farther and farther away to hunt, and on their journeys they encountered many people—some of whom were like the Navajos and spoke the same or a similar language. And many of these people came to live among The People and new clans were added in this manner.

A number of Utes visited the Navajos there once. They came when the corn ears were small and remained till the corn was harvested. They worked for the Navajos, and when their stomachs were filled, all left except for one family, which consisted of an old couple, two girls and a boy. These at first intended to stay but a short time after their friends had gone, but they tarried longer and longer and postponed their going from time to time, till they ended up staying with the Navajos until they died. One of the girls, whose name was Sage Brush Hill, lived to be an old woman and the mother of many children, and from her is descended the clan of Sage Brush Hill.

Some years later a large band of Apaches from the South

came to the settlement on the San Juan and told the Navajos that they had left their old tribe forever and desired to become Navajos. They all belonged to one clan among the Apaches and were admitted to the tribe as a new clan with their old name, Trap Dyke. About this time there was a famine in Zuñi and some people from that pueblo came and were admitted into the tribe, but they were not formed into a new clan but were added to an existing one. The Zuñi clan was formed much later.

More and more, bands of Navajos came among The People on the San Juan and were admitted as clans, as well as the people from an old pueblo named Klógi which was near where Jemez now stands. These people, who were starving, formed the clan of Klógi.

Before this time the Navajos had been a weak and peaceful tribe, but now they found themselves becoming a numerous people and they began to talk of going to war. Of late years they had heard much of the great pueblos along the Río Grande, but how those people had saved themselves from the Naye'i the Navajos did not know. A man named Napáilinta got up a war party and made a raid on Red House pueblo and returned with some captives, among whom was a girl, and from her is descended the Red House clan.

The captives from Red House were, at first, slaves among the Navajos, but their descendants became free and increased greatly and from them came the clan of Many Goats.

In this way the Navajo people grew in number and their power increased. It was about this time that the people from the shores of the great water in the West came to join the Navajos.

One night two strange men entered the Navajo camp. They spoke the Navajo language and told The People they were the advance couriers of a multitude of wanderers who had left the shores of the great waters in the West to join the Navajos along the San Juan river, of whom they had heard. The ancestors of these people were made by Changing Woman, who became lonely in her home in the West and created them for company. When she had made these people from the skin from under her left arm, from the skin under her right arm and from other parts of her body, she said to these people: "I wish you to dwell near me, where I can always see you, but if one day you choose to go east to where your kindred dwell, you may go."

When these people had lived on the shore of the great water for many years, some of them went to Changing Woman and told her that they wished to go and live among their kindred in the East as The People were few where they lived and had many enemies and they felt that they would be better off where there were many of their kind.

On the appointed day they set out on their journey to the East, and after they had travelled for twelve days they crossed a high ridge and came in sight of a great treeless plain, in the center of which they observed some dark objects in motion. They continued on but tried to avoid the dark objects, which they suspected of being men, by keeping among the foothills and under the cover of the timber that surrounded the plain. As they went along they could see the dark objects more plainly and discovered that these were indeed human beings.

In spite of the precautions taken by the travellers, they had been seen by the people of the plain, and when they camped at night two of the latter visited them. The visitors said they were the Kiltsói (Mohave) and the plain in which they lived was extensive, and that they had watermelons getting ripe, with corn and other food in their gardens. The travellers decided to remain with these people for a while and rest.

The second night two more visitors came into the camp and one of them fell in love with a maiden of the western people and stayed with her in the camp as long as her people remained in the valley, except for the last two nights when she went and stayed with his people. These gave the wanderers an abundance of the produce of their fields and they, of course, fared well. When the travellers were prepared to move on, they implored the young husband to go with them. He wanted his wife to stay there, among his people, but in the end the woman's relations prevailed and the Kiltsói man joined them on their journey. In the meantime four other men of the Kiltsói had fallen in love with maidens of the wanderers and these enamored young men also left their kindred and joined the travellers.

As these people continued on their journey east, they encountered many difficulties, for they soon came to a land in which they could find no water. For five days they walked across a parched wasteland before finding water in a hole. A woman was the first to taste it. "It is bitter water," she cried.

"Let that be your name and the name of your people," one who had heard her said, and thus did the clan of the Bitter Water People receive its name. A few days later another woman found some water but it was muddy, and from her is descended the clan of Mud People.

The wanderers travelled steadily for thirty-one days after leaving the Kiltsói, until they reached the San Francisco mountains. Here they stopped for several days to rest and built a stone wall around their camp, which still stands. When they again resumed their journey they were forced to travel much slower as there was little food and the men had constantly to stop and hunt.

It was late autumn when they stopped to rest the second time, and this is where these people from the West became divided into two parties. One group wanted to remain where they were, in hopes that some of their kindred people, whom they knew must be somewhere nearby, would find them. The second group wanted to push on and find the kindred people themselves, so they left. But soon after they had gone, those who remained in the camp sent out two messengers, and later they sent out two more, to induce their people to come back to the camp. The first two couriers, searching for these people, came to a place where the runaways had divided into two bands, one of which travelled east and it is from this group that the Jicarilla Apaches are descended. The other band wandered off to the North and became those kindred tribes who live far to the North (Canada and Alaska) who speak a language much like the Navajo.

The second pair of messengers pursued this band, travelling north for a great distance, but finally gave up the task and returned to the camp. The first pair followed the band travelling east but soon despaired of overtaking these people and turned south toward the San Juan River, where they found the long-sought Navajos. These two messengers were the men of whom you have heard before, who entered the camp of the Navajos and told of the coming of the people from the West.

The wanderers stayed in their camp all that winter, but with the coming of spring they resumed their journey. Along the way, for one reason or another, groups of them stopped to remain at places that they found favorable. One group stopped to live at a place where a great lone tree stood and these people became the clan called People of the (Lone) Tree. Another group stopped at Deer Springs and became the clan of that name but the main body of immigrants continued on and soon joined their kinsmen on the San Juan River.

As the years passed several bands of Apaches joined the Navajos on the San Juan River and became clans. Then another party of Zuñi Indians were taken into the tribe, and a new people with painted faces who came from the West and are supposed to have been Mohaves were also adopted into the tribe.

In this manner all of the old clans of the Navajo were formed and all this happened long ago, before the Spaniards came into the land. Later some Utes raided far to the South and captured a Spanish woman, whom they sold to the Navajos, and from her is descended the clan of the White Stranger People, or Mexican Clan. During the Pueblo wars with the Spaniards many fugitives came among the Navajo to live, and from the women of these people are descended still other clans.

And it has always been told that this is the manner in which the Navajos became a tribe.

PART THREE

Strangers in the Land

ONE

The Spanish Enter New Mexico

The legend of a long-lost white brother, a bearded white or alien god who would return one day from the East or South, was prevalent among many Indian tribes of pre-Columbian America and especially among those tribes living in what is now the American Southwest, Mexico and Central America. To the Mayas of Guatemala he was the bearded white god Kukulcan, and to the Toltecan and Aztecan peoples of Mexico he was the god of civilization, Quetzalcoatl. The Hopis, living in propinquity to the Navajo, called their long lost white brother Pahána (One from Across the Water). There is a basis of at least a common root for the belief in the lost white god among some tribes. For example, the Hopis believe that in their wanderings, before they settled down and built their pueblos, located within what is now Navajoland, they paused to build many cities and remained in each of them for some years, and that the Toltecs, Mayas and Aztecs, all of whom spoke a related language are Hopi tribes who remained in those cities and did not continue the march of exploration.

The Navajo god of the moon, Klehanoai, was thought to be light-skinned and, as related earlier, was credited with creating the Mexicans as subjects for the divine gambler, Nohoílpi, as well as the strange domestic animals that the Spanish brought to the New World. In Navajo legend Nohoílpi came to their land in the person of Juan de Oñate to "a place north of Santa Fe. There they (the Mexicans ceased building, and he then returned to Old Mexico, where he still lives and where he is now God of the Mexicans."

Since the Navjos borrowed freely from the cultures with which they came into contact, assimilated what they chose to use and rejected what they did not choose to use, it is probable that the Navajo moon god was derived from the older Hope god Pahána.

Prophecy plays an uncanny role in the arrival of the Spanish *conquistadores* among the Indians of Mexico and New Mexico. The Aztec priest and astrologers had long predicted that their Quetzalcoatl, benevolent god of light, culture and civilization, would return to them in the year of *Ce Acatl* (One Reed) or 1519 in the Christian calendar, and in that year he came in the person of Hernando Cortés. The Hopis, also by means of astrology and divine prophecy, had long anticipated the coming of Pahána and, either by coincidence or because of a common root of the legends, Pahána was due to visit the Hopi in the very same year that Quetzalcoatl was expected to return to the Aztecs. He arrived some twenty-one years later in the person of the Spaniard Pedro de Tovar, one of Coronado's *conquistadores*, and was the first white man to be seen by the Hopis and very probably the Navajo. Unlike the Aztecs, the Hopis put this Spanish Pahána to a series of tests, and when he failed them they sent him on his way.

Like the Navajos, the Aztecs were borrowers of culture, and their legend of Quetzalcoatl, the Feathered Serpent, came down to them from the Toltecs who preceded the Aztecs to prominence in Central Mexico. Quetzalcoatl was not only the god of light, culture and civilization, he was also the patron of agriculture and that virtue singularly lacking among the Aztecs, humility. When the Aztecs conquered the valley of Mexico and subjected the descendants of the Toltecs, they incorporated Quetzalcoatl and other gods of the older civilization into their theology. According to legend, Quetzalcoatl had descended from heaven, assumed mortal form, taught his subjects civilization and tried to persuade them to stop the practice of human sacrifice.

The latter angered the principal deity of the Toltecs, Texcatlipoca, the Mirror that Smokes, who demanded sacrifice so that the sun would make its way across the heavens each day, and Quetzalcoatl, the man-god, white and black-bearded, was driven out by the people. He and his court boarded a raft on the coast near Tabasco and sailed to the East, promising to return in a One Reed year and re-establish his rule after which the Aztecs would enter a period of great enlightenment. Preceding One Reed years, which occurred every fifty-two years, the Aztec priests and astrologers were particularly attentive to omens and signs from the heavens that would signal the coming of Quetzalcoatl. Such signs came in abundance in the decade preceding 1519 in the form of earthquakes, floods, strange dreams and a brilliant comet with a large tail which was seen in the sky for several nights and was said by Nezahual-pilli, the king of Texcoco, to be an ill omen. According to Fray Diego Durán, Nezahualpilla visited Moctezuma (Montezuma), the high king of the Aztecs, and said: "Terrible, frightful things will come . . . in all our lands and provinces there will be great calamities and misfortunes, (and) not a thing will be left standing. Death will dominate the land!"

About the same time a message of a somewhat more immediate, if less divine, emergency came to the king of the Aztecs in the form of reports from the Gulf Coast of strange men who had landed at Tabasco and Champoton in large floating castles. Mystic and priest-ridden, Moctezuma chose to become frightened out of his wits over the former and all but ignored the latter. But he did send emissaries to investigate the strangers who, upon their return, reported that they had seen men with white skins, dressed from head to foot in hard metal and carrying arms of the same material.

Actually these strange white men were the expedition led by Juan de Grijalva, sent out by the governor of the newly discovered island of Cuba, Diego Velásquez, to explore the area west of that island in April, 1518. The governor had sent an earlier expedition, under the command of Francisco Hernández de Cordoba in February, 1517, which had found the coast of Yucatan and fought and lost a battle with some unfriendly Mayas. The men of the Córdoba expedition escaped with their lives and some gold ornaments which, of course, prompted the second expedition. Grijalva followed the same course taken by Córdoba and encountered more unfriendly Mayas but, instead of returning to Cuba, turned north for further exploration. At Tabasco the Grijalva party encountered some very friendly Indians who spoke a language different from that of the Mayas. These natives were quite amenable to trading and gave the Spaniards gold in return for some glass beads. Quite without realizing it, Grijalva had traded beads for gold with the emissaries of Moctezuma completely ignorant of the existence of the latter or of the vast inland empire he ruled that in many ways, both culturally and artistically, far surpassed anything the Spaniards had ever known or dreamed could exist. But within a matter of years it would all be reduced to ashes and the city of Tenochititlan, where Moctezuma awaited the return of the emissaries and their report on white strangers, would furnish the building blocks for Mexico City, the Spanish capital of the New World. From Mexico City the Spaniards would, within two decades, launch their conquest of the American Southwest and of the Pueblo Indians, which would bring them to their first direct contact with the Navajos.

Much has been made of Cortés' conquest of Mexico with five hundred fifty-three men pitted against the army of one hundred fifty thousand at Moctezuma's disposal, but the true story is infinitely more complicated than a mere matter of comparing manpower and one that we will not go into in detail about here. Moctezuma true to his nature, did absolutely nothing about the strangers but listen to the contradictory advice of a horde of vassals none of whom, by law, could look upon his face, and worry about where he should hide if the prophecies of Nezahualpilli came true. Instead of going about the very badly needed task of tightening the reins of his vast domain, he busied himself with securing a new sacrificial stone, one that would reflect the grandeur of Mexico, as he considered the one his grandfather had set up too small and too cheap!

Cortés set sail from Cuba on February 10, 1519, with five hundred eight swordsmen, one hundred sailors, thirty-two crossbowmen, thirteen musketeers, sixteen horses, several brass guns and four falconets. He landed at Tabasco, routed a small force of Indians, and took possession of the land in the name of King Charles I of Spain. After a second pitched battle with the Tabascans, Cortés sailed up the coast into Mexican territory and landed at the present-day port of San Juan de Ulloa. In the Christian calendar it was Good Friday, April 22, 1519; in the Aztec calendar it was nine Wind Day of the One Reed year—the exact date on which Quetzalcoatl was expected to return to the Aztecs. The coincidence threw Moctezuma into a state of panic. Moctezuma's hysteria, coupled with the fact that the Aztecs had burdened their subject nations to the breaking point in their demand for both goods and victims for their sacrificial altars, sealed the doom of Tenochititlan.

Far to the North, in another world, deep winter snows were just beginning to melt on the mesas of the land of the Navajos, but that world and this were, irrevocably, on a colliding path.

Cortés, with a horde of Indians, enemies of the Aztecs who quickly allied themselves with the Spaniards, made short work of the Aztecs. With Tenochititlan conquered and the Aztec civilization all but reduced to dust, Cortés began carefully to lay plans for an *entrada* into the vast uncharted region to the North where he, as well as other Spanish leaders, thought the fabled "Seven Golden Cities of Cibola" of Spanish legend might be found. The legend of the seven golden cities was almost four hundred years old and was firmly entrenched in Spanish mythology, dating from the Moorish capture of Mèrida in 1150. According to the legend seven bishops of Mèrida, along with their followers, had escaped the Moors and had fled by ship across the western ocean. After weeks of travel the fugitives had landed on "blessed isles." These blessed isles had been the objective of every Spanish explorer since Columbus.

But a very wary King Charles was not amenable to Cortés' *entrada* into the northern lands. Suspecting, with sound reasoning, that Cortés was obsessed with dreams of empire, he decreed that an *Audiencia* (governing council) be established in New Spain. Ostensibly, the *Audiencia* was established to manage the affairs of the crown in the new land but actually its purpose was to hold the indomitable Cortés in check. For several years, until the arrival of Don Antonio de Mendoza in Mexico City in 1535, power balanced precariously between Cortés and the *Audiencia* with some members of the assembly occasionally leaning heavily toward Cortés—especially after Nuño de Guzmán, head of the *Audiencia,* visited the village of Pánuco, near the east coast, and was told by an Indian from the northern lands of seven large, rich cities located just forty days' travel farther north.

Appointed viceroy of New Spain by King Charles, Mendoza arrived in Mexico City just in time to curtail the aging Cortés' ambitions and domination of affairs. Mendoza was an astute administrator and spent his time manipulating the affairs of state and paid little attention to rumors of the lost golden cities of the North. In spite of the fact that Mendoza cared little for conquest he could not ignore the rumors forever. Time and greed were against him.

Other men were already in search of the Seven Cities of Cibola (notably the scoundrel Nuño de Guzmán). And the search pointed to the lands that would become the American Southwest, the home of the Indians the Spaniards would call the Pueblos and the others they would call Querechos. The latter were called the Apachu Nabahu by the Tewa.

In 1528 the Cuban governor sent out an expedition of three hundred men under Pánfilo Narváez to explore Florida in search of treasure. The expedition vanished and nothing was heard of it until eight years later when Nuno de Guzmán came upon a small party of wanderers in northern Mexico. Guzmán had, in the years between 1529 and 1536, ravaged north and west of Mexico City, carving out the province called Nueva Galicia in a fruitless if relentless search for the wealthy cities he'd been told about by the Indian from the northern lands. With heavy hand he'd subdued tribe after tribe of Indians in northern Mexico and had just suffered his first defeat, a stinging blow at the hands of the Cahitas in Sonora, from whom he'd retreated to Culiacán, when the four lone survivors of the Narváez expedition fell into his hands.

The expedition had been shipwrecked on the Texas coast and the survivors found by Guzmán—Alvar Nuñez Cabeza de Vaca, Castrilla Maldonado, Andrés Dorantes and the latter's Negro slave Estevan—were among the group of two hundred and fifty men who had reached shore. Within a year all but these four and another, Lupe de Ovieda, who would be left behind, half-crazed, to die among the Indians, had perished.

The story of Cabeza de Vaca is one of the great sagas of history. First a slave to the Indians of Texas who took him captive, he became a healer, then a trader. It is from his journals that we are able to understand the extensive channels of trade which were established among the Indians thousands of years ago. This prehistoric trade extended from Canada to Central America and virtually from coast to coast of what is now the United States.

Trade languages had developed among the Indians long before Cabeza de Vaca. Sign language was the trade language of the Plains; the Indians of the Northwest spoke, in trading, what would come to be called the Chinook jargon, and the Indians of the Southeast used the language of the Mobilian Indians.

Prehistoric trade trails were long, indeed. As John Upton Terrell points out: "When the first *voyageurs* from French Canada—who regrettably, cannot be identified with certainty--reached the upper Missouri River country, the Dakota (Sioux) possessed dentalia shells from the Pacific and wampum from the Atlantic." (Terrell, 1967: 78.)

Cabeza de Vaca wandered about Texas for years trading among the Indians and finally came upon Maldonado, Dorantes and Estevan who had been on a different ship of the Narváez expedition and were being held as slaves by the Mariames Indians. They made their escape from the Mariames on the night of September 23, 1534, and in the summer of 1536, almost eight years after they had been shipwrecked, they arrived by escort in Mexico City and received a tumultuous welcome and honors from the Viceroy.

Cabeza de Vaca, too, had heard from the Indians with whom he'd traded of the wealthy cities of the North, as had the others. While living with the Opatas of the upper Sonora valley they had been told of a region to the North that was populated by a prosperous people and which contained many large cities. As a matter of fact, the Negro, Estevan, had actually been shown a trail leading to these rich cities. There could be no doubt now that the Seven Cities of Cibola not only existed but lay only a short distance to the North, for these were not untrustworthy Indians telling of them, these were Spaniards.

Upon hearing Cabeza de Vaca's story even cautious Antonio de Mendoza became interested in the possibility of a new empire to be conquered. Mendoza purchased Estevan from Dorantes as the slave had not only readily adapted to the Indian cultures during his stay among them, he also spoke at least six of the varied dialects of the northern tribes and knew the all-important sign language. Mendoza also retained the Indians who'd been with the Cabeza de Vaca party when they were found and put them, along with Estevan, under the charge of a Franciscan priest, Fray Marcos de Niza, whom he sent to the North to verify the rumors of the great cities. Not only was Fray Marcos charged with the task of exploring the regions and learning what he could of the treasure-holding cities, he was also instructed to inform all Indians he encountered that they were now Spanish subjects. Viceroy Mendoza's orders to Fray Marcos were: "You must explain to the natives of the land that there is only one God in heaven, and the emperor on earth to rule and govern it, whose subjects they must all become and whom they must serve." We may presume the Indians found that bit of information highly enlightening.

Fray Marcos set out on his journey from San Miguel de Culiacán on March 7, 1539: a journey that would lead to a complete change of life-style and culture for the Pueblos and Navajos. Because the early histories of the American Southwest were written by the Spanish, it is usually insinuated, by omission if not directly, that the Spanish "discovered" the Indians, causing great surprise when they came upon them. Such was not the case. Cabeza de Vaca, in his famous *Relación*, tells us of the extensive trading network that existed among the Indians and that the traders carried news from tribe to tribe. Therefore we may presume that the Pueblos and even the more primitive Navajos had long since been aware of the existence of the strange white men of Mexico and that the entry of Estevan and Fray Marcos into their lands, therefore, came as little surprise.

At any rate, and for one reason or another, when Fray Marcos' party reached Vacapa (Matapa, in central Sonora), the good father sent Estevan on ahead of the expedition. According to Pedro de Castañeda, soldier-chronicler and member of the later Coronado expedition: "After the

Friars I have mentioned and the Negro had started, the Negro did not get on well with the Friars because he took the women that were given him and collected turquoises and got together a stock of everytning. Besides, the Indians in those places through which they went got along better with the Negro because they had seen him before. This is the reason he was sent ahead."

It seems, in light of later events, that Fray Marcos was not a very brave man and sent the slave ahead to pave the way for his arrival. Estevan, as he was instructed, sent what information he obtained regarding the country ahead back to Fray Marcos. His information told of seven large cities, with houses of stone and lime, and many other cities with houses decorated with turquoise in the provinces farther on. These cities were, of course, the adobe pueblos of New Mexico, and to the hut dwelling natives of Sonora who told Estevan of them they were, indeed, large and rich.

Fray Marcos reached the land of the Apaches, the country in and about the present White Mountain Apache reservation in Arizona, on May 9 and learned, twelve days later, that Estevan had been killed by the natives of Cibola, actually Hawikuh, one of the Zuñi ruins near Ojo Caliente, about fifteen miles south of the Zuñi pueblo, New Mexico.

There are several versions of the story of Estevan's death. Possibly he was killed because he sent, as a calling card, a decorated gourd rattle to the natives that had been made by a tribe with whom the people of Hawikuh were at war. Casteneda was told by the natives of Hawikuh the following year that the slave had been killed because he demanded treasures and women. The story that has been preserved among the legends of the Zuñi tells of a "Black Mexican" who came among their ancients, sending ahead of him a pebble-filled gourd with two plumes, one white and one red, the emblem of a tribe with which the Zunis had long been at war. The Zuñis had already been warned by the Apaches that this "Black Mexican" was a very bad man and had assaulted their women. The Zuñi still tell the story of Estevan: "They and our ancients did much harm to one another. Then our ancients killed one of the Black Mexicans, a large man with chili lips (lips swollen from eating chili peppers) and some of the Indians they killed, catching them. Then the rest ran away and were chased by our grandfathers back toward their country in the Land of the Everlasting Summer."

It has never been established exactly what Fray Marcos did after he learned of Estevan's death. He claims, in his chronicles, that he was taken by the Indians of his entourage to a point where he could obtain a view of the "city of Cibola" which he reported as "the best and largest of all those that have been discovered . . . the settlement is larger than the city of Mexico." The members of the Coronado expedition had reason to doubt that he went one step farther toward "Cibola" after leaning of Estevan's death when they arrived there and found naught but a mean mud village the following year.

Nevertheless, Fray Marcos returned to Mexico with glowing accounts of fantastically rich kingdoms and was hailed as a new Columbus who had not only found the Seven Cities of Cibola but because he reported, falsely, that he had sighted the seacoast which "in latitude thirty-five degrees turns west" had discovered a new route to the spiceries of India. His glowing accounts of "fantastically rich kingdoms" only served to heighten interest in the expedition already being readied under the command of Francisco Vásquez de Coronado. On September 2, 1539, in Mexico City Fray Marcos certified an oath to the veracity of his report and on February 23, the following year, Coronado started out on his famed expedition to the American Southwest.

As far as the Indians of New Mexico were concerned, the Coronado expedition came seeking revenge for Estevan's death. At least that is the way the Zuñis still remember it: " . . . by and by they came back, these Black Mexicans, and with them many men of Sonora. They wore coats of iron, and war bonnets of metal and carried for weapons short canes that spat fire and made thunder, so said our ancients, but they were guns, you know. They frightened our bad-tempered fathers so badly that their hands hung down by their sides like the hands of women. And this time these black, curly bearded people drove our ancients about like slave creatures."

Cortés destroyed powerful Mexico with five hundred fifty-three men. Coronado was somewhat better prepared to crush Cibola. His own contribution amounted to fifty thousand pesos—nearly one million five hundred thousand dollars at today's value—and Viceroy Mendoza not only matched Coronado's contribution but raised it by ten thousand pesos. Over three hundred Spanish foot soldiers led an Indian force of eight hundred men; there were five hundred war horses, adorned with their own coats of mail hearing armored cavalry, followed by almost a thousand work horses and mules for munitions and provisions, and bringing up the rear were hundreds of sheep and cattle for food. Many of the soldiers brought along their wives and children, ready-made colonists to hold the land once Cibola had been defeated.

Two years later, in the summer of 1542, less than a hundred members of the expedition straggled back to Mexico City, a ragged, disgraced band. Coronado found, much to his sorrow, that Fray Marcos' reports were outright lies. Instead of a city larger than Mexico, he found a series of small mud towns, without gold and with very little turquoise, none of which encrusted the buildings. And instead of a confused, superstitious Moctezuma he found, at every turn, war chiefs who were willing to fight to the death and who were clever enough to send him off *(mas alli)* on a fool's errand searching for the "true Cibola" through the empty plains of what is now Texas and as far north as Kansas. Twelve years later he died in disgrace at the age of forty-four.

But the impact the expedition made on the Pueblos of New Mexico and their neighbors, the Apaches and Navajos, was staggering. Not only were there strange men in the land but there were sheep and cattle. Indeed, these strange men dressed in metal came to be, in Navajo legend, the people the Navajo god of the moon had made and given to the divine gambler, Nohoilpi, to punish the *Dineh* for the way they had treated him!

The Spaniards left death and distruction wherever they journeyed. They took Hawikuh by force and killed many men of that pueblo in a battle in which Coronado was severely wounded. Next they travelled to the group of pueblos called Tiquex, near present-day Albuquerque, where they were welcomed as friends and repaid the friendly Indians by ordering them to vacate one large pueblo so it might be occupied by the army and told the displaced Indians to find homes where they could. But that was only the beginning. With winter coming on, the soldiers from the Land of the Everlasting Summer visited

149

each of the twelve pueblos of Tiquex, one by one, and demanded what goods were stored.

Casteñeda wrote: "Under these circumstances the natives could do no more but remove their own cloaks and give them over to the Spaniards until what had been requested was obtained." The people of Tiquex were stripped of their garments in their own homes by their guests, the pueblos were robbed of corn, salt, meat and all else that caught the eye of the soldiers. Rapine followed robbery and this final insult caused the proud people of Tiquex to rebel. They bravely defended their homes at Arenal pueblo, killing many of the Spaniard's Mexican allies and seriously wounding a dozen Spaniards, but they were finally smoked out. A hundred were killed, two hundred were captured.

Casteñeda wrote of the fate of the prisoners: "On the ground the mounted men and some of the Mexican allies from New Spain built some heavy fires in the lower rooms where they had broken holes, so that the Indians were forced to call for peace. Melgosa and López were in that place and they answered the Indian's signs for peace by making similar signs which consisted of making a cross. The natives then laid down their arms and surrendered to their mercy. They were taken to the tent of Don Garcia who, as is affirmed, did not know of the sign of truce and thought they were surrendering as defeated men. As the general had ordered that no one was to be taken alive, so as to dispose a punishment that would intimidate the others, Don Garcia at once ordered two hundred stakes to be put into the ground to burn the Indians alive. No one could tell him of the truce that had been agreed upon because the soldiers knew not of it and those who arranged the peace terms did not speak of it considering it none of their business. When the Indians saw that their friends were tied and the Spaniards had started burning them, nearly a hundred of them who waited in the tent began to defend themselves with whatever they could find: . . . our footmen stormed the tent on all sides with swords that forced the Indians to flee and the mounted men fell upon them. Since the ground was level no one escaped alive except for a few who remained hidden in the pueblo and who fled in the night."

Other pueblos of Tiquex rebelled, having seen all they

wanted of Spanish justice and of the Spaniards too, for that matter. One by one all twelve pueblos were crushed and hundreds of men, women and children were killed. In the night of winter the survivors silently, and without goods, vacated their homes and retreated to the surrounding mountains, never to return as long as the Spaniards were at Tiquex. Of course the Navajos knew about Tiquex, and possibly observed the battles there from afar and might have taken in some of the refugees as they would do later when another force of Spaniards destroyed Jemez.

The Pueblos decided to rid themselves of the iron-clad savages by trickery. When Coronado's expedition first arrived in Cibola, Indians from several pueblos, including Cicuyé (Pecos) in what is now northeastern New Mexico, came, by Coronado's invitation, to visit the strangers and hear what they had to say. Later Hernándo de Alvarado, one of Coronado's lieutenants, visited Pecos and confiscated a slave whom the Spaniards called El Turco because of the peculiar turban he wore. After the people of Tiquex had fled their homes, the Spaniards began giving their attention to the fascinating tales El Turco told of his homeland. The Turk said that in his country there was a river in the level country which was two leagues wide in which there were fish as large as horses, and large numbers of very big canoes, with more than twenty rowers to a side, and that the canoes carried sails. The lords of the land, he added, sat on the poop under awnings, and on the prow they had a great golden eagle. He added that the lord of that country took his afternoon nap under a great tree on which hung a great number of little gold bells which put him to sleep as they swung in the air. No doubt the gold-hungry hearts of the Spaniards were gladdened when the Turk told them that also in that land, which he called Quivira, even ordinary dishes were made of wrought plate and the jugs and jars were of gold, which he called *acochis*. The Pueblos who had made up the story and charged the Turk with repeating it to the Spaniards knew their foe well. Coronado decided that this land of Quivira, surely, was the true Cibola and ordered the army to prepare to march.

On April 23, 1541, the entire expedition, army, Mexican allies, women and children started out for Quivira and at the head of the column, beside Coronado, rode the Turk, a Pawnee slave wearing the distinctive turban of his prairie tribe, leading the Spanish *conquistadores* to the promised land.

The expedition wound its way northward to Pecos where Coronado secured two more Indian slaves from Quivira, a second Pawnee named Xabe, who confirmed the Turk's tales of riches and a Wichita named Sopete who said El Turco was a liar. But the Spaniards wanted to believe the story of golden Quivira. Coronado knew he could not return to Mexico empty of hand.

From Pecos the expedition turned southwest, following the Pecos River, then eastward to what is now the New Mexico-Texas border near Nara Visa, New Mexico. Here, abruptly, the Turk turned the expedition southward. Soon they came upon some nomadic natives of the Texas plains they called Querechos and a second tribe called Tejas. The latter gave the state of Texas its name. The Querechos were Athapascans, plains Apaches, and were described by Coronado as having "the best bodies of any people I have seen in the Indies." Castañeda extolled these Athapascans, the one people that the Spaniards would never subdue, as the finest appearing, most warlike and most feared of all the Indians they met on the expedition. "They do not eat human flesh, they are gentle people and are not cruel; they are faithful friends," he said. As A. Grove Day has said: "Thus was described the Apache Indians at the time when white men first came into contact with them. In the years intervening between the journey of Coronado and the early settlement of Texas by Anglo-Saxons, either the Apache temperament or that of the white men had changed, for, under the names of Jicarilla and Mescalero, the descendants of the free-living Querechos were shot at sight by American ranchers as one would shoot a murderous prowling beast." (Day, California; 1964: 235-36.)

The Querechos told Coronado that there was a very large river in the East and that one could go along this river through an inhabited country for ninety days without a break from settlement to settlement. In spite of the fact that the Turk had talked to the Querechos in their own language before they told Coronado, in sign language, of these eastern settlements, the Spaniard believed them—and pushed on.

For weeks the expedition wandered about the trackless plains beneath an energy-sapping sun, drinking brackish water and killing buffalo as their only means of substenance. Finally, when they reached the eastern rim of the Llano Estacado in northern Texas, Coronado, finally heeding the words of Sopete, turned the Turk over to his soldiers. Under torture the guide confessed that the Pueblos had charged him with leading the Spaniards out into the vast plains and losing them or, at best, so depleting their resources that they could be destroyed when they returned to the settlements. The Turk was put into chains.

The expedition was now two hundred fifty leagues from Tiquex and without provisions. Coronado chose thirty horsemen and six foot soldiers to go north in search of Quivira and send the rest of the expedition back to the Río Grande.

Coronado found no gold in the Wichita huts to which Sopete guided him in what is now Kansas. In September, after having the Turk executed, he returned to Tiquex and on April 1, 1542, after wintering on the Río Grande, the Coronado expedition straggled back to Mexico, its captain in disgrace, leaving behind three priests who were soon killed by the Indians.

Between Coronado's aborted expedition and that of Juan de Oñate in 1598, five lesser-known reconnaissances entered the American Southwest.

In 1581 an expedition of eight soldiers and two priests, under the leadership of Fray Agustín Rodriguez and Captain Francisco Sanchez Chamuscado, twelve men in all, and apparently completely unaware of Coronado's expedition, marched up the Río Grande valley to reconnoiter the area for possible mining ventures and, of course, to convert the Indians to Christianity. The expedition returned the following year having found neither mines nor converts, leaving behind the two priests to be executed by the Indians. The third priest, Fray Juan de Santa María, had already been killed by the Tiwa.

A year later Antonio de Espejo, a fugitive seeking refuge, led an expedition of fourteen soldiers and one priest into the Southwest, supposedly looking for the two priests left behind by Chamuscado, and covered nearly the entire area, from Texas to the Hopi villages of Arizona. The Espejo expedition is important because it was the first to record contact between the Spaniards and the Navajos.

On February 28, 1583, the Espejo group set out from Zia to Zuñi. They skirted the eastern slopes of Cebolleta mesa and near Mount Taylor, the Navajo's sacred mountain of the south, encountered some *Indios serranos,* mountain Indians, undoubtedly Navajos, who were not only peaceful but brought goods to trade with the foreigners at the site that was later to become Laguna pueblo. After visiting the Hopi villages, the expedition left Zuñi on May 31, 1583, to return to the Río Grande.

At Acoma some of the expedition's servants fled, one of which, notably, was a "Querechos woman" who had been given to a member of the expedition, Francisco Barreto, by the Hopis. The Acomas "and the neighboring mountain people" took up arms against the Spaniards and the foreigners did not recover their servants. These mountain people or Querechos were Navajos living in the vicinity of Mount Taylor and cultivating corn from which they made tortillas. Hammond and Rey say of this incident: "The entire incident is of special historical interest because it shows that the Querechos were found from as far west as the Hopi pueblos, where Barreto had obtained the girl, to Mount Taylor." (Hammond and Rey, New Mexico, 1966: 26.) The Navajos, therefore, were occupying virtually the same territory in 1583 that they were three hundred years later when they were finally defeated by the Americans under Kit Carson.

There were two expeditions in 1590, an illegal one led by Gaspar Castaño de Sosa and a second one, under the command of Juan Morlete, who was sent to arrest the members of the Castaño de Sosa group. Finally a group of adventurers under the leadership of Captain Francisco Leyva de Bonilla and Antonio Guitérrez de Humañ marched up the Rio Grande valley and west into Texas in 1593—and were killed by the Indians—before Juan de Oñate led three hundred colonists into New Mexico in 1598 to settle the land in the name of Christ and for Spain.

TWO

The Colonization of New Mexico

Juan de Onate, as he reached his middle years, was one of the richest and most influential men in New Spain and, in the words of one of his contemporaries, "possessed a brave heart and noble pride." A direct descendant of both Cortés and Moctezuma, Oñate was the son of a former governor of New Galicia who was one of the discoverers of the rich Zacatecas silver mines. But as the entry into New Mexico had brought about the downfall of Coronado, it would also serve Oñate.

Oñate petitioned the viceroy, Don Luis de Velasco, several times for permission to colonize New Mexico at his own expense. In his first proposal he offered "to take at least two hundred men, furnished with everything necessary, including provisions sufficient to reach the settlements (of the Pueblos) and even more, this all at my cost." He pointed out that the crown would not be "obligated to pay (the soldiers who accompanied him) any wages besides that which I may willingly give them from my estate" and that he would supply all necessary food, animals, raw materials, manufactured implements, rations for the troops and his own personal equipment as well as "great herds of horses with saddles, mules, coaches, carts and sets of armor with weapons of every sort."

Oñate's request was refused several times but on August 24, 1595, the petition was granted. After several delays, Oñate's expedition left Santa Barbara, then the last outpost in conquered territory, on February 7, 1598. The army of soldiers and colonists numbered about four hundred in all. There was a baggage and supply train of eighty-three wagons and carts, carrying maize and wheat, and about seven thousand head of stock, including horses, cattle, sheep, hogs, mules and jackasses.

On April 30, after celebrating a Solemn High Mass, Oñate took possession of the "newly discovered land" on the south side of the Río Grande at the site of the present-day city of Juarez, Mexico, in the name of Philip II and God. The next day the march was resumed; the river was forded at the site of the modern El Paso, Texas, and the expedition continued, travelling up the east bank of the Río Grande.

Oñate, riding ahead with an advance party, after much difficulty, finally "came in sight of a splendid pueblo" (the Tewa pueblo of Ohke) where the Chama entered the Río Grande. The date was August 11, 1598. The Spaniards renamed the pueblo, set amid willows and cottonwoods, San Juan de los Caballeros and began building a temporary capital. The church, the first in New Mexico, was completed and dedicated to San Juan Bautista with a great deal of ceremony, including a sham battle between Christians and Moors, on September 7. Oñate called the Pueblo leaders of the region to San Juan and, on September 9, persuaded them to receive Christian missionaries—after telling them they not only would burn in hell throughout eternity, but would be burned alive on this earth by the Spaniards if they disobeyed the friars. The province was divided into seven mission districts and seven Franciscan friars were placed in charge. There were several reasons, other than the threat of being burned at the stake, why the Pueblos submitted so meekly, at least on the surface, to Christianity. Possibly one of the reasons was because the area had suffered from a long drought, and the day after the Spaniards arrived and blessed the area in the name of San Juan Bautista a heavy rain fell. Oñate convinced the Indians that the rain was the work of the Christian God.

Too, the Indians did not understand that by embracing the Christian God they would be required to give up their old gods but intended only to add another divine deity to the retinue. Fray Francisco de Zamora was given the Picurís province, Taos and other pueblos in northern New Mexico as well as "the Indians of the snowy mountains"—the Navajos and the ancestors of the Jicarilla Apaches.

The first winter at San Juan was fraught with hardships. Not only were the friendly Indians unable to provide sufficient food for the colonists, but several mutinies developed and had to be put down by the Spaniards. Then, on December 4, the Indians of Acoma revolted. According to Villagra, Oñate's chronicler, the revolt was caused by a man named Zutacapan, "one of the least important among his people." But in his account of the events preceding the revolt Villagra attributes several flowery speeches to Zutacapán and his son, Zutancalpo, who supposedly opposed the revolt, containing concepts completely alien to Pueblo culture. Since the Acomans had already fought and won one pitched battle with the Spanish expedition under Espejo, it is safe to presume that they did not submit willingly to the Spaniards as did the people of other pueblos.

Significantly, the revolt occurred while Juan de Zaldívar, Oñate's favorite nephew, and a patrol of eighteen men were visiting the sky city, requisitioning an excessive amount of supplies for use by the Spanish colonists.

Zaldívar and ten of his men, along with some Indian servants, were killed. Four of the Spaniards escaped by jumping off the three hundred fifty-seven-foot-high mesa into the sand dunes below. Oñate sent a force of seventy men, under the charge of Vicente de Zaldívar, brother of the slain Juan, to revenge the death of his soldiers.

The expedition left San Juan on January 12 and reached the rock on the twenty-first, having "gathered provisions" from the pueblo of Zia (Tsia) on the Río Jemez. Upon reaching Acoma, Zaldívar halted his column at the foot of the great cliff and called upon the Acomans to surrender. According to Villagra, in canto twenty-six of his *Historia*, a great force from the "Apache nation" under a war chief named Bempol had joined the people of Acoma to do battle with the Spaniards. Lummis tells us that Zaldívar's summons to surrender "was met with wild and insulting derision, all the Acomans and hundreds of Navajo allies dancing and shrieking defiance from the top of their impregnable cliffs." (Lummis, 1925: 189.) When Villagra wrote and published his *Historia*—it was published in 1610—the Spaniards had not yet differentiated between the Apaches and the Navajos, and Lummis is no doubt correct in his assumption that the Acoma allies were Navajos from the Mount Taylor area.

The battle began on January 22, 1599, and raged until January 24, when the Spaniards gained the top of the mesa and, loading two cannon with "two hundred balls" decimated the Indian ranks. The pueblo was fired and burned to the ground. The revolt was crushed by superior arms but the Indians were told that the Christian god ordained their defeat. In fact Villagra tells us that the Indians clearly saw a vision of St. Paul fighting for the Christians during the conflict. The Acoma casualties were estimated at a minimum of eight hundred men, women and children, including Navajo allies. Seventy or eighty warriors and five hundred women and children were made prisoners. Zaldívar, to revenge the death of his brother, had many of the Indian prisoners cut to pieces and thrown over the cliff. The Spaniards set an example at Acoma. Indians at other pueblos who had been entertaining thoughts of rebellion took heed. Two years later when two Spanish soldiers—deserters—were killed by the Indians at the Jumano pueblos, Oñate sent Vicente de Zaldívar on another mission of revenge. During the six-day battle eight hundred or nine hundred men, women and children were slaughtered; all three Jumano pueblos were burned. Each soldier was given one of the four hundred prisoners as a slave.

The prisoners of Acoma were taken to Santo Domingo pueblo and stood trial early in February, 1599, charged with killing eleven Spaniards and two servants, and of failure to submit peacefully when Vincent de Zaldívar came to punish them. On February 12, Juan de Oñate pronounced his sentence: All males of more than twenty-five years of age were condemned to have one foot cut off and to give twenty-five years of personal service; all males between the ages of twelve and twenty-five years of age and all females of more than twelve years of age were sentenced to twenty years of servitude. Girls under the age of twelve were turned over to Fray Alonso Martinez to be, by Oñate's orders, "distributed in this kingdom or elsewhere." The boys under twelve were given outright to Vicente de Zaldívar. They were, in fact, sold into slavery in spite of the fact that forced servitude was then illegal in New Spain. Two Hopi Indians captured at Acoma had their right hands chopped off and were sent home as a warning to others of their tribe. Villagra makes no mention of "Apache" prisoners. Apparently if any of the Navajos were taken prisoner they were treated as Acomans. In a leaflet by Villagra, printed at Madrid probably in 1612, he tells of taking, on the orders of Oñate, sixty or more young girls who had been captured at Acoma to Mexico and delivering them to the viceroy for distribution among the convents of the city.

Oñate left San Juan, which he had recently renamed San Gabriel, on June 23, 1601, to visit Quivira, and traveled as far east as the vicinity of the present-day city of Wichita, Kansas, traversing many sections of the country visited by Coronado sixty years before. When he returned to the Río Grande on November 24, he found, much to his surprise, San Gabriel all but deserted. During his absence the Franciscans, long discontented with affairs in New Mexico, had talked the soldiers and colonists into returning to Santa Barbara, having found there was no gold, in fact nothing but corn, pumpkins, squash, beans, and Indian souls to be gathered in the unfriendly North. And the missionaries had learned that the Indian souls did not stay gathered for long.

Only a handful of the colonists were on hand to greet Oñate's return. But Vicente de Zaldívar followed the colonists, secured new missionaries and settlers and brought back the deserters, many of whom were arrested and sentenced to death by Oñate. Later he relented and pardoned all of them.

Oñate's dreams for New Mexico were doomed and his failure was heralded in the words of his grandfather-in-law who said: "I came to get gold, not to till the soil like a peasant." On June 7, 1606, Philip III issued an order that no more explorations were to be made in New Mexico and that Oñate was to return to Mexico City immediately. Most of the settlers had already returned to Santa Barbara. The viceroy appointed Don Pedro de Peralta governor with

159

specific instructions to found a new capital. Oñate remained in New Mexico until the arrival of Peralta and in the spring of 1610 left for Mexico. On the way home, a ruined man, Oñate's party was attacked by Indians and his son Don Cristobal de Oñate was killed. Peralta founded Santa Fé in 1610 and moved the capital there.

While the life-style of the Pueblos was certainly changed by contact with Oñate's Spanish colonists and priests, the change was minimal in comparison to that of the Navajos. Prior to the coming of the Spanish colonists to New Mexico, the Navajos were hunters, seed-gathers and seasonal farmers. Living in the land they called *Dinehtah*, they apparently had been in the process of mixing both racially and culturally with other groups of Indians for some time, possibly centuries. They lived in primitive forked-stick hogans and grew patches of corn, beans, and melons. Their communities were comprised of extended family groups and were located on high mesas near their fields. They had already learned weaving probably from the Pueblos, and were utilizing the wild cotton that grew in *Dinehtah* to fashion rough mantles and clothing. But primarily they, as did their Apache cousins, depended on skins obtained from the hunt for protection against the elements. In spite of the fact that they were referred to as nomads by the Spaniards, indications are that they lived a semi-nomadic life, changing their place of residence only as the need for new farming land arose or because of raids from their enemies, the Utes who lived north of them.

In the early years of Spanish occupation there was apparently very little physical contact between the Navajos and the foreigners, although there was probably more than the Spaniards, who referred to all non-Pueblos of New Mexico as "mountain Indians" or, categorically, as "Apaches," realized.

As the pueblo strongholds fell one by one to the Spanish onslaught, the Navajos faded back into their canyons and retreated to their mesas and watched from a distance. And what they watched, besides the virtual enslavement of the Pueblos, were the animals that the Spaniards brought with them which The People must have considered truly to be gifts from the Holy Ones. How and when they secured their first livestock is not known, but secure them they did, and the livestock brought about a drastic change in life-style for the Navajos within a matter of a few years. As the Spaniards began to put Pueblo Indians to work herding horses, sheep and cattle as early as 1600-1601, and since the Pueblos often fled to take refuge among the Navajos, it is likely they obtained their first stock from runaway Pueblo herdsmen soon afterwards. While the Pueblos were taught to tend the herds and to weave wool by the Spaniards, it was illegal for them to own stock. And since the pueblo villages were subject to frequent visits by the Spanish soldiers, it is not likely that they obtained stock of their own until after the 1680 rebellion.

But the Navajos neither knew nor cared to know the meaning of the word illegal. The acquisition of livestock led to rapid changes in the economy and the way of life of The People. By the end of the seventeenth century the Navajos were depending primarily upon their herds of cattle, sheep, goats and horses for a living. Where once they had been the victims of raids, as soon as they acquired horses they began raiding outlying pueblos as a means for the acquisition of livestock by those members of the tribe who had none, as well as a means for accelerating the growth of herds by persons who did not have enough. Navajo raids depleted the livestock holdings of the Spanish settlers to such an extent that, in 1775, it was necessary to import horses from Spain to make up the deficit.

Of course there is no record of how many Pueblos sought refuge among the Navajos in the first few years of the Spanish occupacy of New Mexico—nor how much livestock they took with them—but the number was probably considerable due to Oñate's heavy-handed policy of colonization.

While the Pueblos nominally accepted Christianity, they continued to practice their old ways, or "devil worship" as the Franciscan friars put it, in their secret kivas. And for such forbidden worship they were punished, often severely, by the missionaries. Adding to the Pueblos' problems was the fact that they were the pawns in a bitter conflict between the church and the crown. As part of his colonization program Oñate made grants of land to soldiers and colonists who participated in the conquest. These grants, or *encomiendas*, carried with them the right of *repartimiento*, the right to employ Indians living on the grants. The produce of the Indian labor was divided between the crown and the owner of the land. Lands not in use by the Pueblos, some quite near villages, were parceled off to Spaniards. The result was persistent conflict between Spaniards and Indians—and between Spaniard and Spaniard. The civil authorities, who drew their power from the crown, were servants of the landowners and, as such, they regarded the Indians as laborers of inferior status whose work, possessions, and even persons existed for the convenience of their proprietors.

On the other hand, the Franciscan friars looked upon the Indians as human creatures, if inferior, with mortal souls to be saved in the name of Christ. Not that they treated the Indians too much better than the landowners did. The missionaries forced the Indians to work for them on their churches, in their fields and with their herds, while the colonists forced the Pueblos to work without wages in *their* fields and homes. Not only did the Pueblos till the soil, tend the livestock and fetch water for the foreigners, but every month the Spanish soldiers visited each of the various pueblos to collect maize and other types of food, leaving very little for the Indians. Each Indian household was taxed a cotton blanket or a tanned deerskin every year, even if the blanket had to be forcibly removed from the back of the lady of the house. According to the testimony of one missionary, Fray Francisco de San Miquel, "the soldiers leave them nothing to eat, nothing that is alive" and the Pueblos were reduced to eating "tree branches, charcoal and ashes."

The missionaries accused the civil authorities of practicing slavery, forbidden by law when applied to converted Indians, and the authorities countercharged by calling attention to the missionaries' practice of whipping Indians who failed to follow the discipline of attending mass and for other offenses. The conflict raged back and forth and grew so bad that investigators were sent from Mexico City to examine the charges. They found corruption among both state and church officials. In the meantime the Pueblos were fleeing to the mountains to join the Navajos—and taking some of the Spaniards' livestock along with them. The conflict between church and crown accomplished two things. It made it possible for the Navajos to obtain horses and other livestock soon after the arrival of the Spanish in New Mexico and it gave impetus to the Spanish practice of slave-raiding expeditions among the Athapascans which caused a war that lasted, off and on, for nearly two hundred and fifty years.

The first recorded instance of Navajos raiding for livestock came in 1606. That year a Spanish colonist named Juan Martínez de Montoya was granted an *encomienda* of the Jemez Indians which, of course, entitled him to the fruits of their labors. The Navajos, living in close contact with the Jemez and probably aided by refugee Jemez, soon began making raids on Montoya's livestock. Montoya, it is recorded, organized several raids in an attempt to recover his stock and punish the culprits in 1606 and more the next year. The Navajos had obtained and learned the value of horses within one decade after the Spaniards brought them into New Mexico and they very quickly extended their hostilities. In the summer of 1608, almost ten years to the date that Oñate established his headquarters there, they attacked San Gabriel itself. That same year when Fray Lazaro Ximénez travelled to Mexico City to report to the viceroy on the poor situation in New Mexico he complained of the Indians who were "carrying off the horse herds."

A year later the Navajos had already set the stage for all future relations with the Spanish, a people they no doubt already recognized as a threat to their beloved *Dinehtah*. In Viceroy Velásco's instructions to Peralta, dated March 30, 1609, he pointed out that the "Apaches" (Navajos) gave refuge and "shelter to our enemies (Pueblo refugees) and there they hold meetings and consultations and hatch their plots against the whole land and set out to plunder and make war."

In 1622 the Christian converts of the Jemez pueblos of Patoqua and Gyusiwa were raided so frequently by the Navajos that the pueblos were abandoned and the Jemez Pueblos were scattered. Apparently the Jemez learned the error of their ways and a great many of them allied themselves with the Navajos. The very next year the Navajos began aiding the Jemez in a very bitter war against the Catholic Tewas and the Spaniards that lasted until 1626.

The first known historical reference to the Navajos by name was made by Father Zarate-Salmerón in his report on California and New Mexico in 1626. He mentioned that the Jemez Pueblos spoke of a people living north of them between the Chama and San Juan rivers as Apaches of "Navaju." In 1627 the Franciscans became sufficiently interested in the souls of the "Navaju" to construct a mission for them at the Tewa village of Santa Clara, on the west side of the Río Grande below San Juan. The mission was founded by Father Alonso de Benavides, the Custodian of Missions of New Mexico. The mission was all but ignored by the Navajos. In describing the adventure in his *Memorial to the King of Spain,* written in 1630, Benavides indicated that the name "Navajo" was learned from the Tewa and meant "great planted fields." After describing the Gila Apaches in his *Memorial* Benavides said that more than fifty leagues north of these "one encounters the Province of the Apaches of Navajo. Although they are the same Apache nation as the foregoing, they are subject and subordinate to another Chief Captain, and have a distinct mode of living. For those back yonder (the Gila Apaches) did not used to plant, but sustained themselves by the chase; and today we have broken land for them and taught them to plant. But these of Navajo are very great farmers, for that is what Navajo signifies—great planted fields."

Benavides added: "All those fifty leagues from Xila (Gila) up to this Navajo nation are settled with rancherieas, and the territory of the latter extends for another fifty leagues of frontier." Benavides' report, therefore, agrees with modern archaeological indications and the Navajo tradition of a precontact Navajo occupancy of virtually all of northwestern New Mexico and extending as far west as the Hopi villages. Benavides also stated that the Navajos, in spite of being a more sedentary people than the other Apaches, were "the most warlike of the entire Apache nation" and "proven to be the crucible of Spanish valor." We may safely assume that Benavides was exaggerating when he reported that the Navajos assembled two hundred thousand warriors on one occasion.

The Navajos not only tested "Spanish valor" for the purpose of increasing their herds, they also raided for retaliation. The Spaniards needed slaves for household servants and laborers and soon found that the slave markets of the various pueblos were not sufficient to meet their needs. Gradually they began to provoke fights between the Pueblos and the Navajos on the West and the Apaches to the East and North of the Río Grande pueblos for the purpose of taking captives of such fights as slaves. In 1627 or 1628 the

Spanish governor, Phelipe Sotelo Ossorio, sent a slave raid against the Eastern Plains, or Vaquero, Apaches who had not only always been at peace with the Pueblos and Spaniards but frequently visited the Río Grande villages for trading purposes. The raid provoked a rebellion throughout the province when the Vaqueros declared war on the Spaniards and their allies but apparently the Navajos did not take an active part in this war as the records indicate that they were more peaceful than hostile toward the Spaniards from 1629 until 1638.

In 1637 Luis de Rosas, a man of few scruples, was appointed governor of New Mexico. Rosas was obsessed by a desire for wealth and there was only one means of acquiring quick riches in New Mexico and that was through the slave trade. He had not been in office for a year before his slave raiding activities had increased Apache hostility, but apparently he did not undertake any campaigns against the Navajos and there are indications that he came to some sort of clandestine agreement with The People. Rosas was charged by the Franciscans with allowing Navajos to carry off horses that belonged to the missions, a most serious charge considering past relations between the two factions. Too, the governor provoked hostilities with the Utes, enemies of the Navajos, and a people who had reportedly always been friendly with the Spaniards and their Pueblo allies. Rosas led a slave expedition into Ute territory and killed a great number of them and captured eighty slaves which he sold into Mexico along with some Apaches.

The rupture between Rosas and the missionaries caused the latter to abandon all of the pueblos and missions and unite at Santa Domingo in 1640 where they were joined by settlers who chose to side with the church. The friars and settlers not only fortified Santa Domingo but they raided the *encomiendas* of those settlers loyal to the governor and actually stole horses and livestock belonging to Rosas himself. After Rosas was murdered in the summer of 1641, the friars and their supporters undertook several campaigns against the Navajos who seemed to be the primary object of their wrath. In a concentrated effort throughout the latter part of 1641 and the first half of 1642, they burned Navajo fields, killed many, and took prisoners to such an extent that the Navajos were forced to sue for peace. But the peace did not last. The Navajos continued to raid the Spaniards and their allies the rest of the decade and in 1650 entered in an agreement with Christian Indians—who turned over to them droves of horses and mares belonging to the Spaniards—to attack the foreigners simultaneously throughout the district and drive them from New Mexico. The plot was discovered and the Pueblo leaders, from the pueblos of Isleta, Alameda, San Felip, Cochita and Jemez, were executed and many of their followers were sold into slavery. A short time later a second plot, between the Navajos and the Jemez, was aborted when Governor Hernándo de Ugarte y la Concha sent a campaign against the Navajos.

Apparently Bernardo López de Mendizábal, who arrived in New Mexico in 1659, was of the same ilk as Luis de Rosas. Shortly after he arrived he sent an army of eight hundred and forty men to raid the Navajos. This raid, according to the Franciscan friars, was nothing but an excuse to take slaves which López sold to the Parral mines in New Spain. López was accused by Fray Juan Ramírez of sending "squadrons of men to capture the heathen Indians to send them to the *real* and mines of El Parral to sell" at a time when the province was in danger of attack. The *Audiencia* of Guadalajara later convicted López of treacherously attacking peaceful Navajos who had visited Jemez to trade, of murdering the men and enslaving the women and children. Because of López's slave raids, the Navajos again began raiding the frontier in earnest.

If anything, López's successor, Diego de Peñalosa, who was governor from 1661 to 1664, was even worse. Under his reign slaves became so numerous that an Apache woman could be purchased for twenty-six pesos. Peñalosa once bragged that he had so many slaves that he gave away more than a hundred of them. Toward the end of the decade, under a new governor, the slave raiding was eased and the Navajos occupied themselves with tending to their flocks of sheep, which were of considerable size by this time. But intensified war broke out again in 1669 when, according to Fray Juan Bernal, "the whole land is at war with the widespread heathen nation of the Apache Indians." By 1671 the Navajos had grown so bold that they were raiding during daylight hours. According to one report all but a few flocks of sheep were carried off and between 1672 and 1678 six pueblos were reported to have been deserted.

In 1675 the situation had deteriorated into an all-out war between the Navajos, some bands of Apaches, and the Spaniards, which prompted the long-suffering Pueblo Indians to begin to show their real feelings toward their Spanish conquerors. That year four Puebloans were hanged, about four dozen were whipped and enslaved and many more were imprisoned, including Popé, future leader of the revolt of 1680, for leading a movement to return to the old religion of the Pueblos. The specific charge was that the Pueblos "bewitched" the Spaniards and caused five to seven priests to die by witchcraft. Actually the priests were probably poisoned.

Long entertaining plans of a revolt against their conquerors, plans that were encouraged by the Navajos, the Pueblos took their first overt step toward that end. A group of Tewas descended upon the governor's palace in Santa Fe and demanded that Governor Juan Francisco Treviño release the prisoners who had been arrested for practicing "idolatry." Faced with about seventy angry Pueblos in his rooms, the governor released the prisoners. Actually Treviño had little choice. The Navajos were destroying towns and churches and killing Christians on all fronts. The Spaniards' defensive force consisted of only about five able men at each frontier station and these not only lacked sufficient arms to defend themselves but had lost most of their horses to the Navajos and Apaches.

Marshaling their forces, the Spaniards raided the Navajos in the summer of 1677, killing fifteen and capturing thirty-five of The People as well as releasing six converted Indians and a captive Spanish girl. Again, in July and October of 1678, *entradas* were made into *Dinehtah,* much damage was inflicted on the fields and food supplies of The People, and many women and children prisoners—fifty in July alone— were taken. But the Spanish effort was too little and too late. The Navajos, Apaches and Pueblos were finally ready to combine forces and drive the enemy from New Mexico.

Actually the 1680 revolt had been fermenting for decades. In their kivas where they had continued to secretly practice their forbidden ceremonies and had passed on the ancient tribal lore from generation to generation, the Pueblos had long dreamed of a war that would rid them of the tyrant *Castillos,* as they called the Spaniards. Over the past thirty years dozens of Pueblos had been hanged for "sorcery and communion with the devil" as well as for plotting rebellion with the Navajos. The seeds of rebellion had always been there but lacked a leader to give them impetus. As the 1670s drew to a close the Pueblos not only found a leader in the San Juan Indian named Popé, but found even more reason than ever for revolution. As Navajo depletions increased, so did Pueblo hardships, for it was they who were taxed to continue the war with the Athapascans. By 1680 even the most docile of the Pueblos—with the possible exception of the Christian Pecos—could see that they were caught in a vise between the warring factions, and that the Spaniards were the weaker of their tormentors. Popé, taking advantage of the situation from Taos, which he made the center of his revolutionary efforts, appealed to the Pueblos' sense of tradition and reverence for the old ceremonies. Supporting him were strong leaders at Santo Domingo, Picuris, Jemez and Taos.

The revolt was well-planned. All the tribes except the Piros in the South were brought into the conspiracy along with at least two Athapascan groups. Oddly the Navajos did not participate in the revolt to the extent that one would expect considering their past relations with the Spaniards. Possibly they already looked upon the Spaniards—as they definitely would later—as their herdsmen, the men who raised the sheep for them to steal. Later they would brag of always leaving behind breeding stock so that the Spanish or Mexican rancher might replenish his flock for their taking at another date.

A knotted cord was passed to each of the pueblos, each knot representing a day before the revolt was to take place on August 13, 1680. Despite the precautions taken by the Pueblos—no women were told of the plot and Popé killed his own son-in-law, suspecting him of treachery—the Spaniards learned of the trouble on August 9, when some Tano Indians turned over two of Popé's Tewa messengers to them. Governor Antonio de Otermín immediately sent couriers warning the Spanish settlers and priests south of San Felipe to flee to Isleta and those to the North were instructed to start immediately for Santa Fe or Santa Cruz de la Cañada. Upon learning that the Spaniards knew of his plans, Popé called for immediate action and before dawn on the morning of August 10, Indians from Taos and Picuris, aided by

Jicarilla Apaches, attacked the missions and farms of the northern pueblos and killed all the Spaniards except one soldier who managed to escape. By August 13, the rebellion had spread throughout the province and no Spaniards were spared who fell into the hands of the Indians except for a few women who were kept as captives. The Jemez shot their missionary, Fray Juan de Jesus María, full of arrows at the altar of the San Diego mission. Each of the twenty-one friars who fell into Indian hands was served in a like manner. In all, the Indians killed slightly over four hundred of the twenty-four hundred Spaniards in New Mexico in the first four days of fighting.

Meanwhile Governor Otermín made preparations to defend Santa Fe. On August 14 a force of Tanos, Pecos and Keres warriors appeared on the outskirts of the capital and were soon joined by Tewas, Taos, Picuris, Jemez and Apaches—about five hundred in all. As none of the contemporary Spanish sources mention Navajos, most earlier writers assumed that none of The People took part in the revolt. Since each band of Navajos acted independently—there was no central tribal authority nor was there until after the Navajos were conquered by the Americans—it is unthinkable that at least some Navajos did not take part in the conflict.

On August 15, Otermín induced a Tano chief, who had previously been friendly with the Spaniards, to enter the capital for a conference. The chief informed Otermín that the Indians had brought two crosses with them to Santa Fe; one red and one white. The red cross indicated war and the white cross was a token of peace, and it was up to the Spaniards to choose the cross of war or the cross of peace. The Tano chief stated that if the Spaniards chose the cross of peace they would have to agree to quit New Mexico and added, for the benefit of the priests present, that the Indians had killed God and Santa María. And, indeed, symbolically, they had. After killing their priests, the people of the pueblos burned the churches, buried the bells and crucifixes, shed their priest-given cognomens and began calling themselves by their old names. They even took soapweed baths to wash off the stains of Christian baptism.

According to a letter that Otermín wrote three weeks later, the Tano chief also demanded, in the event the Spaniards chose the white cross and peace, that all the natives who were in Spanish power be turned over to them, "both those in the service of the Spaniards and those of the Mexican nation of that suburb of Analco. He also demanded that his wife and children be given up to him, and likewise that all the Apache men and women whom the Spaniards had captured in war be turned over to them, inasmuch as some Apaches who were among them were asking for them." As virtually all the recent Spanish *entradas* of recent years had been directed toward the Navajos, it is safe to assume that some, if not most, of the Apache captives referred to were actually Navajos.

But the Spaniards did not give up their captives; Otermín chose the red cross. A week later, on August 20, the Christians succeeded in driving the Indians from Analco after cutting off the water supply to the Indian suburb. The Spaniards killed three hundred Indians and executed another forty-seven captives. Among the dead were Athapascans as well as natives from virtually every pueblo in northern New Mexico, which indicated to Otermín, contrary to his earlier supposition that the revolt wasn't widespread, that all the natives of the province had revolted. The next day the governor prudently decided to abandon Santa Fé and "march to the relief of Isleta." That same day the Spaniards—about one thousand persons in all—began their exodus from Santa Fé, each carrying his own baggage, with the sick and the wounded riding the horses and mules. The Pueblos let them go, content that, at last, they were rid of the Castillos. Otermín's party reached Isleta on August 27, only to learn that the refugees who had gathered there had left thirteen days earlier for the south, thinking that all in the north had been killed and fearing for their own lives. By the end of the month the entire Spanish force was encamped at El Paso del Norte, modern El Paso, Texas. Many of the refugees abandoned the company and travelled on to the Chihuahua settlements, but a few months later the viceroy sent supplies and reinforcements to El Paso along with orders that preparations be made to reconquer the lost province.

THREE

The Conquest of the Pueblos

Otermín blamed the Apaches—actually the Navajos as well as the Apache tribes of northern New Mexico—for the loss of the northern province because of their ceaseless warfare on the Spaniards and constant attempts to get the Pueblos to rebel and, furthermore, felt that unless New Mexico was immediately reconquered, Sonora would fall.

But several factors contributed to the failure of a quick try at retaking New Mexico, not the least of which was the fact that the fires of rebellion did spread to the Athapascan tribes of northern Sonora—the Mansos, Sumas and Janos. In fact, the Sumas, protesting the sudden appearance of the refugees from New Mexico—who took up residence on their lands—revolted on August 29. As the remainder of the northern refugees poured into the El Paso area, where the Franciscans had established the mission of Guadalupe some twenty years before, the Mansos, Sumas and Janos were pushed out and spread the word of the revolution to other captive tribes of northern Mexico. In spite of the fact that it was apparent to Otermín that New Mexico must be reconquered if the Spaniards were to hold northern Mexico, he soon discovered that he had his hands full just holding El

Paso. Another factor that contributed to the Spaniards' failure to try to regain New Mexico immediately was a series of squabbles between Otermín and other officials of Sonora and Nueva Vizcaya.

Meanwhile the Navajos, Apaches and Pueblos of New Mexico were once again masters of their own fate. But in the eighty years the Spaniards had occupied New Mexico the balance of power had drastically changed. Where once the Navajos had been poor farmers and hunters living on the fringe of the more advanced Pueblo culture, they were now the masters of the land, rich in sheep and horses. And the Spaniards actually expected the Navajos to help them, at least indirectly, in reconquering New Mexico. As The People had raided the pueblos almost consistently during the period of Spanish occupation, the Spaniards hoped and even expected they would continue to do so and that eventually the Pueblos would welcome the Christians back with open arms to protect them from the Navajos. On December 23, 1681, Fray Francisco de Ayeta, *custodio* of the New Mexican missions, wrote that it was the opinion of all the Spaniards of El Paso that the Pueblo Indians would be anxious for the return of the Europeans and the protection they offered from the raids of the "Apaches." Such was not the case.

In November, 1681, Otermín led an army of one hundred and forty-six Spaniards and one hundred and twelve Indian allies into New Mexico, expecting to find the pueblos destroyed by the Navajos and the Pueblos in slavery. Instead he found that while the Athapascans and the Pueblos had not exactly embraced each other in total peace, they had not fought a war to the death either. Ayeta wrote: "The Apaches have not destroyed any pueblo or even damaged one seriously. It happened that, although during the discussions of peace to which the apostates invited them (after the expulsion of the Spanish), they spent some months in dances, fiestas, and entertainments, in the end the Apaches were unwilling to accept it and left, still at war, as in fact they are at present (December 23, 1681); and it is seen that this notwithstanding they (the Pueblos) have maintained themselves without the Spaniards."

Ayeta notwithstanding, later writers would have us believe that the "Apaches"—or Navajos—all but destroyed the Pueblos. The respected American historian, Hubert Howe

Bancroft, writing of the period of Spanish expulsion, stated that "Barbarism darker than that of aboriginal times settled down upon this northern land." (Bancroft, 1189: 185.) And Juan A. Niel would have us believe that the rebels suffered the wrath of God . . . "For seven years it rained ashes, while for nine years no water fell, and the streams all dried up. . . . Finally, by the sacrifice of a virgin, water was restored to the bed of the Río Grande, and thus life was saved, and their stubborn, insolent apostasy was confirmed."

Disappointment followed disappointment for Otermín during his 1681 experimental *entrada*. Hoping to find that the Pueblos had seen the "error of their ways" and were ready to welcome the Spaniards—and Christianity—back with open arms, he found them, instead, belligerent and housing cattle in the ruins of the churches, causing Fray Ayeta to comment: "They have been found to be so pleased with liberty of conscience and so attached to the belief in the worship of Satan that up to the present not a sign has been visible of their ever having been Christians." Near Cochiti, Otermín's lieutenant Juan Domínguez de Mendoza was confronted with an army consisting of members of all the Pueblo tribes except the Hopis, under the leadership of a mestizo named Alonso Catiti. This is the same Alonso Catiti that the Spanish historian Silvestre Velez Escalante, writing in 1776, tells us was destroyed, presumably as punishment for having opposed the Spaniards and rejecting Christianity by "bursting suddenly, all of his intestines coming out in the sight of many Indians," as he entered a kiva to "worship Satan."

At any rate Catiti pretended, at first, to welcome the Spaniards and asked them for gunpowder to use in fighting the Navajos. But Domínquez had already learned that Catiti's Pueblos were on the most friendly of terms with the Athapascans and refused the request. Catiti and Domínquez talked peace for the better part of two days until the Spaniard finally realized that the Indian leader was only stalling for enough time for the Navajos and the Hopis to join his force for a combined attack on the Spaniards. When Domínquez finally pressed Catiti to show penitence for the errors of the past, the rebel leader let it be known that he was not about to be swayed by Spanish promises and reminded the invaders of how they had once killed a group of Navajos at

Jemez while negotiating with them under the guise of discussing peace terms. This exchange is significant in that it indicates the Navajos were very friendly with most of the Pueblos, including the Hopis, sixteen months after the Spanish expulsion in spite of what Bancroft, Niel, Escalente and others would have us believe.

Dominquez returned south to join Otermín who awaited him at Sandía. Harassed by a force of mounted rebels, the Spaniards retreated down the Río Grande after destroying eight abandoned pueblos and sacking three others. Otermín reached El Paso the second week in February, 1682, his *entrada* having accomplished virtually nothing. But it did serve to remind the Indians of New Mexico of the persistent threat of Spanish slavery. In his report to the viceroy, Otermín stated that it was not possible to retake New Mexico. Not only were the Pueblos unwilling to submit again to Spanish rule, but the Apaches had begun to raid the El Paso region frequently. Therefore the Spaniards had no choice but to strengthen their position at El Paso.

In autumn, 1683, Otermín was replaced as governor by Domingo Jironza Petriz de Cruzate, who made several raids on the Pueblos during his three-year term of office but always found the Indians well-fortified and was unable to do much damage to them. He was replaced by Pedro Reneros de Posada in 1686. Pedro Reneros led a raid against the pueblo of Santa Ana that accomplished very little and subsequently attacked Zia but was repulsed. Complaints of his inefficiency resulted in the reappointment of Domingo Jironza.

Jironza led the army consisting of eighty soldiers and an indeterminate number of armed settlers against Zia in August, 1689, soon after his reappointment. The Spaniards reported that more than six hundred Keres were slaughtered at Zia and many others were burned alive when Jironza had the pueblo set to the torch for resisting.

Ninety captives who escaped the flames were carried back to El Paso and sold into slavery, excluding approximately twenty elderly persons who were immediately shot. Fearing subsequent raids, the Keres of Santo Domingo, San Felipe, Cochiti and other pueblos abandoned their villages and retreated to more easily defended settlements in the mountains.

In the fall of 1692 the Spaniards came back to New

Mexico under the leadership of a new governor, Diego de Vargas Zapata y Luján—and this time they came with the intent of reconquering the province. Vargas not only possessed the daring, ability and ambition of Cortés, he was as cruel as Vincente de Zaldívar had been. When he conquered a pueblo it stayed conquered. All captives, whether they surrendered or were taken in battle, were immediately baptised and executed.

Appointed governor in early 1691, Vargas immediately began gathering as much information as he could about the people of New Mexico and planning the reconquest. By summer of the next year his preparations were complete and he left El Paso with most of the presidio soldiers, backed by the viceroy and the crown. Marching up the Río Grande, Vargas found Santo Domingo and Cochiti abandoned and arrived at Santa Fé on the morning of September 13. The capital had been fortified by the Tewas and Tanos but Vargas immediately had his soldiers surround the town, cutting off the water supply and all communications with the outside.

Vargas' arrival at Santa Fé was timely. Not only was Luis Tupatu, the leader of the Santa Fé Tanos and Tewas as well as of his own people, the nearby Picuris, away visiting some Navajo allies, but the Pueblos had divided themselves into at least three factions. The surrounding Athapascans were also disunited and were allied with, or members of, the various Pueblo factions. While the records are somewhat obscure, it seems that the faction which included the pueblos of Taos and Pecos, the Keres of Cochiti, San Marcos, San Felipe, Santo Domingo Zia and Acoma, the Jemez, Hopis, most of the Navajos, the Gila Apaches, the Utes living near the Hopis and various other, smaller Apache bands, including those to the East of Santa Fé, were at war with the Tupatu faction. A third faction included the Zuñis and the Salinero Apaches who were at war with the Navajos. The Zuñis, in fact, had been forced to abandon their outlying pueblos and concentrate at the penol of Caquima. Whether Tupatu's "Navajo allies" were allies in war or only for trading purposes is not known. Notably the Jemez and at least most of the Navajos were allies and the Jemez considered the Tupatu group their principal foe.

Luis Tupatu, who returned to Santa Fé with his brother

Lorenzo soon after the arrival of Vargas, tendered his allegiance to the Spaniards and asked them to aid him against his enemies. Vargas prudently decided to take advantage of the situation and accepted Tupatu's offer of friendship. On September 21, fifty soldiers from Parral, sent by the viceroy, arrived to reinforce Vargas' force. Eight days later the Spaniards left to surprise Pecos but found that pueblo abandoned, the people there having been alerted by Apache scouts. A few captives were taken and the pueblo was sacked of maize.

Returning to Santa Fé, Vargas left for Taos on October 7. Again the Indians had been warned and had abandoned the pueblo and fled to the mountains. A week later Vargas arrived back in Santa Fé and wrote a report to the viceroy that he "conquered for the human and divine majesties" all the pueblos for thirty-six leagues and had baptised nearly one thousand children "born in rebellion." He also asked for another hundred soldiers and fifty families and recommended sending convicts from Mexican jails as teachers and to search for metals. Meanwhile, to the West, somewhere near Acoma, there was a great junta of chiefs and headsmen of the Hopis, Keres, Pecos, Apaches, Coninas and, interestingly, Navajos and Zuñis who apparently decided to forget their differences for the time being.

For the remainder of the month Vargas continued to visit the various Río Grande pueblos and hold talks, making it explicitly clear to the Indians that they had to conform to the Spaniards' dictums in regard to religion and culture. Only the Jemez remained hostile, entertaining, at the time of Vargas' visit, a number of Navajos in their village. Leaving Jemez, on October 30, with an army of eighty-nine men, Vargas visited Acoma and Zuñi, taking a roundabout route via Isleta to avoid the land of the Navajos. At Acoma the Spaniards were confronted with belligerent hostility. The Indians that Vargas talked to informed him that the Acomas and the Navajos were allies and, furthermore, they had been warned by the Apaches not to believe the Spaniards when they came to speak of peace because under the sign of peace the foreigners would cut off the hands of the Indians, hang the men and carry the women off to El Paso as they had done with those taken captive in the past. Fearing that the Acomas were talking with him only in order to give their Navajo allies time to arrive, Vargas hurried away from Acoma and on to Zuñi.

There he was received cordially, but on the night of November 10, some Navajos succeeded in stealing sixteen of the Spaniards' horses. Next Vargas visited the Hopi villages, was met by almost one thousand Hopi warriors who had been warned by the Navajos that the Spaniards were coming and, while they managed to placate the warriors, they actually accomplished very little else—except to learn that a large *junta* of Navajos was camped in the vicinity. Returning to Zuñi, Vargas found that tribe had been penalized nine horses, taken by the Navajos for having entertained the Spaniards. From Zuñi Vargas travelled directly to El Paso, arriving there on December 20, after having fought a battle with some Apaches in which he lost two men.

Diego de Vargas' 1692 *entrada* into New Mexico accomplished one thing: it caused the Indians of New Mexico to attempt to put their house in order. To an extent they succeeded. In the face of an invasion they knew was surely coming, even the Zuñis and the Navajos made a truce to resist the Spaniards as did most of the splintered Pueblos.

In October of the next year Vargas came back with soldiers and settlers—over eight hundred persons in all—and set up camp near present-day Bernalillo and took Santa Fé in a battle on December 16. Most of the Tano and Tewa warriors living there escaped, but the women and children were divided among the Spaniards. All males who were captured in battle or surrendered were immediately baptized and executed. Four hundred women and children were distributed as "hostages" among the settlers. The Tewas, living in nearby villages, immediately abandoned their pueblos. A few took refuge with the Navajos while other went to Taos, but the majority congregated at the penol of San Ildefonso.

On February 26, 1694, Vargas led an army of one hundred soldiers against San Ildefonso but, after a siege lasting until March 20, had to return to Santa Fé leaving the penol in Indian control. The Tewas and Tanos were supported by Keres, Acomas, Zuñis, Hopis, Navajos and probably some Gila Apaches. While the Spaniards busied themselves raiding deserted villages for supplies, the Indians, especially those living at San Ildefonso, and the Jemez and the Navajos, concentrated their efforts on raiding Spanish livestock.

On April 17 the Spaniards attacked the new Keres pueblo of Cieneguilla. Apparently the attack caught the Keres and their allies unawares for, in spite of strong resistance, the pueblo was taken and sacked. Three hundred and forty-two women and children were taken prisoner along with fourteen men. The Spaniards also captured nine hundred sheep and seventy horses, which they sorely needed. Again the women and children were divided among the settlers, and the men were promptly shot.

In July the Spaniards marched against Jemez in company with a force of Keres who had allied themselves with the invaders. Jemez, a stronghold of the anti-Spanish Indians, was completely sacked and burned in spite of a gallant defense by its natives and their Navajo allies. Three hundred and sixty-one women and children were captured. The Jemez who escaped scattered. Thirteen families sought refuge at Taos, others joined the Keres of Cochita and still others fled to the mountains to live with the Navajos. A month later a group of Jemez men came into Santa Fé to make peace and ask for the return of their families. Vargas agreed providing the Jemez would aid him in taking San Ildefonso, to which they reluctantly gave their consent. The Tewas and Tanos of San Ildefonso resisted but in the end had to agree to peace. On September 11, the Jemez were allowed to return to their pueblo with their women and children.

By the end of the month the Keres of Cochiti and Santo Domingo agreed to submit to the Spaniards, and priests were being placed at San Felipe, Pecos, Zia and Jemez. By the end of the year only six Río Grande pueblo villages, the Acomas, Zuñis, Hopis, and all of the Apaches and Navajos still held out against the invaders, but it was an uneasy conquest. The Pueblos had accepted peace only to gain time and in the hope of catching the Spaniards off guard later. The Navajos remained free and continued to aid the Pueblos and urge them to resume hostilities throughout 1695. The stronghold of Navajo-Pueblo resistance was shifted from Jemez to Acoma.

The uneasy truce came to an end the first week of June, 1696, when the Taos, Picuris, Tewas, Jemez and the Keres of Santo Domingo and Cochiti revolted and killed five missionaries and twenty-one other Spaniards and, in most cases, abandoned their pueblos and fled to the mountains. If the Navajos were not the primary instigators of the revolt, the role they played was a major one. Navajo warriors joined the Tewas at San Idelfonso and others joined with a force of Hopis, Zuñis, Acomas and Apaches at Jemez with the intent of aiding the people of that pueblo in attacking and taking Santa Fé. The plan to capture the capital was aborted on July 23 when the Spaniards made a surprise attack on the rebels, killing ten and scattering the remainder of the rebel force. But The People continued to take in refugees from the various pueblos. On July 30, Vargas reported to the viceroy that the rebels had killed the twenty-six persons mentioned above, burned the newly built churches and "were going to live with the Navajos." A Spanish woman taken prisoner during this revolt possibly gave birth to the Mexican clan of the Navajos. Among the refugees the Navajos took in during the summer, 1696, revolt were Tanos, Tewas, Keres and Jemez, many of whom were absorbed into the tribe through intermarriage. This infusion of Pueblos had a great impact on the lifestyle, religion and crafts of the Navajos and was certainly a contributing factor to the beginnings of the war The People waged on the Spaniards on and off for the next one hundred and fifty years.

Several campaigns against the Pueblos were made by the Spaniards in August, September and October of 1696, but they accomplished little as most of the villages were almost completely deserted, the natives having fled to the Navajos or to the western pueblos. Five men were captured at Acoma and executed on August 15, and eighty-four women and children taken at San Juan on October 26 were distributed among the settlers. By the end of the decade all of the Río Grande pueblos had again submitted to Spanish rule, including the new pueblo of Laguna, north of Acoma, which had been founded by refugees from Cieneguilla, Santo Domingo and Cochiti.

Intermittently during the last years of the seventeenth century and throughout the remainder of the time that Spain was to hold the Southwest, the Zuñis allied themselves with the Europeans, leaving only the Navajos, the Hopis and various Apache bands as a threat to Spain's stranglehold on New Mexico. Only the Navajos were strong enough to seriously challenge the Spaniards—and challenge them they did. Too, toward the turn of the century the Spaniards began to fear a French invasion from the North and East that never materialized, although the presence of the French along the Mississippi and in the Missouri country did play a role in the balance of power in New Mexico at times. Niel, Bancroft and others tell us that the Navajos were also at war with the French. According to Bancroft, "In 1698 the French almost annihilated a Navajo force of four thousand men . . . " (Bancroft, Bancroft, 1889: 222.) While the Navajos did occasionally cross arms with the French, who were supplying their enemies, the Ute-Commance alliance, with arms, it is highly unlikely that they ever lost anywhere near four thousand warriors in such a confrontation or, for that matter, that they were ever able to raise an army even approaching that number. In 1697-98 the Navajos were at war with the Pawnees, also allies of the French, but George E. Hyde and Gotteried Hotz have both stated that the large force of "Navajos" destroyed by the French were probably Plains Apaches (Hotz, Oklahoma, 1970: 174.) As the Navajos were allies with most of the Apache bands at that time there it is probable that the force was a combination of Navajos and Apaches.

FOUR

Lords of the Earth

Navajo history of the period between the defeat of the Pueblos and the conquest of New Mexico by the United States in 1846 consists of little more than a long list of raids and counter-raids, of expeditions and punitive expeditions. With the exception of one notable period of uneasy peace between 1720 and the last quarter of the eighteenth century, The People were virtually constantly at war with the Spaniards of the Río Grande and occasionally joined their Apache allies to raid Spanish ranches deep in Mexico. Too, there was the matter of the Ute-Comanche alliance, an ever-present and irritable threat from the North and East. By 1725 the French were supplying the Comanches with better guns than any Spanish soldier in New Mexico was permitted to carry. Thus equipped and with the encouragement of their kinsmen, the Utes, the Comanches were soon raiding Navajo rancherias to obtain slaves to sell to the Spaniards at their annual "Comanche Fairs"—Indian trade days in the Río Grande pueblos. Navajo-Hopi relations were fairly stable during this period, a situation most advantageous to the Hopis who desired only peace and freedom to go their own way, which was possible only as long as the Navajos living between the Hopi villages and the Spaniards of the Río Grande acted as a buffer.

So bold and strong did the Navajos become after the defeat of the Pueblos that Spanish contempt for the *indios barbarós* was soon tempered by awe and they came to be known as *Los Dueños del Mundo*— Lords of the Earth. Navajo sheep flocks already numbered in the tens of thousands at the beginning of this period and increased yearly as The People looked upon the flocks of the Spaniards and Pueblos as theirs for the taking. On the other hand the Spaniards looked upon Navajo women and children as *theirs* for the taking and took as many of them as they possibly could. Ostentatiously, Navajo captives were taken out of a sense of Christian duty, to be chained, literally in some cases, to a church pew, taught the rudiments of Catholicism, baptized and given "benefits of a Christian home." On the sandstone face of a canyon wall in Canyon del Muerto is a Navajo petroglyph of a Spanish slave-raiding expedition accompanied by a priest. In reality the "conversion" of Navajo captives was a formality required by the church, preceding their "adoption" into a family. It was, in effect, a socially accepted manner in which to acquire slaves, which had little, if anything, to do with a desire to convert the Indians. An anonymous observer in 1852 described the conditions of recent Navajo captives thusly: "I have frequently seen little children eighteen months to six years of age led around the country like beasts by a Mexican who had probably stolen them from their mother not more than a week (before) and offered for sale from forty to one hundred and twenty dollars." As time passed, in fact, a most unique "bachelor's party" evolved in Spanish New Mexico. Preceding the wedding, the groom and all of his friends would make an expedition into Navajo land to capture as many women and children as possible to be presented to the bride as household servants—after the required baptism, of course.

The first recorded baptism of Navajo captives was that of four young children in 1705 soon after the defeat and surrender of a Navajo force to Roque de Madrid at Belduque Creek. There are numerous recorded baptisms of "Apaches who came from Nabaxo" prior to 1720, a period marked by almost constant warfare between the Navajos and the Spaniards which was actually a continuation of the Pueblo Revolt. Too, some of the twenty-four "Apache" captives baptized prior to 1720 were probably Navajos. Just prior to 1720 a long period of peace began between the Navajos and the Spaniards of the Río Grande that was only occasionally interrupted by insignificant raids on one part or the other. In fact, relations had grown so cordial by 1744 that the Navajos allowed two priests to visit *Dinehtah* and, a few years later, the establishment of two missions at Encinal and Cebolleta near the base of Mount Taylor by Fray Juan Michael Menchero.

The Franciscans never gave up the hope of inducing the Navajos to settle down like the Pueblos and about four or five hundred of the The People moved to the vicinity of the missions. But an overwhelming majority of Navajos still looked upon the Christians and their strange beliefs with disdain and to this day The People still refer to the descendants of the mission Navajos living in the Cebolleta area as *Dinehanaih*—"the People who are Enemies." The Spaniards had to abandon the Mount Taylor missions in 1750 when it became only too apparent that the Navajos had not been attracted to them to embrace Christianity but because Fray Menchero had been most liberal with gifts and the promise of more. Christianity and the sedentary life of the Pueblos held no charm for the Navajos and if the priests had no more goods to give, then why bother? But the Navajos of the Mount Taylor area, the *Dinehanaih*, did remain friendly with the Spaniards even at times when the rest of the nation was at war with them.

The People living on the northern fringe of *Dinehtah* were constantly harassed by Utes and Comanches, who took slaves, as stated before, for the purpose of selling them to the Spaniards. Finally, in 1774, it became apparent that the supposedly neutral Spaniards were behind the Comanche-Ute raids. Too, the Spanish governor had recently granted land in the area of the Rio Puerto to European settlers. That year the Navajos drove the settlers from their lands, killing at least eleven persons. The Spaniards with Acoma and Laguna allies retaliated and nearly sixty Navajo children "in the absolute power of" one or another Spanish official were baptized during 1774-75. In September, 1775, two Navajo headmen made peace with the Spaniards at Santa Fé and exchanged captives as a sign of their good faith. But in reality the Spanish-Navajo truce was all but over, and the fact that Navajo children referred to as "servants" or "purchased" continued to be baptized at Acoma, Laguna and elsewhere indicates that the Spanish slave raiding continued.

In 1786 Viceroy Bernardo de Gálvez instructed General Jacob Ugarte y Loyola to introduce a new Indian policy in the northern provinces—a policy of divide and conquer that was to end any semblance of peace between the Navajos and the Spaniards for all time. The policy called for unrelenting warfare on all tribes to secure treaties, free trade and gifts to tribes at peace, the creation among the Indians of needs that could only be supplied by the Spaniards, the distribution of guns and powder of inferior quality to those tribes allied with Spain, and the liberal distribution of spirits to demoralize those tribes that were not. And, finally, Ugarte was instructed to promote wars of extermination between the tribes that would not sign treaties with Spain. The groundwork for an alliance with the Comanches had already been laid by officials in New Mexico before Ugarte assumed his general command. Under Ugarte's direction it was finalized on April 21, 1787, never to be broken. Both parties recognized the benefits of such a treaty. On one hand the Comanches would have access to the lucrative markets of the Río Grande Pueblos and on the other Spain gained a powerful ally on her northern frontier. But the Spanish-Comanche alliance left the Navajos caught in a vise.

For some years prior to the signing of the Spanish-Comanche alliance, the Spaniards had been trying to break up one between the Navajos and the Gila Apaches, living to the south of *Dinehtah* in what is now southeastern Arizona. On at least one occasion the Navajos had supplied a large mounted force for a combined attack on the Nueva Vizcaya presidio and settlement at Janos. In the early part of 1785 the New Mexican governor, Juan Bautista de Anza, had induced one group of Navajos to sue for peace by a formidable display of the forces under his command—the presidial troops of Santa Fé, a militia of armed settlers, and a host of Pueblo auxiliaries—and a warning that the Utes would be urged into action against them if they failed to comply. In June of that year, in fact, one hundred and fifty Navajos actually joined the Spanish forces in a campaign against the Gilas and a few others participated in two other attacks on the Apaches. But the final rupture of the Navajo-Gila alliance did not come until after the Spaniards signed their alliance with the Comanches and came as a result of the latter.

The Navajos of 1786 were living very much in the manner of the pastoral Navajos of today: in fixed settlements of extended family groups. They sowed corn and other vegetables, raised livestock, and manufactured coarse cloth, fine blankets, and other woolen goods which they had, in times of peace, traded to the Pueblo Indians and the Spanish settlements. Their dilemma was that, while dependent upon livestock and agriculture for a livelihood which required that they remain in their scattered villages, they were now surrounded on three sides by mutually antagonistic peoples—the hostile Utes and Comanches on the North and East, and the Spaniards and Pueblos on the East and South, and the Comanches were threatening to exterminate the Navajos if they did not join the alliance with the Spaniards against the Apaches. Too, the Navajos were split on the issue. Those living near the Spaniards, and particularly the *Dinehanaih*, relented and finally made an alliance with the Spaniards, while those in the western part of *Dinehtah* desired to remain allies with the Apaches. While nominally allied with the Spaniards, the eastern Navajos were clever enough to all but remain neutral in the war between the Apaches and the Spaniards-Comanches. A few Navajos did take part in campaigns against the Mimbres, Chiricahaus and other Apache bands, but indications are they were members of the *Dinehanaih*. Spanish efforts to foster friendly relations between the Navajos and the Comanches resulted only in a temporary truce, however. In late 1792 a force of Navajos, smarting to avenge earlier humiliations, organized a raiding party that surprised a Comanche village and captured a large number of women and children—and actually talked some Utes in joining them. The Comanches retaliated by destroying a large Ute camp, which caused a breach in that alliance that lasted for several years.

The Navajos continued at peace with the Spaniards until 1796 when they joined the Gilas in a series of raids on settlements both in Mexico and New Mexico. An uneasy truce was established that ended in 1800 when Spaniards moved onto Navajo land at the base of Mount Taylor, the sacred Turquoise Mountain of the People. The respected Navajo headsman of the Tachii'nii Clan, Narbona, then about thirty-six years of age, and other Navajo leaders called on the Spanish governor, Fernando Chacon, in an effort to regain the land peacefully only to learn that the Spaniards intended to use it to establish a military site at Cebolleta. When it became only too apparent that their requests that the Spaniards remove themselves from the Mount Taylor area were not going to be heeded, the Navajos declared war in April, 1804. The delay in declaring war on Spain was probably caused by the fact that the Navajos, allied still with the Utes, were at war with the Havasupai during the first few years of the 1800s. At any rate the declaration of war on Spain brought an end to the Navajo-Ute alliance for the time being. Never again were The People to know any extended period of peace until after their defeat by the Americans in 1864.

The Utes and the Jicarilla Apaches allied themselves with the Spaniards. The Navajos, under Narbona and other headmen, raided the Cebolleta settlement several times, sending a force of almost a thousand warriors against the Spaniards in August, 1804, in an effort to reclaim the area of the sacred mountain. In the raids against Cebolleta and subsequent forays against Valle Grande, Santa Clara and other pueblos, the Navajos killed a number of Spaniards and their Indian allies. As a last resort, Chacon requested and received additional troops from Sonora to hold the military settlement of Cebolleta.

Spanish Lieutenant Antonio Narbona led a strong force, comprised of Spanish troops and Opata Indian auxiliaries from Sonora, against the Navajos in January, 1805, and handed the Navajos a stinging defeat in Canyon del Muerto on the 17th. The Navajo warriors, retreating, concealed their aged, women and children in a natural cave high on the face of a sandstone cliff near the head of the north branch of the canyon, then tried to lure the soldiers out of the abyss. The Spaniards were retreating when an old woman, a former slave of the Europeans, began taunting them from the mouth of the cave. The soldiers gained access to the cave by ricocheting bullets off the slanting roof of the cave, killing many. Entering the cave they finished off the Navajos, the aged, hysterical mothers and crying babies, to the last person. Then they methodically crushed the skulls of the dead and dying with their gun butts and cut off the ears for trophies. The marks made by the Spanish bullets can still be seen about Massacre Cave where none survived that day. Riding back down the canyon, the Spaniards laid waste to Canyon de Chelly, destroying Navajo hogans and stores and taking almost four hundred head of livestock and thirty-three women and children captive.

The Canyon del Muerto massacre broke the Navajo spirit and resulted in the initiation of treaty negotiations. The captives taken during the war of 1804-05 were to become a major source of contention during efforts to re-establish peace. At least fifty-one Navajos, probably all women and children, had been taken by the Spaniards and over thirty of them were given to the Sonoran troops brought north by Antonio Narbona. In April the Navajos demanded a complete exchange of prisoners. A treaty was completed on May 12, and among other provisions the Spaniards agreed, in return for Navajo prisoners, to return their captives "and that in case of there being other prisoners among them or among us they will be handed over reciprocally . . ." Cebolleta remained in Spanish control and was to become the major gathering point for launching slave raids against The People.

Apparently Governor Joaquin Alencaster, who arrived in New Mexico to replace Chacon during the peace negotiations and who agreed to the exchange of prisoners, was not aware of how many Navajo captives were held in the New Mexico towns and were at forced labor on ranches throughout the province, not to mention those that had been sold as slaves in Sonora and as far south as Mexico City. Too, the Spaniards did not consider those Navajos who had been baptized into the church as "prisoners." For example, when the Navajos demanded that three little girls held by the Spaniards be returned in June, it was decided that since two of them had already been baptized, they had to be kept among Christians even though they neither understood the Spanish language nor the baptisimal ceremony. The third was allowed to return to her people only because she had not been baptized. The Spaniards quickly baptized the remainder of their prisoners.

While the Spaniards had agreed to cease their slave-raiding expeditions in the treaty of 1805, church baptismal records for the next ten years show that they did not keep the agreement. Too, Spanish ranchers increasingly sent their herds and flocks onto Navajo grazing lands. The Navajos soon took the only action that seemed to have any effect—raiding the livestock which had fattened on their grass. The old pattern of raid and raid alike was soon re-established in Navajo land.

Spurred on by the Spaniards, the Comanches increased their raiding against both the Navajos and the Utes, causing many Navajo bands to move west to seek safety in the Chuska-Tunicha mountains. As soon as the Navajos moved out, Spanish ranchers moved onto their land, assured of Comanche protection. Councils convened across *Dinehtah*. The headmen of the tribe unified behind Narbona, now almost fifty years of age, and began striking directly at the Spaniards in June, 1818, again in alliance with the Utes. Preoccupied with the Mexican rebellion in the South, the Spaniards had withdrawn many of their soldiers from the northern frontier, leaving it weakly protected. From their stronghold on Beautiful Mountain the Navajo warriors launched their war, attacking Cebolleta, still a sore point, first. Attacks on Belén, Laguna and Cochiti followed before the Navajos crossed the Río Grande and killed settlers at Sandia. Suffering from the drought that struck *Dinehtah* that year, the Navajos were forced to conclude a treaty with the Spaniards in August, 1819. Again the Spaniards promised to release all the Navajo slaves they held and again they refused to return those who had already been baptized.

The reasons for the next outbreak of hostilities are obscure, but apparently it was caused by a considerable increase in Spanish slave raiding in the summer of 1821. Two large forces of New Mexicans entered *Dinehtah* early that summer, killing at least thirty warriors and taking a considerable number of captives. In autumn the New Mexicans sent two columns of armed settlers and soldiers into the field to operate simultaneously against the Navajos. The southern column killed seven Navajos and captured an unweaned baby near Bear Spring while the northern column, operating in the vicinity of Sanostee, killed twenty-one Navajos and captured seven more. While the warfare of 1821 was primarily a New Mexican matter, with the New Mexicans repeatedly entering *Dinehtah,* and there is evidence of only limited Navajo retaliation, the next year was to be a different matter.

The first week of March, only a month after the citizens of Santa Fé celebrated Mexico's independence from Spain, twenty-four Navajo emissaries of peace were treacherously killed at Jemez and The People ceased all efforts to make peace with the New Mexicans. General Thomas James, an American trader in Santa Fé, described the murder of the Navajo emissaries: " . . . sixteen Navajo chiefs came . . . and requested the commander of the fort to allow them to pass on to the Governor at Santa Fé, saying that they had come to made peace. The commander invited them into the fort, smoked with them, and made a show of friendship. He had placed a Spaniard on each side of every Indian as they sat and smoked in a circle, and at a signal each Indian was seized by his two Spanish companions and held fast while others dispatched them by stabbing each one to the heart. A Spaniard who figured in this butchery showed me his knife, which he said had killed eight of them. Their dead bodies were thrown over the wall of the fort and covered with a little earth in a gully.

"A few days afterwards five more of the same nation appeared on the bank of the river opposite the town, and inquired for their countrymen. The Spaniards told them they had gone on to Santa Fé, invited them to come over the river, and said they would be well treated. They crossed, and were murdered in the same manner as the others. There again appeared three Indians on the opposite bank, inquiring for their chiefs. They were decoyed across, taken into the town under the mask of friendship, and also murdered in cold blood. In a few days two more appeared, but could not be induced to cross, when some Spanish horsemen went down the river to intercept them. Perceiving this movement, they fled and no more embassies came in."

The murder of the peace emissaries, coupled with the fact that the Navajos were only too aware that over two hundred and fifty of their women and children had been taken by slave expeditions since they'd signed the last peace treaty with the Spaniards, caused the Lords of the Land to begin an aggressive series of attacks, killing Spaniards at Valverde, Las Hertas and elsewhere. In describing a raid of the Navajos "in great force," James, whose

189

sympathies leaned toward the Indians, said: " . . . they killed all of every age and condition, burned and destroyed all they could not take away with them, and drove away the sheep, cattle, and horses. They came from the South directly towards Santa Fé, sweeping everything before them and leaving the land desolate behind them. They re-crossed the Del Norte (Río Grande) below Santa Fé and passed to the North, laid bare the country around the town of Taos, and then disappeared with all their booty. While this was going on, (Governor Facundo) Melgares was getting out the militia and putting nearly all the inhabitants under arms, preparatory to an expedition. I was requested to go but I preferred to be a spectator in such a war." (James, 1966: Citadel, 164-66.)

Melgardes' expedition, which James said "beggared all description," was singularly unsuccessful, capturing only one Navajo too old to run and two or three horses. By summer the Navajos had increased the tempo of their campaign, raiding Tome several times, Laguna, Mora, ranches near Belén, Albuquerque and elsewhere, and killing at least twenty-seven New Mexicans to revenge the murder of the peace chiefs. Melgardes' second expedition of 1822 against the Navajos in August was as unsuccessful as the first and he sued for peace in October.

José Antonio Vizcarra replaced Melgares as governor and met with the Navajos at Paguarte to negotiate a peace treaty on February 12, 1823. Vizcarra again proposed a mutual exchange of captives, but demanded also all "fugitives" among the Navajos while reserving the right to retain all Navajos who did not wish to return to their people, stating that "if they should wish to receive the beneficial waters of baptism it does not seem proper for Catholics to deny them, but on the contrary to favor them and exhort them to the end that the number of the faithful adorers of the true God of the Christians be multiplied." He also suggested "that it be proposed to them with energy that they be converted to the Catholic Religion, resettling themselves in pueblos that will be found in the places that might be convenient in order to attain this goal that the faith of Jesus Christ be propagated and that we complete with the perfect attributes of Christians the reduction of an infidel nation to the fold of the Catholic Church."

The Navajos of 1823 found Christianity even less palatable than had the ancestors who had been approached by the conquistadores with virtually the same words centuries before. When the Navajos found that Vizcarra was not willing to surrender any Navajo captives until the entire nation agreed to become Christians they rejected the treaty and renewed the war. Which was just as well. At the same time Vizcarra was suggesting that the New Mexicans "with the perfect attributes of Christians" attempt to bring the Navajos into the fold of Catholicism, he and his lieutenants were busy drafting a new plan of war on The People and debating how to divide the booty and captives that such a campaign would surely net! Two months later six new Mexicans were buried at Socorro who had "died at the hands of the gentile enemies." At the end of May the Spaniards reported an "atrocious invasion" of Sabinal by Navajos that left another eight Spaniards dead.

On June 18 Vizcarra set out on the most ambitious campaign of the period, one that lasted over three months and took him to the mouth of Canyon de Chelly and west of the Hopi towns. While losing nine men of his own, the Mexican governor killed fifty Navajo men and captured thirty-six women and children. The Navajos struck back by raiding Socorro again, then swept across the land, striking Tome, Albuquerque, and the outskirts of Santa Fé itself. On the way home they attacked Socorro again. But apparently the Spanish raids also continued to take toll. Between September 4 and November 17 at least eighteen small Navajo children who had been captives but a short time were baptized at various pueblos and during the following year there were seventy-one recorded baptisms of Navajos described in the baptismal entries as "purchased," "sold," or "ransomed."

Narbona, working through the Navajo headman-interpreter from Cebolleta, Sandoval, tried again and again to make peace with the Mexicans over the next ten years, a period for which there is no record of a single death of a New Mexican attributed to the Navajos. Yet Navajo children continued to be baptized in the various churches of the New Mexicans, indicating that slave-raiding parties were still active and especially in 1825-26 when one hundred fifteen were added to the baptismal roles. Too, the 1820s brought a severe drought to *Dinehtah* and recovery was slow. While the Navajos rebuilt their strength they refrained from war with the Spaniards.

But the New Mexicans' need for more slaves soon caught up with the Navajos. In the spring and summer of 1834 slave-raiding expeditions were launched against the Navajos from Abiquiu, Cubero, Cebolleta, Sandia, Jemez and Cochita. A Mexican offical named Blas de Hinojos led an undisguised slave-raiding expedition into *Dinehtah* that lasted from October 13 to November 17, 1834 that failed to take more than three captives but did kill sixteen Navajo warriors. Hoping for better results, Hinojos organized an expedition of nearly one thousand armed men and left Santa Fé on February 8, 1835 but this time the Navajos were ready for them.

Led by Narbona, two hundred Navajo warriors divided into small groups and concealed behind rocks and bushes lining the trail ambushed the double column of Mexicans in what was later to become known as Washington Pass. Very few of the Mexicans escaped the rain of Navajo arrows that were released simultaneously at the signal of the owl hoot that February 28. An old Navajo, recalling the ambush years later, said, "we killed plenty of them." After celebrating the Enemy Way, the Navajos took to the warpath and killed three Mexicans at Tome on March 9, four days before the survivors of the Washington Pass ambush straggled back into Santa Fé to report the death of Hinojos and the others. Striking Tome again, and Socorro and Lemitar, the Navajos forced the Mexicans to come into *Dinehtah* to talk peace in August. Again the Mexicans made impossible demands and again they broke the peace by sending an expedition into *Dinehtah* in October under the command of Don José Chaves. Ralph Emerson Twitchell, having inherited the anti-Navajo bias of the Hispano historians, stated that this raid was in retaliation for the "many Mexican children carried into captivity." And that "the settlers, by way of retaliation and the infliction of punishment upon the Indians, in their campaigns into the Indian country, would also take captive children, bring them to the settlements, where they would either be sold or retained as servants. These captives were always treated with the greatest kindness by the Mexicans."

Regardless of Twitchell's opinion of the reasons for the slave raiding of the New Mexicans and the treatment of the captives, the Chaves expedition, consisting of fifty young men, was organized purely for the purpose of taking Navajo slaves and livestock and with the hope, as he paradoxically states, of "bringing droves of horses and sheep and numerous captives, which last, at this time, were worth five hundred dollars each." The expedition travelled all the way from Cebolleta to Río Chaco without seeing a Navajo. On the sandy banks of the stream beneath a sandstone cliff the expedition was ambushed by the Navajos, again led by Narbona. The only survivor was Manuel Chaves, sixteen-year-old brother of the leader of the expedition, whose account of the ambush was retold by Twitchell, who incorrectly placed the site of the ambush in Canyon de Chelly:

" . . . in the terrible battle which ensued, lasting all day, every one of the expedition was either killed or wounded. Only two survived—Manuel Chaves and a civilized Navajo boy . . . Chaves had seven arrow wounds, one arrow having pierced his body through and through; the boy was also wounded in the breast, but not so severely as to prevent his hiding in the rocks of the cañon. When night came the Indians moved to their camps, believing that every one of their enemies had been slain. After much effort Chaves succeeded in finding the dead body of his brother, which, with the aid of the (Navajo) boy, he carried to a nearby arroyo and buried in the sand." (Twitchell, New Mexican, 1925: 293-94.)

Young Chaves and the Navajo boy, after two days, arrived at the site of what is now Fort Wingate, New Mexico, where the latter died. Chaves made his way back to Cebolleta, recovered and later became prominent in New Mexican affairs.

The battles between the Navajos and the New Mexicans continued to wage back and forth throught 1835-36, with the Navajos more than holding their own. By November 1, 1836, the Mexicans had sent three more expeditions against The People, the last of which killed nineteen men and one woman. On November 23, the Navajos attacked Albuquerque and killed five Mexicans.

Desperate, the Mexican government encouraged private citizens to become scalp hunters, paying a high bounty on Navajo scalps. But the government officials in Santa Fé couldn't tell one swatch of black hair from another and ended by paying silver for the scalps of their allies as well

193

as quite a few that had been lifted from their own countrymen. This policy only served to incense the Navajos and they pillaged every settlement they could along the Mexican frontier from Socorro to Abiquiu. The Mexicans sent out a campaign from Santa Fé on September 13, 1838, that ranged from the Tunicha mountains to the Gila river which, according to government reports, killed seventy-eight warriors and took fifty-six captives—most, if not all, of whom were Gila Apaches who had, until this time, not overtly involved themselves in the recent war with the New Mexicans. Another campaign left Abiquiu on December 8 and attacked a rancheria near Tocito, killing two men, one woman and capturing "six little slaves of all sexes."

These raids only increased the fury of the Navajos, now joined by both the Utes and the Gila Apaches in their war against the New Mexicans. Clutching for a straw in the wind, New Mexican Governor Manuel Armijo appointed Sandoval, the headman of the *Dinehanaih* at Cebolleta, as "captain" of the Navajo nation and concluded a treaty with him at Jemez on July 15, 1839. Sandoval was given a gleaming sword, a fancy suit of clothes, and a land grant like those the Mexican ranchers held to show "legal" ownership of property, and was charged with "maintaining the warriors of the Navajo nation in good order." The warriors of the Navajo nation expressed their opinion of "Captain" Sandoval rather explicitly two months later when they raided Cebolleta. Later Sandoval led a force of his *Dinehanaih* and Mexicans against the Navajo strongholds to the West.

Peace negotiations were initiated, primarily through the efforts of Sandoval, in December, 1840, and continued into the following year. The treaty proposed by the Mexicans included a provision that the Navajos give up all the captives among them "without demanding equal recompenses" and allowed Navajo slaves to gain their freedom only if they successfully escaped their masters and returned to *Dinehtah* without being caught! The Navajos pointed out that they had made ten treaties with the Spaniards and each time had surrendered the captives they held but the Spaniards had never once made more than a token effort to return the Navajos they held in their power. During the discussions of peace that continued throughout 1841 and into 1842 Narbona, now past seventy-five years of age, managed to keep the Navajos off the raiding trails, but when it became apparent that there was no hope of getting back the thousands of Navajo women and children who were slaves to the Mexicans, he quit trying to hold them back.

Mexican settlements and ranches paid dearly for the never-ending slave expeditions of the Mexicans such as that led by Pedro Herrera in January, 1843, which killed nineteen Navajos, took another nineteen captive and returned to the Río Grande with one thousand eight hundred animals. In return the Navajos raided as far east as San Miquel del Vado, where they killed five men who were buried on November 20, 1843. The next month Tome was again the object of their wrath and they left two men dead there. The New Mexican governor, Manuel Armijo, and his officers continued to approach the Navajos with offers of peace, claiming with justification that the war was slowly consuming the department, but they adamantly refused to discuss the release of Navajo slaves. Narbona and the other headmen, with the notable exception of Sandoval, refused to discuss peace as long as Navajo children were being offered for sale in the Santa Fe marketplace for one hundred fifty pesos.

Sandoval, long a liaison between the Mexican officials in Santa Fe and his Mount Taylor Navajos were caught in a quandary. Caught between the war leaders of the western Navajos who persisted in their attacks on the Mexicans and who began to look upon Sandoval's peace efforts with suspicion and the Santa Fe officials who continued to insist on a peace treaty that made no mention of Navajo captives, the *Dinehanaih* found themselves in a position of being subject to possible attack from both East and West. A small group of Mexicans actually did attack the rancherias of the *Dinehaniah* and drove off about forty head of livestock belonging to Sandoval although it is not known whether or not the raid was officially sanctioned by Governor Armijo. But Armijo did help Sandoval get his livestock back and this, coupled with the fact that the headsmen of the *Dinehanaih* found that he was no longer welcome at the Navajo *Naachid*, the important council of headmen held periodically to determine future policy and action toward the Mexicans, caused the Mount Taylor Navajos to throw their lot in with the Mexicans.

In April, 1846, Sandoval asked Armijo for permission to enlist men for an expedition against the western Navajos, which was granted. Dressed like a Mexican and shouting orders in Spanish, Sandoval led his force directly into Navajo strongholds on a highly successful riad later that same month and sold the captives he took into slavery. He was prevented from leading subsequent raids against his people only because Armijo learned that the United States had declared war on Mexico and thought it best not to further antagonize the Lords of the Land in face of the threat of an invasion from the East.

Then, in the summer of 1846, a rumor spread across *Dinehtah* like wildfire. The Americans, those whites of the far east of whom one heard to much but knew so little about, were marching on New Mexico with a large army. If the Americans should defeat the Mexicans would not their women and children be returned to them at long last? One dared hope and so the Navajos took to the war trail to help the Americans crush the Mexicans, thinking that any enemy of the latter must, perforce, be an ally of theirs. This illusion was quickly shattered. And Sandoval, the Navajo headsman who had so recently led a raid against *Dinehtah* and sold women and children of his nation into slavery, would be appointed by the Americans as the liaison between themselves and the *Dineh*.

PART FOUR

The Burning Ground

ONE

The Navajos and The American Conquest

The rights of the Navajos and other Indian tribes of the West to the land on which they had lived for centuries before the first Puritan set foot on Plymouth Rock were given no consideration when John O' Sullivan wrote in the *United States Magazine and Democratic Review* for July-August, 1845: "It is our manifest destiny to overspread the continent allotted by Providence for the free development of our yearly multiplying millions," and thereby coined a phrase to fit the prevalent expansionary mood of the United States—manifest destiny. The Indians who were yet trying to hold onto their ancestral homelands and tribal unity were not numbered among O' Sullivan's "multiplying millions" and the United States' "manifest destiny" to possess two-fifths of the territory then claimed by Mexico—a claim still disputed by the original Indian owners of the land—would bring destruction to their hereditary way of life.

The American of the 1840s was energetic, vigorous, idealistic and had unwavering faith in his democratic institutions, a faith that would prevent his ability to grasp a rudimentary understanding of the pure democracy of the Navajos. Unlike the United States, the *Dineh* had no President James Knox Polk who was able to quelch all opposition to a declaration of war. Each Navajo band was ruled by a headman, a *Naataani,* who exerted leadership by the strength of his personality, his abilities and by the esteem granted his person by his followers. Not even the revered Narbona could speak for the tribe as a whole. Promises made by the headman on one band or group were not necessarily binding to others nor, for that matter, to members of his own band who might disagree with the action. The Americans, accustomed to thinking of all Indian tribes as savage bands ruled over by a hereditary chief—a political organization not unlike that of most contemporary European states in a more simple form—would fail to recognize the fact that a treaty with a Navajo "chief," to be effective, had to be agreed upon by the entire nation much as the same treaty had to be ratified by the United States Senate. This lack of understanding of the Navajo tribal structure would eventually lead the Americans to think of the *Dineh* as the most treacherous, treaty-breaking tribe with whom the westward-expanding Americans had yet come into contact. As a result the Navajos, who looked upon the Americans as allies at first, soon found themselves faced with the most formidable foe they had ever encountered and one who would, within less than two decades, conquer and all but destroy them.

The annexation of Texas by the United States in 1845 set the stage for the American War with Mexico, a war that had long been expected by the Mexicans. As early as 1810, New Mexico's first and only delegate to the Spanish Cortés, Don Pedro Bautista Pino, warned King Ferdinand: " . . . I expect, Sir, that your Majesty will take note of this truth, that resulting from the purchase of Louisiana, by the United States, the door is left open to enable them to arm and incite the savage tribes, as well as for themselves to invade our province; once lost, its recovery is improbable."

The manifest destiny contingent in Washington not only wanted Texas but it already considered all territory owned by Mexico that is now within the boundaries of the continental United States as but unconquered territory. The United States offered to buy the territory, which now comprises all of the states of California, Nevada, Utah,

Arizona and New Mexico excluding the Gadsen Purchase territory as well as parts of Wyoming and Colorado, for thirty million dollars, but Mexico refused to negotiate, whereupon President Polk ordered General Zachary Taylor, who had already landed with a force of United States troops at Corpus Christi, Texas, to proceed to the Rio Grande. Polk wanted "the whole hog, not just the trotters," and the chance to acquire it came in the form of a group of dispatches from Taylor that arrived at the White House at daybreak on the morning of May 9, 1846. "Hostilities may now be considered as commenced," reported Taylor. The dispatches were dated April 26 and stated that a force of sixty-three dragoons, commanded by Captain Seth B. Thornton, had been ambushed by Mexican cavalry the day before. Sixteen Americans were dead and forty-seven had been captured and were prisoners of the Mexicans.

Polk had already called his cabinet into session the day before and polled its members on the "Mexican question." "I . . . propounded the distinct question to the cabinet, and took their opinions individually, whether I should make a message to Congress on Tuesday, and whether in that message I should recommend a declaration of war against Mexico," Polk recorded in his diary. "All except the Secretary of Navy (George Bancroft) gave their advice in the affirmative. Mr. Bancroft dissented but said if any act of hostility should be committed by the Mexican forces he was then in favour of immediate war."

Polk sent his message to Congress and, after considerable debate, mostly in the Señate, and some rather violent objection from the Whigs and from the South Carolinian John C. Calhoun, who later wrote that if a single Democrat of standing had "come to my side" war would have been averted, a declaration of war against Mexico was passed. President Polk signed the act recognizing the existence of a state of war shortly after one p. m. on May 13, 1846. Congress authorized Polk to raise an army of fifty thousand volunteers and a sum of ten million dollars was voted for the prosecution of what critics, including Abraham Lincoln and Ulysses S. Grant, would soon call "Mr. Polk's War."

Polk wrote in his journal that night: "I told him (Secretary of State James Buchanan) that though we had not gone to war for conquest, yet it was clear that in making peace we would if practicable obtain California and such other portions of the Mexican territory as would be sufficient to idemnify our claimants on Mexico and defray the expense of war which that power by her long continued wrongs and injuries had forced us to wage."

Colonel Stephen Watts Kearny was ordered to organize the Army of the West at Fort Levenworth, Kansas, for a descent to occupy the broad territory stretching from New Mexico to California and, if practical, to cooperate with other branches of the army in operations farther south. By June, Kearny was on his way to Santa Fe and reached Bent's Fort on the Arkansas the last week of July. On August 1, from a camp nine miles south of the fort, Kearny sent a delegation to call upon Governor Manuel Armijo, under the command of Captain Philip St. George Cooke, who was the only officer on the frontier whom Kearny would trust with the large sum of gold that was being sent to Santa Fe to bribe the governor to leave New Mexico without fighting the American Army of the West. Accompanying Cooke was a trader named James Magoffin who had spent several years in New Mexico and who knew Armijo. Arriving in Santa Fe on August 12, Magoffin and Cooke called on Armijo and asked him to "submit to fate" and peacefully turn New Mexico over to Kearny. A large amount of gold—probably in the amount of twenty-five thousand dollars—exchanged hands at the governor's palace that day and Armijo did "submit to fate" after making a blusterous show of defending his department.

Then Kearny, without opposition, marched directly to Santa Fe and, on August 22, 1846, issued a proclamation declaring New Mexico a possession of the United States by right of conquest and raised the American flag over the ancient governor's palace without having fired a shot. Ignorant of the particulars of the war between the New Mexicans and the Navajos, Kearny, recently promoted to the rank of Brigadier General, assumed the role of the protector of the New Mexicans and stated " . . . the Navajos come down from the mountains and carry off your sheep and your women whenever they please. My government will correct all this. They will keep off the Indians, protect you in your persons and property."

During the construction of Fort Marcy, which Kearny ordered built on a commanding hill northeast of the city, the American general abruptly came face to face with the "Navajo problem" that had plagued his predecessors in the New Mexican capital. The Navajos not only raided several of the nearby Río Grande settlements but a small force of warriors drove off a flock of horses belonging to the American army. Learning about Sandoval and the role he'd played in Mexican-Navajo affairs, Kearney sent for the headman and charged him with surveying all of the Navajo headmen to see if they were "inclined to make peace." Whether Kearny knew that Sandoval was considered a traitor by his people and of the raid he'd made on them only six months previously is not known, and it is highly doubtful that he "surveyed" any members of the tribe except his own Mount Taylor *Dinehanaih*. Nevertheless he sent word to Kearny a few days later that he "had seen all the headmen of his nation" and they had expressed a desire to make peace with the Americans. An American scouting party did reconnoiter *Dinehtah*, and Narbona, now about eighty years of age, was asked to call on Kearny in Santa Fe to discuss peace terms.

Narbona considered accepting the American invitation but he was only too aware that two Navajo peace parties had recently been ambushed while on their way to Santa Fe and sent word to Kearny that he would only talk peace with the Americans in the safety of his own homeland. Kearny agreed to Narbona's terms and replied that he would soon send word about the meeting time and place.

Meanwhile, curious about the manner of these new men, Narbona chose a few companions and, taking a back trail which took them into the mountains north of Santa Fe, went to observe the Americans himself. Impressed with the regimental drills, the parades and the sounds of the thunderous cannon fire which he could see and hear from his secret vantage point in the hills above Fort Marcy, Narbona returned to his home in the Tunicha Valley and urged his people to follow the peace trail with the Americans. Those under his sphere of influence listened to the aged headman and began to make preparations for the coming of the Americans by grooming and decorating their horses, and bringing out their best garments and jewelry. But many of the younger men and particularly the followers of the young war chief, Manuelito, Narbona's son-in-law, questioned the wisdom of entering into peace negotiations with the Americans, suspecting correctly that they were but another—and infinitely more serious—threat to *Dinehtah*. Too, they were aware that for years the Navajos had signed one peace treaty after another that neither brought peace nor returned their captive women and children to them.

Kearny left Santa Fe' for California on September 25, leaving Colonel Alexander William Doniphan in charge of the department until the arrival of Colonel Sterling Price and a force of about one thousand two hundred Missouri volunteers, expected momentarily, whereupon Doniphan was to lead an expedition against Chihuahua. A week later he sent Doniphan a dispatch from his camp near Socorro revising his orders with instructions for the Colonel to lead an expedition against the Navajos before marching on Chihuahua.

Acting on orders from Doniphan a force of thirty Americans under the command of a Captain Reid left Cebolleta on October 20 to call on the Navajo headmen and ask them to meet with Doniphan the next month to sign a peace treaty. Guided by Sandoval, the Americans penetrated the heart of *Dinehtah*. In a wide valley near Narbona's camp in the Tunicha mountains, the aged chief met the Americans accompanied by nearly two thousand Navajo men and women on horseback. Captain Reid wrote John T. Hughes a letter describing the meeting which contained some interesting observations of the Navajos and revealed the prevailing American attitude toward The People at the time of the first formal contact between the two societies: "This was the most critical situation in which I ever found myself placed; with only thirty men in the very centre of a people the most savage and 'proverbially treacherous on the continent. Many of them were not very friendly. Being completely in their power, we, of course, had to play the game to the best advantage. As there was no pasturage near the camp, we had to send our horses out. Our numbers were too few to divide, or even altogether to think of protecting the horses, if the Indians were disposed to take them. So I even made a virtue of necessity; and putting great confidence in the honesty of their intentions, I gave my horses in charge of one of the chiefs of these notorious horse stealers. He took them out some five miles to graze, and we, after taking supper, again joined in the dance, which was kept up until next morning. Our men happened to take the right course to please the Indians, participating in all their sports, and exchanging liveries with them. They seemed to be equally delighted to see themselves clothed in the vesture obtained from us, and to see our men adopting their costume. The emboldened confidence and freedom with which we mixed among them seemed to win upon their feelings, and make them disposed to grant whatever we asked. They taxed their powers of performance in all their games to amuse us, and make the time pass agreeably, notwithstanding our imminently precarious situation.

"We had not arrived at the place of our camp before we were met by all the head men of the nation. The Chief of all Narbona, being very sick, was nevertheless mounted on horseback, and brought in. He slept in my camp all night. Narbona, who was probably seventy years old, being held in great reverence by his tribe for the warlike exploits of his youth and manhood, was now a mere skeleton of a man, being completely prostrated by rheumatism, the only disease, though a very common one, in this country. Conformably to a custom of the chief men of his tribe, he wore finger nails very long, probably one and a half inches—formidable weapons! He appeared to be a mild, amiable man, and though he had been a warrior himself, was very anxious before his death to secure for his people a peace with all their old enemies as well as with us, the 'New Men,' as he called us.

"Upon the evening of our arrival we held a grand talk, in which all the old men participated. Most of them seemed disposed for peace, but some opposed it as being contrary to the honor of the Navajos, as well as their interest, to make peace with the Mexicans; though they were willing to do so with us . . . "

Among those who objected to making peace with the Mexicans or treating with the Americans were Manuelito and Narbona's wife, the only woman allowed to attend the solemn council. Narbona's wife, addressing the Navajo headmen, pointed out that there were only a few soldiers present and asked why the Navajos didn't overpower them and be done with it. Asserting his authority, Narbona dismissed her from the council and assured Reid that he desired peace.

Reid continued: " . . . the night passed off in a variety of diversions; and in the next morning, notwithstanding the most urgent desire on the part of our entertainers that we would stay, I thought it prudent to return, as we were running short of provisions. Our horses were forthcoming without a single exception, and as soon as we caught them, we turned our faces towards camp (Cebolleta).

"Although this expedition was one of much hazard, yet it turned out to be one of much pleasurable excitement, and attended with no loss or harm. The people . . . who were the object of our visit, are in many respects singular and unlike any other of the aboriginal inhabitants of this continent. Their habits are very similar to those of the of the Tartars. They are entirely a pastoral people, their flocks constituting their sole wealth. But little addicted to the chase, and never indulging in it, except when the game may be taken on horseback. Their weapons of war are the spear or lance, the bow, and the lazo, in the use of all which they are not excelled. They may be said literally to live on horseback. Of these animals they possess immense droves, and of a stock originally the same with the Mexican horse, yet wonderfully improved. They pay great attention to the breeding of their horses, and think scarcely less of them than do the Arabians. They also possess many mules, but these are generally the proceeds of their marauding expeditions against the Mexicans. Indeed the whole of New Mexico is subject to the devastating incursions of these lords of the mountains. Of this, however, you know as well as I." (Hughes, James, 1848: 171-73.)

The objections of Manuelito and Narbona's wife to treatying with the Americans were well founded. The American occupation of New Mexico had not changed the situation for the Navajos in the least. The New Mexicans, generally, did not concern themselves greatly with the exchange of governments and looked upon the Americans as new allies—and a new market for Navajo captives. Lieutenant J.W. Abert, of the topographical engineers, reported of being offered a Navajo woman at a ranch between Bernalillo and Santo Domingo only a few days prior to the meeting between Narbona and Reid: "Old Montejo (Abert's New Mexican host) offered to sell me a Navajo squaw, who happened to pass as we were bargaining for the mule; and he then related a long story about the depredations committed by the Navajos: that they kept all of New Mexico poor, whilst they themselves rolled in wealth."

Too, the American opinions of the Navajos, particularly that of Congress which had, of course, great bearing on their treatment and the particulars of treaties made with the tribe, were formed by such men as Colonel William H. Emory who reported to Congress from Kearny's command: "I saw here (near Albuquerque) the hiding places of the Navajos, who, when few in number, wait for the night to descend upon the valley and carry off the fruit, sheep, women and children of the Mexicans. When in numbers they come in daytime and levy their dues. Their retreats and caverns are at a distance to the west in high and inaccessible mountains, where troops of the United States will find great difficulty in overtaking and subduing them, *but where the Mexicans have never thought of penetrating.* Few in numbers, *disdaining the cultivation of the soil* (emphasis mine) and even the rearing of cattle, they draw all their supplies from the valley of the Del Norte (Río Grande) . . . They are prudent in their depredations, never taking so much from one man as to ruin him. (Governor) Armijo never permitted the inhabitants to war upon these thieves. The power he had of letting these people loose on the Mexicans was the great secret of his arbitrary sway over a people who hated and despised him. Any offender against Armijo was pretty sure to have a visit from the Navajos." Years would pass before more than a handful of Americans realized to what extent the Navajos were also the victims of raids by the New Mexicans.

Kearny had promised the New Mexicans religious freedom when he occupied the province and this apparently was interpreted by the citizens of the province to include freedom to baptize Navajo captives, for the baptism of Navajo children continued at just about the same pace as before the arrival of the Americans. Even as Reid and Narbona sat in council discussing means of establishing a lasting peace between the two factions, Kearny had already issued an order that, by its very wording, would prevent the Americans from considering the Navajo position and, hence, peace. Near Socorro where Kearny camped on his way to California, the American general learned that a party of Navajos had recently raided that community, killing seven or eight men, taking as many more women and children captives and driving off ten thousand head of sheep, cattle and mules. In a dispatch dated October 2, 1846, to Colonel Doniphan, at Santa Fé, Kearny stated: "As the chiefs of the Navajos have been invited to Santa Fé by the commanding general, for the purpose of holding a council, and making a peace between them and the inhabitants of New Mexico (now forming a part and under the protection of the United States), and as they have promised to come, but have failed doing so, and instead thereof continue killing the people and committing depredations upon their property, it becomes necessary to send a military expedition into the country of those Indians, to secure a peace and better conduct from them in the future.

"For reasons set forth in the foregoing paragraph, Col. Doniphan, of the first regiment Missouri mounted volunteers . . . will march with his regiment into the Navajo country. He will cause all the prisoners, and all the property they hold, which had been stolen from the inhabitants of the territory of New Mexico, to be given up—and he will require of them such security for their future good conduct, as he may think ample and sufficient, by taking hostages or otherwise . . ." (Hughes, ibid, 1848: 143-144.) It was that dispatch, in which Kearny completely ignored the Navajo grievances, that prompted Reid's meeting with Narbona. Two days after sending the dispatch to Doniphan, Kearny, eager to be on his way to California where he hoped to gain glory and fame, destroyed all hopes of any lasting peace between the Navajos and the Americans when he published permission "for the people of New Mexico to retaliate and make war on the Navajos . . . to form war parties, to march into the country of their enemies, the Navajos, to recover their property, to make reprisals and obtain redress for the many insults received from them."

Kearny, unintentionally, had given the New Mexicans his explicit permission and encouragement to continue to make slave-raiding expeditions on the Navajos and, as it would come to pass, to do so under the protection of the United States military.

Hoping to settle the "Navajo problem" before the winter snows made the mountain passes of *Dinehtah* impassable, and be on his way to Chihuahua, Doniphan dispatched directions for an American force stationed at Abiquiu under the command of Major William Gilpin to proceed to Bear Spring by a northern route, and a second force stationed at Cebolleta to march there by a southern route, while he, himself, left Santa Fé on October 26 with the intent of leading a third force through the center of *Dinehtah*. With such a show of American force Doniphan hoped to frighten the Navajos into coming to a quick and amiable agreement. Doniphan's party caught up with that from Cebolleta at Cubero on November 5, the latter having been beset with injuries and illnesses and delayed, and also that of Captain Reid returning from the meeting with Narbona. The Reid party was allowed to return to Albuquerque and Doniphan started out for Bear Spring (*Shas Bitoo*, later the site of Fort Wingate) on November 15 after sending a message to Gilpin's northern force, camped on the San Juan, to meet him at the rendezvous on the 20th and summon all the Navajos he should meet to the council.

Doniphan's party was delayed by snow and did not reach Bear Spring until the morning of the 21st. While his force did encounter some hardship it did not, as stated by his biographer, rival "the passage of the Carthaginian general over the Apeninines" nor "the march of Bonaparte and McConough over the snow-capt peaks of the Alps." The American commander found his northern force awaiting him at Bear Spring along with about five hundred Navajos, including most of the headmen. Doniphan immediately got to the task at hand, stating that power had been delegated to him by the government of the United States to conclude a lasting peace between the Navajos, the New Mexicans and the Americans. Both sides delivered speeches alternately throughout the first day of negotiations and adjourned at sunset.

Addressing the Navajo headmen the morning of November 22, Colonel Doniphan explained that the United States had taken military possession of New Mexico and had extended her laws over the territory; that the New Mexicans would be protected by the Americans against violence and invasion and their rights preserved; the United States was also anxious to enter into a treaty of lasting peace and friendship with "her red children, the Navajos" and that the same protection would be given them against encroachments and usurpations of their rights as had been guaranteed the New Mexicans. He added that the United States claimed all the country—which included the land of the Navajos—by right of conquest and that the Navajos as well as the New Mexicans were now "the children" of the United States and, further, if the *Dineh* refused to treat on terms honorable to both parties, he was instructed to prosecute a war against them.

Whereupon a bold young headman the Mexicans called Zarcillas Largo (Long Earrings), known to his people as Nataallith, stood up and faced the American commander: "Americans! you have a strange cause of war against the Navajos. We have waged war against the New Mexicans for several years. We have plundered their villages and killed many of their people, and made many prisoners. We had just cause for all this. *You* have lately commenced a war against the same people. You are powerful. You have great guns and many brave soldiers. You have therefore conquered them, the very thing we have been attempting to do for so many years. You now turn upon us for attempting to do what you have done yourselves. We cannot see why you have cause to quarrel with us for fighting the Mexicans on the West, while you do the same thing on the East. Look how matters stand. This is *our war*. We have more right to complain of you for interfering in our war than you have to quarrel with us for continuing a war we had begun long before you got here. If you will act justly, you will allow us to settle our own differences."

Doniphan then explained that since the New Mexicans had surrendered the whole country and everything in it had become the property of the United States by conquest, when the Navajos now stole property from the New Mexicans they were stealing it from the United States; when they now killed New Mexicans they were killing American people and such would not be suffered any longer. He went on to point out that it would be greatly to their advantage for Americans to settle in New Mexico as the Navajos would then be able to trade and obtain all their needs from his countrymen "in exchange for furs and peltries." Furthermore, he pointed out, if they entered into a peace agreement, they would be allowed to go to the United States and learn trades that would be valuable to their people, and if they wanted to continue to fight they might join him in fighting Mexicans in Chihuahua! The assembled Navajos expressed an interest in going to the United States but none in fighting Mexicans in Chihuahua, having no quarrel with those people.

In reply, Zarcillas Largo said: "If New Mexico be really in your possession, and it be the intention of your government to hold it, we will cease our raids and refrain from future wars upon that people; for we have no cause to quarrel with you, and do not desire to have any war with so powerful a nation. Let there be peace between us." After discussing terms of the peace, the treaty was signed by Doniphan, Lieutenant-Colonel Congreve Jackson and Major William Gilpin for the Americans and by fourteen headmen, including Zarcillas Largo, Narbona, Manuelito and Sandoval for the Navajos.

The treaty called for "a firm and lasting peace and amity between the American people (which specifically included the New Mexicans and the Pueblo Indians) and the Navajo "tribe of Indians," as well as for mutual trade and the rights of "Americans, Mexicans and Pueblos to visit all portions of the Navajo country, and the Navajos all portions of the American country without molestations, and full protection shall be mutually given." Article four of the treaty also called for a mutual restoration of all prisoners, "the several parties being pledged to redeem by purchase such as may not be exchanged for each other" and "all property taken by either party from the other, since the 18th day of August last, shall be restored."

While Doniphan's intentions were honorable, his treaty was as worthless as the dozens made with the Navajos by the Spaniards and Mexicans. In exchange for vague promises the Navajos had, once again, agreed to give up their captives and to allow Pueblos and New Mexicans to come into *Dinehtah* in safety. Doniphan and his successors in New Mexico did not have the means to enforce the treaty and there weren't enough American soldiers in the Southwest to cause the return of Navajo captives held by the New Mexicans even if they had been so inclined nor, for that matter, to protect the life of a single Navajo who might desire to visit all or any "portions of the American country." Congress failed to ratify the treaty, an omission of little importance.

After an exchange of presents—the Navajos giving Doniphan a number of fine blankets which he sent to the war department in Washington as specimens of Navajo manufacture—the commander led his Missourians southward to the pueblo of Zuñi, taking three Navajo headmen with him. They completed the sixty-mile march in two days and there, on the 26th, Doniphan caused a treaty to be made between the Navajos and the Zuñis who had lately been at war. Then he returned to the Río Grande and left in early December for Chihuahua, having secured two treaties that would not endure as long as the snow that covered the mountains of *Dinehtah*.

TWO

The "New Men"

The "New Men," as Narbona called the American
soldiers, did not overtly concern themselves in the quarrel
between the New Mexicans and the Navajos at first except on an official level. Generally the American volunteers
looked upon all the people of the conquered province—
Mexicans and Indians alike—as members of an inferior
society although they did give deference to the Navajos for
their superior horsemanship. T.B. Thorpe, editor of the
New Orleans *National* newspaper and a personal friend of
Colonel Doniphan, published an article that indicated
that the American commander was possessed of an un-
abashed admiration for the *Dineh*. Quoting Doniphan,
Thorpe wrote: "The Navajo Indians are a warlike people;
have no towns, houses, or lodges (?); they live in the open
air, or on horseback, and are remarkably wealthy, having
immense herds of horses, cattle and sheep. They are celebrated for their intelligence and good order. They treat
their women with great attention, consider them equals,
and relieve them from the drudgery of menial work. They
are handsome, well made, and in every respect a highly
civilized people, being as a nation, of a higher order of

beings than the mass of their neighbors, the Mexicans. About the time Col. Doniphan made his treaty, a division of his command was entirely out of provisions: the Navajos supplied its wants with liberality."

John T. Hughes, Doniphan's biographer, added: "The art and skill which they possess in manufacturing woolen fabrics (the texture of which is so dense and fine as to be impervious to water) and apparently with such limited means, is really matter of astonishment. The Navajos can easily muster fifteen hundred warriors for battle; and their aggregate numbers cannot be less than twelve thousand. They are certainly the noblest of the American aborigines." (Hughes, Ibid 1848: 103.)

Neither the contemporary American policy toward all Indian nations nor the New Mexicans' hatred and fear of the Navajos would allow such favorable opinions to long prevail.

Once they arrived in Santa Fé, Sterling Price's Missouri volunteers, having missed the conquest, such as it was, proceeded to act like nothing less than conquerors and soon antagonized the citizenry. Within a week after their arrival Charles Bent, a longtime American resident of New Mexico who had been named civil governor by Kearny, protested their actions and asked Doniphan to interpose his authority to compel the soldiers to respect the rights of the inhabitants, stating that outrages committed by the Americans were becoming so frequent that he apprehended serious consequences if measures were not taken to improve the conduct of the volunteers. Too, a few influential New Mexicans, mostly former government officials and members of the clergy, did not yet consider the province "conquered" and were plotting to overthrow the American government even before Doniphan left for Bear Spring. On October 15, Governor Bent wrote Secretary of State James Buchanan that he suspected plots were being made against the Americans and that the Pueblo Indians would "join in any revolutionary enterprise to which they might be instigated by those whose orders they have long been accustomed to obey with blind submission."

The arrogant attitude of the American soldiers toward the natives added fuel to the fires of rebellion. Too, the New Mexicans realized that Doniphan's treaty with the Navajos was worthless. They wished for, even expected, the Americans to completely crush the Navajos—something they had never been able to do. The St. Louis *Weekly Reveille* of February 22, 1847, printed a dispatch from Santa Fé summoning up the prevailing attitude toward the treaty in that city: " . . . Col. Doniphan's treaty has been discussed. It is said to be very defective, and not likely to effect any very substantial peace. Gentlemen here, well acquainted with the Navajos, expect every day to hear of new outrages being committed by them. The achievement of this treaty does not, therefore, seem to confer many laurels; but we ought to remember that making Indian treaties is a new business to the Col., and if he has not made a very good one on the first trial, he may do infinitely better the next time. But the Navajos, it is here thought, will continue to steal sheep and commit other outrages, until they are well whipped a few times." No doubt the high regard in which Doniphan held the Navajos was known in Santa Fé and possibly contributed to the dissatisfaction of the New Mexicans.

News from the front was slow in reaching the East in 1847. By the time the St. Louis newspaper printed the dispatch from Santa Fé not only had the Navajos returned to the war trail but Governor Charles Bent and several other Americans had been killed in an insurrection at Taos. The rebellion, instigated by the disgruntled New Mexicans and executed by the Taos Indians, came on the morning of January 19, 1847. After murdering Bent in his home in Taos, the Indians fanned out and killed every American in northern New Mexico who fell into their hands before Sterling Price's Missouri volunteers put down the insurrection by bombarding the Taos pueblo on February 4. The Navajos did not take part in the rebellion. In fact, as far as they were concerned, it mattered little how many the Pueblos and the *Bilagáana*—the Americans—killed of each other. But they were interested observers. For the first time the Americans in New Mexico had engaged in battle and while Price's raw recruits did put down the rebellion of a weak and outnumbered foe, they did not appear, in doing so, as formidable in combat as they had on the parade ground. The Navajos returned home with a considerably lowered opinion of the *Bilagáana* and with the secure knowledge that most of the Americans had left the territory to fight in Mexico. And if the New Mexicans had no intention of keeping Doniphan's treaty—the baptism of Navajo women and children had not abated in the least—then neither did they.

In the time between the signing of the Doniphan treaty in November and midsummer, 1847, the Navajos, travelling in small, elusive parties and intent primarily on stealing livestock rather than warfare, visited the Mexican ranches along the Río Grande time and again, driving tens of thousands of sheep and horses back up the sand valley of the Rio Puerco and through the well-worn trails of the Zuñi mountains to their strongholds in the Chuska-Tunicha mountains. Among the seven New Mexicans killed that spring by the Navajos was Juan Cruz Piño, the son of a prominent rancher, who held numerous Navajos in slavery. The New Mexican ranchers reminded the Americans at Fort Marcy that they had been promised protection from Navajo raids by Kearny. Grandiose plans were formulated by the New Mexicans and laid before the American authorities calling for the total annihilation of the tribe or, more profitably, complete enslavement of the Navajos.

José Manuel Savedra led an unsuccessful expedition into *Dinehtah* in May, but it was the first week of September before the Americans, their numbers few and widely scattered in performing garrison duty, deemed it necessary to send a military expedition against the Navajos. A well-equipped battalion of Missouri volunteers, under the command of Major W.H.T. Walker, left Santa Fé on September 10 with the intent of invading *Dinehtah* and giving the Navajos a thorough chastising. The troops carried along a small detachment of artillery and provisions for two months, but the Walker expedition was to accomplish virtually nothing—possibly because, as the Santa Fé *Republican* pointed out on the day of departure, "nearly every man left (Santa Fé) drunk."

Walker's troop of one hundred forty men, which took ten days just to reach Albuquerque, saw a lot of the country but very few Navajos. From Albuquerque the expedition travelled due west to Bear Spring where they left their supply wagons, then proceeded to Laguna Colorado (Red Lake) from which point Walker sent out detachments to contact the Navajos. His troops found fields ready to harvest, hogans recently deserted and sheep trails, but the only Navajos they saw were always some distance away. Regathering his command at Laguna Colorado, Walker next marched them to Canyon de Chelly with the intent of penetrating that stronghold of the Navajos. Once they entered the deep chasm with its towering vertical walls, the Americans realized that their position was precarious at best, whereupon they quickly backtracked and returned to Santa Fé, arriving at the capital on October 13.

A few days after the Walker expedition arrived back at Fort Marcy a group of Navajo headmen that did not include Narbona, Zarcillas Largo, Manuelito or any other person of importance in the tribe visited the capital and offered to treaty for peace. Undoubtedly this offer was a ruse to keep the American soldiers out of *Dinehtah* until the crops were gathered. In the council that was called the headmen agreed to a peace, the details of which are lost, and kept it for a few months. But shortly after the first of the year the Navajos began raiding again. By March, 1848, they were striking all along the frontier, from Abiquiu to Socorro. The pueblos of Santo Domingo, Jemez and Zuni were struck repeatedly and ranches near Cubero and Cebolleta suffered losses of livestock but there are no records of deaths attributed to Navajos during this period. Very few records of the early American occupation of New Mexico exist and the few that remain do not mention any raids on the Navajos by the New Mexicans, but expeditions to secure slaves and in reprisal were made throughout the latter months of 1847 and early in 1848 without army sanction as nine Navajo children "captives" were baptized prior to May 15.

On March 27, 1848, the new military commander of New Mexico, Colonel Edward W.B. Newby, realizing that his troops were virtually helpless in putting a stop to the Navajo raids, gave his official sanction to expeditions made by New Mexican irregulars, thereby further encouraging undisguised slave raiding. From his headquarters at Fort Marcy, Colonel Newby issued Orders Number 22: "The Colonel Commanding is deeply pained at the intelligence which he daily receives of the frequent outrages committed upon the persons and property of the peaceful inhabitants of the Territory . . . by the Navajos . . .

"This painful feeling, not a little enhanced by the fact that three-fourths of the force remaining in this Department are infantry, and are powerless against the rapid movements of mounted men, who are familiar with every inch of the country, and that, in consequence, his garrisons are compelled to sit still while murder and robbery is committed under their very eyes.

"In consideration of the circumstances, that as the only means of protection remaining, it is ordered that the Mexican inhabitants of this Department, be authorized to arm and equip themselves—organize in parties or hands and hold themselves in readiness to repel all incursions and to recover the property that may have been taken from them by the Indians." (Santa Fé *Republican*, April 2, 1848.)

Legalizing the expeditions of the New Mexicans served only to cause the Navajos to increase the tempo of their own raids which, in turn, made it necessary for the Americans to invade *Dinehtah*. Leaving Santa Fé May 1, the two hundred men under the command of Colonel Newby arrived at Jemez on the fourth. Newby, in a letter to Roger Jones, Adjutant General of the United States, dated June 17, 1848, said that after an "arduous march of six days" after leaving Jemez: "I reached the outskirts of the Navajo Territory, and in the immediate vicinity of which, as informed by spies, numbers of the Indians (were) herding their stock and preparing to sow their grain. Late in the evening of the sixth day I perceived some four or five men on horseback at a short distance in advance and instantly ordered out the best mounted portion of my force to give chase. I soon perceived, however, from the extreme ease with which the Indians made their escape, that an attempt to march openly upon them would be folly and blast every prospect of the successful issue of the expedition. The difference between the speed of their animals and *ours* infinitely surpassed my expectations and convinced me that as much secrecy as possible would have to be used."

Proceeding with "secrecy" Newby's force was met by "two of the Principal Chiefs who proposed making a treaty, and promised to visit our camp in a few days for that purpose" the very next day.

The headmen of the tribe, including Narbona, Zarcillas Largo, José Largo and Chapitone, a Naatáaní of the San Juan Navajos, did meet Newby at "Monte del Cayatana," present-day Beautiful Mountain near Sanostee, and signed a treaty on May 20. The Newby treaty was never ratified by Congress. The third article of the treaty stated: "There shall be an entire restoration of all prisoners that are held at the date of this treaty by either of the parties, and the people of New Mexico; such restoration to be full and complete without regard to the number of prisoners held." The treaty also called for the Navajos to deliver three hundred sheep and one hundred head of mules and horses, "such delivery to be made as indemnity in full for the expenses incurred by the people of the United States in this campaign."

The treaty did not mention property held by the Navajos that was claimed by the New Mexicans simply because, as Newby pointed out in his letter to Adjutant General Jones, "the Mexicans had succeeded previously to my departure from this place (Beautiful Mountain), in taking from the Indians by stealth, immense numbers of cattle and sheep, leaving the Indians with about as much as properly belonged to them." Newby added that, as of June 17, "the exchange of prisoners have been fully complied with, and that twelve Mexican captives have been restored to their relatives." Newby, who was mustered out of service October 16, 1848, did make an effort to return Navajo children to their parents in accordance with the terms of the treaty, but no contemporary records exist to indicate the degree of success attained. Later records suggest it was not great. Once again the Navajos had signed "paper" with the Americans and once again they had returned captives and had watched their sheep and cattle— some obtained by stealth and some not—driven off by their enemies. And, once again, they waited in vain for the return of their women and children held by the New Mexicans. They no longer admired nor feared the "New Men" but now held them in contempt as worthy allies of the *Hispanos*.

Fort Sumner, on the Pecos River near the New Mexico-Texas border. A majority of the Dineh, already poor, hungry and demoralized, were rounded up by troops under the command of Kit Carson (along with Ute allies), and taken there in 1864.

*This action was taken on the part of the Federal commander
at Santa Fe, General James H. Carleton, because he was convinced that gold and "great mineral riches" could be found
in Dinehtah once the Navajo were "removed to a reservation."*

Bosque Redondo (Fort Sumner), was four years of pure horror for the Navajos. Crops failed, shelter and firewood were virtually non-existent and Comanches raided almost at will.

The situation became so desperate that Senator Charles Sumner of Massachusetts denounced General Carleton and Governor Henry Connelly in Congress for practicing "Indian slavery."

Barboncito, the eloquent spokesman who succeeded in gaining permission for the Navajos' return to Dinehtah in 1868.

Pedro and Anrelina, a young married couple, were photographed by Ben Wittick in the 1880s. The clothing, no doubt, reflects the Navajo mode of dress at the time. Certainly the abundance of silver jewelry is an indication of how well the Navajos had recovered since returning from Ft. Sumner.

Fort Defiance, 1869, only a year after the Navajos signed a treaty with the United States and were allowed to return from

"The Long Walk." The gathering was probably one of the monthly "ration days" when food and supplies were dispersed.

Another view, probably taken on the same day as the photograph on the preceding pages. Beef, flour, coffee and salt—

and occasionally tobacco and sugar—were distributed along with seed, sheep and farm tools to heads of families.

The famed headman Ganado
Mucho (Tot'sonii Hastiin), wearing deerskin trousers and buckskin
leggins with silver buttons is
flanked by Mariano (right) and
another headman. Along with
Barboncito and Manuelito,
Ganado Mucho made up the trio
of most respected headmen in the
years before The Long Walk.

The delegation that met President Grant on December 10, 1874. General Arny is standing at left; Manuelito sits at front center, flanked by his wife Jaunita (left) and his sons, Manuelito Segundo and Tiene-suse, at right.

After the return from Fort Sumner, their herds of sheep became the most important source of the Navajos' livelihood. At left

is an old style forked-stick or "male" hogan. Very few hogans have been built in this style in recent years.

Black Horse, the sternly defiant man on the left, was one of those who strongly opposed the idea of sending Navajo children to the white men's schools. Manuelito led the pro-school faction until his sons contacted an infectious disease and died at a boarding school in Pennsylvania.

THREE

The Death of Narbona

In spite of the fact that the Americans failed to honor the Newby treaty, at least to any degree of success in returning Navajo captives, Narbona and the other Navajo Naataani were able to keep Manuelito and his followers, the "war party" of the Navajos, from raiding the stock of the New Mexican ranchers throughout the remainder of 1848 and until August, 1849, at which time Americans were in the field with the largest expedition yet sent against the Navajos.

Newby was replaced in Santa Fé by Colonel James Macrae Washington who was appointed to serve in the dual role of military commander and civil governor of the territory. Where Doniphan had been most favorably disposed toward the Navajos and Newby had authored a treaty that, had it been carried out to the letter, would have given the *Dineh* reason to cease warring on the New Mexicans, Washington, on the other hand, did not consider appeasing the Indians a part of his duties. Interpreting his orders to the letter, he concluded that his job began and ended with the protection of the Spanish-American settlements. With that goal in mind he mustered an auxiliary force of 393 volunteers in early spring, 1849. The auxiliary force, comprised of a cross-section of society that included a number of American adventurers recently arrived in New Mexico, was divided into four companies. They were sworn in to serve for a period of six months at a cost to the United States carefully calculated by Washington, of $43,433. One member of the volunteer force, a thirty-two-year-old lawyer from Missouri named Henry Linn Dodge, was to play a very important role in Navajo affairs in the years to come.

Washington could not help but have been aware that a goodly number of his new troops were *Hispano* slave raiders. Too, he must have known that the New Mexicans were breaking the peace within weeks after he took over his command—an unsanctioned expedition took two small Navajo girls captive in January, 1849—but there is not one mention of the slave-raiding activities of the New Mexicans in his official correspondence. An experienced Indian fighter in campaigns against the Creeks and Seminoles in the South, Washington, as an artillery expert, also played a passive role in helping remove the Cherokees to Oklahoma along the tragic "trail of tears" that brought about the death of one-fourth of the people of that highly civilized nation. No doubt that experience recommended him for his post in New Mexico. As Frank McNitt has pointed out, ". . . in his official orders and letters as military governor he reveals nothing of himself beyond the vague, faceless image of authority—stern, though not overbearing, and among his officers inclined less to gregariousness than to aloof reserve." (McNitt, Oklahoma, 1964: xlv.) The unbending Washington was to become a formidable foe indeed to the Navajos and especially to the aged Narbona who wished only to see his people make an honorable peace with the Bilagáana before his death.

On July 22, James S. Calhoun arrived in Santa Fé, having been appointed the first Indian agent to the New Mexico Territory by President Zachary Taylor. A resident of Georgia and a veteran of the Mexican War, Calhoun was a political appointee with little or no previous knowledge of the Indians in his charge. Both Annie Heloise Abel, who collected Calhoun's official letters while he was Indian agent and later civil governor of New Mexico, and H.H. Bancroft have stated that there was much more to Calhoun's appointment than his modest office might indicate. According to Bancroft, Calhoun "declared that he had secret instructions from the government in Washington to induce the people to form a state government. For a time the plan received but little support, but in the course of the summer and fall an excitement was raised (by Calhoun and several prominent New Mexicans), and both parties, state and territorial, published addresses to the people..." (Bancroft, IBID, 1889: 446-47.) Apparently Calhoun was sent to New Mexico solely for national political purposes and was to let Washington take care of the Indians—at least in the beginning.

While some historians have credited Calhoun for devising the "show of might" sent against the Navajos less than a month after he arrived in Santa Fé that brought about the murder of Narbona, indications are that Washington had already formulated plans for the offensive and Calhoun merely took credit for it. In a letter dated July 7, 1849, two weeks before Calhoun arrived in Santa Fé, Washington write Adjutant General Roger Jones: "Within the last three weeks several of the inhabitants have been murdered... and a considerable quantity of their stock run off. In these outrages, which have been confined to the Eutaws (Utes) and Apaches, the Navajoes and Comanches appear also to have been recently engaged. From their numbers and formidable character, greatly increased exertions have become necessary to suppress them." In a second letter to Jones on August 5, Washington wrote: "From the repeated depredations committed on the settlements of New Mexico by the Navajoe Indians, and which have lately been attended by the murder of some of the inhabitants, it has become necessary to make a campaign against them. Accordingly I expect, in a few days, to set out in sufficient force to insure the most favorable results—one of which will probably be to lay the foundation of a lasting peace." Perhaps Colonel Washington had been misinformed or deliberately planned a campaign against the Navajos to gain favor with his superiors. More likely, he was acting under secret orders from Washington. The latter possibility will be taken up later.

As several historians have pointed out, including David Brugge who has done extensive basic research on the period, there is not one single piece of evidence in either the official archives or the church records that indicate the Navajos broke the Newby treaty. No deaths are attributed to the Navajos from the date of the signing of the Newby treaty until *after* Washington was in the field and at least eight Navajos had been killed by members of his expedition. Nor, for that matter, is there any contemporary report of a specific case of Navajos taking livestock during the period.

Considering Washington's past performance, his conduct on the expedition, and his personality, the possibility that he devised the campaign purely for personal gain and duped Calhoun into going along with it certainly exists. Only a week after Calhoun arrived in Santa Fé, he wrote a letter to Indian Commissioner William Medill, dated July 29, 1849, stating, ". . . it is the opinion of Colonel Washington that any attempt to conciliate the tribes who have caused the recent and present troubles in this territory, would have a very serious tendency. The Indians presuming upon their knowledge of safe retreats in the mountains, and our entire ignorance of all avenews (Calhoun's spelling), excepting established military roads and well-known trails, are not to be subjected to just restraints until they are properly chastised. When they shall feel themselves so chastised, they will sue for peace."

Washington issued orders for the expedition, typically planned to the last detail, on August 14. Early on the morning of August 16, the column, consisting of 178 soldiers, 123 New Mexican civilians, and a force of sixty Pueblo Indians left Fort Marcy. Bringing up the rear was a pack train of mules, carrying, among other things, one six-pound field gun, three twelve-pound howitzers, thirty days' rations for 500 men and tents for everyone. Calhoun accompanied the expedition, and numbered among its ranks were Henry Linn Dodge, who would serve as Indian agent to the Navajos from 1853 until his death three years later and gain a lasting place in the hearts of the *Dineh* for his interest in their welfare; Major Henry Lane Kendrick, who would command Fort Defiance from 1852 until 1857; Lieutenant James Hervey Simpson, who authored a detailed journal of the expedition, and Sandoval, the traitorous Navajo headman from Cebolleta.

The expedition reached Jemez on the eighteenth and left that pueblo four days later, taking a line of march directly toward Canyon de Chelly. It entered the southeast outskirts of *Dinehtah* on August 24, an event occasioned by the desertion of seven of the New Mexican mounted militia. Lieutenant Simpson, who accompanied the expedition to make "such a survey of the country as the movements of the troops will permit," later stated that: "The object of the expedition was to coerce the Navajos into a compliance with a treaty which they made three years previous (actually one year and three months previous), under Colonel Nuby (Newby) of the volunteers; and at the same time extend the provisions of the treaty, so that they would be put in the same relation to the government of the United States, as the tribes counterminous to our old western frontier are, to wit: the Creeks, Choctaws, Cherokees, Seminoles, Winnebagos and others." (Simpson, 1852: 5.)

The expedition camped on Torreon Arroyo August 25, where three more of the New Mexican militia deserted. The area was then, as now, heavily populated by Navajos. Simpson in his detailed journal does not mention making contact with the Navajos there. But the *Dineh,* living in their small isolated ranches, were well aware of the advance of the large column into *Dinehtah* and deserted their homes and fields, took to the canyons and mountains, and watched the soldiers destroy their hogans and crops.

While Navajo scouts kept the expedition in sight at all times, the first physical contact was not made with any of The People until the troops camped at Badger Springs, the present site of the Naschiti Trading Post, on August 29. Richard Kern, a civilian working as Simpson's assistant, recorded in his diary under that date: "When near camp saw a large band of Indians to the north—Our valiant escort (of New Mexican militia) brandished their arms & shouted most valiantly—One fellow in particular who had painted his face, hands, shirt & every part of his clothing as well as his mule, red, seemed particularly brave & to have centered in himself all the courage of Santa Anna & the sublime Mexican Republic—When within a mile of camp a large band of Indians appeared to be coming between us & it & we came in at a round gallop—Found the Navajos around & in camp—Three had been captured by the command & we had taken corn from their fields for our animals . . ."

That afternoon the camp of the soldiers was visited by several Navajos—members of Narbona's band—both men and women, who had collected fifteen horses and mules

241

and fifty sheep to turn over to the Americans as Washington had demanded of them. Within Simpson's diary entry for that date is the first known description of Navajo women in their natural habitat: "The women I noticed wore blankets, leggins, and moccasins—the blankets being confined about the waist by a girdle. They bestrode their horses *à la mode des hommes.* One of them, on horseback, had a child at her breast confined on its back to a board, the upper portion canopied by a frame of willow-work to protect its head from the weather."

While Simpson's journal would indicate that the Navajos gave up the livestock willingly at Badger Springs and relations with the Americans were most cordial, that was hardly the case indicated by Richard Kern's entry for the same date: "Had a talk with some Navajo Chiefs—all talk—they said if we were friends why did we take their corn, and they had nothing (to do) but submit although it was hard—Disavowed all connexion with those *(Dinehanaih* Navajos) beyond the mountains—Would not promise to meet us at Ché (Canyon de Chelly) but agreed to come in council tomorrow at 12 oclock & make peace—(Colonel Washington) sent off a large force to seize enough corn for our animals."

Actually Narbona, well aware of the presence and intent of the column of troops and militia in *Dinehtah,* requested a meeting with Washington. Colonel Washington had already sent word to the various headmen that he expected them to meet him at Canyon de Chelly to discuss the terms of a new peace treaty. Narbona and José Largo, another headman who was past the age of seventy, requested a meeting to name proxies to represent them at Canyon de Chelly as neither of them was strong or well enough to make the trip. In sending the sheep and the horses to Washington, the old headman requested that the troops leave the fields unharmed, a request that the American commander ignored. As quickly as possible the Navajo families of the Tunicha Valley gathered what food they could and fled to the safety of the mountains. The "Chiefs" who talked with Richard Kern were actually a group of men that Narbona had sent to ask for a meeting with Washington. Next Narbona had the young men of his band round up a thousand sheep and some cattle—much of it his own livestock—which was turned over to the expedition as "captured goods" being returned. Washington agreed to the meeting with Narbona and José Largo.

The following day, August 30, 1849, Narbona led several hundred—possibly a thousand—warriors to meet the Americans. Simpson wrote, ". . . dressed as they were in their costumes, they formed quite an interesting and formidable group. Several of the Navahos, I noticed, wore helmet-shaped caps which were in some instances heightened in picturesque effect by being set off with a bunch of eagles' feathers.

"One of them, I observed, had hair approaching to red and looked, as was observed by several, very much like a white man painted. Another man (Narbona), who was quite old and of very large frame, had a grave and contemplative countenance not unlike, as many of the officers remarked (I hope the comparison will be pardoned), that of General (George) Washington."

With the Navajos leading the way, the column advanced to Tuntsa Wash, a tributary of the Chaco, and camped about a mile southwest of the present Two Gray Hills Trading Post, where the troops, once again, laid waste to all the cornfields in the vicinity. While Narbona protested the destruction of the crops upon which the Navajos depended to see them through the coming winter, he did everything in his power to appease the Americans as indicated by the fact that he willingly turned over such a large number of his own livestock to them. That afternoon Washington and Calhoun told Narbona and the other headmen present that the troops had invaded *Dinehtah* to see that the Navajos complied with the Newby treaty; that they give up all Mexican captives (they, for the most part, had already done so) and all murderers of Mexicans who had secreted themselves among the tribe and all Mexican stock they had driven off since the establishment of the government of the United States over them (which they had done at the time of the signing of the Newby treaty). No mention was made of the fact that both the Americans and the New Mexicans had failed to fulfill the promises they had made in the Newby treaty. A meeting was scheduled for noon the next day.

Narbona, José Largo and a third headman, Archulette, rode into the American camp the following day and sat down in council with Washington and Calhoun. Through an interpreter, James Conklin of Santa Fé, Simpson wrote that "something like the following colloquy took place:

"Colonel Washington: Tell them that I wish them to go to Chelly, so that a treaty may be made with the whole nation. Tell them the treaty I wish to make with them is to establish the conditions they promised yesterday to comply with (which was to honor the Newby treaty). Tell them the treaty I propose to make with them will be based upon the demands I have already made; and the object, in addition, will be a permanent peace.

"Calhoun: Tell them they are lawfully in the jurisdiction of the United States and they must respect that jurisdiction . . . Tell them that after the treaty is made, their friends will be the friends of the United States, and their enemies the enemies of the United States. Tell them when any difficulty occurs between them and any other nation, by appealing to the United States they may get redress. Are they willing to be at peace with all the friends of the United States?

"Interpreter: They say they are willing.

"Calhoun: Tell them that by the treaty which it is proposed to make with them, all trade between themselves and other nations will be recognized as under the regulations to be prescribed by the United States.

"Colonel Washington: And the object of this is to prevent their being imposed upon by bad men.

"Calhoun: Tell them if any wrong is done them by a citizen of the United States, or by a Mexican, he or they shall be punished by the United States, as if the wrong had been done by a citizen of the United States, and on a citizen of the United States. That the people of the United States shall go in and out of their country without molestation, under such regulations as shall be prescribed by the United States. Tell them that, by this treaty, the government of the United States are (sic) to be recognized as having the right to establish military posts in their country wherever they may think it necessary, in order to (assure) the protection of them and their rights. That the government of the United States claim the right to have their boundaries fixed and marked, so as to prevent any misunderstanding on this point between them and their neighbors.

"Interpreter: They say they are very glad.

"Calhoun: For and in consideration of all this, and a

244

faithful performance of the treaty, the government of the United States will, from time to time, make them presents, such as axes, hoes, and other farming utensils, blankets, &c."

According to the interpreter, Conklin, Narbona, José Largo and Archulette all agreed to the vague terms of the proposal. As both Narbona and José Largo were very old and ill, possibly they did, but it does not seem probable that they would agree to let military posts be established in *Dinehtah* and give the United States the right to establish boundaries for a few "axes, hoes, and other farming utensils, blankets" and fail to mention the all-important matter of the return of Navajo captives. Ironically, Calhoun's ignorance of Navajo culture is only too apparent in the mention of blankets. At that time blankets of Navajo manufacture were already eagerly sought throughout the West.

At any rate both Narbona and José Largo signed papers granting full authority to two younger men, Armijo and Pedro José, to act for them at the proposed Canyon de Chelly council "in the same manner and to the same extent as they would do were they present."

Following the council Sandoval addressed an assemblage of, according to Simpson, two or three hundred Navajos, explaining the terms of the treaty that was to be signed at Canyon de Chelly. During this harangue a New Mexican member of Washington's command spotted a horse that he said had been stolen from him. Whereupon Washington demanded that the horse be immediately returned to the New Mexican. The man on the horse fled but Washington said that unless they restored the horse immediately the assembled Navajos would be fired upon. The Navajos, sensing the hostile intent, turned and fled, some on horseback and some afoot. Washington ordered the guard to start firing.

Richard Kern wrote in his diary: "Navajoes crowding around us in great numbers—Council met—Agreed to the terms & some agreed to meet us at Ché in person & two old chiefs Narbona (head chief) & José Largo by deputy and gave power of attorney to others—The council was dissolved, when a Spaniard (one of the Mexican militia) said a horse had been stolen from him some time ago—the horse was among the Navajoes & he could identify him—The Col.

ordered the horse to be given up—The Mexican advanced to get him, when Narbona said Something in Navajoe & the horseman rode off—Col. W. gave the word to fire—the guard did so & at the first shot the Indians broke & fled up a ravine to the N(orth). The six pounder was fired 3 times at them, and a force sent in pursuit—Narbona the head chief was shot in 4 or 5 places and Scalped." According to Robert V. Hine, biographer of Richard Kern's brother, Edward, who was also present, both the Kerns were later furious with themselves because, in the excitement, they had not secured Narbona's head for a scientist friend.

Calhoun wrote a letter, dated October 1, 1849, to Indian Commissioner William Medill describing the events of August 31: "As an ernest of their intentions, (the Navajos) delivered to us one hundred and thirty sheep and some four or five mules and horses (Calhoun's count was, of course, far short of the actual number). This accomplished, orders were given to prepare to resume our march. In the mean time, the Indians were all permitted to descend from the heights, and to occupy a level space, commencing within fifty paces of the Governor's Quarters—The Actings and doings of the parties were duly explained to them by a long and noisy harangue from a Navajo (Sandoval). They were further informed that a certain horse, which was pointed out to them, was the property of a Pueblo Indian then present, and that the horse must be delivered to the proper owner at once. The fact of having stolen the horse was not denied, but a statute of limitation was suggested by the reply, that the horse had been rode back to the country from where the animal was taken, and that that was the time to have claimed him, and ended by the enquiry why he was not then claimed—This conversation was reported to Governor Washington in the presence of several Chiefs, who were distinctly notified by him that he required the immediate delivery of the horse—The Chiefs, among them the Senior Chief (Narbona) . . . left the Governor's tent, as was supposed, to instruct their people what they should do. The Governor, having waited a sufficient length of time without the return of a single Chief, or any report from them, ordered a small detachment of the guard to proceed to the crowd, with instructions to the officer of the guard to demand the immediate surrender of the horse, and walked out, in person, to superintend the execution of the order—

The demand not producing the desired effect, Lieut. (Lorenzo) Torez, the officer of the guard, was directed by the Governor to seize the horse and his rider, and to bring them before him. The moment the guard was ordered forward, every Navajo Indian in the crowd, supposed to number three to four hundred, all mounted and armed (again Calhoun is incorrect), and their arms in their hands, wheeled, and put the spur to their horses; upon which, the Governor ordered the guard to fire. The Senior Chief, Narbona, was left lifeless upon the ground, and several others were found dead in the vicinity. The Indians did not attempt to fire until their own and our forces were scattered, when feeble efforts to kill and cut off small parties were unsuccessfully made. Except for the killing of a few horses, and the loss of a few mules, we sustained no injury."

As for Colonel Washington, he immediately ordered the command to break camp and march on toward Canyon de Chelly, apparently considering the murder of Narbona and seven others of little importance.

At sunset, having prepared his body for burial, two of Narbona's sons carried the corpse, wrapped in a buffalo pelt with his jewelry, his buckskin war helmet and bows and arrows and dropped it into a deep crevice. They stayed for four days and nights on a nearby hill, mourning for the respected headman who had been instrumental in keeping the Navajos off the war trail. Word of his death quickly spread across *Dinehtah.*

Zarcillos Largos, long the most zealous advocate of peace among the Navajo headmen, mourned the death of his old friend and decided he would neither attend the Canyon de Chelly council nor sign any peace treaties with the Americans. Not only had they failed to keep their promises to have Navajo slaves freed and to protect the *Dineh* from Mexican slave-hunters made in the last treaty, but now they had invaded *Dinehtah* for no good reason, destroyed crops everywhere they went and killed the most revered of all Navajos. The time for talking peace had passed. Zarcillos Largos decided to fight.

Manuelito, Narbona's son-in-law, had long openly and violently disagreed with the aged headman's efforts to make peace with the Americans and had already led many young men away from his influence.

Now many others flocked to his side, shocked by the murder and utterly repulsed by the scalping of Narbona—a practice the *Dineh* looked upon with absolute abhorrence. Manuelito promised to drive all white men out of Navajo country. As Colonel Washington blithely marched on toward his "peace meeting" at Canyon de Chelly, Manuelito went on the warpath behind him and began what was apparently a concentrated effort to steal every head of sheep and cattle in New Mexico. One bold foray followed another with Manuelito leading but a few warriors who struck the frontier ranches suddenly, then vanished back into the mountainous timberlands taking hundreds of heads of livestock with him. As soon as the sheep and cattle was distributed among Navajo families, he led still another raid from his home near Dibébito.

On the very day that Washington reached the vicinity of Canyon de Chelly, September 5, a group of Navajos—probably followers of Manuelito—ambushed two messengers carrying mail to the expedition about forty miles east of Tunicha. The Navajos were prudent in not attacking the main column of Americans but they did harass its flanks. On the day after Narbona was killed a Navajo guide attempted—and failed—to lead a small force under the command of Major Henry L. Kendrick into an ambush. Lieutenant Simpson decided that the Navajos were "tricky and unreliable!"

On the morning of September 5 a party that included Simpson, Washington, Calhoun and the Kern brothers visited what Simpson called "the renowned Canyon de Chelly." Continuing, the chronicler of the Washington expedition wrote: "This canyon has been for a long time of distinguished reputation among the Mexicans, on account of its great depth and impregnability—the latter being not more due to its inaccessibility than to the fort which it is said to contain. This fort, according to Carravahal (a Mexican guide), is so high as to require fifteen ladders to scale it, seven of which, as he says, on one occasion he ascended, but not being permitted to go higher he did not see the top of it."

Actually the party was a bit lost and was, as McNitt has pointed out, "exploring the head of Canyon del Muerto." (McNitt, Ibid, 1964: 82n.) McNitt and others have suggested that the Navajo fort referred to by Carravahal was probably Massacre Cave which is located near the head of Canyon del Muerto, but I disagree. The small, natural indention called by that name can be seen from the floor of the Canyon and could never be mistaken for a fort. Actually the legend of a "Navajo Fort" that was supposed to exist deep in Canyon de Chelly dated back at least a hundred years among Spanish soldiers. As for the Carravahal story about the seven ladders, I suspect he was lying in an attempt—apparently successful—to impress the Americans.

At dusk the next afternoon the expedition reached the wide valley west of the mouth of Canyon de Chelly and camped on the bank of the Chinle Wash, near the present Thunderbird Lodge in the midst of Navajo cornfields that furnished "an abundance of forage for the animals and fine roasting ears for the men . . ."

Simpson wrote: "It was somewhat exciting to observe, as we approached the valley of Chelly, the huts (hogans) of the enemy, one after another, springing up into smoke and flame, and their owners scampering off in flight." According to Kern the hogans were set aflame by the Navajos "as signals"—but signals for whom? The hogans were burned by the troops on orders from Colonel Washington.

On the morning of September 7, Sandoval went out looking for Navajo "chiefs" and brought in one headman, a man with little influence named Mariano Martínez, who was presented to Washington as the "principal chief of the Navahos." Mariano Martínez, dressed in a sky-blue greatcoat of American manufacture, buckskin leggins and moccasins, and a narrow-brim Mexican tarpaulin hat, assured Washington that he and his people desired to make a peace with the Americans. He promised the American commander that he and the other "chiefs" would gather at the American camp in two days—September 9—to sign the peace treaty and was presented with a list of "stolen property" that was to be restored on demand from Washington: 1,070 head of sheep, thirty-four head of mules, nineteen head of horses and seventy-eight head of cattle. While protesting that the Apaches must have stolen the cattle, he promised to replace the stock and apparently sent a subordinate off to round it up and to inform the "chiefs" of the peace council for he, himself, accompanied Lieutenant Simpson, with an escort of sixty men, who made a reconnaissance of

Canyon de Chelly the next day.

Entering the mouth of the canyon, the Simpson party took the left, or north branch—Canyon del Muerto—and travelled for a distance of nine and a half miles looking for the mythical "famous fort of the Navajos." The party saw Navajo hogans, peach orchards, fields and numerous Navajos who "appeared very friendly" but found no fort. Lieutenant Simpson did make tactical observations that would, in 1864, prove most valuable to the New Mexican militia under the command of Colonel Christopher "Kit" Carson. Simpson wrote: "Should it ever be necessary to send troops up this canon, no obstruction would be found to prevent the passage of artillery along its bottom. And should it at the same time, which is not at all unlikely, be necessary that a force should skirt the heights above to drive off assailants from that quarter, the south bank should be preferred because less interrupted by lateral branch canons."

The next day two "chiefs," Mariano Martínez and Chapitone, the headman of the San Juan Navajos who had signed the Newby treaty, met with the Americans in council, bringing with them 104 sheep, four mules and horses and four captives, with the promise to deliver the remainder of the stock the Americans asked to be restored to Jemez within thirty days. One of the captives was a man named Josea Ignacio Anane who asked to remain with the Navajos. Calhoun, in his *Official Correspondence*, says that Anane was captured "when quite a boy, by a roving band of Navajoes, at Tuckalotoe (Tecolote). His parents then lived in Santa Fe, where he supposed they now reside. He is the fortunate possessor of two wives and three children, living at Mecina Gorda (Big Oak), north of Cheille two and a half days' travel. I do not think he is under many restraints, for he prefers most decidedly to remain with the Navajoes . . ." The other captives were identified by Calhoun as "Anto Josea, about 10 years old, taken from Jemez where his parents now live . . . He was well treated . . . Teodosia Gonzáles, twelve years of age, was taken about six years ago, from a corral near the Río Grande . . . He was well treated . . . Marceito, eighteen years of age, was taken at Socorro . . . He has evidently been a captive many years, as he has entirely forgotten his native tongue. The novelty of a home, as explained to him, seemed to excite him somewhat."

The treaty that Mariano Martínez and Capitone—and also Sandoval—signed, representing themselves and their actions as binding to the whole of the Navajo nation, spelled out the terms presented to Narbona, José Largo and Archulette, and while it called for the Navajos to surrender all the prisoners they held, it did not mention those held by the New Mexicans. Lieutenant Simpson and apparently Washington too were satisfied with the treaty and considered it binding on the part of the *entire Navajo nation.* Simpson said: "All that could be accomplished by the expedition, then, may be considered as having been accomplished. A full and complete treaty had been made with the Navajos, by which they have put themselves under the jurisdiction and control of the government of the United States, in the same manner and to the same extent as the tribes bordering the United States. The portion of the captives and stolen property near enough to be made available have been given up, and the remainder has been promised to be restored within a determinate period. Added to this, what is of no inconsiderable value, the troops have been enabled to penetrate into the very heart of their country, and thus a geographical knowledge has been obtained which cannot but be of the highest value in any future military demonstration it may be necessary to make.

"It is true that the Navajos may fail to comply with the terms of the treaty . . . but should any future coercion become necessary, it would be but a just retribution and, in a manner, their own act." Ironically, the Washington treaty, effected by an expedition that served only to renew hostilities between the Americans, the New Mexicans and the Navajos, was one of only two made with the *Dineh* that were ever ratified by Congress.

In the afternoon following conclusion of the treaty, a hundred Navajo warriors entered the American camp and traded blankets, dressed skins and peaches from the Canyon de Chelly orchards for trinkets and accouterments from the uniforms of the soldiers. In concluding the treaty Mariano Martínez brought what Simpson described as "a beautiful mule" into the camp to present to Washington as a present which was "graciously declined" by the Colonel. Under the given circumstances and in consideration of the Navajo custom, such a refusal was an unforgiveable insult to the

251

Navajo headman.

The troops took up the line of march toward the Southeast at seven o'clock in the morning on September 10, having received a report that the Apaches had attacked Zuñi and killed a number of the inhabitants of that pueblo, and camped at Cañoncito Bonito (the future site of Fort Defiance) on the eleventh. They arrived at Zuñi on the fifteenth only to learn that the report of the Apache attack on the pueblo had been false. The Canyon de Chelly Navajos, aware that their eastern brethren had already taken to the war trail, probably made up the tale of the attack on Zuñi to speed the expedition out of *Dinehtah*. Soon after they arrived at Zuñi, and were given a cordial welcome by the governor of the pueblo, two Navajos rode in and turned a fourteen-year-old male captive Mexican over to the Americans.

Observing the body of a dead Indian a short distance from the pueblo, Washington was told by the Zuñi governor that it was that of a Navajo prisoner taken captive during a recent raid on the pueblo's sheep and killed by the Zuñis at the direction of some emigrants bound for California. The emigrants had outraged the Zuñis by commandeering, in the name of the government of the United States, a quantity of food and a number of horses and mules. Richard Kern, having failed to secure the head of Narbona, rode out "after supper" and cut off the head of the dead Navajo to send to his scientist friend.

The expedition terminated at Atrisco, a suburb of Albuquerque, on September 22, with orders for the different commands to march independently to Santa Fé as soon as practicable. Washington, Calhoun and Simpson arrived back in the capital on the twenty-third, apparently unaware that the Navajos had already invaded the Río Grande Valley. The next day they struck near the pueblo of Sandia and killed five New Mexicans virtually within shouting distance of the returning infantry. A week later Calhoun wrote to Indian Commissioner William Medill that "not a day passes without hearing of some fresh outrage, and the utmost vigilance of the military force in this country is not sufficient to prevent murders and depredations and there are but few so bold as to travel alone ten miles from Santa Fé."

For whatever purposes and intent it was made, Washington's campaign was a failure. His "show of might" failed to impress the Navajos. Instead of laying "the foundation of a lasting peace" he caused a complete rupture in Navajo-American relations, a fact of which he was apparently aware. On the day he returned to Santa Fé he wrote the adjutant general in Washington: "The vigilance and activity of our troops in protecting the inhabitants of the Territory against the numerous bands of hostile Indians have been unceasing and with few exceptions their efforts have been successful. The services rendered by the four companies of Volunteers which were mustered in last spring have contributed largely towards this result, and as the time of their engagement draws to a close, I am reminded of the necessity of retaining those companies that are mounted a while longer."

Two days later he got around to writing Adjutant General Jones about the death of Narbona. "After marching over a barren, badly watered, and, in many places, rough country for eight days, I arrived in the vicinity of the labores, or cornfields, of the Navajoes, at Tuna Cha. Here I first met with the Indians, and on the next day a party of them was fired upon by our troops, which resulted in killing and wounding several of them. Among the dead of the enemy left on the field was Narbona, the head chief of the nation, who had been a scourge to the inhabitants of New Mexico for the last thirty years." Once again Washington was terribly misinformed or was deliberately lying.

Later in the same report he said: "To secure a firm and durable peace with them, it will be necessary to plant a military post in their country," and recommended Tuna Cha (the Chuska Valley) or Sienega Grande (Cienega Amarilla, just south of the site where Colonel Edwin Vose Sumner would establish Fort Defiance in 1851) as sites for the proposed post.

Washington's expedition, penetrating *Dinehtah* under a flag of peace, had served to bring about war. The Navajos had seen their property taken and destroyed at will, their hogans burned and their most respected headman, a man who had advocated making peace with the Bilagáana, wantonly shot down; and were now expected to honor a peace paper signed by a traitor and two local headmen who were in no position to commit the *Dineh* to anything even if they had understood what they were doing.

FOUR

Calhoun's War on the Navajos

The possibility that there was an ulterior motive behind the Washington expedition looms ominously, and that Colonel Washington and Indian agent Calhoun were acting under secret orders from President Zachary Taylor and Adjutant General Roger Jones to reconnoiter *Dinehtah* to select possible sites for a future fort is a distinct possibility. In 1849, as Howard Roberts Lamar has pointed out, "New Mexico's future had become extremely involved with several national questions: the North-South fight over the extension of slavery into the Mexican Cession: the admission of California as a free state—which implied that New Mexico must declare for slavery in order to retain the traditional slave state-free state balance in the Senate . . ." (Lamar, Yale, 1966: 72.) Calhoun was a southerner and a Whig, as was the newly elected president who appointed him to the Santa Fé post, and they both advocated statehood for New Mexico. Annie Heloise Abel said, "Calhoun was most certainly sent to Santa Fé for a purpose but what the real purpose was does not appear (in his official correspondence). Somewhere, no doubt, and very probably in the *confidential* files of Interior, War, or State departments, there are papers that hold the secret." If New Mexico was to enter the union as a state some definite control would have to be placed over the Navajos and a fort placed within *Dinehtah* would have been—and would prove to be—the logical first step toward that objective. Too, the fact that Lieutenant James Hervey Simpson, of the Topographical Engineers, made such a detailed survey of *Dinehtah,* with special emphasis paid to the availability of grazing grass and water supply at several campsites and frequent references made to "future military expeditions" indicates that the primary purpose of the expedition was other than to "secure a lasting peace" with the Navajos. Just such a post—Fort Defiance—was established in the heart of *Dinehtah* exactly two years after the Washington expedition by Colonel Edwin Vose Sumner.

The San Juan headman, Capitone, apparently attempted to comply with the terms of the treaty he'd signed with Washington and reached Paguate, below Cebolleta, reportedly with additional captives and "stolen" property, early in October. He sent a message to Calhoun and Washington that he would be at San Ysidro on October 28 or 29 to turn over the captives and property to them but was probably deterred by mounting violence all along the frontier. Too, at about the time Capitone visited Paguate, Mexican traders in the vicinity were spreading a rumor that all the Pueblos, the New Mexicans and the Americans were planning a large new expedition with the intent of completely exterminating the *Dineh.*

Navajos attacked the Mexican village of Le Bugarito, also near Cebolleto, on October 5 and killed two residents and made off with a female captive. On October 15, a group of Zuñis, including the governor and the war captain, called on Calhoun and asked for arms, ammunition and permission to make a war of extermination on the Navajos. Meanwhile, Lieutenant Simpson, with an escort of dragoons, was in the vicinity of Cebolleta selecting a site for a new military outpost which was not established until the next autumn— at which time Calhoun reported that the Navajos and the Apaches had stolen 12,887 mules, 7,000 horses, 31,581 cattle and 453,293 sheep since the Americans had taken over the government in Santa Fé.

The new outpost was apparently a source of amusement to the Navajos. Two months after post commander Colonel Daniel T. Chandler arrived in Cebolleta with a force of seventy men, a small force of Navajos descended on the neighboring Mexican ranches and drove off several thousand head of sheep. In the next twelve months Colonel Chandler wore out all of the garrison's horses marching his troops all over the eastern outskirts of *Dinehtah* but was never able to engage the Navajos in a single battle. Washington was succeeded as military commander of the department by an interim commander, Colonel Edward F. Beall, who was replaced by Colonel John Munroe on October 23. Washington remained at Fort Marcy until April, 1850, when he was transferred to Fort Constitution in New Hampshire. Three years later, bound for a new command in California on the steamer *San Francisco,* he was washed overboard with three other officers and 180 soldiers off the capes of the Delaware. All but two perished, among them the dour Scotsman John Macrae Washington.

Colonel Munroe was a territorialist and was soon at loggerheads with Calhoun on virtually every phase of administering the department, including the control of the Navajos. The Indian agent recommended several measures for controlling the *Dineh.* Within a week after he returned from the Washington expedition he wrote Indian Commissioner Medill suggesting that the Navajos be put on a reservation, the limits of which would be "circumscribed, and distinctly marked out, and their departure from said limits to be under certain prescribed rules, at least for some time to come. Even this arrangement," he added, "would be utterly ineffective unless enforced by the military." This recommendation was, interestingly, a direct contradiction of Article III of the Newby Treaty which gave the Navajos permission "to visit all parts of the United States and of New Mexico."

Again in November Calhoun urged that the Navajos as well as the Utes, Apaches and Comanches be placed on reservations. In an effort to control unscrupulous traders—both Mexican and American—who were furnishing not only the Navajos but also the Utes, Apaches, Puebloans and Comanches with arms, ammunition and liquor, Calhoun posted the following notice the same month: "Licenses to trade with Indians will be granted by the undersigned, upon the following conditions, provided they are approved by His Excellency, Governor Munroe, Military Commander of this Department.

"Applicants must be citizens of the United States, produce satisfactory testimonials of good character, and give bond in a penal sum not *exceeding* five thousand dollars, with one or more sureties, that he will faithfully observe all the laws and regulations made for the government of trade and intercourse with the Indians tribes of the United States and in no respect violate the same, and they will not trade in fire-arms, powder, lead, or other munitions of war. Applicants will distinctly state what tribe they wish to trade with, and under a license granted, they will not be authorized to trade with others.

"For the present, no license will be granted authorizing trade or intercourse with the Apaches, Navajos or Utahs."

Of course there was no way to enforce the trade laws or to stop the illegal traders who, from the frontier towns of Abiquiu, Cebolleta and Cubero, ranged *Dinehtah* with impunity.

The Navajo offensive slackened during the winter months, but by spring, 1850, they were again on the war trail. In January a large expedition from Cebolleta entered *Dinehtah* and one of its victims was Capitone, the San Juan headman. Capitone's death only served to increase the fury of the Navajos, who kept the towns, ranches and pueblos on the west side of the Rio Grande constantly on the alert and in a state of anxiety throughout the year. In June direct attacks were made against both Jemez and Acoma, and from that month until October Zuñi substained almost constant attack. On October 12, 1850, Calhoun wrote Indian Commissioner Orlando Brown: "The Navajos a few days since made another attack on Zuñi, with a force, it is apprehended, that will have proved disastrous to the Pueblo, by the destruction of their crops." The siege the Navajos had put upon the pueblo was alleviated only when Colonel Munroe transferred a company of dragoons from the post at Cebolleta and armed the Zuñis with a shipment of obsolete muskets from army stores. In November another large expedition of New Mexicans invaded *Dine-* another large expedition of New Mexicans invaded *Dinehtah* to recapture 2,000 sheep the Navajos had taken from a Colorado, the expedition continued to Black Mesa where they attacked several Navajo camps, taking fifty-two prisoners as well as 5,000 sheep, eleven oxen and 150 horses and mules.

Meanwhile, President Zachary Taylor had died on July

9, 1850, and with him perished any chance of immediate statehood for New Mexico. In September Colonel Munroe was informed that Congress had organized a territorial government for New Mexico and that henceforth he was to "abstain from all further interference in civil as well as political affairs of that country." Near the close of the year Calhoun was nominated by President Millard Fillmore as governor of New Mexico, bringing an end to four years of military rule over the territory. His appointment was confirmed by Congress in January, 1851, and on March 3 he was installed as the first civil governor of New Mexico and also assumed the duties of Superintendent of Indian Affairs for the territory. The very next day he issued the following proclamation: "To the Caciques, Governors and Principals of (all the Pueblos of New Mexico): The savage Indians who are daily murdering and robbing the people of New Mexico, in which I include your Pueblo, must be exterminated or so chastised as to prevent their coming into or near your Pueblo. For this purpose you are directed to abstain from all friendly intercourse with the Navajo Indians and should they dare to come into your neighborhood, you are authorized to make war upon them, and to take their animals and such property as they may have with them, and to make divisions of the same according to your laws and customs."

The "savage Indians" did not include Sandoval and his *Dinehanaih.* Sandoval had led at least one expedition against the Navajos the year before and a week after Calhoun took office as governor a Baptist missionary named Hiram Reed who was visiting Cebolleta wrote: "A famous half-tamed Navajo Chief named Sandoval who resides in this vicinity, came into town today to sell some captives of his own nation which he recently took prisoners. He sold one young man of 18 years of age for thirty dollars."

Sandoval took advantage of the Navajo war by pursuing slave raiding with great vigor, as did the New Mexicans engaged in the profession. He followed up the raid reported by Reed almost immediately. On March 20, Calhoun reported in a letter to Commissioner of Indian Affairs Luke Lea: "Sandoval, our Navajo friend near Cebolleta, returned about the 20th of the month from a visit to his Navajo brethren with eighteen captives, a quantity of stock and several scalps."

This expedition was made against some Navajos living near Laguna Colorado who had been making peace overtures and considered themselves, at that time, allied with Sandoval's band. In a council with Colonel Daniel T. Chandler at Cebolleta, they complained: ". . . they stole everything we had, our horses, wives, children and even the sheepskins we slept on, and if we are killed it will not be much loss to the tribe. Besides we have relations with Sandoval and . . . thought his people would not hurt us."

Meanwhile Governor Calhoun had issued a proclamation, in granting permission for a large New Mexican militia expedition against the Navajos, that declared open season not only on the *Dineh* but on all Indians in the territory. On March 18, Calhoun was presented with a proposal drawn up by a New Mexican named Manuel Chavez requesting the governor's permission for Chavez to raise six companies of militia, 100 men to each company, to undertake a campaign against the Navajos. The proposal asked for the government to supply the expedition with 100 mules, 600 rifles, and ammunition in sufficient quantity to enable the militia to conduct the campaign to a successful termination. The New Mexicans asked for no pay, the only recompense they desired being to have "the disposal of the interests of the country they are to conquer, such as the disposal of captives, animals, cattle, etc."

Chavez, in offering to "pursue the Navajos to their extermination or complete surrender," took advantage of Calhoun's feud with Munroe by requesting that his volunteers not be subject to the "ineffectual" command of any officer of the regular army and promised they would, instead, "always be ready to obey the orders of the Civil Government of the Territory of New Mexico." Calhoun fully sanctioned the Chavez proposal and authorized the recruitment of the volunteers, but could not furnish them with the requested rifles as the issuance of weapons was under the sole control of Colonel Munroe. In giving his permission Governor Calhoun specially stated: "I further direct and order that the property which may be captured from any hostile tribe of Indians, by any company raised under the foregoing provisions, shall be disposed of in accordance with the laws and customs heretofore existing in this territory—until legislative action shall be had upon the subject, either by the Congress of the United States or

259

the Legislative Assembly of the Territory."

Following Chavez' success, the office of the governor was flooded with similar petitions from New Mexicans who desired official sanction of their expeditions into *Dinehtah* which, of course, were to be made for the explicit purpose of garnering a quick profit on captives and stolen property. Calhoun granted permission for each and every petition as long as he was in power to do so and, of course, his actions only incited the Navajos to further depredations. The Navajos, masters at offensive warfare, had long been in the habit of vanishing into the mountains when invaded rather than make a defensive stand. But as expedition after expedition invaded their homeland they began to alter their tactics. For example, early in June when a large expedition of New Mexicans invaded *Dinehtah*, they stood their ground and killed eight of the New Mexicans while losing two men and one woman. Following the expedition back toward the Rio Grande, they attacked Laguna and raided nearby ranches.

Calhoun's proclamation officially sanctioned Indian slavery—and Indian slave raiding—and that was the way matters stayed in New Mexico until a federal law outlawed such slavery in 1867. Both institutions continued "unofficially" for several more years.

On July 19, 1851, Colonel Munroe was replaced as commander of the Ninth Military Department, which included almost all of New Mexico and Arizona, by Colonel Edwin Vose Sumner. Sumner arrived in Santa Fé with specific instructions from Secretary of War C. M. Conrad to strengthen frontier defenses and with drastic plans to reorganize the costly command. Conrad's orders to Sumner were to "revise the whole system of defense (for the) protection of New Mexico (and) the defense of the Mexico territory, when we are bound to protect against the Indians within our borders . . . to remove the troops out of the towns where they are now stationed and . . . more towards the frontier and nearer the Indians." Conrad added: "From all the information that has reached the Department, it is induced to believe that no permanent peace can exist with the Indians, and no treaty will be regarded by them until they have been made to feel the power of our arms. You will, therefore, as early as practicable, make an expedition against the Navajos . . ."

Sumner was also instructed to "act in concert with the Superintendent of Indian Affairs in New Mexico, whom you will allow to accompany you in the expedition into the Indian territory . . ."

"My first step," Sumner reported later, "was to break up the post at Santa Fé, that sink of vice and extravagance . . ." He also withdrew the garrisons from Las Vegas, Rayado, Cebolleta, Albuquerque, Socorro, Dõna Ana, San Elizario and El Paso; transferred one company of dragoons and two companies of infantry to Fort Fillmore, which he established at Cottonwood, midway between El Paso and Dona Ana to restrict the Apaches and the south plains tribes from making their frequent forays into Mexico; erected a new post which he named Fort Conrad at Valverde and another near Mora which he named Fort Union and designated as departmental headquarters to replace Fort Marcy.

Governor Calhoun and the citizens of Santa Fé, of course, protested the removal of the troops from Fort Marcy, to which Sumner replied to Adjutant General Jones: "I understand that many applications have been made to the government, by the people of Santa Fé, to have the troops ordered back there. I have no hesitation in saying that I believe most of these applications proceed directly or indirectly from those who have hitherto managed to live, in some way, from the extravagant expenditures of the government. I trust their petitions will not be heeded."

If Santa Fé disgusted him, the citizens of his new command fared no better. In Sumner's opinion: "The New Mexicans are thoroughly debased and totally incapable of self-government, and there is no latent quality about them that can ever make them respectable.

"They have more Indian blood than Spanish, and in some respects are below the Pueblo Indians, for they are not as honest or as industrious."

And as for Calhoun, Sumner said: "No civil Government emanating from the Government of the United States can be maintained here without the aid of a military force; in fact, without its being virtually a military government . . . All branches of this civil government have equally failed—the executive for want of power, the judiciary from the total incapacity and want of principle in juries; and the legislative from want of knowledge." Later he seriously recommended that the status of the territory be reduced to that of a protectorate and that the military, for which supplies were brought at great expense from the East, be withdrawn. Fortunately, for New Mexico, his suggestion received no support in Washington.

Sumner immediately saw that the New Mexican militias sanctioned by Calhoun were a source rather than a deterrent of Indian troubles and suggested that they be stopped and the Navajos put under the surveillance of the regular army for their own protection as well as that of the Mexican, Pueblo and Anglo population of New Mexico. His disapproval of Calhoun's administration and Indian policies soon deepened to the level of personal contempt. Most historians have maligned Sumner and sided with Calhoun in the bitter feud. Annie Heloise Abel, among others, attributed Calhoun's health failure and death in May, 1852, ten months after Sumner's arrival in New Mexico, to harrassment and opposition on the part of the military commander. Since Calhoun died of a combination of jaundice and scurvy such speculation cannot be taken seriously.

While he was bullheaded and arrogant, Sumner's opposition to Calhoun's administration was, for the most part, justified, as was his sincere belief that he, himself, was the logical director of Indian affairs in the territory. Calhoun's militia of New Mexicans had inflamed the whole department in an all-out war. He gave arms to Sandoval's band while paying heed to such statements made by that traitor to his people as: "All Navajos ought to be whipped badly, or they will not keep any treaty made . . . Destroying their corn fields and taking their stock, would be a greater punishment to them than the loss of a few men."

On the other hand Sumner was able to bring an end to the Navajo war, at least temporarily, by ignoring Calhoun's policies and instituting his own. With the removal of the garrisons to their new posts, Sumner began making preparations to comply with Conrad's instructions to initiate a campaign against the Navajos. Calhoun, of course, expected to accompany the expedition but much to his surprise—and in direct disobedience of Conrad's orders to the contrary— Sumner refused the request of the civil governor to accompany him into *Dinehtah*. Next Calhoun asked permission for three newly appointed Indian agents to be permitted to accompany the expedition. Not only was this request refused but Sumner also refused to furnish a military escort to see the Indian agents to their posts. It was Sumner's opinion, and a correct one under the circumstances, that Indian agents did more harm than good. Calhoun made one final request. As he had never visited either the Hopi villages or the Apaches, he asked the military commander for an escort to do so. As it would have taken virtually every man in Sumner's command to see Calhoun safely through *Dinehtah* to the Hopi villages and to protect him from the Apaches who were also at war, he was again refused.

Colonel Sumner assembled four companies of cavalry, one of artillery, and two of infantry at Santo Domingo and marched out on the morning of August 17, followed by a van of forty wagons carrying supplies, ammunition, two mountain howitzers, and camp equipment. Skirting the southern boundaries of *Dinehtah*, the expedition visited Laguna and Zuñi, halting at each pueblo long enough to confirm the friendship of the inhabitants and to recruit a few Indian allies. From Zuñi the command marched north, retracing the trail taken by the Washington expedition after they left Canyon de Chelly, and camped at Cañoncito Bonito. Called Tsehootsooi (Meadows Between the Rocks) by the Navajos, Cañoncito Bonito had been singled out by Simpson for not only its beauty but also for the availability of a plentiful water supply and "green luxuriant grass." At that time the site was a favorite rendezvous for the Navajos not only because of the existence of several springs in the vicinity but also because it was considered holy.

While camped at Cañoncito Bonito, the Americans were visited by one lone Navajo who was sent by Sumner to inform all the headmen in the vicinity to assemble for a council. The Navajos, still at war, did not trust the American and ignored Sumner's request, whereupon the commander moved on to Canyon de Chelly with part of the artillery, the two mountain howitzers and the cavalry, leaving the remainder of the artillery, the infantry and the wagon train at Cañoncito Bonito under the command of Major Electus Backus. Colonel Sumner's intention was, in his own words, "to attack the Indians" at Canyon de Chelly and force them into submission.

But as the troops penetrated deeper into the redrock country of the Navajos, it soon became apparent that they were outnumbered and the anticipation of attacking the Indians was soon replaced by fear of ambush. When they neared the western mouth of the canyon, Navajos began to gather about the command's flanks in ever-increasing numbers. Dragoon James A. Bennett wrote in his diary on the night of August 27: "The Indians still keep with us by day. At night we can occasionally see their fires. A little after dark last night, the enemy fired several shots into our camp. Wounded one man in the leg."

The next day Sumner entered the mouth of Canyon de Chelly with part of his command and, heeding the advice of Lieutenant James Hervey Simpson, sent the remainder of his troops, a small detachment of mounted dragoons, to skirt the heights of the south rim and ward off assailants from that quarter. Sumner cautiously led his command up the canyon floor, burning hogans and fields of ripening corn and destroying the orchards of peach trees—from which the troops first filled their pockets and haversacks. Expecting at any moment to confront a large force in this "stronghold of the Navajos," Sumner was surprised as an ever-increasing number of Navajos gathered on the north rim of the canyon to watch the progress of the Americans. Out of range of the guns of both detachments of the Americans, the Navajos shouted taunts and insults at the invaders and "commenced an attack upon the column with a few muskets and arrows, and by rolling down stones" from the top of the steep walls. Sumner ordered his men to scale the cliffs and dislodge the attackers, but they found it "utterly impractical to do so." Nightfall found the command encamped fifteen miles from the mouth of the canyon and the appearance of what one trooper described as "at least 1,000 little fires" above them on the heights with "the dark form of savages . . . moving around them."

Sumner decided, prudently, that it would be unwise to penetrate farther into the canyon, or, for that matter, to remain where they were for the duration of the night. At ten o'clock, under the cover of darkness, the troops re-saddled their mounts, retraced their steps back out of the canyon and bivouacked in Chinle Wash for the remainder of the night. The next morning the troops headed bck to Cañoncito Bonito, constantly harrassed by the Navajos.

Exactly when the decision to build an American fort at Cañoncito Bonito was made is not a matter of record.

264

Certainly the decision was made prior to the departure of Sumner's expedition from the Río Grande. And the possibility that the site was selected soon after the return of the Washington expedition certainly exists. At any rate, on the very day that Colonel Sumner left on his ineffectual reconnaissance of Canyon de Chelly, the construction of an adobe and log fort, built around a rectangular parade ground, was commenced under the supervision of Major Backus. Sumner paused at Cañoncito Bonito only long enough to rest his escort before returning to the Río Grande, leaving behind Major Backus and most of the troops to garrison the new post. The fort, located in the heart of *Dinehtah* and on a site considered holy by the Navajos, was named, appropriately, Fort Defiance by Colonel Edwin Vose Sumner.

FIVE

Fort Defiance

In establishing Fort Defiance at Cañoncito Bonito Colonel Sumner not only hoped to put an end to the Navajo war but also to stop the incursions against the Navajos by the New Mexicans. In a letter explaining his actions to Adjutant General Roger Jones dated November 20, 1851, Sumner said: "This predatory war has been carried on for two hundred years, between the Mexicans and the Indians, quite time enough to prove, that unless some change is made the war will be interminable. They steal women and children, and cattle, from each other, and in fact carry on the war, in all respects, like two Indian nations.

"This system of warfare will interfere very much with my measures, and indeed do away with all the advantages, that I confidently expect to reap from the establishment of Fort Defiance. This large post in the very midst of the Indians cannot fail to cramp them in all their movements, and it will harass them so much, that they will gladly make peace . . . provided they find that the post can protect, as well as punish."

But Colonel Sumner's plan to bring peace to New Mexico came close to being aborted even before Fort Defiance was officially established. Upon the return of the expedition to the Río Grande, Sumner learned that none of the factions involved—the Navajos, the New Mexican slave raiders, the Territorial Assembly nor Governor Calhoun—intended to cooperate with his plans. While Sumner was in the field the Navajos had made several successful raids in the Río Arriba country of the upper Río Grande and, following in the tracks of the returning troops, perpetrated a raid only eighteen miles from Santa Fé.

Calhoun, upon learning that Sumner's expedition had not as much as engaged the Navajos in a single military confrontation, again advocated sending armed civilians to war against the *Dineh* and was supported by the Territorial Assembly. Speaker of the House of Representatives Theodore D. Wheaton presented a petition to Calhoun a few days after Sumner's return requesting that the "hundreds of citizens who are anxious to make a campaign against the Navajos" be allowed to do so. Pointing out that the citizens he represented were no better armed than the Navajos, Wheaton requested that "arsenals and arms be distributed through (out) this country, so that these people could be furnished with arms and ammunition." In spite of the fact that the civilian militias had never proven effective against the Navajos, Wheaton said, "They could do more in one year to protect not only this but the Mexican frontier from the ravages of the different nations of Indians which surround us, than the regular army could do in three."

Calhoun, of course, agreed with Wheaton and wrote Secretary of State Daniel Webster: "Col. Sumner's expedition to the Navajo Country has been productive of no good, as yet, and if an effort I am now making fails, the people of the Territory, to some extent, will be forced to take care of themselves, or consent to lie down quietly, and be plundered and butchered."

On September 18, Sumner issued an order officially authorizing the construction of Fort Defiance. Actually the post had been under construction since Sumner left Cañoncito Bonito. Major Electus Backus was appointed commander of the fort. The post's garrison consisted of Company "G," First Dragoons; Company "K," Second Dragoons; Company "B," Second Artillery; and Company "F," Third Infantry. Sumner instructed Backus to treat the Navajos "with the utmost rigor, till they show a desire to be at peace. . . ." Calhoun, continuing to advocate the use of

267

civilian militias which would fall under his jurisdiction rather than that of the military commander, wrote to Daniel Webster on October 1: "It is folly to suppose that *less than two mounted regiments* . . . can preserve the quiet in this territory." He also informed Webster that he thought that the executive branch of the territorial government should have at its command munitions of war and authority to call out the militia at any time. Apparently—and fortunately for all concerned—Webster did not agree with the governor.

Meanwhile work on Fort Defiance, located seventy miles north of Zuñi and 190 miles west of Albuquerque, progressed, but not without difficulty. The most distant post from Washington of any in the army in point of time, Fort Defiance created tremendous supply problems for Colonel Sumner. He put the forty quartermaster wagons which had accompanied the expedition to use in transporting supplies and materials from Albuquerque to the new post. The Navajos watched with interest and alarm as the post, consisting of ten sets of officers' quarters, each eighteen feet square, five barracks, each 100 by 200 feet with accompanying kitchens, messrooms and company storerooms all built around a parade ground 200 by 300 yards, began to take shape. Later a hospital with the same dimensions as the barracks, with a kitchen to its rear, a combination guardhouse, office and smoke house, quarters for laundresses and miscellaneous storerooms were added to the post.

But as Sumner and Calhoun continued their war of words, the Navajos continued to make war on the Bilagáana into the fall of 1851. The construction of the fort only a few yards from springs considered holy by the *Dineh* so disgusted Zarcillos Largos, still the leader of the peace faction, that he personally led an attack on supply wagons taking materials to the site of the fort. The Navajos wounded several soldiers, but following this warning attack Zarcillos Largos again began advocating peace with the Americans. No doubt he saw that the American soldiers had come to *Dinehtah* to stay and that it would be foolish to continue fighting so large a force located near Navajo ranches and homes.

Calhoun, in a grandstand play by which he hoped to have Sumner replaced as military commander of New Mexico, wrote Daniel Webster and suggested that since "the Civil and Military Authorities of the Territory but with few exceptions are in hostile array *one* or *both* should be relieved from duty in this territory." Since the governor was a political appointee there is no doubt about which one he hoped would be relieved from duty.

Sumner was convinced that the new post would become the determining factor in establishing a peace and began to work toward that end by contacting the Navajo headmen through Major Backus at Fort Defiance. He was also aware that in order to establish peace he had to keep the civilian militias out of *Dinehtah*. But Calhoun was just as determined to hold the upper hand in the administration of New Mexico affairs and when an American adventurer named Preston Beck, Jr., commander of an itinerant militia company being organized in Santa Fe, brought a request for arms to him on November 9, he blissfully endorsed it and forwarded it to the military commander. Calhoun was quite aware that Sumner was in contact with the Navajo headmen and had already made plans for a peace parley with them to be held at Jemez later in the month. Much to the governor's surprise, Colonel Sumner gave his assistant adjutant general, First Lieutenant J.C. McFerran, permission to furnish Beck's militia with seventy-five flintlock muskets, cartridge boxes, bayonet scabbards, belts and plate from military stores at Fort Union. Convinced that such adventurers as Beck were, through Calhoun's office, keeping alive the Indian troubles just to fleece the government, Sumner affixed several conditions to the use of the weapons before turning them over to Beck. The muskets were never to be used in hostile forays into Indian—specifically Navajo—country, unless the volunteers were acting in conjunction with regular troops and the weapons were to be returned to the army upon immediate orders of the department commander. Beck felt that Sumner's restrictions would so limit his activities that he was forced to decline acceptance of the arms and wrote to Calhoun complaining that he felt that the commander of the Ninth Military Department had no authority over the movement of civilian companies but that he would gladly comply with he will of the governor. Sumner had taken the teeth out of Beck's militia but when he was informed by Calhoun that an expedition of civilian militia was going to ride against the Navajos regardless, he warned the governor that he would use federal troops against the civilians if necessary in keeping them out of *Dinehtah*.

Sumner's efforts to establish peace with the Navajos finally paid off. On November 15 he and Governor Calhoun met a large group of Navajo headmen at Jemez and "to the great amusement of the Indians" proposed another treaty. When the Navajos refused to consider the proposition, Sumner pointed out that the troops at Fort Defiance could and would prevent them from raising a single field of grain unless they remained at peace. The headmen, after holding what was described as an "exciting council" among themselves, agreed to sign the treaty made with Washington at Canyon de Chelly. To consummate the agreement, Calhoun, against the wishes of Sumner, distributed several thousand dollars worth of gifts to the headmen including agricultural implements, calico, bayeta and brass wire. Sumner felt that the Navajos should earn such gifts as a reward for remaining at peace with the Americans for at least six months. It is impossible to determine which headmen attended the Jemez council as no copy of the treaty has ever been located. But apparently it was an influential group as the Navajos immediately quit raiding. Sumner, by building Fort Defiance in *Dinehtah* and by keeping the civilian New Mexican militias from raiding the Navajos, had, in a few short months, accomplished what the armies of Spain Mexico, and the United States had tried so vainly to do for centuries.

As the winter of 1851-52 wore on, a particularly severe one in *Dinehtah*, more and more Navajos began to visit Fort Defiance, having decided that the Belagáanas were sincere in their offer of friendship. On January 4, Major Backus wrote Sumner: "The Navajo Indians continue on friendly terms with us, and daily visit the Fort. Zarcillos Largos, the most influential Chief, made me a visit today, with his brother, known as the 'Governador Gordo'. They all recognize the Treaty of October 26 (sic) as binding upon the whole Nation, and they seem anxious to carry it into effect They will be prepared to enter into a detailed Treaty, for that purpose, at Cañon Boníto, or at some place west of the Río Grande, in preference to Santa Fé or Fort Union. They do not wish to come in collision with the Mexican people many of whom entertain no kind feelings toward them."

Actually the *Dineh* were visiting the frontier towns as well as Santa Fé that winter to trade and confer with Calhoun or one of his agents. In January a delegation of headmen, including Zarcillos Largos, took three captives to Santa Fe to deliver to Calhoun in accordance with the treaty made at Jemez. When agent John Greiner pointed out that the people living in the Río Abajo area of the lower Río Grande Valley had complained that some Navajos had taken their children and livestock, one of the headmen, Armijo, replied that his "people are all crying in the same way. Three of our chiefs now sitting before you mourn for their children who have been taken by the (New) Mexicans. More than two hundred of our children have been carried off and we know not where they are. The Mexicans have lost but few children in comparison with what they have stolen from us ... from the time of Colonel Newby we have been trying to get our children back again. Eleven times we have given up our captives—only once have they given us ours. My people are yet crying for the children they have lost. Is it American justice that we must give up everything and receive nothing?"

In his report to Governor Calhoun, Greiner pointed out that "there is too much truth in what these Indians complain of. It was the custom of the Mexicans to fit out expeditions against them every year, everyone claiming what he stole of his plunder ... these Indians are now what the U.S. Government is striving to make of all the wild Indian tribes—a farming community. I was so well convinced with the truth of the remarks of Armijo that I confess I had but little to say."

In spite of the fact that he had both advocated and sanctioned expeditions that had taken Navajo captives, Calhoun forwarded the letter to Commissioner of Indian Affairs Luke Lea, adding his own opinion that the Navajo statements were true. Again no effort was made to return the Navajo captives, which now included the families of two nephews of Zarcillos Largos. Only a few days before he visited Greiner in Santa Fé, a band of New Mexicans had attacked the homes of his young nephews near Ganado, killed the men and taken their families captive as his wife, on her way to visit the family, watched from her hiding place.

In an effort to cement friendly relations with the

Navajos, Calhoun appointed Spruce M. Baird as Special Agent to the tribe and established agency headquarters at Jemez. The pueblo of Jemez had long served as a center for both clandestine trading activities and as a starting point for slaving expeditions invading *Dinehtah*. Trading restrictions which had been placed on commercial intercourse with the Navajos were lifted and, as was expected, traders began to flock into Navajoland. It was hoped that, from Jemez, Baird would be able to oversee the activities of the traders and prevent trouble from erupting between them and the Navajos. But Baird was a poor choice. In the opinion of Calhoun's successor, William Carr Lane, who replaced him with Henry Linn Dodge, Baird "gave little attention to his official duties, and gave most of his time to his private business—as lawyer, farmer, editor of a newspaper, politician, ec., ec., ec.,"

Colonel Sumner, continuing in his efforts to gain the friendship of the Navajos, sent them 500 sheep, seeds of various types and agricultural implements from quartermaster stores in March. In spite of the fact that there had been no trouble with the Navajos for several months, Sumner did not suppose that all hostilities had ceased. In a letter he wrote to Secretary of War Conrad on March 27, 1852, he said: "They are educated to believe that the stealing of horses, is an act of prowess, and a few young men may occasionally band together for this purpose, but the propensity will soon wear out."

Nor were all the New Mexicans inclined to keep the peace. Not only did unscrupulous traders persist in supplying the Navajos with liquor, arms and ammunition, but others continued to steal Navajo livestock. Just two weeks after he'd arrived in Jemez to establish the agency headquarters, Spruce Baird apprehended a trader named Vincente Romero on his way to *Dinehtah* with powder, lead and liquor, and revoked his license. Perhaps if Special Agent Baird had been more diligent in performing his duties others would have been apprehended and some of the future troubles could have been avoided. Then, a few weeks later, Armijo was back in Santa Fé to call on John Greiner, accompanied by another influential headman named Black Eagle to complain that the New Mexicans had recently stolen several horses.

Governor Calhoun became increasingly ill and began

making plans to return home. John Greiner, an ardent Whig who had authored William Henry Harrison's campaign song, "Tippecanoe and Tyler Too," was appointed acting Superintendent of Indian Affairs on April 13. Calhoun, stoically leaving the sick bed in which he had been confined for several weeks, order his coffin built, loaded it on a wagon and, with his two daughters and their husbands, joined a merchant train headed for the States the last week of May, 1852. He died on the trail and was interred at Independence, Missouri.

Strangely, all of Calhoun's biographers have lauded his efforts. Perhaps the job he was charged with in New Mexico was too big for him but the fact remains that, either through blind ignorance or stiff-necked arrogance, the man was responsible for prolonging the troubles between the New Mexicans and the Navajos during his tenure.

President Millard Fillmore appointed William Carr Lane, another Whig politician, as the second territorial governor of New Mexico. Lane, a prominent physician in his early sixties, had been elected nine times as mayor of St. Louis. He arrived in Santa Fé on September 9 and was immediately installed as governor and ex officio Superintendent of Indian Affairs—and just as immediately took up Calhoun's feud with Colonel Sumner. In an undated letter to Colonel Sumner Lane expressed his frustration on the state of affairs in New Mexico at the time of his arrival: "Never was an executive officer in a more pitiable plight than I was at this time. I was an utter stranger to my official duties, without having any competent legal adviser, and with scarcely an official document on file to direct or assist my official actions; the secretary of the Territory (John Greiner) was likewise lacking in experience. . . . (There was) not a cent of money on hand, or known to be subject to the draft of the governor, superintendent of Indian affairs, or the secretary of the Territory; not a cent in the city, county or Territorial treasuries, and no credit for the county. There were no policemen and no constabulary force for either city or county . . . nor was there a single company of militia organized in the whole Territory, nor a single musket within reach of a volunteer, should there be an offer of service by anyone; and you, Colonel Sumner, must have been, from your official position, duly informed of these things."

Lane felt it was better to feed Indians than fight them and evolved a policy of attempting to keep the tribes quiet by the issuance of rations. A few months after he took office he authorized Baird to expend $2,237.65 for the purchase of "an outfit of hoes, spades, knives, axes and other necessities for the Navajos."

That summer the Navajos tended their flocks and fields, free for the first time in years from the burdens of war and worried only by persistent rumors that New Mexican slave raiders were riding against them. Late in August Zarcillos Largos heard from Navajos recently returned from Cebolleta that a band of five hundred Americans and New Mexicans were planning a campaign against The People. Riding to Fort Defiance at the head of a small delegation, he called on Captain J.H. Eaton, who had replaced Backus as commander of the post. Eaton assured the headman that the soldiers knew of no such planned raid and that the American troops were stationed at the post to protect the Navajos as long as they remained at peace. But Captain Eaton, aware of the vacillating mood of the New Mexicans, suggested that Zarcillos Largos post scouts in the direction of Cebolleta as a precautionary measure. Apparently no such raid was planned. Possibly Sandoval started the rumor, for two months later he was accused of starting rumors among the Navajos to the effect that Colonel Sumner had been sent to New Mexico to establish Fort Defiance for the purpose of initiating a campaign to exterminate the *Dineh*. Sandoval was summoned to departmental headquarters by the military commander to account for the rumors and Governor Lane sent presents to the Navajos in an effort to squelch "Sandoval's treacherous reports."

Now that he could no longer raid his own people with inpunity, Sandoval began raiding the New Mexicans with hopes that the Navajos would be blamed. In May, 1853, about thirty or forty Navajos stole a flock of 5,600 sheep from a ranch northwest of Socorro. One of the marauders was recognized as Sandoval's son. Zarcillos Largos called on Captain Henry Lane Kendrick, who had replaced Eaton as commander of Fort Defiance, and told him "that this and other evils are the results of the machinations of Sandoval himself; that if he were out of the way, everything would be quiet." Sumner wrote to Governor Lane regarding Sandoval: "I have suspected this fellow for a long time, with his half Pueblo, half Navajo band, and I have no doubt but he has had something to do with these difficulties. He is an unprincipled scoundrel and it is plain that he has everything to gain by a war between the Navajos and the whites, for then he can steal from both sides.

Kendrick was not as sympathetic toward the Navajos as his predecessors at Fort Defiance had been but, fortunately, his influence was balanced by that of Henry Linn Dodge, who was appointed agent to replace Baird in early 1853. Dodge was the youngest son of Senator Henry Dodge of Wisconsin and brother of Augustus Caesar Dodge, Senator from Missouri. While his appointment to the position by President Franklin Pierce was politically motivated, he was an excellent choice both by aptitude and experience. He had lived in the West for several years and commanded one of the New Mexican volunteer forces during the Washington expedition. Afterwards he served as commissary agent for the garrison of troops stationed at Cebolleta and engaged in trading ventures with Navajos and Pueblos and, with a man named Hezikiah Johnston, made one of the earliest gold strikes in New Mexico near the headwaters of the Gila River. Dodge surprised both his countrymen and the Navajos by immediately moving the agency from the relatively comfortable station at Jemez to Fort Defiance and proceeded to travel extensively throughout *Dinehtah,* often alone. The fact that he showed no fear and indicated sincere concern for their welfare immediately gained him the respect of the headmen, who called him "Red Sleeves" and promised to protect him.

Dodge's appointment came none too soon. While most of the tribe continued to enjoy the peace, a few young men, in an effort to gain status and wealth, began raiding the New Mexican flocks and herds in the spring of 1853, Too, the Navajo bands living on the eastern fringes of *Dinehtah,* particularly those in the Zūni mountains, had continued to suffer losses at the hands of intinerant expeditions of Anglos and New Mexicans. As a result of the raids on their large flocks and the kidnapping of two small girls and possibly some women that spring, the Navajos were growing belligerent. Then, on the night of May 3, five young Navajos from Black Eagle's band murdered a New Mexican rancher named Ramón Martin at Vallecitos and took his eight-year-old son, Librado, and his nephew, José

Claudio, and three shepherds captive. The shepherds were released and told to inform their people that when a "paint horse and a mule, stolen from the Navajos, were given up, then the boys would be delivered."

Governor Lane, informed by the alcade of Chamas of the murders and kidnappings, ordered Donaciaro Vigil, territorial secretary, to *Dinehtah* to ascertain the identity of the murderers and to proclaim to the tribe that a failure to relinquish the culprits and the captives would result in "beginning hostilities against the whole of the Navajo tribe." Colonel Sumner sent a letter to Major Kendrick at Fort Defiance stating: "If they do not comply with this demand, I shall march a strong force in their country and destroy all their fields, and inflict upon them, in every way, as much injury as possible. . . . I wish you to send for as many of the principal chiefs as you can find, and to say to them, that if I do not receive a letter from you by the 6th of July (the next full moon), informing me that you have the murderers, that I shall immediately commence moving troops into their country. The whole force will be assembled at Fort Defiance amounting to 600 or 700 soldiers, with cavalry and artillery, and if the murderers are not immediately delivered up to me, I shall immediately commence to lay waste to their country, in accordance with the promise I made to them some time ago at Jamaz (sic), if they violated the treaty. I shall put to death every man I catch. I shall destroy every field of grain, and at the time when it will be too late to plant again this year—and I shall take all the flocks that I can find. Say to Zarcillos Largos and the other chiefs, to some of whom I am personally known, that it will give me great pain to destroy their crops and to leave their women and children to starve, but the word I have pledged to them must be kept, and they must be made to know once and for all the difference between American and Mexican governments. If the chiefs and principal men are desirous to preserve the peace, the only thing for them to do is go in a body at once to Black Eagle's band, and get these five murderers either by council or force . . . If they do this, there will be an end of all difficulty between us, and they can sit down in peace, and enjoy the prospect of an abundant harvest for themselves and families."

Donaciaro Vigil, accompanied by nine Jemez Pueblos,

travelled to the valley of Tunicha, where he held a council with Armijo and a second headman named Aguila Negra. Upon his demand, the captives were turned over to Vigil, but when he also demanded that the murderers be turned over to him in accord with the orders of Governor Lane, he was told by Aguila Negra that they belonged to another band over which they had no control and any attempt to force their surrender would precipitate a civil war. Vigil returned to Santa Fé with the captives after persuading Armijo and Aguila Negra to journey to the capital to confer with Governor Lane about the grave situation. The two headmen did visit Lane but failed to impress upon him that it was beyond their powers to arrest members of Black Eagle's band and turn them over to the Americans. But Lane was adamant and insisted that the murderers and the stock, stolen by the Navajos, be given up, otherwise he would declare war against them. Lane was in the midst of a political campaign against Padre José Manuel Gallegos for the office of congressional delegate from New Mexico and felt that if he was instrumental in bringing in the Navajo murderers he would increase his chances of defeating the popular priest. Lane demanded that the headmen return with the murderers or send word of their captivity within a week.

When the week had passed and the governor had not heard from Armijo and Aguila Negra, he called on Colonel Sumner. While Colonel Sumner agreed that it the headmen failed to turn over the guilty parties a campaign would be organized by the army and the militia against the tribe, he refused, perhaps perversely, to cooperate with the governor in declaring immediate war against the Navajos and questioned the propriety of holding a tribe of ten to twelve thousand people responsible for the acts of five young men. He also pointed out, much to Lane's consternation, that a war against the Navajos would be both costly and futile as it was impossible to engage the Navajos in decisive battles and about all his few troops could hope to accomplish was the destruction of the *Dineh's* crops and the capture of their flocks. If anything, Sumner cared even less for Lane than he had for Calhoun and realized that the governor's concern for the life and property of the citizens of New Mexico was politically motivated. The fact that Lane had attempted to apprehend the murderers before consulting the military commander—and failed to gain the glory he sought—no doubt amused the Colonel. But he did promise to send orders to Kendrick at Fort Defiance to bring in the culprits.

In an effort to impress upon the Navajós the seriousness of the situation, Captain Kendrick, accompanied by Henry Linn Dodge, toured the eastern portion of *Dinehtah* and talked to large groups of Navajos at Ojo Caliente, Tunicha and Chuska. Dodge called on Zarcillos Largos and was told by the headman that while his band had nothing to do with the murders or the recent stealing of sheep, he would see what he could do. A short time later the stolen sheep were returned; Zarcillos Largos could do no more than that.

Meanwhile Captain Kendrick reported to Sumner: "(The Navajos) are quite adverse to war ... we met the Indians in large numbers at various points and told them very distinctly that war would result unless satisfaction was given; that this war would be the last one which it would be necessary for us to have; that the Americans would be let loose upon them, their flocks seized, their men killed, their women and children taken captive, and ultimately the mountains made their eastern limit ... in relation to Sandoval, I have now to say that these people are anxious to get rid of him fearing him greatly, whereas we ought to sustain him and use him as a scourge ... the most effective rod in terrorism to be held over these people is the fear of permission being given to the Mexicans to make captives of the Navajos and retain them. ..."

With election time approaching and the murderers of Martin—upon whom Lane had pinned his political future—still free, the governor called on Colonel Sumner and said, in effect, that if the military did not intend to bring the matter to a close, he would take it upon himself to do so. His intention, Sumner learned, was to raise a civilian militia of five hundred men to invade *Dinehtah*. For the second time Colonel Sumner threatened to use his troops against a New Mexican militia to prevent them from invading the Navajos, whereupon Governor Lane challenged him to a duel, a challenge that the military commander refused. Lane resigned his office but continued to campaign for the congressional seat. The voting on September 5, 1853, gave him a majority but Congress refused to accept the ballots cast by the Pueblo Indians, which left his opponent the victor.

With Lane out of the way the matter of Martin's murder was all but forgotten and a quiet peace settled over *Dinehtah*. Henry Linn Dodge spent most of the month of August visiting his charges and was successful in keeping the young men off the war trail. From Fort Defiance, he rode to Canyon de Chelly, and made notes about the large orchards of peach trees and extensive corn fields he found there. Then, from the western mouth of Canyon de Chelly, he followed the Chinle Valley north to the San Juan River and the land of the Utes, then turned south and east, visiting Chuska and Tunicha. Everywhere he travelled the Indian agent found the people prosperous; he estimated their livestock at 250,000 head of sheep and horses. He also estimated the population to be considerably larger than the ten to twelve thousand figure accepted at the time. As McNitt points out: "With the possible exception of Thomas Keam, who as special agent deeply affronted the Indian Office later with the same reprehensible habits (neglecting to write daily reports, Dodge was rarely to be found in agency quarters. He spent much of his time hobnobbing with the Fort Defiance officers, on some trip to a distant band of Navajos or on a hunting trip through the Chuskas with Indian friends), no Navajo agent in the next sixty years travelled as far into the country of his Indian charges or spent as much time among them." (McNitt, Ibid, 1964:186.)

President Franklin Pierce appointed David Meriwether to replace William Carr Lane as governor of New Mexico. Unlike Calhoun and Lane, Meriwether brought some knowledge of his charges to his office as Superintendent of Indian Affairs. He had worked for the American Fur Company as an Indian trader and, in 1819, had visited Santa Fé in company with a party of Pawnee Indians with the intent of opening trade with New Mexico. He was arrested as an American spy but was released for lack of evidence after being imprisoned a month. Meriwether arrived in Santa Fé and took office on August 9. Two weeks later he got what was probably the surprise of his life when his Navajo agent paid him a visit.

On the morning of August 31, 1853, Henry Linn Dodge rode into the capital at the head of a deputation of one hundred Navajos, including Zarcillos Largos, Manuelito,

Ganado Mucho, Armijo and all of the other important headmen with the exception of Archuleta, leader of the San Juan Navajos. Archuleta and his followers were still antagonistic toward the Americans. Much to the alarm of the new governor, Dodge caused panic among the citizens of Santa Fé by leading his charges directly to the plaza before the governor's palace. The women of the city called their children inside, locked and barred their doors and windows, and the men kept their distance in uneasy silence. These tall, lean, dignified Navajos, dressed in their finest raiment of buckskin and blankets, adorned with silver, turquoise and coral, and carrying lances and shields and some with bows over their backs and others with rifles across their saddles, were the most feared men in all America. And Henry Linn Dodge was the only man outside their tribe that trusted them. The Navajos remained in the capital until the morning of September 4 and, much to the surprise of the citizenry, not one incident marred their visit. Not only was their conduct most cordial toward their hosts but not one member of the delegation was seen to take a drink. In a letter reporting the visit to Commissioner George W. Manypenny, Governor Meriwether lauded the "remarkable sobriety and general good behavior of the delegation."

Meriwether met with Dodge and the Navajo headmen in council the day after their arrival and discussed peace and a mutual exchange of captives. He stated that he intended to keep the peace by hearing "the complaints of the white man with one ear and the red man with the other; weigh both and then give . . . a decision with impartiality." He added that his decision would be "irrevocable and must be obeyed." As a gesture toward future relations and to show his faith, he agreed to extend his pardon for all past offenses, including the murder of Martin.

Apparently what Governor Meriwether referred to as the "remarkable" sobriety and general good behavior of the Navajos also impressed the Anglo and Hispano citizenry of Santa Fe. Virtually the whole town turned out for the ceremony on the evening following the council and watched as the governor presented medals to the principal headmen and designated Zarcillos Largos as "head chief" of the Navajo Nation by presenting him with a cane as staff of office. The townspeople relaxed and enjoyed the dance the Navajos staged in the plaza and mingled among them throughout the next day. Henry Linn Dodge then led his charges back to *Dinehtah,* satisfied that, by bringing them face to face with their ancient enemy, he had done much to alleviate future troubles.

In his report to Commissioner Manypenny, Meriwether pointed out that in his opinion the Navajos were "certainly very far in advance" of any other Indian tribe in agriculture and manufactures, managed to raise an abundance of corn and wheat, owned numerous herds of horses and sheep and "on the whole, live in a degree of comfort and plenty unknown to the other wild Indians of this section of the Union." He also expressed misgivings regarding their visit to Santa Fe: "I am inclined to doubt the policy of bringing these Indians into our settlements for many reasons. In the first place it is expensive, then it brings them acquainted with our country, its roads and settlements, which would be a decided advantage in time of hostility. And last though not the least objection which I will mention is that I think it best for both races that they should have as little promiscuous intercourse as possible with each other."

Soon after he returned to Fort Defiance from Santa Fe, Dodge removed his agency to Sheep Springs, near Washington Pass. The only apparent reason for this move is found in a Navajo legend which had Dodge falling in love with a niece of Zarcillos Largos whom he is said to have married in a Navajo ceremony.

From Sheep Springs Dodge, sometimes alone and often accompanied by groups of warriors and headmen, continued to visit the widely scattered settlements throughout his immense jurisdiction to familiarize himself with the people and their problems. The fact that he was seldom found at home when visiting officials from Santa Fe or Washington called at his agency coupled with the fact that he was derelict in that most important traditional function of an Indian agent—writing daily and weekly reports—caused some high level criticism of his methods. Typically, Dodge replied that if he had anything to report that required the attention of Washington he would report it. His critics could not ignore the fact that since Dodge's arrival in *Dinehtah* the Navajos had remained at peace. He managed to keep the *Dineh* off the war trail in spite of political machinations in Santa Fe that winter of 1853-54 that would have, in other times, caused an immediate outbreak

281

of hostilities.

New Mexican and American ranchers, with greedy eyes on Navajo grazing lands, had long pressured the territorial legislature to pass a bill permitting them to move their herds into *Dinehtah*. Refused by the legislature, they turned to Federal District Court, which ruled that under the laws of Congress there was no Indian country in New Mexico. Thus the court of the land opened *Dinehtah* not only to the encroachments of stock raisers but also to the illegal commerce of traders in arms and liquor.

On February 10, Captain Kendrick reported from Fort Defiance that New Mexicans were already herding in traditional Navajo lands and tht sheep belonging to them were being grazed as far west as Zuñi, more than one hundred miles from the nearest frontier town. Realizing that the 250,000 head of sheep and up to 60,000 head of horses owned by the *Dineh* already threatened overgrazing of the limited grasslands of *Dinehtah,* Kendrick wrote Governor Meriwether: " . . . I know not what explanation to make of such criminal recklessness, unless I am furnished the key to it in the remarks made to me by one who seemed more anxious to protect his two or three mules than to recover his large flock of sheep, which had been stolen—*viz*: 'If I lose my sheep the Government will pay for them.'

"Now that our peaceful relations with the Navajos have a fair prospect of becoming consolidated, it is to be regretted that owners of flocks, instead of allowing us time necessary for such a result, are placing an almost irresistible temptation to robbery before a people, under whose exactions New Mexico has groaned for a third of a century."

The Navajos complained bitterly to agent Dodge of the encroachments and he wrote one of his few letters to Washington pleading that Congress set aside Navajo tribal lands for their exclusive use.

In the spring of 1854 Dodge led a second delegation of Navajos to Santa Fé in an effort to obtain agricultural tools. Meeting with acting superintendent of Indian Affairs, William S. Messervy—Governor Meriwether was out of the city on business—Dodge was told that there was a total lack of funds to accommodate the request. When Dodge pointed out that if the Navajos were allowed to return home empty-handed it could put further strain on relations between them and the Americans, Messervy requisitioned a few tools in the capital. Reporting the visit to Commissioner Many-penny, Messervy pointed out that Washington was continuing to offer virtually nothing to keep the Indians at peace beyond the beggarly expenses of a few agents.

There is substantial evidence that Dodge used most, if not all, of his annual salary of·$1,550 to help the Navajos. At Fort Defiance and later at Sheep Springs his expenses were kept at a minimum, yet soon after he visited Messervy, he applied to his father for a loan of one thousand dollars. The senator forwarded the money and Dodge arranged for the loan to be taken out of his salary beginning the following January. There is little doubt but that he used the money to buy agricultural tools for the Navajos that Washington could not, or would not, supply. Upon occasion Governor Meriwether delved into his personal funds for the same reason. Dodge brought a blacksmith, George Carter, to his agency to instruct the Navajos in the fundamentals of iron forging. He also hired a Mexican silversmith named Juan Anea (or Anaya) as an assistant to Carter. The few spades, hoes and plows and the seeds that Dodge had managed to obtain contributed to the bountiful Navajo crops of 1854 and further cemented the cordial relations between the Navajos and the Americans.

Exactly one year after Dodge led his first delegation of Navajos to Santa Fé, Governor Meriwether reported to Commissioner Manypenny that while in the past the people of the territory had charged many wrongs to the Navajos, "under the judicious management of Agent Dodge, who has taken up his abode among these Indians, we have but little cause to complain of them during the present year."

The respect the Navajos accorded to Dodge prevented a senseless incident from developing into a crisis early in October, 1854, when a Navajo killed a soldier near Fort Defiance. It was originally reported that the soldier was killed from ambush (and this is the version of the story told in most white histories), but later evidence indicates that the soldier provoked a fight and was shot dead for his trouble. Dodge, accompanied by a Lieutenant Alley and twenty-five soldiers, set out immediately in pursuit of the murderer. They tracked him northward to Laguna Negra, through Washington Pass, down the Chuska Valley and to the vicinity of Armijo's ranchero near Ojos Calientes (Bennett's Peak). Dodge called on Armijo and demanded that he surrender the culprit to the military for trial, pointing out that failure to do so would, in one swift blow, destroy the friendship between the *Dineh* and the Bilagáana.

Armijo agreed that retribution had to be made but offered, in the custom of the Navajos, to give the Americans sheep and horses as compensation. Dodge explained that, while he respected the Navajo custom of absolving guilt by the payment of livestock, the custom of the Bilagáana was different; the person guilty of a crime and not his relatives had to be punished. While Armijo failed to see what the corporal punishment of the culprit would accomplish, he finally promised to have the man brought to the *silaoo*—the soldiers—within seven days. Armijo sent several of his men to take the fugitive, who put up a fierce fight and was taken only after being severely wounded. On November 13, 1854, Dodge reported to Governor Meriwether:

"It is with the greatest of pleasure that I have the honor of announcing to you the delivery to me, by the Navajo tribe of Indians, the murderer of the soldier belonging to this Post. I left this escorted by Lieut. Alley and twenty-five Infantry soldiers on 28th October, crossed the Tunicha mountain near the Ojo Calientes with the view if possible of expediate (sic) the apprehension of the murder. Upon my arrival Armijo assured me that the murderer would be brought to this house in seven days, and if he was not I could have his son as a hostage for his delivery at the Fort. On the 5th November he was delivered to Lieut. Alley badly wounded by an arrow shot in the loins, he having made fight to the last. The man that shot him is a nephew of Armijo's, who says that but for a shield that he had provided himself with, he would have been killed, that thirty eight arrows were shot at him many of which struck the shield in the center. On the 6th we took up the line of march for Fort Defiance where we arrived on the evening of the seventh. Captain H.L. Kendrick and myself at the urgent request of Armijo and the civil Chief and Zarcillos Largos, the war Chief, and one hundred other principal men of the Nation, and after his identity was proven by a Sergeant and two Soldiers, had him hung until he was *dead dead dead*."

In reporting the incident to Commissioner Manypenny,

Meriwether said: "The hanging of this Indian in this summary manner, without legal trial, is to be regretted, but there is no jail or other means of confining such a prisoner in this Territory until next spring when our civil courts are holden, and it became necessary that an example should be made to impress other bad Indians."

The Navajo headmen—and particularly Armijo who requested a plow—were so impressed with the increased crop yield brought about by the tools that Dodge had secured for him that they begged him for more. During the winter of 1854-55 the agent wheedled or appropriated every agricultural implement that he could from Meriwether in Santa Fe, from the military stores at Fort Defiance and elsewhere, including one hundred and fifty hoes and twelve axes reluctantly furnished by the Indian Bureau. Dodge was positive that by improving Navajo agricultural methods and thereby increasing the yield of their crops, the temptation to gain wealth by raiding New Mexican flocks would be eliminated. In the spring he turned over the new tools to the Navajos and travelled about demonstrating their use.

But that spring a new trouble appeared on the northern horizon of *Dinehtah;* one that would have far-reaching consequences for the Navajos. The Utes allied themselves with the Jicarilla Apaches and went on the warpath, striking hard at ranches in northern New Mexico and westward into the lower valleys of the San Juan. By June the New Mexicans had lost large numbers of cattle, sheep and horses and counted twenty dead in addition to several women and children carried off. From their Utah strongholds, the Utes made daring sweeps westward and, picking up Mohave allies along the way, raided as far west as San Bernardino, California. Strutting with success, they called on the Navajos and tried to coerce them into joining them in their war and taunting them for farming like Pueblos.

In April Dodge was told by the Navajos that a force of nearly one thousand Utes and Apaches were encamped southwest of the La Platas. On April 17, 1855, Dodge wrote Meriwether: "The Utahs (camped nearby) has said to them that we are an easy prey for them, that they had killed eight hundred of our people since the war commenced. In trying to induce the Navajos to join them, the Utes boasted of the great numbers of livestock they had captured and offered to trade even the best of animals for

285

almost nothing ... The Navajos replied that they would buy mules and cows if they could see them, and believe that the Utahs have lied with the view of deceiving them. They have begged the Navajos not to plant this year but to join them and drive the Americans from the Territory. The Navajos reply that we are the best friends they have ever had and they will not do anything to make us enemies ... a few days since, five Mexicans came out to the (Utes') camps from Arbiquiu to sell them corn and ... they killed them and got the corn for their trouble."

Their friendship and respect for Henry Linn Dodge was the determining factor in moving the Navajos to spurn the proposed Ute alliance—an act that almost immediately caused a war between the two tribes.

In June Governor Meriwether called Dodge to Santa Fé. Eleven months before, on July 31, 1854, the United States Congress approved an Indian Appropriation Act which allowed the New Mexico Superintendency $30,000 to negotiate treaties with the Navajos, Utes and Apaches. Commissioner Manypenny instructed Governor Meriwether to: "... make such arrangements as will provide for the Indians, within the country which they may respectively reside and the possession of which they claim, a suitable tract or tracts, limited in extent, for their future permanent home; and will guarantee to them the possession and enjoyment of the reserve assigned to them, with provisions that hereafter the President may cause the land reserved to be surveyed, and to assign to each single person over twenty-one years of age, or head of family, a farm containing from, say twenty to sixty acres, according to the number of persons in such family."

Certainly Henry Linn Dodge was aware, as probably not one other white American was, that the institution of individual land ownership was not only foreign to Navajo—and almost all Indian—cultures but the very idea was repulsive to the *Dineh*. One did not own the land. A man used only what was necessary to supply his needs. Too, the suggestion of allotting twenty to sixty acres of land to a family in *Dinehtah* with its great deserts, broad grazing lands and few isolated canyons, river bottoms and mountain slopes suitable for farming was typical of the prevailing ignorance of Washington officials, not only in 1855 but for decades to come.

286

Nevertheless—and pointedly ignoring the specifics of Manypenny's instructions—Dodge and Meriwether went ahead with plans to make a new treaty with the Navajos, a treaty that would firmly establish the boundaries of *Dinehtah*. While Dodge was in Santa Fe he penned one of his infrequent letters to Manypenny: "At the commencement of this fiscal year," he wrote, "war was raging on our borders with the Apaches and Utahs and every effort that was possible for me to make had to be put forth to prevent the poor, viciously disposed part of the tribe from joining the enemy. During the year large and petty thefts have been committed upon the property of our citizens and murder perpetrated upon the body of a soldier near Fort Defiance by the party anxious for war . . . they had every prospect of peace and contentment for the year to come but for recent depredations committed upon their lives, and property by the Utahs, who it is evident—to revenge themselves for a recent defeat received from our troops in which they lost many lives (and) all of their horses and camp equipage— attacked the Ranchos of two rich Navajos living on the south side of the Río San Juan killing them both, capturing their children, and running off one hundred head of horses. This has produced a panic in all their farming operations for the present and caused the rich to flee to the mountains with the women, children, flocks & herds, where they have concentrated in a body for mutual protection.

"It is impossible to say what will be the result of this war. The Utahs have fine rifles, live by the chase, and are the most warlike tribe in New Mexico. The Navajos have but few guns of inferior quality, live by the cultivation of the soil and the produce of their flocks and herds and are not warlike, and if this war is persisted in without prompt and efficient aid is received by them from our Government, must fall an easy prey to the Utahs.

"A treaty will be made in the early part of next month with them by Gov. D. Meriwether at which Genl. Garland the commanding officer of this military department (General John Garland had recently replaced Colonel Sumner) has assured me he will be present, & that the Navajos shall have every assistance against their enemies that it is possible for him to give. That a friendly visit to the heart of their country by the Governor and the Genl. commanding the Military arm of our Government in this

Territory will have a happy influence upon these people and secure a treaty of limits and friendship which will last for years, I have every reason to believe.

"A liberal and enlightened policy towards this tribe for a few years will fix their destiny as an agricultural, manufacturing, and stock raising community. That these results can be speedily attained by them no person will doubt who is acquainted with their habits of industry, temperance, and ingenuity . . ."

Governor Meriwether, while supporting the treaty, was ill disposed toward personally visiting *Dinehtah*. Pointing out that the trip would consume weeks—a slight exaggeration—and that other duties required his presence in Santa Fe, he suggested that Dodge have the Navajo headmen come to the capital to negotiate the treaty. Dodge responded emphatically in the negative. If the new treaty was to be taken seriously by the Navajos it would have to be presented and discussed with all the headmen in council by the governor himself. Dodge also felt that the Navajos would be more favorably inclined to accept the proposed treaty if it was presented to them at a gathering in their homeland, and recommended Laguna Negra, twenty-five miles north of Fort Defiance, as the council site.

Meriwether reluctantly agreed and left Santa Fe, accompanied by his son Raymond, his secretary, W. W. H. Davis, and two servants on July 5 to rendezvous with General John Garland at Fort Defiance.

Dodge hurried back to *Dinehtah* to make preparations for the council. After sending messengers to all of the headmen, he prepared a camp and had a large *ramada* of poles and cedar boughs built on the shores of Laguna Negra.

When Governor Meriwether and General Garland arrived at the council site on July 16, it was apparent that Henry Linn Dodge had done his job exceedingly well. Gathered on the low, red, sandy valley on the western approach to Washington Pass (about four miles west of the present Crystal) were, by Dodge's estimate, two thousand Navajos awaiting the white officials. Dressed in their finest bright-hued clothes and riding their best steeds, the Laguna Negra gathering, in a setting of great natural beauty, was an overwhelming spectacle to the visitors from the East. Dodge reported that every headman with the exception of Sandoval was present although there is no record that indicates that Archuleta and his San Juan Navajos attended the meeting. They had not been friendly toward the Americans since the death of Capitone and, while they had not joined them in their war, they were on friendly terms with the Utes.

Henry Linn Dodge almost saw all his hopes dashed before the council started when a minor headman named Delgadito *(Cach'osh nez* or Tall Syphilis as he was known to the Navajos) made a blustering and denunciatory speech against the Americans at the first assemblage. When Delgadito and his small band of followers forced their way into the *ramada,* hurled curses at the Americans and threatened to kill Meriwether, Manuelito came to the rescue. The young headman, still known as Hastin Chihajin (Man of Blackweed) to the Navajos, grabbed the renegade while others jostled his followers aside.

When quiet had been restored, Governor Meriwether passed around tobacco and addressed Zarcillas Largo, Armijo, Manuelito and the rest of the headmen: "I have come here," the governor began, "to meet the Navajos and am glad to see as many present. I am glad the Navajos and the whites have been at peace so long a time, and hope they will remain at peace. I have come to see you to agree upon a country the Navajos and whites may each have, that they may not pasture their flocks in each other's lands. If we have a dividing line so that we know what each other's country is, it will keep us at peace. I will explain the kind of treaty I desire to make with you; and when I am through I want you to council with each other whether you will agree to such a treaty, and want an answer in the morning."

Meriwether then outlined the terms of the treaty which established the boundaries of *Dinehtah*. It is assumed that the southern boundary, which was not specifically mentioned, was to be the Little Colorado River. The western boundary was to be a line running, approximately, from the present location of Mexican Hat on the San Juan River to the confluence of Chevalon Creek and the Little Colorado between Holbrook and Winslow, Arizona. The eastern boundary—and by far the most important—was to follow the San Juan River from the present Four Corners to the northern extreme of Cañon Largo in New Mexico and then in a southerly direction along the canyon and from its southern extreme, in a southwesternly direction to the Zuñi River at a point just east of the pueblo of Zuñi. This, of course, was a considerable reduction of the territory the Navajos claimed. According to Meriwether himself, before the treaty the Navajo country "extended from the Río Grande to the Colorado and from about 35° to 37° latitude." Still the proposed treaty gave the Navajos considerably more of their land than the New Mexican stock raisers wanted them to have. Upon completion of the governor's speech the council disbanded and the Navajo headmen withdrew to discuss what they had been offered while their families and friends spent the remainder of the day visiting, trading, horse racing and gambling.

The council resumed the next morning, July 17, and began on a note of surprise when Zarcillas Largos failed to appear. The aged headman, whom Dodge and Meriwether had hoped would be instrumental in bringing the negotiations to an amicable conclusion, sent the staff of office and medal that had designated him as "principal chief" with word that he wished to resign the office as he was "too old." Actually the title conferred on Zarcillas Largos in Santa Fe by Meriwether was more honorary than factual and had not affected his considerable influence among his people one way or the other. Those that had followed his advice before had continued to do so and he had prudently chosen not to attempt to impose his will on those who he knew would not accede to it. The Navajos continued to regard the old man as their principal headman until his death in 1862 and his sudden resignation at Laguna Negra—which caused considerable consternation among the Americans who were not sure what effect his actions might have on the council at this critical stage—was merely a tactful manner by which he excused himself from participating in the negotiation of a treaty that he found wanting.

Meriwether accepted the staff and medal and asked the other headmen if they would meet in council and choose one of their numbers as Zarcillas Largos' successor as "head chief of the Navajo nation." Actually Dodge was fully aware that there could be no such thing as a "head chief" of the Navajos but went along with the sham, as did the Navajo headmen, to satisfy the American governor. After discussing the matter among themselves for about two hours, the headmen told Dodge that they had chosen Manuelito, then about thirty-seven years old, to replace Zar-cillas Largos. However Manuelito refused to accept the staff and, at first, the medal returned by Zarcillas Largos saying that these things represented the power of the old headman and should remain with him. Meriwether than presented his own steel cane to the young headman and Manuelito was persuaded to place the medal around his neck only after it had been. restrung. Then the council resumed with Man-uelito acting as spokesman for the Navajos.

Governor Meriwether reopened the council by reminding the gathering of the propositions he had made the day before and stating that they would discuss each term of the treaty after it had been "reduced to writing" by his secre-tary. Again gifts of tobacco were distributed with which W. W. H. Davis reported the headmen "quickly made them-selves cigarritos, and went to smoking with great gravity and gusto. The Indians of New Mexico never use the pipe, but smoke an ordinary Mexican cigar instead." As the assemblage sat smoking Davis transcribed the treaty terms. Perhaps, also as they waited Dodge told Meriwether, as he reported later, that while Manuelito was highly respected and, at the present time, a strong advocate of peace, he also possessed an unshakable belief that the Navajos had been unfairly treated in the past and would not hesitate to defy the Americans if he felt it necessary. At any rate Meri-wether was soon to learn that the new "head chief" was shrewd, intelligent and a brilliant orator.

While waiting for Davis to finish his work, Manuelito asked one of the interpreters to tell Governor Meriwether: "We are sorry our people treated you badly yesterday, and I am ashamed to show myself." He did not explain what he meant when he added, "I am now appointed in place of Zarcillas Largos and things will be different." Meriwether accepted Manuelito's aplogies, saying that the matter was forgotten and "the boys will behave badly."

When Davis had finished, Meriwether read the treaty terms with the interpreters translating the document into Navajo. Manuelito raised no objections until Meriwether read the fourth article which set forth the boundaries of *Dinehtah*. Standing, he skillfully and vehemently objected to the proposed boundaries, pointing out that the *Dineh* claimed a much larger country than that set forth in the treaty and that they were in the habit of going to Mount

Palonia and other places considered sacred by the Navajos that were outside the proposed boundaries. Too, as long as his people could remember, the Navajos had journeyed to the salina near Zuñi for salt and, most important, only one of the four sacred mountains which marked the traditional limits of *Dinehtah* were within the new boundaries.

Meriwether, attempting to dispel the air of uncertainty that had come over the council as Manuelito spoke, traced the new tribal boundaries on a map prepared for the purpose by Lieutenant Parke of the Topographical Engineers. The map, of course, was incomprehensible to the Navajos. Putting it aside, Meriwether explained that Manuelito was wrong. The Carrizo Mountains (Mount Palonia) were within the limits of the reserve. Meriwether said he "hoped this one sacred mountain would be sufficient" and that while the salinas were outside the boundary, he would issue a special order permitting the Navajos to gather salt there.

Manuelito also objected to surrendering all lands east of Chaco Canyon and pointed out that the Navajos had lived in that region for centuries; it was their ancestral homeland. Meriwether replied that the Navajos would not really be giving up this area as it was the proposed buffer zone and, too, they would be recompensed with annual payments of $10,000 for this area.

With Dodge giving his full support to the treaty which he hoped would prevent future wars between the Americans and his charges, the Navajo headmen approved it after a short council. Manuelito raised one more objection. The ninth article of the treaty called for the surrender by the tribe of all Navajos committing depredations. Manuelito explained that this portion of the treaty was considered offensive by the headmen, and while they had turned over malefactors in the past, it was all "very unpleasant to them." Furthermore, any headman attempting to cause the surrender of a tribesman did so at the risk of his own life. The *Dineh*, he explained, would much prefer that the Americans come and claim such criminals, as this would not conflict with the social and ethical values of the tribe. Meriwether explained that Americans coming into *Dinehtah* would not recognize the guilty from the innocent and could very well arrest the wrong man. After much deliberation the headmen finally agreed to accept article nine and on the following day, July 18, 1855, the treaty was signed.

And so at Laguna Negra the *Dineh* put pen to the first of a series of treaties that reduced their lands to but a fraction of what had been historically *Dinetah*. Dodge was pleased, and with blind faith in the federal government he firmly believed that Congress would fulfill the commitments that he and Meriwether had made with the Navajos. But his enthusiasm was to be short-lived. The supplies, farming implements, and funds promised the Navajo headmen at Laguna Negra failed to materialize and the treaty was not ratified by Congress. Nevertheless, and as we shall see, the Navajos were expected, in the coming years, to uphold *their* part of it to the letter. And by signing the worthless treaty in good faith the Navajos had also allied themselves with the Americans in their war with the Utes.

Too, not all the Bilagáanas shared Dodge's enthusiasm and respect for the *Dineh*. Meriwether was not only a racial bigot but he proved to be dishonorable and dishonest. Exactly one week after he'd signed the treaty and promised the Navajos an annual stipulation of $10,000 for the lands they were giving up in the East, he wrote Commissioner Manypenny: "The necessities of the Navajos does not require the payment of a large sum annually to enable them to live in comfort and improve their condition. Indeed, these Indians now may be considered in a prosperous condition; they have a large number of horses and sheep, together with their domestic animals; have planted some four thousand acres of grain this season, and by another year will be able to raise a sufficient amount to feed the whole tribe plentifully, after which time I hope they will have a surplus sufficient to supply the wants of Fort Defiance, which now has to be hauled over one hundred miles at great cost to the government." He further stated that the treaty was no bargain for the Navajos as the proposed reservation contained only about seven thousand square miles and "the entire reservation does not contain over one hundred and twenty-five or thirty square miles susceptible of cultivation, and this in small detached portions."

Meriwether's secretary, W. W. H. Davis, writing of the Laguna Negra council after his return to Santa Fé, left us the only really beneficial thing to come out of the whole meeting; an unprejudiced American's observations of the *Dineh* of 1855. After writing that the Navajos "appear superior in intelligence to all the other North American tribes," he added: ". . . They have ever been known as a pastoral and peaceful race of men, and live by raising flocks and herds, instead of hunting and fishing. They own some two hundred thousand sheep, and more than ten thousand head of horses and at times one single chief is worth as much as fifteen thousand dollars in stock, owning thousands of sheep and hundreds of horses. They raise corn, wheat, beans, pumpkins, melons, peaches, wild potatoes, etc. They sometimes grow as many as sixty thousand bushels of corn in a single season, and the present year (1855) they are supposed to have five thousand acres under cultivation. They number about twelve thousand souls, and can muster twenty-five hundred mounted warriors. They are industrious and laborious, and the men, women, and children are generally kept employed. They manufacture all their own wearing apparel, and make their arms, such as bows, arrows, and lances; they also weave a beautiful article of blankets, and knit woolen stockings. They dress with greater comfort than any other tribe and wear woolen(s) and well-tanned buckskin. The skin breeches come down to the knee, where they are met by blue stockings that cover the lower half of the leg; the breeches fit tight to the limb, and the outer seams are adorned with silver or brass buttons. The coat reaches below the hips, with a hole at the top to thrust the head through, and opens at the sides; it is made of wool, often in bright colors, and is fastened around the waist by a leather belt, highly ornamented with silver when the wearer can afford it. They wear numerous strings of fine coral, and many valuable belts of silver, and generally appear with a handsome blanket thrown over the shoulder in the style of a mantle.

"The Nabajo Indian is seldom seen on foot, a horse being as indispensable to him as to an Arab of the desert. They manufacture their own saddles and bridles, bits, stirrups, etc. as also the looms on which they weave their handsome blanets, which are quite an ingenious affair. It is a noted fact that they treat their women with more respect than any other tribe, and make companions of them instead of slaves. A Nabajo never sends his wife to saddle his horse, but does it himself when he has no peon. The modern doctrine of 'Women's Rights' may be said to prevail among them to a liberal extent. The women are the real owners of all the sheep, and the men dare not dispose of them without their permission; nor do the husbands ever make an important bargain without first consulting their wives. They admit women into their councils, who sometimes control their deliberations; and they also eat with them. They are mild in disposition, and very seldom commit murder; but they consider theft one of the greatest human virtues, and no one is thought to be at all accomplished unless he can steal with adroitness."

Davis might have added that stealing was considered a virtue only when New Mexicans and members of other tribes who also stole from them were the victims. Davis penned the above soon after his return from Laguna Negra and it was published in his book *El Gringo: or New Mexico and Her People* in 1857.

The Navajos returned home from Laguna Negra, having given up much of their homeland in return for a promised peace with the Bilagáanas. But the time would come to pass, within a few short years, when the *Dineh* would find themselves caught in a vise between the Americans and the Utes, allied against them in a war of extermination. Such were the ever-changing alliances in American New Mexico.

But the word for Agent Dodge and Governor Meriwether meant nothing to Mexican and Anglo ranchers who continued to graze their herds where they pleased, which included the Navajos' best grazing lands west of the eastern boundary line. The *Dineh* complained to Dodge, who in turn protested to government officials. But since the treaty had not been made official by Congress, it continued to be binding only on the part of the Navajos.

Throughout that summer, Henry Linn Dodge continued to visit the major rancheros and was able to report to the Navajo headmen that General Garland was making a series of campaigns against the Utes. Garland's efforts did cause the Utes to stop raiding the Navajos for the time being and allowed them to gather a bountiful harvest that fall—their last such for almost two decades.

Dodge, in an effort to at least particlally fulfill the promises he and Meriwether had made to the headmen at Laguna Negra appealed to Commissioner Manypenny for funds or equipment to furnish the *Dineh* with four flour mills, which he pointed out "would not cost, including the transportation of the stones from the Río Grande to this point, no more than one hundred and fifty dollars each. This would enable them to have flour and meal instead of using the grain in its entire state." He also requested that the government establish a school for the Navajos—the first such request—and that they "may be furnished with four sets of blacksmith tools and one thousand pounds of iron. They have," he pointed out, "eighteen native blacksmiths who work with the hand bellows and the primitive tools used by the Mexicans with which they make all of the bridle bits, rings, buckles & c." There is no record indicating that the Indian Office acted on any of the agent's requests.

Gradually, that fall of 1855, things began to change and the serenity that had come over *Dinehtah* after the Laguna Negra council and Garland's containment of the Utes was soon replaced by uncertainty and then overt animosity, even toward Henry Linn Dodge. A devastating winter arrived early in the Southwest that year and by early November *Dinehtah* was covered by snow. The Rio Grande was frozen over so solidly at Albuquerque that it was reported a horse and cart could be driven over it. On December 25, the temperature at Fort Defiance was thirty-two below zero. The severe weather continued through March and Navajo stock froze by the thousands. Blizzards left deep snowdrifts that caused most of the *Dineh* living in the highlands to move south. When spring finally came the herds and flocks had been devastated and many families had eaten their seed stock to stay alive. Dodge was only too aware that the situation was explosive and, with no help coming from the government, there was not much he could do about it.

And with the coming of spring, the Utes renewed their raiding of the settlements south of San Juan, forcing more Navajos to flee to the Fort Defiance area for protection. The Comanches joined the Utes, as did the Kiowas, in raiding *Dinehtah,* and a band of the Plains Indians struck Manuelito's camp in February and stole his favorite horse. The headman and several warriors chased the thieves hundreds of miles into Utah territory. When they finally gave up and turned back homeward, the Comanches followed them, attacked Manuelito's camp for a second time and wounded the headman. Manuelito lay with a high fever for several days while Zarcillos Largos prayed over him and administered herbal medicines. He recovered but with a changed attitude toward the Americans. It was only too clear that Dodge and Meriwether's promise of protection was worthless; the Navajos were being raided with impunity. Near the first of March members of his band drove off a New Mexican herd of horses and mules from the valley of the Rio Puerco. It was a warning that the *Dineh* had had enough.

As Kendrick had predicted, the flocks belonging to New Mexicans grazing in Navajo territory were raided. On March 27, a New Mexican rancher named Antonio José Otero reported that 11,000 head of sheep had been run off by Navajos who had left three herders dead. Kendrick and Dodge were ordered to investigate and, much to their surprise, discovered that the leaders of the raid were not the usual poor young men looking for quick wealth and fame; they were the offspring of *ricos*—wealthy families. One was the son of Narbona, two others were sons of Archuleta, leader of the San Juan Navajos who were still friendly with the Utes, and the remaining two were the sons-in-law of an important headman named Cayatano. Dodge was also told that Otero had lied; the number of sheep stolen was not more than 4,000, and in a subsequent investigation by Governor Meriwether it was learned that the New Mexican had, indeed, grossly exaggerated his losses.

Dodge was able to get back some of the stolen livestock. Armijo and Many Horses, son of Ganado Mucho, rounded up 1,400 sheep and forty horses and returned them to the agent at Laguna Negra on May 31. They also offered to give up three servants, probably Pauite slaves, in restitution for the three Mexican herders that had been killed, an offer that was refused by Dodge and Kendrick. As for turning over the perpetrators of the raid to the Americans, the headmen were unanimous in their refusal. Dodge reported to Meriwether that the "headmen with whom I have conferred say that it is impossible to give up the murderers, that it would produce a civil war among themselves in which the Utahs would take part on the side of the offenders." Dodge also pointed out that "it would be madness in the extreme to effect anything with the small force at Fort Defiance at the moment, as any small party going out to capture the murderers would be surrounded by a thousand warriors before going twenty-five miles."

Dodge, who was forced to his bed by illness the first week of June, hoped for a peaceful settlement and had secured the promise of the return of the remainder of the stolen sheep. But he knew that the situation had deteriorated to the point that the slightest incident would destroy all that he had accomplished as agent. Only a few days before the Laguna Negra meeting with Armijo and Many Horses, he had visited the Hopi pueblos and had found the Navajos in the region armed with fine new silver-mounted rifles. When he asked about the weapons the Navajos belligerently replied that they had obtained them from the Mormons in trade for horses. The Mormons who had fled religious persecution in Illinois, Missouri and England to establish their Zion in Utah were being harassed by the United States and were encouraging the southwestern tribes to drive the "Gentiles" out. They, the Navajos related to Dodge, were asking why the *Dineh* did not drive the Americans away from Fort Defiance.

Two weeks later Dodge received word that the Navajos would return no more of Otero's sheep. Four young Navajos had raided another New Mexican flock and two of them had been killed. Too, it was now the middle of June, 1856, almost a year since the headmen had signed the Laguna Negra treaty, and not only had the Indian Bureau failed to supply the promised money, supplies and farming implements, but New Mexicans were still grazing their livestock on Navajo lands. And while there had been no large raids by New Mexicans that spring, none of the children held as slaves by the New Mexicans had been returned. It was apparent to the agent that the Navajos were not going to abide by the restraints placed upon them by the Laguna Negra treaty and, as he confided to Governor Meriwether, in view of the circumstances and the failure of the government to honor its commitments, he could not blame them.

To make matters worse, Manuelito had become belligerent. He had been grazing his herds on lands set aside for the Fort Defiance livestock and when Captain Kendrick called on him June 13 and asked him if he intended to respect the treaty reserving the grazing lands for the horses of the fort, he replied that the agreement was foolish and meant nothing. When he was ordered by Kendrick to remove his herds, the headman replied: "Your army has horses and wagons, mules and many soldiers. They are capable of hauling in feed for their own livestock. We Navajos have only our feet, and must take our sheep and cattle wherever there is good grazing, and that land around the fort has been ours since I was a boy and will remain so after my death."

On the other hand, Manuelito added, Kendrick could drive him from the grounds that he occupied if he thought his force was sufficient. Then the headman said that he could call a thousand warriors around him in less than a day and flung the gauntlet of war at the post commander, defying him to attempt to remove his herds. Dodge reported that Manuelito added that, from what he had seen, he had more warriors than the governor and general of the Americans and closed the discourse by taunting, "The Americans are too fond of sleeping, eating, drinking and had white eyes and could not see to catch them (the Navajos) when they chose to keep out of their way."

Dodge advised that no action be taken as "the soldiers are barely able to protect themselves and the government herds without attempting an offensive movement against the Navajos . . . they are no fools and see at a glance that the troops of this place are too few to prevent them killing and stealing . . . That the dreadful scourge of war should not be visited upon the Navajos I have labored and suffered many privations, but I fear to little purpose," he sadly prophesied. In closing his report to Governor Meriwether he added, "I have this moment received information from a Navajo that a war party headed by the son of Jon Largo, a rich man who lives at the hot springs (is out) to steal and kill all persons that may be so unfortunate to fall in their hands."

As Meriwether and Garland continued to receive reports of Navajo raids and of Manuelito's increasing belligerence throughout the remainder of June, they, for once, took Dodge's advice and sent reinforcements to the fort. The additional troops put a stop to Manuelito's threats and he removed his livestock from the garrison grounds for the time being, but more Americans in *Dinehtah* could not quiet his anger. And in spite of the ominous threat of war, New Mexican ranchers continued to graze their herds on Navajo ranges and neither the military nor Governor Meriwether did anything to stop them.

But it was already too late for the Navajos. Their best

grazing lands east of the Chuska mountains were too tempting to the Americans, who had already caused them to retreat a hundred miles to the West since their arrival in New Mexico only ten years before. On October 18, 1856, the Santa Fé *Weekly Gazette* published an editorial that attempted to justify the encroachments of the New Mexicans and that heralded the doom of old *Dinehtah:* "New limits should be established for the Navajos, so as to give more room for our citizens to graze their stock. There is no necessity for these Indians to have grazing grounds east of their settlements, for they have far better pasture lands west of them, and there there will be no interference from any quarter." The editorial was written, presumably, by the publisher of the *Weekly Gazette,* one James L. Collins, who was soon to become Superintendent of Indian Affairs in New Mexico!

Only one man stood between the *Dineh* and the steady westward movement of New Mexican and Anglo ranchers into *Dinehtah*—Henry Linn Dodge. Then he, recovering from the illness that had persisted all summer, accompanied Kendrick and a small detachment of soldiers on a patrol of the hilly country south of Zūni to track down a band of Coyotero and Mogollon Apaches who had been raiding Zuni and Navajo herds, and got himself killed. Early on the morning of November 19, Dodge left the patrol camp some thirty miles south of Zuni to go hunting, taking the trail he knew the soldiers would follow that day.

The troops followed but when they camped at nightfall near Laguna Sal there was no sign of Dodge. The next morning he still had not returned and it was discovered that several horses belonging to the troops had been run off during the night. Kendrick, concerned, instructed the Indian scouts to find Dodge's trail and follow it until they determined what had happened to him. About noon the next day, Kendrick reported, "the place where he had been taken evidently by stealth, was discovered, some four or five miles from the camp where he had left us . . . No violence appears to have been used, but after having been taken, it seemed—judging from the signs which were carefully examined . . . that a conversation was had between them, after which they went off in a southeastern direction."

Kendrick was so certain that Dodge had been kidnapped

and was being held for ransom that he sent an urgent message to Major Van Horn, commanding at Albuquerque, to notify the Apache agent, Dr. Michael Steck at Fort Thron, "by whom it is presumed Capt. Dodge's liberation can be effected." He also sent letters to Governor Meriwether requesting a full and quick investigation of the alleged abduction. Three weeks passed before Dr. Steck received a discouraging report from the Apache leader, Mangas Colorados. He knew nothing of Dodge.

It was not until the first of the year that it was determined what had happened to the agent. Late in the day on January 2, 1857, Jose Mangus, the brother of Mangas Colorados, reported to Dr. Steck that he had learned that some Apaches, led by renegades named Cautivo and Tsna, had surprised Dodge while he was hunting alone and "he was shot with a carbine on the spot." After killing Dodge the Apaches continued to Laguna where they stole a flock of sheep. Crossing the Rio Puerco valley, they ran off another flock before descending to the Gila country.

Upon receiving details of Dodge's murder, Colonel Benjamin Louis Eulalie de Bonneville, Garland's second-in-command, directed three columns of dragoons and infantry against the Apaches. The troops were in the field from May until September, 1857, but failed to inflict much damage, perhaps because Bonneville wasn't much of a soldier. An 1819 graduate of West Point, his entire career had been marked by unsavory episodes which had long caused public criticism of him both by prominent civilians and by his military superiors. The New Mexico Department was to be his last command but before he left it he and *Weekly Gazette* publisher James L. Collins would hold the fate of the Navajos in their hands.

Bonneville asked the Navajos to participate in the campaign against the Apaches but they refused, knowing that such action would cause a war between them and their kinsmen. But Sandoval joined the expedition with a band of his *Dinehanaih,* no doubt for the purpose of sharing the spoils taken from the Apaches. While he was in the field with the Americans, about August 1, the Utes attacked his ranchero, killed four men and one woman from his band and a woman from Laguna. They also carried off six captives, five boys and one woman. When Sandoval returned and learned of the raid, he protested to Bonneville who wrote both James L. Collins, new Superintendent of Indian Affairs, and General Garland of the incident: "Sandoval, a chief of the Navajoe Indians, has been several times to see me to relate his grievances. When I say Navajoe chief, I must not be understood to fix him as one of that tribe, for as far back as Genl. Kearny he and his people have joined our troops ... always with us, ever against the disaffected of his own tribe; for this they now look upon Sandoval and his band of 100 warriors, not only with jealousy, but even with hate. He was with me on the Gila, and to my kowledge gave substantial aid ... Now he returns home, after being with us, and finds that during his absence and that of his warriors, his people have been killed and captives taken. Sandoval assures me that his people have never been permitted to make war on the Utah, never killed their people nor stole their stock; true, he says, the other Navajoes and the Utahs have long been at war, and parties come and go frequently. He begs your kind interposition on his behalf to have his captive people restored to him, and hopes some steps may be taken to have a peace made between them (and the Utes)."

There is no record indicating the return of the captives to Sandoval's band—nor is there any telling that he returned the two young sons of the Apache chief Eskitila that he brought home with him from the Gila. A few weeks later Sandoval's niece and two men of his band took a captive girl, a Navajo, to Albuquerque and sold her for $150. Falling in with some Mexicans, they drank liquor "pretty freely" and were attacked and robbed of the money they'd received for the slave. The niece, a girl of about sixteen, and one of the men were killed.

Meanwhile, in *Dinehtah*, the Navajos, and particularly Zarcillos Largos mourned the death of "Red Sleeves." Not only had the aged headman lost a friend but he also probably realized that the *Dineh* had lost their last hope of peace with the Bilagáana.

SIX

The Fearing Time

The Navajos remember those years between the death of Henry Linn Dodge and the final defeat by Christopher (Kit) Carson in 1864 as the Fearing Time—*Naahondzod*. They were surrounded by enemies on all sides; a man never knew when he might return home from hunting to find his wife dead and his children abducted by the Utes or the New Mexicans and their Pueblo allies to be sold into slavery.

Captain H. L. Kendrick, already overburdened with his duties as commander of Fort Defiance, was appointed temporary agent to the Navajos and was immediately faced with the overwhelming problem of keeping the peace. Not only were the Navajos raiding New Mexican herds grazing on their lands east of the Chuska mountains, but a few young men raided a ranch near Cochiti on the Río Grande soon after Dodge's death. With the coming of spring the Utes intensified their raiding of Navajo rancheros in the northern part of *Dinehtah*. In February, 1857, they rode down and killed eight Navajos in the Chuska mountains. The Navajos retaliated by raiding a Ute camp and killing five warriors, causing the Ute agents, Christopher Carson and Albert W. Pheiffer, to lodge a complaint with the authorities. And still the New Mexicans persisted in using Navajo grazing lands. Kendrick wrote William A. Nichols, adjutant general of the department on February 11, 1857, and suggested: "Under the supposition that we are to have difficulties with other Indians, it would be well if the Mexicans were induced to keep their flocks out of the way of the Navajos, at least until these difficulties are over; this is the more important from the reduced state in which this garrison will soon be found." In April he again advised New Mexican stockmen to move their flocks "well in toward the Rio Grande, or even east of the river."

An extreme drought during the spring and summer of 1857 was as devastating as had been the severe winter of 1855-56 and brought ruin to the crops of *Dinehtah*. When winter came that old monster Hunger picked an opportune time to return to haunt the Navajos. And with James L. Collins chaotically administering Indian affairs in Santa Fe the situation quickly became explosive. On the North, Mormons were still hopeful of inducing the Indians to drive the "Gentiles" out of the Southwest and were furnishing guns and ammunition to the Utes, Piutes, and some Apaches who used them instead to raid the Navajos. Neither the military nor the Indian bureau did anything to discourage the Comanches and the Kiowas from raiding *Dinehtah*, although they were not yet explicitly encouraging them—that would come later. The western Pueblos were also raiding Navajo herds and the New Mexicans, instead of returning Navajo slaves, as the headmen hoped, stepped up their independent forays against the *Dineh* for the purpose of taking more captives. Meriwether, with all his faults, was replaced by Abraham Rencher, a North Carolinian who had once been a Congressman. Rencher had no Indian policy of any sort. Not that it mattered for with the change in civil administration, that office was separated from the governorship and placed solely in the charge of James L. Collins. Then, at the end of the year, Captain Kendrick was replaced by a brass-bound fool—one Major Thomas Harbaugh Brooks of Ohio.

Considering the provocation, it is amazing that the Navajos were able to remain off the war trail as long as they did. In January, 1858, a large party of Utes crossed the Colorado below the mouth of the San Juan and penetrated *Dinehtah* as far as Canyon de Chelly where they killed a respected headman named Pelon. Navajo headmen protested to Major Brooks, pointing out that the army was supposed to protect them as one of its duties and that all Navajos living north of Fort Defiance were moving south because of Ute incursions. Brooks' only action was to request additional troops for the post as he felt the Navajos were "growing restless."

Then, in mid-March, a party of Utes and New Mexicans left Abiquiu under the pretense of recovering some livestock that had allegedly been stolen by Navajo raiders. Instead they rode due west and attacked the first Navajo ranchero they came to, killing five and returning with three young captives who were placed on the slave block and sold—with Ute agent Albert W. Pheiffer looking on.

A few days later another dispute broke out over the Fort Defiance grazing grounds. Because of the drought grass was scarce and Manuelito, who still claimed the pasturage around Ewell's camp twelve miles north of the fort, turned his livestock into the area. When the military protested, Zarcillos Largos advised Manuelito, in light of the deteriorating relations with the Americans, to keep his herds away from the grazing lands claimed by the post. Then both headmen rode to Fort Defiance to advise Major Brooks that Manuelito would remove his herds. Major Brooks, instead of showing appreciation of this remarkable gesture on the part of Manuelito, took the visit as an insult. Looking upon the Navajos as savages who were to be treated as children, he upbraided the "head chief of the Navajos" for not having called on the new commander of the post during the three months he had been at Fort Defiance. He considered the matter of the grazing grounds of little importance. In his opinion Manuelito had no business letting his stock graze there in the first place.

A short time later Brooks reappointed Zarcillos Largos "head chief" and demanded that he and Manuelito gather up sheep that the New Mexicans claimed the Navajos had stolen and bring them into the fort. In April the two headmen led a large band of Navajos to Gray Mountain and returned with 117 sheep. Later that month Zarcillos Largos brought in eight mules that had been stolen from Albuquerque by Delgadito's band.

Although Manuelito had promised Zarcillos Largos that he would remove his herds from the disputed grazing grounds, he, either because of Brook's attitude or because he was too busy with spring planting and rounding up sheep to turn over to the commander, had not done so by the end of May. When he was told that the army was driving off all the animals at the hay camp, he rode to Fort Defiance and tool Brooks virtually what he had told Kendrick two years before: that the water and grass there had always been his to use and he had more right to it than did the army. Major Brooks reminded Manuelito of the Laguna Negra treaty and dismissed him, saying that he and his band were no longer considered friends of the Americans.

As soon as Manuelito rode away from Fort Defiance, Brooks ordered his troops to ride out to the grazing grounds and kill all the livestock that was still there. On May 29 the soldiers mercilessly slaughtered nearly sixty head of livestock, most of which belonged to Manuelito. A *Naachid*—a meeting of the entire nation—was called as a result to discuss going to war. At the meeting, held near Canyon de Chelly, Zarcillos Largos eloquently pleaded for peace and his influence among the important headmen carried the day. But a few days later, on July 7, Brooks usurped more Navajo grazing lands at the end of Canoncito Bonito and detailed a squad of soldiers to harvest hay there for the garrison's horses. This high-handed measure infuriated the Navajos. During the night a war party stole within firing range of the camp and shot a barrage of arrows at the soldiers as a warning, killing a dog. Major Brooks reported that he "made no complaint of the matter to Zarcillos Largos and some other chiefs ... merely cautioning them that it might be a dangerous experiment to try again." Five days later, on July 12, 1858, there finally occurred the senseless incident that plunged the Navajos into a devastating war with the Americans. On that day a Navajo rode into Fort Defiance and, apparently without reason, shot an arrow into the back of Major Brooks' Negro slave, a man named Jim.

As Jim lingered between life and death, Major Brooks sent for Zarcillos Largos and angrily demanded that the culprit be turned over to him immediately. Apparently the old headman, like most of the *Dineh,* had had enough of Brooks and his demands. He pointed out that it had been six weeks since the soldiers had killed Manuelito's livestock and the army had neither paid for nor replaced them, implying that since the major expected restitution for his property it was only fair that he repay Manuelito in kind.

Brooks considered the reply impertinent in the extreme. Furious, he shouted that the Navajos would suffer drastic consequences if his requests were not obeyed to the letter. With deliberate calculation and considerable indifference, Zarcillos Largos said that he was on his way to visit Zūni and he would look into the matter upon his return. He left for Zuñi and two days later Jim died. Major Brooks, at last, had an excuse to give vent to his wrath.

On July 21 Zarcillos Largos was again summoned to Fort Defiance and told by Brooks that the Negro had died. He was given until September 8 to deliver the murderer and if he failed, Brooks said, a state of war would exist between the Navajos and the United States as of that date. Upon learning that the murderer belonged to a band of *ricos* living in the Tunicha mountains, Brooks started organizing an expedition to go after him. When he was told that the members of the murderer's band would fight and die to a man before they would turn him over to the Americans, Major Brooks began preparing for war by gathering intelligence pertaining to Navajo settlements and locations of planting and grazing grounds, and by sounding out various headmen as to the attitudes of the tribe as a whole. According to Brooks' official report the murder of his slave stemmed from a marital understanding between the killer and his wife. It was alleged that he wanted her to go some place with him and when she refused he started out to kill someone outside the tribe to appease his wrath.

Considering Brooks' attitude and the general dissatisfaction of the *Dineh* at the time, this story may or may not be true. At any rate Brooks was not going to be easily appeased. On July 22 he wrote to the adjutant general of the army and suggested that a large force of troops take the field against the Navajos not later than early September. He suggested that an irregular company of New Mexicans from Albuquerque called "Lucero's Spies" be utilized as guides, pointing out that this group could be hired at a very low cost, if a portion of the booty taken during the campaign was offered as payment for their services. Major Brooks' final suggestion indicates the extent that relations with the Navajos had deteriorated in the six months since he'd replaced Kendrick: he urged that the Utes be encouraged to resume raiding the *Dineh* in earnest.

Encouraged by James L. Collins, General John Garland

endorsed Brooks' war plans, excusing the action by proclaiming that the Navajos had started a war "which forces upon me the necessity of opening a campaign against them with not less than one thousand men." Acting under orders from Garland, Lieutenant Colonel Dixon S. Miles arrived at Fort Defiance on September 2 at the head of Company "A" of the Regiment of Mounted Rifles and Company "C" of the Fifty Infantry, a total of 124 men. Two days later Miles summoned Sandoval and sent him to notify as many headmen as he could—or as he dared—that the Navajos had until eight o'clock on the morning of September 8 to deliver the murderer of Jim.

Sandoval reported on September 5 that the murderer had been seen at Bear Springs. The next day he told Miles that he was hiding out in a cave near Laguna Negra. Later that same day he rushed into the garrison and reported that he had been captured near Chuska and promised to return the next day with the prisoner. But on the morning of September 7 the headman of the Enemy People reported that the man had died from wounds sustained during his capture and requested a wagon with which to bring in the body. Miles refused to give him a wagon but furnished him with a blanket instead.

Soon after sunrise on the morning of September 8, Navajos began congregating at the post in such numbers that by mid-morning there were an estimated 300 to 500 mounted and armed warriors milling about Fort Defiance. At eleven o'clock Sandoval arrived with the body. Suspecting treachery, Colonel Miles immediately ordered a careful medical examination of the corpse. Assistant Surgeon J. Cooper McKee conducted the post mortem examination and his findings substantiated Miles' suspicions. He reported that the corpse was that of a man about five feet, two or three inches tall and not over eighteen years old. "The body was perfectly fresh and pliant as in life. There was no rigor mortis anywhere except some little in the left elbow. The face and hair were daubed and smeared with mud and dirt. After washing, and examination I found the following wounds: The most marked was one immediately over the left eye, involving the eye as well as the ridge above it . . . the bone extensively shattered. The weapon must have been very close, and the ball a very irregular one to have made such a wound. The ball did not pass out. Another bullet wound—very regular—was over the region of the stomach, running upwards. Another, very irregular through the right shoulder blade into the cavity of the chest. This bled freely. Another regular wound, just above the left collar bone. Upon opening the cavity of the chest and abdomen, I found the ball which entered the region of the stomach had passed upwards, wounding in its course the left lobe of the liver, passing through the diaphragm into and through the right lung, going out through the ribs and shoulder blade. There was a quantity of uncoagulated blood in the cavity of the chest, and very considerable heat in the intestines. This wound could not have been immediately a fatal one. The ball above the left collar bone had penetrated into the integraments of that region, and was not a wound of much import. Upon opening the cavity of the cranium, I found a battered and flattened slug lying in the brain near the wall of the skull opposite to where it had entered, having passed directly through the brain . . . This wound was an immediately fatal one.

"The wounds were all fresh—there being not the least suppniation (sic). The blood was uncoagulated—the skin perfectly natural. The uninjured eye still preserved its natural appearance. All the organs and tissues were healthy. The blood had not gravitated or settled in any part of the body. From these evidences I am certain that the man had not been dead over eight hours. I am of the opinion that he was first shot through the liver and lungs by a rifle ball while he was in a reclining position—probably asleep. This not being fatal, he was dispatched by a pistol held near his head. This was the immediately fatal wound.

"The Indians asserted that he had been badly shot some days ago, and had died last night after lingering with his wounds. The anatomical evidence—which never deceives—proves positively to the contrary. They also assert that he died some forty miles from the post. The evidence indicates that the boy was murdered in the neighborhood. The man who shot the Negro boy was known from his appearance to be at least forty years of age. This man was not over eighteen . . .

"They have added another murder to their long account, not saying anything of the falsehood and deception attempted to be practiced upon the government."

And so upon McKee's findings and the word of

Sandoval—a man ostracized by his people and despised by them to the man—a state of war was declared between the United States and the Navajos. A general council was called with all the headmen. Opening the council, the newly appointed Indian agent to the Navajos, Samuel M. Yost, told the *Dineh* that his function as their agent had ceased and turned the council over to Major Brooks. Brooks, speaking for Colonel Miles—who refused to see or speak with the headmen—told the Navajos that "their falsehood had been exposed, that further talks were useless," and from that time on a state of war would exist between them and the United States. That very day Colonel Miles penned a formal declaration of war:

"I. Since the arrival of the commanding officer at this Post . . . sufficient time has been given the Navajo tribe . . . to seek, secure and deliver up the murderer of Major Brooks' Negro; to atone for the insult to our flag, and the many outrages committed on our citizens. They have failed to do so; our duty remains to chastise them into obedience to the observances of our land, and after tomorrow morning war is declared against them.

"II. At 8 o'clock tomorrow morning the column designated by Order No. 2 will be in readiness to march with 12 days' rations to fight these Indians wherever found."

So that he might keep his troops continuously in the field and at full strength, Miles requested that Assistant Adjutant General, Major William A. Nichols, take proper measures to open supply channels to Fort Defiance and urged that all means at the disposal of the army be utilized against the *Dineh* and particularly "all the surrounding tribes and inhabitants"—the Utes and the New Mexicans—be encouraged to take the field.

The Navajos quickly withdrew to their strongholds, realizing too late that a different breed of Bilagáana had replaced Henry Linn Dodge and Colonel Edwin Vose Sumner. Brooks, Miles, Garland and particularly James L. Collins were for various reasons as eager to make war on *Dinehtah* as were the New Mexicans and the Americans arriving in New Mexico who wanted Navajo grazing lands. And if the *Dineh* were exterminated in a trumped-up war over the death of a Negro slave, then all the better. That would certainly eliminate any further question as to the use of Navajo grazing lands.

Hoping to find a large concentration of The People in that "Navajo stronghold," Canyon de Chelly, Miles started out for there on the morning of September 9, leading companies "A," "I," and "F" of the Mounted Rifles and two companies of the Third Infantry. As Major Brooks had suggested, Blas Lucero's "Spies" from Albuquerque had been hired and were acting as guides along with some Zūni Indians—and some of Sandoval's Enemy Navajos. The command travelled only twelve miles the first day and camped at Ewell's Camp. Moving out early the next morning they were still fourteen miles from Canyon de Chelly at nightfall. But the Navajos had now had two days in which to get themselves organized and harassed this bivouac throughout the night with sporadic sniping.

The Miles expedition arrived at the Monument Canyon arm of Canyon de Chelly at noon the next day and was guided down a narrow path to the floor of the gorge by one of the Indian scouts. After resting, two companies of the Mounted Rifles were ordered to sweep down the canyon and, if possible, reach its mouth at Chinle Wash before dark. Miles, in the meantime, pressed on with the infantry and the rest of the riflemen. Colonel Dixon S. Miles' march down Canyon de Chelly was reminiscent of Colonel Sumner's reconnaissance of the gorge on August 29, 1851. Again as the setting sun threw long shadows across the canyon floor, Navajos began to appear in ever-increasing numbers on the heights above, shouting insults to the troops and rolling large rocks off the cliff tops to frighten them. An occasional gunshot, followed by the puff of spent powder high on a canyon wall, echoed through the gorge and kept the troops on edge. At sunset the two companies of Mounted Rifles returned, having failed to reach the mouth of the canyon. They had encountered and fought a small party of Navajos and reported killing at least one. Miles chose a wide area on the canyon floor to bivouac for the night. As darkness fell Navajos gathered on the heights "as crows to a feast" and kept campfires burning throughout the night.

The troops, with a great deal of pleasure, resumed the march down the canyon at dawn the next morning. Finally reaching Chinle Wash, they encamped "amid extensive fields" and feasted on the corn and peaches of the Navajos. Miles reported that they were "glad enough to get rid of that remarkable hole in the earth." The only thing that he had accomplished by his reconnaissance of Canyon de Chelly was the capture of a Navajo who told him that many of his people had taken refuge with their flocks at Bekihatso Lake twelve miles to the South. Two companies of Mounted Rifles, under the command of Captain Elliott, were detached at midnight in an attempt to get through the Indians without being detected, while the infantry followed with the first rays of dawn. The movement of the troops was under the constant surveillance of Navajo scouts but the refugees at Bekihatso Lake did not have time to move all of their livestock and lost 6,000 sheep to the Americans. Miles, after burning the fields at Chinle, took up the line of march for Fort Defiance on the morning of September 14. Harassed constantly by Navajo snipers and slowed by the wounded and the captured stock, the troops were forced to camp near Ganado, Arizona, that night. It was a long night. Nearby was the ranchero of Manuelito and his band kept the troops awake and nervous by crawling within firing range and shooting into the camp. The expedition started out at daybreak the next morning and marched the twenty-eight miles to Fort Defiance that day.

Miles, who had predicted that he felt "confident no one, two, or three scouts, with as many battles, would end this war," no doubt realized his prognostication had been painfully correct. His troops had captured about 6,000 head of stock, killed six men at the most and captured one man and six women and children but had lost two killed and several wounded. However, Miles was able to report that the expedition had not been in vain. One of the captives, he wrote Major William A. Nichols, told him that the corpse that had been brought to Fort Defiance as the murderer of Brooks' slave was actually the body of a Mexican slave. This information dispelled any lingering doubt in Santa Fé as to the justification of the war. Colonel Benjamin L. E. Bonneville, who had replaced General John Garland as commander of the department, in an unusual bit of sanctimonious prose considering the source, wrote Miles: "The murder of the Mexican captive, and the offering him as the murderer demanded, is an outrage of so heinous a character, that when the negotiatings were closed, and agent turned the matter into the hands of the military, you were right in pressing the demands by taking the field against them."

Bonneville, over sixty years of age and heading his first command of any importance, saw the outbreak of hostilities with the Navajos as a rare opportunity to redeem his scandal-ridden reputation. Not only was he a dishonest egomaniac (he once copied maps of the West that had been prepared by Jedidiah Smith, William H. Ashley and others and passed them off to Andrew Jackson as his own work. The only change of note that he made on the plagiarized maps was to change the name of Great Salt Lake to "Lac Bonneville"), but he found killing Indians great sport. The historian H. H. Bancroft, who was of the opinion that any crime perpetrated on the Indians by the whites was justified, wrote of him: "(to Bonneville) to shoot buffalo was rare fun; but men were the nobler game, whom to search out in the retreat and slaughter and scalp were glorious."

Bonneville, seeing his chance, immediately issued instructions to Colonel Miles to undertake a second scout and sent the assistant quartermaster of the department, Captain Van Bokkelen, to Fort Defiance with orders to make sure that the troops were properly supplied. He also sent word that Major Electus Backus, the first commander of Fort Defiance and a man who knew the Navajo strongholds well, was on his way back to New Mexico with six companies of recruits and would be sent to fight the Navajos as soon as he arrived from Fort Levenworth.

But Miles did not wait for instructions from Bonneville. As soon as he returned to Fort Defiance from the Canyon de Chelly expedition, he ordered Major Brooks to take a detachment and attack the ranchero of Zarcillos Largos. The records are obscure but apparently the command left Fort Defiance within the week. They were back at the fort on September 25 when Captain John P. Hatch, commander of one of the companies of Mounted Rifles, wrote up his report of the expedition: ". . . I reached Laguna Negra at 5 o'clock this morning . . . and moved with as much rapidity as possible, by a curcuitous (sic) route, to the wheat fields of Zarcillos Largos, situated about nine miles north of the Laguna. By taking advantage of the inequalities of the ground, I reached without being discovered the arroyo which passes through the fields, about one and half miles below them. Entering this arroyo . . . I succeeded in conducting it within two hundred yards of the ranches of Zarcillos Largos' people before I was discovered by them, arriving there at 7 o'clock a.m. I immediately formed (the company) in columns of fours, advanced to the front of the lodges and dismounted my men within fifty yards of them. I was met by about forty Navajoes, armed almost exclusively with fire arms. The fire was for a few minutes quite warm, when the Navajoes retreated, leaving six dead near the houses, and two certainly of those who escaped severely wounded; one of these Zarcillos Largos himself, the Head Chief of the Navajoes, probably mortally. My force was so small that I was not willing to allow it to be scattered in the thickets of oak near the ranches to look up the dead and wounded. Were it not for this I think I would have reported a larger loss of the enemy. I captured upon the ground over fifty horses, and a large number of buffalo robes, blankets, Saddles & c. Many of these latter articles I caused to be thrown upon the wheat stack which was fired by my orders . . . I bring my command back to this Post in as good condition as when it left here; the only reason I can give for this, is that those Indians are unaccustomed to the use of fire arms; most of them were probably using for the first time arms purchased for this war. Had they been armed with the bow and arrow, I must have had numerous casualties to report, for certainly, no man ever behaved with more gallantry and coolness than did Zarcillos Largos until he had discharged the last shot from his rifle and revolver."

Actually the Navajos were using firearms for the first time to any extent, having purchased them from the Mormons. Zarcillos Largos quickly recovered from the wound he received in the fracas and was soon again advocating peace with the Bilagáana. On the very day that Zarcillos Largos' ranchero was under attack, Sandoval was in Santa Fé to consult with Bonneville "about the country in which the troops will . . . operate" and declaring the neutrality of his *Dinehanaih*.

Four days later, on September 29, Major Miles left Fort Defiance with three hundred regulars and Blas Lucero's Spies to attack the Chuska Valley. Surprising the Navajos there, the Americans easily captured more than 5,000 sheep, seventy-nine horses, burned several large fields, hogans and other property and killed ten Navajos with the loss of only a few wounded.

With the arrival of Major Electus Backus and his recruits in New Mexico the last day of September, Bonneville prepared to deliver the coup de grace to the *Dineh*. His plan was to send two powerful columns, one consisting of Backus' recruits and the other of Miles' veterans to strike the Navajos simultaneously and to operate "among the Navajo planting grounds, on and about the San Juan, and the mouth of Canyon de Chelly, with the view of forcing the Navajos further south, towards the Río Chiquito (Little) Colorado." By coordinating the efforts of the two columns Bonneville was certain it would be possible to "destroy and drive from that part of the country every vestige of this troublesome tribe."

Backus' six companies of infantry and cavalry, marching by way of Jemez, rendezvoused with Miles' troops from Fort Defiance in the Tunicha valley on the morning of November 2 and established a base of operations there. After each man was issued fifteen days' rations, the columns moved out, marching together for fifteen miles north through Washington Pass, where they split up. While Backus led his command north to skirt the eastern slopes of the Tunicha mountains, Miles marched his column up the western slope. They reunited at the northern extremities of the Tunichas. Having failed to encounter Navajos or take any captive property, the combined commands then turned west toward Canyon de Chelly, skirted the northern rim on Canyon del Muerto and again made camp at Chinle Wash. Learning from Ute and New Mexican scouts that a large body of Navajos had fled west of the Hopi pueblos, the troops started in pursuit, marched to Black Mesa, skirted the Hopi villages and back to Fort Defiance. Meanwhile a force of 160 Zůni warriors was sent to attack Manuelito's camp in the Ganado Valley. Manuelito and his people learned of the planned attack in time to escape but his fields and hogans were destroyed. The combined columns of Americans had covered three hundred and fifty miles to kill four Navajos, wound four others and capture—and slaughter—less than three hundred and fifty head of livestock.

Bonneville's plan to "destroy" the Navajos taught Miles what Washington and Sumner had learned before him: it was impossible to force the *Dineh* into a decisive battle in their own country. Upon his return to Fort Defiance Colonel Miles learned from Navajo agent Samuel Yost that Zarcillos Largos and a delegation of headmen—among which Manuelito was not numbered—had visited him and asked for peace. Miles prudently realized that further demands for the surrender of the murderer of Brooks' slave were useless and sent a message to Bonneville asking permission to terminate the war. Yost also wrote James L. Collins suggesting that the "chiefs of the tribe" be called in for a peace conference. Collins, realizing that virtually nothing had been accomplished by the "war" and that his fellow New Mexicans would blame him for its failure, suggested that Yost let the military make peace with the Navajos.

Then Collins met with Bonneville and they decided that the Navajos had not been properly "chastised" and, more to the point (unstated, of course), that neither had the Navajos' eastern grazing lands been opened up for the use of New Mexicans nor had Bonneville's reputation been redeemed. The Indian superintendent wrote Yost instructing him not to do more than "agree to bringing down to Albuquerque a deputation of fifteen or twenty of their chiefs" for the purpose of discussing peace with himself and Colonel Bonneville. However, on November 20, two days before Collins penned his letter, Agent Yost and Colonel Miles met Zarcillos Largos, Armijo, Barboncito and some other headmen in council and agreed upon an armistice of thirty days. Miles reported: "Armijo brought in his little boy, and said he wanted for the sake of such as him—that the children were poorly clad, & could not stand to suffer as they would have to do in war. Zarcillos Largos . . . brought in one of his wives, and said that he wanted peace for the sake of her and the women of the nation. The woman came in foremost, bearing a white flag." At the end of the thirty days the headmen agreed to meet with the military at Fort Defiance to form a new treaty of peace "on a sure basis: and which would be binding on the United States as well as the Navajos." In the meantime the headmen were instructed to deliver all stock taken from the military (the theft of which had not been mentioned in any prior military reports), deliver up the murderer of Jim "should he be caught" and exchange captives with the military.

But Collins and Bonneville violently objected to the armistice terms: they still wanted war. In making "amendments and additions" to the terms agreed upon by Miles, Yost, and the Navajo headmen they, among other things, called for the establishment of a new eastern boundary to *Dinehtah*, moving the line established by the 1855 Meriwether treaty still farther west. The new boundary line would force the Navajos to give up virtually all their arable land—all under cultivation—and most of their best grazing lands. And hereafter the army would have permission to destroy all livestock and crops found east of the new boundary. The "Bonneville treaty" also stipulated that, in the future, the whole tribe would be held responsible for the actions of all its members; the United States government would retain the right to dispatch military expeditions and build posts in *Dinehtah* at any time and place, and the tribe had to select a head chief to represent the entire tribe and to act for it in all future negotiations. It also called for the return of "Navajo prisoners in the hands of the United States" and while no explicit mention was made of those held as slaves by the New Mexicans, the subtle wording of the treaty led the Navajo headmen to believe that those, too, would finally be returned.

On December 1 Collins mailed the amended armistice paper along with a letter severely reprimanding Agent Yost for assuming the responsibility for negotiating peace "without instructions or authority from me."

The peace faction of the Navajo headmen absolutely refused to travel to Albuquerque to negotiate so Bonneville and Collins had to go to Fort Defiance. They left Santa Fé on December 14 and, because of inclement weather, took a week to reach their destination. A heavy snow lay over *Dinehtah* and, on December 25, 1858, the day appointed for the signing of the treaty, the temperature hovered around zero. And no really important headmen showed up to put their marks on the new paper with the Americans. Not even Zarcillos Largos was there. He was ill and sent his son instead. Huerro, a minor headman who was also the post blacksmith, was selected the new "chief" and was given central authority over the entire tribe. Then the treaty, calling for the Navajos to give up their principal grazing grounds, the fertile agricultural lands at Collitas, Bear Springs, Ojo Caliente, at Laguna Negra and in the Chuska and Tunicha valleys, was concluded. The fact that the important headmen had not agreed to the treaty caused Agent Yost to predict that the Navajos would not honor it. He also pointed out that the *Dineh* were being left with only one large fertile area—the mouth of Canyon de Chelly—along with a few scattered slopes and canyon bottoms on which to raise enough corn and wheat to sustain 12,000 people as well as his estimation of 250,000 sheep and 60,000 horses, and that the *Dineh* would either have to break the agreement forced upon them and become plunderers or would be compelled to abandon cultivating the soil and stock raising to become pensioners of the government. But James L. Collins and Colonel Bonneville couldn't have cared less. They instructed Collins and Brooks to get the marks of all headmen who had been absent later and returned to Santa Fe, satisfied that they had, for once and all time, opened up the Navajos' eastern lands to white settlers. But they had left the *Dineh* poor.

And they had not reckoned with the wrath of Manuelito. Zarcillos Largos soon realized that the Navajos would find it difficult, if not impossible, to keep the terms of the Bonneville treaty. After several days and nights of meditation, he called for a *Naachid,* to be held northeast of Chinle at Tsin Sikaad (Standing Tree). Arriving to preside over the council that mid-winter, he directed the building of the ceremonial hogan, dug down into the earth for this particular ceremony. Then for eight days he chanted, instructing the young men and women in the ways of the *Naachid,* while the fires of a thousand families glowed and flickered around the council grounds. On the ninth day, after sunup, the war leaders and the peace leaders gathered in a bush-rimmed clearing. In the center was a pile of war implements, shields, lances, bows and arrows.

Zarcillos Largos told of a black vision that had come to him during his meditation:

"I have seen this. I do not want to think of it, but it comes to me. Our sacred mountains were covered with black couds, billowing so not even the Holy Ones could see the peaks. Throughout our valleys and across our mesas not a breath stirred, not a person moved. All that broke the death silence from the tops of the mountains to the very bottom of the canyons was the howl of wolves and the wail of the black wind, death."

Referring to an earlier *Naachid* when he had advocated war, he said: "I was much younger then. I agreed to follow the war trail, to make medicine for the warriors. I heard the Mexicans of the Río Grande cry when we burned their homes. I saw the soldiers fall when we attacked their supply wagons to Fort Defiance . . .

"Blood revenge for the slaying of my nephews at Wide Reeds has never been taken, and their women and children now work in the homes of Mexicans weaving blankets as slaves. And in the last big ripening I had to watch as soldiers burned my hogans to ashes and my fields."

But still he pleaded for peace. In referring to the Americans, he said: "Look how quickly they overcame the Mexicans. Those you see at Fort Defiance have tens of thousands of brothers in their home camps. They are a great and powerful nation . . . No, my blood has not grown thin. No, I am not afraid to fight. But I have learned in these last years of something better than war. From our friend, Red Shirt, I learned of a better trail. You know that when he spoke, it was in truth."

But when it came Manuelito's time to speak, he angrily and eloquently urged war and for four days he campaigned among the younger men, pleading with them to join him in driving the Bilagáana from *Dinehtah*. Finally several of the peace leaders reluctantly agreed to follow the war trail. Zarcillos Largos left the council determined to continue his efforts to keep the peace. And with him went many frightened families who quickly hurried to their homes and fields. At Tsin Sikaad the Navajos split over the issue of another war with the Bilagáana. But war it would be—eventually—a war that would culminate in their defeat and bring about that horrible time remembered forever as The Long Walk.

PART FIVE

The Long Walk

ONE

Manuelito's War

Zarcillos Largos and a few other headmen, notably Ganado Mucho, his clan kinsman, Juanico, and Aqua Chiquito ignored the war party victory at the Tsin Sikaad *Naachid* and attempted to honor the terms of the Bonneville treaty. In the first four months of 1859 they sent several small lots of livestock to Fort Defiance in an effort to pay New Mexicans who claimed that the Navajos had stolen almost 6,000 animals from them which they valued at more than $14,000. They also brought in several captives, who had been stolen at early ages from the Río Grande settlements, but when these were given the choice of returning to their Mexican families or remaining with the Navajos, they all chose the latter. Agent Yost reported to James L. Collins that the captives told him that the Navajos were their brothers and friends and they wished to remain with them.

Manuelito was unusually quiet throughout the year. Perhaps, as he had in the past, he was giving aid to those displaced Navajos living east of the new boundary. There is no way of determining how many Navajos lived in the area taken from *Dinehtah* by Bonneville and Collins. Based on earlier reports I would estimate the number as no less than 3,000 and perhaps as high as 5,000. Of course not all the people living east of the new boundary moved; most stoically remained in their homes and planted new crops that spring. But the number migrating to the western lands, of which much was worthless desert, was sufficient to cause extreme hardship on their clan brethren who took them in.

Primarily at the urging of Agent Yost and because the peace faction of headmen had made an attempt to return the property claimed by the New Mexicans, James L. Collins decided to distribute the annuity goods that had been withheld during the war. In early April his clerk, John Ward, brought the goods to Fort Defiance and issued "a liberal allowance" to the assembled Navajos, assisted by Major Oliver L. Shepherd. In return he took charge of a few horses brought in by the headmen to turn over to the New Mexicans.

While the American military was no longer harassing the Navajos during the spring planting time, apparently no one had remembered to tell their allies, the Utes, that the war was over. Ute war parties were being organized to ride against Navajo ranches at Abiquiu with the knowledge, if not the explicit encouragement, of their agent, Albert W. Pheiffer. Bowing to Navajo complaints, James Collins called a joint council of headmen from both tribes in mid-March. Armijo, Manuelito, Zarcillas Largos, and a number of headmen represented the Navajos. Sandoval's band, also having trouble with the Utes, was not represented. He had died about the middle of February. The Mauhuache Utes were represented by three chiefs and their agent, Christopher Carson. The Capotes—the Southern Utes who were causing most of the trouble—were represented by their war chiefs, Tamuche, Pantalion, Tomasico and a delegation of forty warriors. Collins reported to Commissioner of Indian Affairs J. W. Denver that the council adjourned with both sides promising to end the conflict and "live once again in peace."

In a letter Collins wrote to Denver dated March 20, he stated that he had been anxious to close the war between the two tribes "ever since I came into office," which, of course, was not true. He had encouraged the Ute participation in the recent conflict and had not once reprimanded his agent, Pheiffer, for allowing the Utes to raid Navajo ranches. He added that his attempts to end the war had always ended in failure "owing to the evil influence of bad disposed Mexicans" who profited from Navajo-Ute conflicts by offering an outlet for stolen property and captives. True

324

enough, but James L. Collins' first bid at making peace between the two nations came in mid-March, 1859, and he had an exact purpose for doing so then. His New Mexican and American friends were anxious to move their herds onto the lands that he and Bonneville had recently stolen from the Navajos and it was not expedient to do so as long as it was being traversed by uncontrollable Ute war parties raiding the Navajos or angry Navajo warriors on their way to retaliate.

Collins' feeble effort as a peacemaker came to naught. The Capote Utes, especially, realized they could continue to raid Navajo herds at will. The Americans were their friends and allies. About May 1, a faction of young Navajos, probably encouraged by Manuelito, raided a Ute camp within three miles of Albert W. Pheiffer's agency at Abiquiu. A few days later Navajos struck a herd belonging to Felipe Chavez, left three *pastores* dead and ran off, Chavez reported, 2,000 sheep. The actual number was less than half of that. The New Mexicans demanded that the murderers of the *pastores* be caught and punished.

Writing to the Indian Commissioner on May 29, Collins said, in his opinion, "the influential men seem entirely unable to control the dishonest portion of the tribe." He added, probably with Manuelito in mind, that he believed some headmen "connive at the robberies committed by their people," and suggested a severe chastisement of the entire nation: "It is true," he wrote, "that since the conclusion of peace the conduct of the chiefs had led me to hope that the tribe would profit by the lesson they received. But their chastisement must be more severe, they must be well punished and thoroughly humbled before we can expect better conduct from them." Obviously the "better conduct" Collins wanted was for the Navajos to stand meekly by while he and his fellow New Mexicans took the last acre of their land, sold their children into slavery, and took all property they owned worth taking.

While admitting that the reports of the Navajo depredations were probably exaggerated by the New Mexicans, Collins, nevertheless, urged a show of armed might that would force the Navajos into compliance with the Bonneville treaty. Actually Colonel Bonneville had already organized an expedition to ride against the Navajos under the command of Major John S. Simonson, and Collins knew it.

Simonson arrived at Abiquiu on June 12 and assumed command of the 700 troops and Ute guides assembled there and left immediately for *Dinehtah*. Splitting the troops into two commands, he led one column from Abiquiu to Fort Defiance by way of Ojo Caliente, crossing the Tunicha Mountains north of Washington Pass. The second column marched by way of Laguna and Cubero to meet him at the post.

In the meantime James Collins wrote his new Navajo agent Alexander Baker, who was already at Fort Defiance, and ordered him to accompany the expedition on its tour of the Indian country so that the Navajos would see that the civil government and the military were working in harmony. Major Simonson reached Fort Defiance about the first of July and immediately called a council of headmen. He instructed those who attended to contact the other headmen and tell them to come to the fort for a council before scouting parties were dispatched to "visit the more troublesome bands." Simonson's next two councils accomplished nothing as few headmen showed up at the fort for them. But a council held on July 14, in a wooded area about a mile from the post, was attended by Huerro, Zarcillos Largos, and Ganado Mucho and other headmen of the peace faction who were offered an "article of agreement" binding them to restore all property stolen from the military and the New Mexicans since August 15, 1858. Zarcillas Largos, particularly, had had enough of the American's paper and he was instrumental in persuading the others not to sign it.

The old headmen had signed many papers with the Americans and they had never accomplished anything. Besides the *Dineh* were constantly giving up property and livestock to satisfy the claims of the New Mexicans. But not once had the New Mexicans returned any of their property, livestock or, most important, women and children. While it was highly unlikely that any of the headmen attending the meeting had stolen anything claimed by the military or the New Mexicans, Major Simonson and Agent Baker did get some of them to agree, verbally, to repay "all that they had stolen." Then Simonson went ahead with Bonneville's plan of making a "show of the might of the United States army" and on July 18 two detachments left Fort Defiance to reconnoiter the countryside. One column marched west to the Hopi villages and on to the Little Colorado River gorge. A second company, commanded by Lieutenant J. G. Walker and accompanied by Agent Baker, marched northwest to Canyon de Chelly, then north to the San Juan and back across the Tunicha mountains over what Baker described as "the most beautiful country I have ever seen in this territory."

Baker reported to Collins that the number of Navajos encountered during the seventeen-day trip convinced him that the *Dineh* were more populous than the previous estimates of twelve to fifteen thousand and that the immense herds of horses, sheep and goats were proof that the Navajos were capable of repaying their debt to the New Mexicans. He added: "It is perfectly useless to postpone a settlement of the present difficulties with them; the longer it is put off the more trouble you will have in the end. Now is the time to take a decided stand against them, while the army is in their country."

Collins, of course, concurred and wrote the Indian Commissioner suggesting a rigid enforcement of the Bonneville treaty. He added: "We should never allow a murder or robbery to go unpunished; each violation of law or treaty stipulation should be followed by prompt and immediate chastisement. They deserve no more mercy at our hands, and should be taught to expect none."

But the military did not agree with Agent Baker and James L. Collins. Captain J. G. Walker, with whom the agent had made his tour of *Dinehtah,* warned that "a war made upon them now by us would fall heaviest upon the least guilty—would transform a nation which has already made considerable progress in civilized arts into a race of beggars, vagabonds and robbers." And in a letter written to Assistant Adjutant General J. D. Wilkens on August 8, Major Simonson said: ". . . Since my last report the conduct of the Indians has been pacific. Herrero Miles (Huerro) and Zarcillas Largas (sic), notwithstanding their refusal to sign a paper reiterating the pledges made in the treaty of December last, have been actively engaged in bringing in stock as indemnity for property said to have been stolen by Navajos. In fact all the wealthy and influential men of the nation are solicitous for peace and are assisting in restoring the reputed stolen property. Doubtless the present state of feeling existing among them. The *ladrones* (or bad men as they call them) are undoubtedly the thieves and commit the depredations. They have nothing to lose and if war were made upon them now, the innocent and those most active for the preservation of peace would be the sufferers. It is an unquestionable fact that many horses and sheep have been stolen on the frontier and settlements by the Navajos but there are reasons to believe that the numbers are very greatly exaggerated; and it is very doubtful if a single murder has been committed by them since the peace of December last. They on the contrary assert that two of their people have been murdered; that many of their horses have been stolen; that they have never been offered restoration for property or people and they claim that their losses should be taken into account. Another complaint is that their agents *(Tatoes)* are frequently changed before they can become acquainted with them; that from the death of Mr. Dodge to the arrival of Major Baker, no agent apparently took interest in their affairs . . .

"They have evidenced no hostility towards the troops, made no objections to explorations of their country and have furnished guides and information when requested. At this moment they are endeavoring to procure contributions of sheep and horses and say they will indemnify claimants for stolen property as far as they are able. Whatever the offenses of these people may have been heretofore, their present conduct will not justify hostilities against them . . ."

Major Simonson, apparently unaware of Agent Baker's letter advocating war, added: "I have the concurrence of Major Baker (their agent) in this opinion."

Baker was serving as temporary agent and was replaced by Silas F. Kendrick who arrived at Fort Defiance in early September. The new agent was instructed by James L. Collins not to waver in carrying out his hard-line policy and in the beginning he complied. A few days after his arrival he called a council at Laguna Negra—on September 15, 1859—that was attended by Zarcillos Largos, Huerro, Ganado Mucho and several other important headmen who rode in with about four or five hundred Navajos. They listened to their new agent tell them, once again, how important it was to pay claims made by the New Mexicans, and rode away. Next Kendrick travelled to Canyon de Chelly where he remained for four days urging leaders there to honor the

New Mexican claims and telling them if they did not their crops and herds would be destroyed. While at Canyon de Chelly, Kendrick learned that the Mormons, who were under attack by the United States Army, were again trying to unite all the tribes between the Colorado and the Río Grande to fight the Americans. Captain Walker, on his recent visit to the area, had been told the same and that missionaries were inviting Navajos to attend a council at Navajo Mountain in October at which guns, powder and other articles of trade would be passed out. The Mormons, Kendrick reported, had advised the Navajos that they were being cheated "out of their land, timber, grass and live-stock."

At a second Laguna Negra council, held on September 25, Kendrick, accompanied by Major Simonson and fifty mounted troops, again urged the Navajos to "meet their obligations." Zarcillos Largos and Ganado Mucho replied that they had paid as much as they were able to in an effort to fulfill the claims of the New Mexicans. They also pointed out that the Navajos had never received any compensation for depredations committed against them by the New Mexicans and Pueblo Indians. Simonson, in his last official letter from Fort Defiance, written to J. D. Wilkens on September 28, agreed: ". . . Another important item, in connection with Navajo affairs, is depredations of Mexican citizens and Pueblo Indians upon the Navajos. Since the troops arrived in the Navajo country, in June last, these depredations have increased under the supposition that the plundering of the Indians could be done with impunity, and less danger encountered; and they have continued to this time."

Ganado Mucho and a few other headmen of the peace faction continued to bring livestock into Fort Defiance and turn it over to the new agent. On October 25 Agent Kendrick calculated that the Navajos had repaid no more than one-tenth of the $14,000 worth of stock the New Mexicans claimed was owed them and turned the matter over to the military, saying that he had exhausted "every means within my power" to get the *Dineh* to comply with the stipulations of the Bonneville treaty. But he made it clear that he was acting under the specific instructions of Superintendent of Indian Affairs James L. Collins. In effect, Collins had ordered his agent at Fort Defiance to place the entire matter of Navajo relations in the hands of the military. This order came only a few days after the amiable Major John S. Simonson, at his request, had been transferred east. In his place Colonel Bonneville had appointed Captain Oliver Lathrop Shepherd. Compared to Captain Shepherd, Major Brooks—whose arrogance had perpetrated the last war—had been a paragon of fairness.

A few weeks after he arrived at the post, Captain Shepherd furnished Kendrick with a military escort so that he could take the livestock the Navajos had relinquished to Albuquerque to be sold or delivered to persons claiming losses. The first night out of Fort Defiance a party of Navajos stampeded the herd and got away with all but eighteen horses. The next morning a Navajo rode into the Americans' camp with two army rifles, which he said he had found. Although the man was a member of Ganado Mucho's band—and that headman and his followers had gathered livestock from one corner of *Dinehtah* to the other and turned it over to the Americans for the past year—the lieutenant with Kendrick suspected that he had been involved in stampeding the herd the night before. The officer ordered him to take the rifles to Captain Shepherd at Fort Defiance and also a note telling the commander of the theft of the livestock. The man, instead of riding directly to the fort, stopped to ask Ganado Mucho what he should do. The headman told him to take the rifles and the note to Captain Shepherd. But because the Navajo took longer to arrive at the Fort than Captain Shepherd thought he should have, he was ordered stripped and flogged.

The undeserved punishment lost the friendship of Ganado Mucho to the Americans, and brought about the beginning of a feud between Agent Kendrick and Shepherd. Kendrick wrote James L. Collins: "Such treatment as this is what destroys all confidence of the Indians in the poisonous justice or common humanity of government officials . . . Ganado Mucho is one of the most faithful and efficient friends of the whites in the whole tribe."

After the wanton flogging of the messenger, few Navajos would venture near the fort for any reason. With but two or three exceptions the headmen who had been wavering between peace and war for the past year called on Manuelito and offered to follow him on the war trail. But Ganado Mucho and his brother, Juanico, still held out hopes for peace. When they learned that the Navajos planned to attack the garrison grazing camp and run off the military livestock, Juanico rode to Fort Defiance on the afternoon of January 15, 1860. Remembering what had happened to his relative, he waited on a hilltop outside the fort until the interpreter came out to see what he wanted. He told the interpreter that Navajos had been riding past his camp all day going in the direction of the hay camp. When this information was relayed to Captain Shepherd, he sent a detachment of thirty men to strengthen the guard at the camp.

Manuelito, having waited a year, now had almost the entire tribe behind him, and shortly after dawn on January 17, he and Huerro led a force of about 200 warriors against the hay camp. The Navajos succeeded in burning the haystacks and running off some cattle but the fire of the soldiers repelled the attack. Later that day four soldiers out on a wood detail were killed near the fort, and at noon the next day a detachment of soldiers who were sawing lumber about three miles from the post was suddenly attacked. The Navajos left another soldier dead and one wounded. Fanning out his warriors, Manuelito posted scouts about the post in an attempt to cut off supplies from Albuquerque. A quartermaster wagon, on its way to Fort Defiance from Albuquerque, was harassed constantly but was saved by its escort of forty-two men under the command of Lieutenant William Dickinson.

Three days after the outbreak of hostilities, Agua Chiquito appeared at the fort and asked to speak to Kendrick. Agua Chiquito, Ganado Mucho and Juanico were all the important headmen that remained of the peace faction, and the headman's purpose in conferring with the agent was to determine a way to stop the war. But Captain Shepherd kept interrupting the conversation, trying to get the friendly headman to talk to him instead of to Agent Kendrick. Agua Chiquito ignored the officer, unable to comprehend his purpose in interrupting. Shepherd lost his temper and told Kendrick that he was in charge and the Indian agent was not allowed to hold conversation with any Navajo without his permission. When Agua Chiquito refused to talk to Shepherd, he was ordered to leave the post immediately. As the headman turned to go, Shepherd signaled for his sentries to shoot him. The headman quickly ran from the fort, under fire, and made his way to safety. All hopes of stopping the war went with him. Major Shepherd wrote the adjutant general that the question of whether there would be a war had been settled in the affirmative.

A few days later Kendrick wrote Collins and complained of Shepherd's conduct: "Up to this occurrence," he said, "Agua Chiquito, Ganado Mucho, Juanico and several other influential members of the tribe, had given every evidence of their sincere desire to bring their people to an amicable adjustment of the difficulties and had rendered many valuable services to me and and also to the military . . . There was every reason to believe in and rely upon their good faith, and they were extremely anxious to second and advance the views and purposes of the Government to the best of their ability. But since the treatment of Agua Chiquito, not one of these Indians has returned . . . to the fort or seek any communications with me or with any other white man. Evidently their good confidence in the good faith of the Americans is entirely destroyed, and if they have not become active combatants themselves, they cannot be expected to cooperate with us." Not only did the Indian agent feel that the military had greatly contributed to the breach in relations, but most of the junior officers at Fort Defiance also felt that the Navajos had been unjustly treated and that the New Mexican claims against the *Dineh's* property were either completely unfounded or greatly exaggerated.

Shepherd informed Kendrick that a state of war existed between the Navajos and the United States and that the agent was prohibited from holding any intercourse with any member of the tribe. Kendrick then wrote Collins and requested permission to return to Santa Fé. Permission was granted and he arrived in the capital in early March and assumed duties as the agent to the Pueblos.

Before the end of January the Navajos carried the war as far east as the Río Grande and harassed the area around Fort Craig, south of Socorro. Then, on February 8, a war party attacked the cattle guard consisting of forty-one enlisted men and three officers at Captain Richard Ewell's Camp and were repulsed only after a hard-fought battle lasting two hours. Not only did the Navajos continue to harass the supply wagons on their way to and from Albuquerque but they fanned out and also began raiding the New Mexicans, burning ranches and running off livestock.

Then, just as the war got under way—a war that had been started, to a great extent, by his personal ambition— Colonel Bonneville was summoned to the East and was replaced by Colonel Thomas T. Fauntleroy. An experienced Indian fighter, Colonel Fauntleroy was convinced that he needed more troops than the approximately 1800 in his command to win a full-scale war against the Navajos. He decided to wait until he could bring additional troops from other posts in the West before launching an offensive against the *Dineh,* and when Captain Shepherd requested aid he was turned down.

Fauntleroy's hesitation infuriated James L. Collins, who started a press war with the commander in his Santa Fé *Weekly Gazette.* Governor Rencher joined Collins in his attack on the military and the old feud of governor versus general was renewed. To complicate matters, New Mexico's Delegate to Congress, Miquel A. Otero, backed Fauntleroy and attacked Governor Rencher in letters to friends and press. Then the New Mexico Assembly authorized the formation of militia companies for the purpose of conducting campaigns independently of the military. But Colonel Fauntleroy refused to issue them arms and Governor Rencher was legally compelled to concur with his decision.

As the war of words between the military and civil administrations raged in Santa Fé, and between the capital and Washington, the Navajos tightened the circle around Fort Defiance. Captain Shepherd again called for reinforcements, but Colonel Fauntleroy sent word that no offensive action would be immediately undertaken against the Navajos. Furthermore he ordered Company "G" of the Third Infantry from Fort Defiance to Ojo de Oso where a new post (Fort Fauntleroy, later Fort Wingate) was being constructed to replace Fort Defiance. The Navajos watched the departure of the troops on April 21 and immediately began making plans to launch a direct attack on the fort. The attack was planned by Manuelito and Barboncito, a headman and Singer from Canyon de Chelly.

During the night of April 29, 1860, the thousand men that Manuelito had said he could call about him at any time gathered at Cañoncito Bonito. They moved in before dawn and surrounded three sides of the fort. Then, about an hour before sunrise, they struck. The first shots were fired at the three sentries at the southwest corner of the fort, near the corrals and powder magazine. Almost immediately a large force attacked the east side of the fort from the rocky hill there, and that attack was quickly followed by the whoops and yells of another force attacking the West. The Navajos quickly took possession of the garden where the woodpiles and fences gave them protection. The post sentries were driven back to the kitchen and laundry quarters before the Long Roll was sounded, sending the 138 men left at the post to the firing line. So swift and well-organized was the assault (even Captain Shepherd would later admit that the attack was "well planned") that the Navajos had taken possession of all the outer buildings, including the storehouse, before the soldiers got their wits about them and began an organized defense. For an hour the battle raged, but with the coming of dawn the Americans were able to achieve stronger defensive positions and Manuelito signaled his warriors to withdraw.

Two companies were ordered to pursue them but the orders were quickly countermanded when the advance company was mistaken for Navajos and fired on by the rear company. As Maurice Frink said: "It was, to be sure, no Little Bighorn with cavalry charges, no Washita with an army band playing the troops into battle, no Wounded Knee with Hotchkiss guns killing women and children. It was just a two-hour hand-to-hand fight in the dark with bows and arrows and muzzle-loading muskets. Casualties were what military men call light. But the issue settled by the battle was momentous to the Navajos." (Frink, Pruett Press, 1968: 48.)

Only one American was killed, Private Sylvester Johnson. The Navajos lost seven, possibly eight men. But the Navajos had raided the post storehouse and given the soldiers a good scare. And the Americans decided to abandon Fort Defiance. As Shepherd pointed out in his official report of the attack, the post had been vulnerable to attack from the time of its establishment due to its "peculiar and extraordinary location."

The Navajos had taken the offensive against the Americans but they were not rid of the Fort Defiance soldiers quite yet. On May 4, Adjutant General Wilkins decided that Fort Defiance should not be abandoned "for the time being"—and as soon as he learned of the attack on the fort, Secretary of War J.B. Floyd declared: "Active operations will be instituted against the Navajos as soon as the necessary preparations can be made. A winter campaign *with infantry,* if inaugurated with secrecy and prosecuted with vigor, will prove the shortest and most effectual plan of operations."

But the citizens of New Mexico were in no mood to wait for a winter campaign. Collins took matters in hand and ordered Albert W. Pheiffer and Christopher Carson to urge the Utes to send war parties against the Navajos--not that the Utes had ever stopped. Pheiffer and Carson were also instructed to assist in organizing forays in which the Utes and New Mexicans would unite to "attack the common enemy."

By the middle of May a force of 400 New Mexicans and Utes was on its way to invade *Dinehtah.* Hitting the Tunicha valley, they burned hogans and destroyed fields. Then, led by Ute guides, they invaded the nearby mountain retreats of the Navajos and took at least thirty-five children captive after killing six men and one woman.

J.B. Floyd immediately began shuffling military units in the Southwest and sent the Fifty and Seventh Infantry regiments, three companies of the Tenth Infantry, and two companies of the Second Dragoons from Fort Floyd, Utah, to Fauntleroy's command. For the next three months the United States Army in New Mexico geared itself for a full-scale campaign, the likes of which the Navajos had never before witnessed. But the army was moving too slow for the New Mexicans, especially after word got back to the Rio Grande in June that Manuelito had won the first really decisive victory of the war. Learning that another expedition of Utes and New Mexicans were on their way from Abiquiu to raid the Chuska valley, the headman quickly martialed a war party to meet them.

The Navajos arrived in the valley before the New Mexicans and prepared an ambush. Dragging fallen logs and large boulders to the edge of the high slopes above a pass they knew the expedition would take, they sat down and waited. As the New Mexicans rode into the pass, parties of mounted Navajos suddenly appeared to their front and rear and began letting arrows fly. The warriors who had remained above on the heights rolled the logs and boulders down on the New Mexicans who were trying to escape by climbing the slopes. Fifty New Mexicans and Utes had ridden out from Abiquiu, but only ten returned. The bodies of the other forty were left behind in the Chuska valley.

A convention was called in Santa Fe at the beginning of August—after the Navajos had turned back another large expedition—to discuss a citizens' war on the *Dineh*. Backed by James L. Collins and merchants and land speculators who agreed to furnish arms for a price, the convention proposed to raise an army of 1,000 New Mexican volunteers and the recruitment of 400 Utes. On the first day of then convention, Collins called for war in his *Gazette* by writing: "For months the bells of your sacred edifices have tolled the obsequies of your slaughtered citizens."

The Navajos managed to hold their own until late September, when the army finally took the offensive. Fauntleroy gave the command of directing the campaign against the Navajos to Colonel Edward Sprigg Canby. Canby, an 1839 graduate of West Point, had fought the Seminoles in Florida, served under General Scott in Mexico, and had for several years commanded posts in the West. Canby was a good soldier and he had the complete confidence of both Colonel Fauntleroy and the Secretary of War, who gave him full control of the operations against the Navajos. His plan of operation was deceptively simple. Three columns would move out from various points on the Rio Grande, would rendezvous at Fort Defiance, then fan out and stay in the field until the Navajos were defeated or harassed into submission.

On September 9 one company of cavalry and two companies of infantry left Fort Craig under the command of Captain Lafayette McLaws for *Dinehtah* by way of Zuñi. Three days later four companies of cavalry and one infantry company left Albuquerque, along with twenty of Blas Lucero's Spies, under the command of Canby's brother-in-law, Major Henry Hopkins Sibley. Sibley marched west and north through the Tunicha valley, then south through Washington Pass to Fort Defiance. Then, on September 18, Canby left Abiquiu with 138 regular troops and a force of 500 Pueblo Indians, by way of Canyon Largo. The purpose of the three columns was to force the Navajos residing east of Fort Defiance to flee west to seek sanctity at Canyon de Chelly and in the Black Mesa region—and it was successful. Canby's troops were immediately followed into the field by a force of about 800 New Mexicans—the "citizens' army" that had been organized at the convention in Santa Fé the month before.

Canby strenuously objected to the volunteer army. Not only did he fear they would complicate the military campaign but he also realized that taking captives would be their primary objective. The New Mexicans were followed into the war by bands of Utes, Apaches and Pueblo Indians after plunder and captives.

Canby sent Captain McLaws and his troops north to patrol the western slopes of the Chuska-Tunicah mountains and to prevent the Navajos who had fled west from returning to their homes east of the mountains. Then he and Sibley led separate commands toward Canyon de Chelly and Black Mesa. Sibley's command left Fort Defiance on October 10, and Canby left the next day. They united at Chinle Wash a week later, and learned, to their amazement, that neither command had encountered any Navajos. It seemed that the entire nation had suddenly disappeared. On October 23, Sibley, on his way back to Black Mesa, came across a large herd of horses and a flock of about 2,000 sheep which he captured after killing five Navajo herdsmen. He also captured three women and two children. On November 6, both Sibley and Canby were back at Fort Defiance. The expedition had, they felt, been a miserable failure. Sibley reported that troops and army horses were completely exhausted. But the campaign of the slave raiders had been successful. During the month of October the New Mexicans alone took over one hundred captives and returned them to the Río Grande to be placed on the slave market. The Utes and other Indians probably took again as many. Agent Pheiffer, leading a large party of Utes, had raided the ranches of the San Juan Navajos and had captured several thousand head of livestock.

But the most devastating blow, at least spiritually, to the Navajos was the death of Zarcillos Largos. Some time just before October 20, 1860, the great peace leader was killed on his way home at Oak Springs from a visit to the Hopi country. According to Navajo tradition, he was riding alone near Sagebrush Spring, south of Klagetoh, when he encountered a party of New Mexican and Zuñi raiders. A Zuñi who knew him tried to shout a warning, but it was too late. Several of the party began firing and Zarcillos Largos returned fire with his arrows, killing four of his attackers. But as he tried to escape, his horse was shot from under him. Taking cover behind the fallen horse, he continued to fight until all his arrows were gone. His attackers then closed in and shot his body full of arrows. Then they proceeded to break his arms and legs, lest he have power to injure them after death. The sinews from his limbs were taken to make war medicine by the Zuñis.

While Canby and Sibley considered the military operation against the Navajos as falling far short of their expectations, they perhaps did not realize how really effective their campaigning, combined with those of the New Mexicans and other Indians, had been. With enemies everywhere, constantly crossing and crisscrossing *Dinehtah*, the Navajos had been forced to abandon their fields, and the fall harvest had been left to rot, or, more often, set to the torch. The *Dineh* would go hungry that winter even if their enemies withdrew.

But Canby did not withdraw. Instead he stationed garrisons at several strategic points throughout *Dinehtah* to harass the Navajos. Leaving a few troops at Fort Defiance for that purpose, he moved his base of operations to Fort Fauntleroy. Scouting parties, led by Ute, Zuñi and New Mexican guides, were kept in the field at all times for the purpose of keeping the Navajos away from their fields and grazing grounds. The Navajos, broken up into small groups and family units, were kept constantly on the move. Finally they had no choice but to give up.

With heavy snows covering *Dinehtah* it became increasingly difficult to avoid the troops and raiders and, toward the end of December, several delegations timidly approached fort Fauntleroy and asked for peace. Canby sent word that a general peace council would be held on January 12, 1861, to discuss armistice terms, if the "chiefs" of the tribe would come in. One by one, Ganado Mucho, Armijo, Barboncito, Delgadito, Huerro, and finally Manuelito came to the new fort. At the council Canby agreed to stop all military operations west of Fort Fauntleroy but, as he believed most of the *ladrones* lived east of the fort, he pledged to continue to scout that area until those people indicated they also wanted peace. Actually, whether he knew it or not, by designating Fort Fauntleroy as the east-west dividing line, Canby was adhering much more closely to the boundary established by the Meriwether treaty than that set by Collins and Bonneville. He closed the council by designating February 5 as the date for another council at which terms for a final peace would be discussed.

Although about 2,000 Navajos were camped about Ojo de Oso on February 5, several important headmen, Manuelito among them, had not yet arrived because of the deep snow covering *Dinehtah*. Canby postponed the council until February 15. On that date thirty-two headmen were present to sign the treaty—yet another "paper" with the Americans. Even Manuelito must have been surprised at the conditions Canby set forth in the new treaty. It was almost a complete reversal of the hated Bonneville treaty. Having come to the conclusion that the Navajos were both impoverished by the various military campaigns and that they were more often the victims rather than the perpetrators of aggression, Canby proposed extremely lenient peace terms calling for all headmen signing the treaty to submit unconditionally to United States authority and thereafter to be held responsible for the acts of all their people; to suppress the *ladrones*, and to collect their people and establish them in the country west of Fort Fauntleroy.

Canby was sincere in his desire to protect the Navajos from the raids of the New Mexicans and other Indians and proposed that Fort Fauntleroy and Fort Defiance be kept at their current strength to both protect the Navajos and prevent them from making raids. But he soon learned that protecting the Navajos was going to be more difficult than keeping them in check. Only twelve days after signing the treaty he wrote Colonel Fauntleroy: "I had the honor in previous reports to suggest the danger to be apprehended in the permanent settlement of the Navajo difficulties from the unauthorized aggressions of the Mexican and Pueblo populations, and recent occurences in this quarter induce me to recur to that subject.

"1. A party of 31 Mexicans from the neighborhood of Taos, who by their own statements had no complaints to make of the Navajos, arrived here a few days since in starving condition. In the course of their operations they had killed one man and six women and children and had captured four women. At this post subsistence was issued to them as a matter of humanity. Their prisoners were taken from them and since have been returned to their families. On their way to Fort Fauntleroy they committed wanton aggressions upon the property of Navajos (Ganado Mucho's band) who have always been friendly. At this post they received subsistence to carry them to the settlements, and them of their number who from debility were unable to travel are now receiving subsistence and medical attendance. They openly avow their intention to disregard the treaty made with the Navajos, and on their return home to organize a new expedition to capture Navajos and sell them on the river.

"2. The inhabitants of Cuvero express the same determination and a few days since, two Navajos who had been permitted (after the treaty) to visit their relations in Sandoval's band were openly killed in the neighborhood of that place.

"3. On the 24th inst. two Navajo guides in the service of the United States, and wearing distinctive marks, were fired upon and one of them killed and scalped by a party from Jemez. These and other occurrences of minor importance indicate I think a settled disposition on the part of some of these people to protract the Navajo troubles indefinitely."

Canby learned of four more expeditions a month later, two of which carried off captives to be sold in Santa Fe or elsewhere. Absolutely nothing was done about the situation by the American authorities, however, and on March 18 Canby reported that still another expedition of New Mexicans had attacked fifteen Navajo ranches in the Tunicha mountains and killed or carried off all the people there. In the same report he also stated that "the Navajo chiefs appear to be carrying out in good faith the conditions of the treaty" in spite of what amounted to almost constant attack from the New Mexicans.

Manuelito had taken his war to the Americans. The Bilagáana had abandoned Fort Defiance and he could now graze his cattle within the very grounds of the hated military post; the Navajo losses, at least in lives, had been light and the *Dineh* had actually seen some of their lands restored. But there was to be no peace. Far away to the East the Bilagáana were mobilizing to fight each other. And the few military men in New Mexico—Canby, Fauntleroy, Sibley—who were capable and desirous of bringing about a permanent peace with the Navajos would soon leave to oppose each other in that conflict.

340

TWO

The Civil War in New Mexico

During that spring of 1861 most national observers believed that New Mexico would cast her lot with the Confederacy. Governor Abraham Rencher remained neutral but the popular territorial secretary, Alexander M. Jackson openly boasted of his close friendship with Confederate President Jefferson Davis and, with considerable native support, campaigned to move New Mexico to join the "coming new order." In the southern part of the state a majority of the population supported the South; and at Mesilla, a small town north of El Paso on the Rio Grande a group of southerners, mostly ranchers who had moved to the area from Texas, joined forces with influential Hispanos and declared all of Arizona and the southern half of New Mexico as the Confederate Territory of Arizona.

The effects of the southern succession were most immediately felt among the military stationed in New Mexico. Colonel Thomas Fauntleroy, a southerner, resigned as commander of the department on March 25 and was replaced by William Wing Loring who served for only two months before declaring his loyalty to the South. The command was then given to the highest ranking officer in the department who was still loyal to the Union, Colonel Edward Sprigg Canby.

In the meantime Colonel Canby's brother-in-law, Major Henry H. Sibley, had also resigned his commission and left New Mexico after telling the men of this command, "Boys, if you only knew it, I am the worst enemy you have!"

Sibley immediately traveled to Richmond to visit Jefferson Davis and convinced the Confederate president that he possessed a workable plan to seize Arizona and New Mexico and also to take, or at least tap, the gold regions of California and Colorado. He also hoped to get the Utah Mormons to support the South. Davis commissioned him as a brigadier general in the army of the Confederacy, and by June Sibley was in Texas recruiting an army with which he hoped to quickly defeat his brother-in-law's force and push on to California.

Meanwhile Canby had his hands full in New Mexico. Half his command had deserted to the South and those that remained had not been paid for six months and a majority of them were without mounts. Canby, knowing that Sibley was in Texas whipping an army into shape to invade New Mexico, had little time to concern himself with the Navajos. With Fort Defiance deserted and the garrison at Fort Fauntleroy, now called Fort Lyons, severely reduced, the Utes realized an opportune time to renew their war on the *Dineh*. Too, that segment of the New Mexicans who were of a bent to deal in the slave traffic did not concern itself with national politics and quickly stepped up their raids. By summer Manuelito realized that the soldiers left at Ojo de Oso were too few and were unable to give the Navajos the protection that had been promised by Canby. While remaining on friendly terms with the soldiers, he again took to the war trail. During June and July he led or directed raids against the Utes, and against the New Mexicans as far west as the Rio Grande.

Canby obtained permission from the war department to raise four regiments of New Mexican volunteers and placed one of them, the First Regiment, under the command of Christopher Carson, the fur trader, explorer and veteran Indian fighter who had, in recent years, been the Ute agent at Taos. As Ute agent Carson's attitude toward the wars between his charges and other Indians had been, "they win a few and they lose a few, so what? They're only Indians."

When, on July 1, 1861, Captain John Robert Baylor, in command of 258 Texas cavalry, occupied Fort Bliss, Canby appealed to Colorado for volunteers and requested that troops be sent from California. A brigade of California volunteers were mustered and placed under the command of General James H. Carleton, who had served in the New

Mexico department from 1852 until 1858 when he was transferred to California.

Captain Baylor moved his Confederate forces northward, occupied Mesilla, and after very little resistance took Fort Fillmore in late July. Canby, realizing that the Confederates would invade either over the Santa Fe Trail or up the Rio Grande, prepared his defenses accordingly.

And while Canby was preparing to defend New Mexico from the Confederates, trouble struck at Ojo do Oso. The precarious peace between the Bilagaana and the Navajos was broken, and by the soldiers. Since the last peace treaty, Navajos, in spite of their war on the Utes and Ne./ Mexicans, often visited the soldiers at the fort to trade. Loving nothing more than a horse race, the Navajos began racing their horses with those of the soldiers. By fall race days had grown into something of a celebration, with hundreds of Navajo men, women and children, dressed in their best clothing and jewelry, attending. On September 22, there were, as usual, to be several races; but the special race, the one in which there was the most interest, was scheduled to be run at noon between Manuelito on his favorite horse and a Lieutenant Ortiz on a quarter horse. The bets were heavy, the Navajos betting blankets, jewelry, and livestock for the soldiers' money, clothing, trinkets and foodstuffs.

Seconds after the race began it was apparent that Manuelito was in trouble and could not control his horse. The horse ran off the track but the lieutenant continued to the finish line. When Manuelito discovered that his bridle rein had been slashed with a knife, he demanded that the race be run again. But the judges, all soldiers, laughed at him and declared that Lieutenant Ortiz had won the race fairly. Immediately the soldiers formed a victory parade and marched into the fort to claim their winnings. The Navajos were infuriated and, protesting, tried to follow the soldiers into the fort, but the gates were slammed shut as soon as all the soldiers were inside. When a Navajo tried to force his way through the gate, a sentinel shot him dead. The carnage that followed was reminiscent of that massacre in which Narbona was killed. The Americans completely lost control. A year later, Captain Nicholas Holt described the slaughter in an official report: "The Navajos, squaws, and children ran in all directions and were shot and bayonetted. I succeeded in forming about twenty men . . . I then marched out to the east side of the post; there I saw a soldier murdering two little children and a woman. I hallooed immediately to the soldier to stop. He looked up, but did not obey my order. I ran as quick as I could, but could not get there soon enough to prevent him from killing the two innocent children and wounding severely the squaw. I ordered his belts to be taken off and taken prisoner to the post. . . . Meanwhile the colonel (J. Francisco Chavez, a New Mexican) had given orders to the officer of the day to have the artillery brought out to open upon the Indians. The sergeant in charge of the mountain howitzers pretended not to understand the order; but being cursed by the officer of the day, and threatened, he had to execute the order or else get himself in trouble. The Indians scattered all over the valley below the post, attacked the post herd, wounded the Mexican herder, but did not succeed in getting any stock; also attacked the expressman some ten miles from the post, took his horse and mail-bag and wounded him in the arm. After the massacre there were no more Indians to be seen about the post with the exception of a few squaws, favorites of the officers. The commanding officer endeavored to make peace again with the Navajos by sending some of the favorite squaws to talk with the chiefs; but the only satisfaction the squaws received was a good flogging."

Colonel Chavez succeeded in keeping the massacre a secret for several weeks by forbidding private letters from being sent from the post. From that day forward no headmen visited Fort Wingate; they had no friends there. Once again they had been betrayed by the Americans. The Navajos have always been blamed for taking advantage of the military's preoccupation with the Confederate invasion to start a new war on the New Mexicans. But the senseless massacre at Fort Wingate that left fifteen Navajos, mostly women and children, dead and as many wounded was the direct cause of renewed hostilities on the part of the Navajos. And, as we shall see, their offensive lasted only to the beginning of 1862.

General Henry H. Sibley led a Confederate force of approximately 3,700 men up the Rio Grande that winter and met Canby's army at Valverde near Fort Craig. There on February 21, 1862, the two men who had fought the Navajos together the year before opposed each other in a furious all-day struggle. Despite heavy Confederate losses, the Union forces gradually gave ground. The aggressive southerners soon broke the spirit of Kit Carson's New Mexican volunteers and Canby was forced to retreat to Fort Craig.

Marching up the river to Socorro, Sibley's army seemed invincible. The Second Regiment of New Mexican volunteers, under the command of Colonel Nicholas Pino, surrendered without firing a shot. But Sibley's supplies were so short that he had to move quickly on to Albuquerque in order to avoid putting his troops on starvation rations. The confederates easily took Albuquerque and Santa Fe, but captured few of the supplies they sorely needed. At Glorieta Pass Sibley's Confederates met 1,300 Colorado volunteers under the command of Colonel John P. Slough. The Union troops were forced to retire but they managed to destroy the Confederate supply wagons, forcing Sibley to backtrack to Santa Fe and then down the river. The Colorado troops joined Colonel Canby's forces at Tijeras and on April 15 fought an indecisive skirmish with the Confederates at Peralta. The Confederates, now painfully low on supplies and with morale slipping, crossed the Rio Grande at Los Lunas. The supply situation became desperate and Sibley and his ragged, hungry men retreated as quickly as possible to Fort Bliss. The Confederate invasion of New Mexico was over.

But it had caused the abandonment of Fort Wingate in February. And as soon as the Confederate army turned back toward Texas, the New Mexicans again turned their attention to Navajo slave raiding. Party after party marched into *Dinehtah* throughout the spring of 1862 for captives that were now bringing up to four hundred dollars each in Santa Fe. Instead of taking to the war trail themselves, Navajo warriors were forced to remain in *Dinehtah* and try to protect their women and children. In commenting on the intensified Navajo slave raiding that year, Dr. Louis Kennon, a long-time resident of Santa Fe, wrote: "I think that the Navajos have been the most abused people on the continent, and that in all hostilities the Mexicans (of the Rio Grande) have always taken the initiative with but one exception that I know of . . . if you asked the Mexicans any reason for making war, they would give no other reason but that the Navajos had a great many sheep and horses and a great many children ... (I believe) the number of Captive Navajo Indians held as slaves to be underestimated. I think there are from five to six thousand. I know of no (New Mexican) family which can raise one hundred and fifty dollars but what purchases a Navajo slave, and many families own four or five, the trade in them being as regular as the trade in pigs and sheep. Previous to the War their price was from seventy-five to one hundred dollars, but now they are worth about four hundred dollars." Dr. Kennon was of the opinion that both the Indian Bureau and the military had encouraged slave raiding since the beginning of the Civil War.

As New Mexican raiding parties continued to ravage *Dinehtah* throughout 1862, the Navajos again were forced to retreat deep into the canyons and mountains of their land and were unable to plant crops to any extent or properly care for their flocks. Yet James L. Collins wrote the Indian Commissioner that the Navajos had "driven off over one hundred thousand sheep and not less than a thousand head of cattle besides horses and mules to a large amount" before summer of that year. Based only on Collins' statement, white historians of the twentieth century, with but one exception that I know of, have all written that the Navajos started a war of "murder and plunder" or that they "inflamed the frontier" that spring. There are official records of only some half-dozen raids made by the Navajos throughout the entire year of 1862 resulting in the death of fourteen New Mexicans.

In late summer General James H. Carleton and his 1,500 California volunteers who had been recruited to turn back the Confederate invasion of the Southwest, arrived in New Mexico after having recaptured Tucson for the Union. Carleton marched his troops through Santa Fé in September, and on to Fort Union. Canby was recalled to the East and promoted to the rank of general, and Carleton was given command of the department. Carleton, then forty-eight years of age, had been trained under Edwin Vose Sumner at the Pennsylvania Cavalry School, had served under Sumner in New Mexico and, recently, in California. In spite of the fact that Carleton had been Sumner's protege, there was a marked difference in the personalities of the two men.

The Military Department of New Mexico had been commanded by two good soldiers—Sumner and Canby—and by fools, cowards, and thieves; but none of them could match General James H. Carleton in his desire for personal glory and unbridled, consuming ambition. And, unfortunately for the Navajos, he was obsessed with the idea of finding a fortune in precious metals, an aberration sometimes called gold fever that he had picked up while serving in California. Ramrod-straight and a picture of indomitable self-confidence, Carleton could neither change his mind nor admit an error. Denied his chance to gain fame on the eastern front, Carleton decided he would win it in New Mexico by getting rid of the Indians and opening their lands—which he was convinced contained uncountable riches in gold and silver—to prospectors.

General Carleton devised a plan of operations against the free Indians of New Mexico that was devilishly simple: His troops would hunt them down and kill or capture them until they agreed to surrender and live on a single reservation where they could be taught Christianity and agriculture. Carleton was an eloquent and convincing speaker and a compulsive and grandiose writer of letters, but had he been a stammering, illiterate idiot he would have found no problem getting James L. Collins to back *that* plan. Collins so wholeheartedly supported Carleton's Indian policy that he was soon hailing him as "the deliverer of the Southwest," and had difficulty in finding new adjectives with which to praise the commander in the *Gazette*. The new governor, Henry Connelly, also endorsed Carleton's Indian program as did Chief Justice Kerby Benedict, the boss of the local Republican party, members of the influential Chavez family and Ute agents Albert W. Pheiffer and Christopher Carson.

Carleton selected a strip of land in the public domain a hundred and seventy-five miles southeast of Santa Fe at a spot where the alkaline Rio Pecos twisted through a stand of ragged cottonwood trees called Bosque Redondo for the proposed reservation. And the "round forest" of cottonwoods were the only trees within miles. Three hundred years before, Castaneda had described the area: "in 250 leagues was seen not a hillock which was three times as high as a man. The country is like a bowl, so that when a man sits down, the horizon surrounds him all around at the distance of a musket shot." But it suited Carleton's plan as it was isolated far from the white settlements. The general wrote glowing reports of the area and his plan to settle "those wolves of the mountains," the Navajos and Apaches there and make "Christian farmers" out of them. Both the Department of War and the Bureau of Indian Affairs quickly agreed to Carleton's proposal, but a board of army officers assigned to inspect the Bosque Redondo vociferously disagreed with Carleton and reported the place was "remote from the depot of supplies, Fort Union, and from the neighborhoods that supply forage. Building materials will have to be brought from a great distance. The water of the Pecos contains much unhealthy mineral matter. A large part of the surrounding valley is subject to inundations by spring floods." They recommended a site near Las Vegas, New Mexico, for the reservation "where the supply of good timber for building and firewood is convenient, the water is pure and abundant, the grazing is very fine, and none of the neighboring country is subject to overflow." But Carleton was a man who knew how to get his way and the War Department let him build his fort, which he named in honor of Edwin Vose Sumner, at Bosque Redondo.

There was one flaw in Carleton's plan that was immediately apparent to New Mexicans who knew the Indians: the Navajos and the Apaches, even if he did manage to round them up and get them to Fort Sumner, would never live together. But General Carleton, with the enthusiastic backing of Governor Connelly and James L. Collins, went ahead with his plans to make war on the Mescalero and Gila Apaches and the Navajos. By the end of the year he was ready to put the campaign into operation. He induced Christopher Carson, known to the Navajos as "the Rope Thrower," to take command of the troops in the field and to spearhead the attack with the volunteer force of New Mexican militiamen recruited to fight the Confederates.

THREE

The Rope Thrower

By the beginning of 1863 the Navajos were a defeated people: poor, hungry and demoralized by the New Mexican slave raids that had continued without respite or interruption since the beginning of the Civil War. The dozen retaliations by Navajo warriors the year before had been but feeble protests. By Navajo and also some white estimations, almost a third of the tribe were slaves of the New Mexicans. Those that remained free grieved for their lost women and children and were constantly haunted by the ever-present threat of the roving bands of New Mexicans and Utes.

Apparently General Carleton did not realize how weak the *Dineh* had become as his correspondence indicates that he expected a strong resistance and a protracted war with them. And with that in mind he decided to get the matter of the Apaches out of the way before making war on the Navajos. He ordered Kit Carson into the field against the Mescaleros and at the same time sent a force of regulars against the Gilas. In the campaign against the Gilas which temporarily subdued the Apaches living in the mountains along the border between Mexico and New Mexico, the impressive Apache chief Mangus Colorados, who ventured into a command camp to talk to the Americans, was arrested and murdered under circumstances that later proved embarrassing.

According to his biographers, Kit Carson's final instructions from General Carleton shocked the Taos mountain man who had once been married to and fathered a daughter by an Indian woman: "All Indian men of that tribe (the Mescaleros) are to be killed whenever and wherever you can find them. The women and children will not be harmed, but you will take them prisoners, and feed them at Fort Stanton until you receive other instruction about them. If the Indians send in a flag and desire to treat for peace, say to the bearer that when the people of New Mexico were attacked by the Texans, the Mescaleros broke their treaty of peace, and murdered innocent people, and ran off their stock; that now our hands are untied, and you have been sent to punish them for their treachery and their crimes; that you have no power to make peace; that you are there to kill them wherever you can find them; that if they beg for peace, their chiefs and twenty of their principal men must come to Santa Fe to have a talk there."

Actually the Mescaleros, poor, hungry and tired, had been in no position for some years to commit the crimes of which they were accused by Carleton. They had been asking for a truce since before the Confederate invasion and were totally unprepared for the savage war that was suddenly launched upon him. The California volunteers, disappointed that they had not arrived in the territory in time to fight the Confederates, were only too glad to fight the Indians. And the New Mexicans, of course, were too. And neither force was of a mind to give any quarter. When an aged chief tried to surrender his small band to Captain James Graydon, the officer ordered his men to attack. Six men and one woman were killed in the first volley. The others turned to run, but the soldiers chased them down and killed five more. Captain Graydon claimed the massacre as a "great victory over the enemy." Kit Carson was appalled at this victory and complained to General Carleton. When another large group of Mescaleros was surrounded and attacked by two companies of Californians under Major William McCleave, the ones who survived made their way to Fort Stanton and asked Carson for protection. Cadete, their chief, said: "You are stronger than we. We have fought you as long as we had rifles and powder; but your weapons are better than ours. Give us weapons and turn us loose, and we will fight you again; but now we are worn out; we have no more heart; we have no provisions, no means to live; your troops are everywhere, our springs and waterholes are either occupied or overlooked by your young men. You have driven us from our last and best stronghold, and we have no more heart. Do with us as may seem good to you, but do not forget we are men and braves."

Cadete's words were the death song of the once-proud Mescaleros. But if General Carleton heard them, they fell on deaf ears. By the beginning of March, 1863, over four hundred men, women and children were imprisoned at Fort Sumner. The rest of the tribe, no more than a hundred, had fled west to join the Gila Apaches, or to Mexico. On March 19, General Carleton wrote his superiors in Washington to say, "now that the Mescaleros are subdued, I will send the whole of Colonel Carson's regiment against the Navajoes, who still continue to plunder and murder the people. This regiment will take the field against them early in May. Already I have commenced drawing the companies in from the Mescalero country preparatory to such movement."

Actually the Navajos had watched the war on their Apache cousins, from afar, with a great deal of alarm, realizing that their turn was next. As early as December a delegation of eighteen headmen, including Delgadito and Barboncito—but not Manuelito—had travelled to Santa Fé to call on General Carleton. They told him that the Navajos were weak and did not want war. Carleton replied, "You can have no peace until you give other guarantees than your word that the peace should be kept. Go home and tell your people so. I have no faith in your promises."

In April General Carleton went to Fort Wingate to "gather information for a campaign against the Navajos as soon as the grass starts sufficiently to support stock." Again Delgadito and Barboncito called on him and offered peace but they were bluntly told there would be peace only when all the Navajos had joined the "contented" Mescaleros at Bosque Redondo. Barboncito told Carleton that he would not fight the Americans but neither would he go to Bosque Redondo. "I will never leave my country," he said, "not even if it means I will be killed."

Carleton returned to Santa Fe and prepared for his war on the *Dineh*. The defeat of the Mescaleros had been but a prelude. The plum was to be *Dinehtah* where the general was convinced there would be found great mineral riches.

On May 10, 1863, Carleton wrote General Henry W. Halleck: "Among all my endeavors since my arrival here has been an effort to brush back the Indians, so that the people could get out of the valley of the Rio Grande, and not only possess themselves of the arable lands in other parts of the territory, but, if the country contained veins and deposits of precious metals, they might be found." A few days later he again wrote Halleck: "There is evidence that a country as rich if not richer in mineral wealth than California, extends from the Rio Grande, northwestwardly, all the way across to Washoe (Nevada)." A month later he wrote Captain J. G. Walker: "If I can help others to a fortune, it will afford me not quite as much happiness as finding one myself, it is true—but nearly as much. My luck has always been not to be at the right place at the right time for fortunes."

General Carleton passed his gold fever on to Governor Connelly who, in addressing the New Mexican legislative assembly, said: "The Navajos occupy the finest grazing districts within our limits (and) infest a mining region extending two hundred miles. . . ." Connelly then, hoping to quiet the few voices being raised in objection to the war that was in its final planning stages, pointed out that an immense white "pastoral and mining population is excluded from its occupations and the treasures of mineral wealth that are known to exist . . . they (the Navajos) too long have . . . roamed lords of the soil over this extensive track of country."

Carleton scorned the very idea of treating or negotiating with the Navajos. On the eve of his invasion of *Dinehtah* he wrote the War Department: "I would respectfully recommend that the only peace that can ever be made with them must rest on the basis that they move onto the lands (at Bosque Redondo) and, like the Pueblos, become an agricultural people and cease to be nomads. . . . Entire subjugation, or destruction of all the men, are the alternatives." Once the *Dineh* had been removed to the reservation, Carleton said, "old Navajos would soon die off, and carry with them all the latent longings for murdering and robbing; the young ones would take their places without these longings; and thus, little by little, the Navajos would become a happy and contented people, and Navajo wars would be remembered only as something that belongs en-

352

tirely to the past."

Carleton called for Christopher Carson to come to Santa Fé from his home in Taos where he was on leave, and, on June 15, 1863, gave him his orders: He would leave Los Pinos on July 1, 1863, and march his 1,000 men to Navajo country. And so began the war of legendary horror aginst the Navajos.

The Navajos were given until July 20 to surrender. After that, in General Carleton's words, "every Navajoe that is seen will be considered as hostile and treated accordingly." Governor Connelly offered to raise several companies of civilian volunteers to aid the troops but the proposal was rejected by General Carleton. He wanted no "unruly contingents" in the field as he felt regular "troops must be kept after the Indians, not in big bodies, with military noises and smokes, and the gleam of arms by day, and fires, and talk, and comfortable sleep at night; but in small parties moving stealthily to their haunts and lying patiently in wait for them."

But before Kit Carson arrived at Fort Wingate, most of the men who would have comprised Connelly's companies of volunteers were on their way to *Dinehtah*, in large and small groups, to take captives. They realized that if the Navajos did surrender to the Rope Thrower, as the Navajos called Carson, the opportunity to turn a quick dollar in Navajo slaves would be gone forever. And they were followed by Utes, Pueblos and Apaches, and Kiowas and Comanches from the plains, always ready to take advantage of a white war on the Navajos to raid, plunder, and take captives. Even the Hopis, who had for the most part remained neutral in the Navajo wars, took advantage of the situation and began raiding their neighbors. Kit Carson urged his Ute guides to take Navajo captives for themselves as a reward for "their continued zeal and activity." In his opinion the captives "would be better off than at Bosque Redondo, as the Utes would sell them to Mexican families who would care for them, thus they would cease to require further attention on the government." Too, he said, by breaking up family groups and distributing members as slaves to the New Mexicans, "that collectiveness of interest as a tribe which they will retain if kept together at Bosque Redondo" would be destroyed.

Soon after the command arrived at Fort Wingate, Kit

Carson sent a letter of resignation to General Carleton. His biographers have said that he was reluctant to wage the savage war planned against the Navajos. In my opinion his reason was nothing so noble. Carson was uneasy in his role as commander of such a large expedition. He was also a very proud man but illiterate and soon after he arrived with the command at Fort Wingate several of his men made him appear foolish. The details of the embarrassing incident were related in a letter written by Captain George H. Pettis, commander of Company K, to Edwin L. Sabin, author of *Kit Carson Days*: "The command arrived (at Fort Wingate) late in the afternoon, and, after getting settled down, one of the men went to the company clerk, and asked him to write an order (to) purchase a quart of molasses" from the post commissary. Such an order had to be signed by the commanding officer, Kit Carson.

The soldier took the order to Carson and "asked him to sign it as he was not well, explaining to the colonel the purpose of the order. The colonel, always the best-natured of men, signed it, and the man got his molasses. The man upon his return to this quarters, informed his friends that he believed the colonel could not read manuscript, and related his experience. It was the regulations of the post that no enlisted man could purchase whiskey at the sutler's except upon the order of the commanding officer. So one of the men, who was anxious to get some whiskey, thought that he would try and see what he could do with the colonel in this direction. He had the company clerk write an order on the sutler for a canteen of whiskey. . . . He accordingly appeared with it before the colonel and told him he was not feeling well and that he would like to get some molasses at the commissary's. The colonel signed the order as before, and the man obtained the canteen of whiskey at the sutler's . . . the news soon spread through the company and for the next two weeks there was a brisk business at the sutler store. It happened that when Colonel Carson made a visit to the sutler's and looking around asked, kindly: 'Well, John . . . how's business?' John answered that it was fine—he had sold two barrels of whiskey by the canteen to H company! Upon this the colonel waxed warm, and he said 'John, don't you know that it's agin regulations to sell whiskey to enlisted men of the post without the written order of the commanding officer?'

John Waters replied that he knew it very well; and he added that every sale had been made upon written order. To prove it, he went behind the counter and showed his order string—a wire set in a block of wood and holding already a foot of orders! After this Colonel Carson would sign no order until his adjutant, Lieutenant Lawrence Murphy, had read it first." (Sabin, 1919, McClurg: 425-26.)

And while the Rope Thrower was resigning his commission and subsequently accepting General Carleton's urging that he reconsider, the Navajos, as best they could, were preparing for the coming war. There was nothing spectacular about Kit Carson's campaign against the Navajos. The *Dineh* were weaker than they had been at any time since the arrival of the Europeans in the Southwest. Their only avenue of defense was to retreat as far as they could into their mountains and canyons and hope to avoid both Carson's volunteers and the hordes of New Mexican, Ute and other Indian raiders who were much more adept than the army was in finding their hiding places. In late July Carson moved up to Fort Defiance and renamed it Fort Canby for the commander who had successfully hounded the Navajos into a peace treaty three years before. Then, following Carleton's plan of operations, he sent patrols of troops into the field. But the Navajos had already fled, deserting their fields and even some of their livestock. Some sought safety along the San Juan and in the wild area north of Monument Valley, but most of the tribe fled west, beyond the Hopi villages and as far as the Grand Canyon and to the area around Navajo Mountain.

It mattered little to the Rope Thrower that few Navajos were to be found—in fact he did not expect his troops to find any but a few stragglers. He would scorch the earth, destroy their livestock and crops, and once the children started starving the *Dineh* would come to him. On July 25 he sent out a detachment of troops under the command of Major Joseph Cummings to bring in all the livestock and to burn all the fields in the Canoncito Bonito area. The Navajos, watching the destruction of their property from their hiding places, became infuriated. They saw, then, that it was to be a war with no quarter. Every Navajo field and food cache that Cummings found was destroyed. A Navajo warrior rode to where Cummings was directing the destruction of a field, got within firing range and shot him out of the saddle, killing him instantly. A few nights later a small group of Navajos crawled into the corral at Fort Canby and stampeded the horses, getting away with the Rope Thrower's favorite mount.

But Carson's campaign was relentless. In August he reported to Carleton that he had left Fort Canby August 5, 1863, "on a scout for thirty days." On the first day out he sent Sergeant Romero with fifteen men after two Indians seen in the vicinity; he captured one of their horses; the Indians made their escape. "On the night of the 4th instant Captain (Albert W.) Pheiffer captured eleven women and children, besides a woman and child, the former of whom was killed in attempting to escape, and the latter accidentally. Captain Pheiffer's party also captured two other children, one hundred sheep and goats, and one horse. The Utes captured in the same vicinity eighteen horses and two mules, and killed one Indian. Captain Pheiffer wounded an Indian, but he escaped. On the 16th, a party who were sent for some pack-saddles, brought in one Indian woman. . . . One of the parties sent out from this camp captured an Indian woman. Total Indians killed, three; captured, fifteen; wounded, one; twenty horses, two mules, and one hundred sheep and goats captured."

That was certainly not the sort of report General Carleton expected. He wanted great victories. On August 18 the general, in an effort to "stimulate the zeal" of the troops in the field, offered to pay twenty dollars for "every sound, serviceable horse or mule and one dollar per head for every sheep" brought in to the commissary at Fort Canby. As the soldier's pay was less than twenty dollars per month, the bounty offer did cause them to try harder. Kit Carson continued his steady but sure destruction of grain stores and fields, but by the first week of September General Carleton was forced to report to Washington that only fifty-one Navajos, men, women and children, had been taken and sent to the Bosque Redondo. He followed up his Washington report with orders to Carson that "henceforth every Navajo male is to be killed or taken prisoner on sight. . . . Say to them—'Go to the Bosque Redondo, or we will pursue and destroy you. We will not make peace with you on any other terms. . . . This war shall be pursued until you cease to exist or move. There can be no other talk on the subject.' "

In one of what amounted to virtually a constant stream of letters the General wrote to Washington, he asked for more troops. An additional regiment of cavalry was needed, he reported, falsely, because a new gold strike had been found just west of the Navajo country and more troops were needed to protect the people going to and from the mines. "Providence has indeed blessed us," he wrote . . . "the gold lies here at our feet to be had by the mere picking of it up!"

Manuelito led his warriors in several skirmishes against the soldiers, but as the first chill of autumn fell over *Dinehtah*, he had his band pack all the food they could carry and led the aged, the women and children west of the Hopi villages. Then he sent the warriors to range through *Dinehtah* to tell clan relatives and others that they encountered to join him there. After a few weeks he led his followers farther west to take refuge in the Grand Canyon for the long winter. With all the fields and livestock between Fort Canby and Canyon de Chelly destroyed, Carson next sent his patrols to destroy ripening crops to the North and West of the Cañoncito Bonito-Canyon de Chelly line. He reported in the middle of November that his troops had destroyed more than two million pounds of Navajo grain. At that time only a total of 188 Navajos had surrendered and been sent on the long walk to Bosque Redondo. Among them were a large contingent belonging to Delgadito's band. The headman led the band, suffering from cold and starvation, in himself. Carleton considered the surrender of Delgadito—the first headman to give up—a matter of great importance, and arranged for his band to be given special treatment. They were issued the best rations available and given the best shelters upon their arrival at Bosque Redondo. Most of the *Dinehanaih*—Sandoval's band—were already at Bosque Redondo, working for the soldiers about the fort, but many of their young men were in *Dinehtah* serving as guides for Carson. Delgadito was so impressed with the kindness of his captors—as was General Carleton's intention—that when he was asked to return to Fort Wingate and persuade other Navajo headmen that life at the Bosque Redondo was better than starving and freezing to death fighting the Americans, he agreed to do so.

With the coming of the first snows, Carson put his second plan of operation in action. He knew that, even with

357

the loss of most of their livestock and crops, the Navajos could still survive the winter on game and wild seeds and plants—but not if they were constantly kept on the move. Again breaking his command up into small patrols, he sent them out to crisscross *Dinehtah* until the Navajos were broken up into small family units and scattered. They could never remain in one place for more than a few days at a time, camped in mountain crevices or caves without sufficient food, shelter or clothing. Very few dared attempt a journey to the faraway salt flats, and the lack of that mineral in their meager diets soon caused many to become ill. By the middle of December most of the weak and aged had died. There is hardly a Navajo family that cannot remember tales of an aged grandfather, a pregnant mother or a lame child that had to be left behind when a camp had to be quickly deserted. The patrols were not interested in taking captives; it was too much trouble to transport them back to the forts. Any Navajos they saw were shot on sight. Mothers were sometimes forced to suffocate their hungry, crying babies to keep the family from being discovered and butchered by an army patrol or taken captive by the slave raiders.

On December 6 Carleton ordered his field commander to invade Canyon de Chelly. Carson immediately began making preparations to lead an expedition against that "notorious stronghold of the Navajos" and before a week had passed he had assembled a pack herd of the best mules available to carry supplies. Members of Barboncito's band, from their hiding places, watched this activity with a great deal of interest. Their home was Canyon de Chelly, and as long as the pack mules were destined to visit them anyway, they supposed they might as well escort them there and put them to better use than carrying army supplies. On the night of December 13, Barboncito and his warriors swooped down on Carson's mules and ran off the entire herd. Nothing of that herd of mules went to waste. Every scrap of meat and intestines and every shred of skin and ligaments were put to use. Even the hooves were pulverized and went into a stew.

Carson sent two detachments in pursuit of Barboncito's raiders but the Navajos escaped under the cover of a heavy snowstorm. But one detachment, commanded by Lieutenant Donaciano Montoya, did find a camp of Navajos which was attacked that resulted in the capture of thirteen women and children. The lieutenant reported: "Indian (man) was shot through the right side but succeeded in escaping through the tangled underwood. His son, a boy of ten years old and very intelligent for an Indian, was taken a short time afterwards, and reported that his father died amongst the rocks in a neighboring arroyo."

Kit Carson reported the loss of his pack mules to General Carleton and asked permission to delay the invasion of Canyon de Chelly. The general was tired of delays. He had expected far greater results from his Navajo war. He promptly replied: "You will not delay the expedition on account of lack of transportation. You will have the men carry their blankets and, if necessary, three or four days' rations in haversacks."

The Canyon de Chelly expedition left Fort Canby on the morning of January 6, 1864, in two columns. The first column, of more than three hundred men, commanded by Carson, arrived at Chinle Wash on January 12. Twenty-seven of its pack animals perished from exhaustion on the short journey in the heavy snow. Albert W. Pheiffer arrived at the eastern extremities of Canyon del Muerto on the same day with a command consisting of about 100 men, and immediately led his troops down into the depths of the gorge. As Pheiffer started westward down the canyon, Carson sent a detachment of about fifty men to scout the mouth of the canyon system. There the troops fought a short skirmish with some Navajos, killed eleven and captured two women and two children and about 130 sheep and goats.

The next morning Carson divided his command into two columns to reconnoiter both the south and north rims of the canyon system. Meanwhile Pheiffer continued to lead his troops down the floor of Canyon del Muerto toward the main branch of the canyon, where the snow lay two feet deep. Once again Navajos appeared on the heights of the canyon walls to hurl stones, pieces of wood and curses down on the Americans. But these half-starved protesters were not the proud warriors of yesteryear. The Americans ignored them but did kill three men who came within range of their muskets. Pheiffer rode on down the canyon, burning hogans and food caches and killing all livestock he found. Arriving at Carson's camp at Chinle Wash, he made his report: "Here (in Canyon de Chelly) the Navajoes sought refuge when pursued by the invading force, whether of neighboring tribes or of the arms of the government, and here they were enabled to jump about on the ledges like mountain cats, hallooing at me, swearing and cursing and threatening vengeance on my command in every variety of Spanish they were capable of mustering. A couple of shots from my soldiers with their trusty rifles caused the red-skins to disperse instantly, and gave me a safe passage through this celebrated Gibraltar of the Navajoes. At the place where I encamped the curl of the smoke from my fires ascended to where a large body of Indians were resting over my head, but the height was so great that the Indians did not look larger than crows, and as we were too far apart to injure each other no damage was done except with the tongue. . . ."

Kit Carson added his comments to the report: ". . . Having accomplished an undertaking never before successful in war-time, that of passing through the Canyon de Chelly from east to west, and this without having had a single casualty in his command . . . he killed three Indians (two men) and brought in ninety prisoners (women and children). He found the bodies of Indians frozen to death in the canon."

While the troops rested in camp that night three Navajo men came in under a flag of truce and requested permission to surrender with their families. Carson gave them until ten o'clock the next morning to bring in their families. Early the next morning sixty ragged, emaciated Navajos arrived at the camp and "expressed their willingness to emigrate to the Bosque." When Carson asked them why they had not surrendered before, he was told that they were afraid to surrender to the patrols as those who had tried had been killed. The Rope Thrower then told some of the men to return to their people and tell them that they had ten days to surrender at Fort Canby, during which time the soldiers would not bother them.

That day the fields at the mouth of Canyon de Chelly were laid to waste. Carson reported, " . . . It took me and three hundred men most of the day to destroy a field of corn." Carson then left for Fort Canby as he wanted to be there when the Navajos came in as he was sure they would now. But before he left he ordered the complete destruction of all Navajo property within the canyon—including the five thousand peach trees there that were the pride of the *Dineh*. By the time Pheiffer and Captain Asa B. Carey were finished with this task and were ready to leave for Fort Canby on the morning of January 17, another two hundred Navajos had surrendered, twenty-three had been killed, thirty-four had been taken prisoner—and the spirit of the *Dineh* had been broken. As news of what the Americans had done at Canyon de Chelly spread through the hidden camps, the Navajos realized they had already lost the land they'd fought to keep. Some fled even farther west to the wild Navajo Mountain area, but most of the *Dineh* had lost heart and decided to give up.

By February 1, there were almost seven hundred Navajos at Fort Wingate, most of whom had been persuaded to surrender by Delgadito. Two weeks later the number that had surrendered at Fort Canby reached 1,200. Very few of them really believed that the Americans would provide them protection and succor at Bosque Redondo. But headmen such as Huerro, who came in a few days later with his band of 300, had no choice. It was easier to hope the Americans were telling the truth than to continue to watch babies starve to death because there was no milk in their mothers' breasts.

At the beginning of March, 1864, the Long Walk of the Navajos to Fort Sumner and the Bosque Redondo was set in motion. That day 1,443 of The People left Fort Wingate, taking with them 473 horses and 3,000 sheep. Ten died en route and three children were kidnapped by New Mexicans among the soldier escort. Those that followed would not fare nearly so well.

FOUR

Bosque Redondo

On February 27, 1864, General James H. Carleton wrote the War Department: "What with the Navajos I have captured and those who have surrendered we now have over three thousand, and will, without doubt, soon have the whole tribe. I do not believe they number now much over five thousand all told. You have doubtless seen the last of the Navajo war—a war that has been continued with but few intermissions for one hundred and eighty years, and which, during that time, has been marked by every shade of atrocity, brutality and ferocity which can be imagined or which can be found in the annals of conflict between our own race and the aboriginal race."

Carleton was well aware that less than half the tribe had surrendered. Manuelito, Barboncito, Armijo and Ganado Mucho were still free. And most of those who had surrendered were already having second thoughts. After the first contingent had been sent off to Fort Sumner, food supplies became scarce at the two army posts in *Dinehtah* and there was no clothing nor blankets to give to the freezing Navajos who gave themselves up. On March 4, a group of 2,400 left Fort Canby, their numbers already reduced by the 126 who had died of dysentery the week before. The night before they left the Navajos were given wheat flour, a food totally strange to them, and were not instructed as to its preparation. Thinking it was the corn meal of the Bilagaana, the Navajo women made a cold gruel in the same manner they made corn meal mush. Those that ate the flour gruel the night before the departure and were stricken with cramps were lucky. They were left behind. The ones who ate it on the first day of the march fell along the trail and were shot by the military escorts. The wagons accompanying the march were already filled with the aged and the lame.

By the second day of the march coyotes began to follow the long line of Navajos, marching a few abreast in family groups, and hawks and crows circled overhead, waiting to make a meal of the next body. The horses weakened and stumbled, and as soon as they fell they were slaughtered and the meat divided among the hungry *Dineh*. Without the horses, many of the aged, too weak to keep up, were left behind. Their relatives gave them a little food and marched on with tears in their eyes. The old, the weak, and the lame sat beside the trail and watched hopelessly as the column passed out of sight. Those that a jeering soldier wasted a bullet on were fortunate. When that group straggled into Fort Sumner 197 had been left behind, dead or dying on the trail.

On March 20 another 800 left Fort Canby and were joined by an additional 146 en route. The officer in command reported: "On the second day's march a very severe snowstorm set in which lasted for four days with unusual severity, and occasioned great suffering amongst the Indians, many of whom were nearly naked and of course unable to withstand such a storm." The army had supplied this group with only twenty-three wagons to transport supplies, the aged and the crippled. When the Navajos reached Los Piños, below Albuquerque, the wagons were commandeered for other use. While waiting for the return of the wagons, the Navajos were forced to camp in the open. By the time the march was resumed, several children had been kidnapped by the New Mexicans. The officer in command reported: "Officers who have Indians in (their) charge will have to exercise extreme vigilance, or the Indians' children will be stolen from them and sold." By the time this contingent reached the Bosque Redondo on May 11, 110 of them had perished.

The Navajos continued to surrender at Fort Canby and Fort Wingate and were marched headlong into the horror of Fort Sumner and the Bosque. That spring, while he was, as ever, writing self-laudatory reports to the War Department in praise of the success of his "Indian policy," General Carleton refused to realize he was facing disaster. Opposition to his tyrannical rule and the Bosque Redondo reservation was growing in Santa Fé. Both the territorial secretary William Frederick Milton Arny and the former Apache agent Dr. Michael Steck had opposed the reservation from the beginning. Arny, a well-meaning religious zealot, had already caused the removal of James L. Collins as Indian superintendent and Dr. Steck was appointed to replace him. Judge Kirby Benedict, who had supported Carleton in the beginning, soon began attacking the general in the Santa Fé *New Mexican* of which he was part owner. In defense of Carleton, James L. Collins wrote in the Santa Fe *Gazette*: "If a person happens to be a contractor and in favor of the Bosque Reservation he is charged with being so because of the profit he can make out of it, and acting the hypocrite in the most approved style." Judge Benedict retorted in the *New Mexican* that the description fit Collins and his friends who were "generally petted with patronage in some form from the military crib."

By July 8, 1864, there were about 5,900 Navajos at Bosque Redondo and another 1,000 were being held at Fort Canby. At this time General Carleton estimated that not more than 2,000 Navajos were still free in *Dinehtah* but others estimated that not more than half the tribe had surrendered. Manuelito had actually travelled to Bosque Redondo with one contingent of prisoners, had not liked what he had seen and quickly returned home. His band still refused to give up as did those of Ganado Mucho and Barboncito.

At Bosque Redondo each family unit was given a plot of land to farm. Those that arrived too late to plant that spring helped others, usually clan relatives, dig irrigation ditches for fields of corn, melon squash and a large field of wheat that was being cultivated under the supervision of the soldiers. But there was never enough to eat and everyone was living in makeshift shelters, as materials were not available to construct hogans. Some families were living in holes they had dug in embankments, others had erected crooked poles and covered them with sheepskins. The families that had been rich back in *Dinehtah* lived alongside those that had been poor, in the same sort of hovels, worked shoulder to shoulder with them scratching in the alkali-permeated soil and drank the bitter water from the Río Pecos that made them ill. They were convinced that their gods—even the benevolent-Changing Woman—had deserted them. Besides, what gods would look with favor upon a people who tried to farm such land and lived in such squalor?

Ignoring the conditions at the Bosque Redondo, General Carleton wrote Kit Carson, "You can send on 7,500 Navajos, including what we have. That number we can feed." Only two weeks later, when he was forced to put troops throughout the department on half-rations, he again wrote Carson: "I cannot believe but that 8,000 will cover all the tribe; and we can manage to feed that number." But General Carleton did not have enough supplies at his disposal to feed half that number. Capturing Navajos had not proven easy but trying to feed them was proving calamitous. The Santa Fe *Gazette* continued to pull out all stops in praise of General Carleton, and the local government—with the exception of Judge Benedict and Arny—supported him so completely that Carleton became virtually the ruler of New Mexico. But he realized that, without the support of the federal government, his entire program would quickly come apart at the seams. He sent James L. Collins with an urgent message of the Adjutant General, Lorenzo Thomas: "Now that they have surrendered and at our mercy, they must be taken care of—must be fed, clothed and instructed. . . . These six thousand mouths must eat, and these six thousand bodies must be clothed." Carleton asked the army for two million pounds of foodstuffs, to be sent in installments of 500,000 pounds, the first to start at once and the next to reach New Mexico in August. The remainder, he suggested, should be sent in the fall and would be used to sustain the Navajos at Bosque Redondo until their crop "comes off" in 1865.

But in the late spring of 1864, when Collins visited Washington, the War Department was in no position to concern itself with the matter of Navajo captives being held somewhere out west. The Civil War was too near at hand; Lee's army was in Virginia and on May 5-6 had fought

General Grant to a standoff. The matter of General Carleton's Navajos could wait. With his troops grumbling about their half-rations, Carleton wrote Major Henry Wallen, commanding at Fort Sumner, and gave him specific instructions as to feeding the Navajos: "The Indians are to be fed at the rate of one pound for each man, woman and child per day, of fresh meat, or of corn, or of wheat, or of wheat meal, or of corn meal, or of flour, or of kraut, or of pickles. . . . Or in lieu of any one of these articles, half a pound of beans or of rice, or of peas, or of dried fruit."

Carleton sent emissaries to several western posts to appeal for food to feed his Navajo prisoners, and in Colorado James L. Collins succeeded in obtaining 500,000 pounds of flour and 2,000 head of cattle from the commissary stores—and for the moment saved Carleton's "Indian policy." But the supplies obtained were far too little to feed the approximately 9,000 Navajos and 400 Apaches who were on the reservation by the end of summer as well as the troops at Fort Sumner. Carleton hoped that the supplies, combined with the crops the Navajos had planted, would be sufficient to last them through the winter on his one pound per person per day quota. But the Bosque Redondo fields of the Navajos were struck by cutworms just as the young corn started to tassel and almost all the crop was destroyed. Then, in October, half of the nearly matured wheatfield that the *Dineh* had cultivated was destroyed by storms. As Kay Bennett said: "It was clear to everyone that the gods did not look with favor on this alien land and were punishing them for leaving the land they had been given. Some of the older Navajos began talking of going back to Navajoland."

Dr. Michael Steck became more open in his criticism of General Carleton and, in fact, travelled to Washington to see if he could find out exactly what his duties were since Carleton had assumed control of Indian affairs in New Mexico. The Indian superintendent's Washington visit greatly angered Carleton and he wrote one of his many letters to the War Department, this one criticizing the Indian department's lack of interest in the Bosque Redondo experiment. He accused Steck and the Indian department of "stifling Western progress." Judge Joseph Gillette Knapp, whose court district was the southern part of New Mexico and included Mesilla, also attacked the general.

Judge Knapp was infuriated that criminal cases often went to the military courts and that he could travel about the territory with only a pass from the tyrannical Carleton. In spite of the fact that the Confederate threat had been repulsed before he arrived in New Mexico, Carleton still insisted on a state of martial law. Others who had decided, for one reason or another, that having the Navajos at Bosque Redondo wasn't such a blessing after all, joined in the attacks on Carleton.

General Carleton accused his critics—one and all—of wanting a return to the time of captured Navajo slaves, and to small wars and raids that were profitable. The general's defense of his military regime was ill-founded. While he had not sanctioned slave raiding himself, he had never taken steps to stop it nor had his field commander, Kit Carson. Faced with mounting criticism—especially from the Santa Fe *New Mexican* which was beginning to make humorous if derisive attacks on his person—and still short of funds and supplies, Carleton called on his old friend Governor Connelly and got him to issue a proclamation announcing "a suspension of arms against the Navajos, (as) the more hostile part of that tribe is now reduced."

While Barboncito and his band had been captured in Canyon de Chelly in September, "the more hostile part of that tribe" was still very much free. Neither Manuelito nor Ganado Mucho had given up. Carleton sent Kit Carson off to fight the Comanches and Kiowas but he left a detachment of soldiers at Fort Wingate to continue to "deal with hostile" Navajos.

With the coming of winter, the situation at Bosque Redondo grew even more desperate for the Navajos. Not only had they worked all summer in the cursed place, digging irrigation canals with hardly any implements and tearing mesquite roots from the tough virgin sod with their bare hands and sharp pieces of wood, only to see the crops fail, but with the first cold they realized there was no fuel to keep them warm through the winter. The strand of cottonwoods, much of which had been cut to construct Fort Sumner, was quickly used up. The Navajos, still without adequate food, or enough clothing or blankets to keep warm, were soon again pulling mesquite roots from the ground—to use for fuel. By mid-winter Navajo men were traveling ten, then fifteen, then twenty miles to haul logs to burn for warmth and for cooking fires. And more captives were arriving from *Dinehtah* almost weekly.

The summer before Congress had appropriated $100,000 and given it to the Indian commissioner to "buy tools, implements, blankets and clothing" for the Navajos at Bosque Redondo. The Indian department commissioned civilian merchants to supply the Navajos with the goods. By the time the appropriation filtered down to the Navajos only about $30,000 worth of merchandise got to Bosque Redondo. Later investigators determined that the merchants had appraised blankets that were worth only about $4.50 at $22.50 and there were far too few of those to go around. Kay Bennett, whose family was at Bosque Redondo, was told years later of the distribution of the goods: "Gray Hat's family (an extended family group of fourteen people) were given about thirty yards of unbleached muslin for clothing, four lightweight blankets, a pair of large scissors, two butcher knives, and a bag of bright-colored beads." (Bennett, 1969: Naylor, 163.) The Navajos at Bosque Redondo, barefoot, dressed in rags and suffering from exposure and dysentery, were as bad off as they had been the winter before in *Dinehtah*. Then, at the beginning of the year, the Comanches started raiding the reservation, striking the small herds of sheep and horses the Navajos had managed to retain.

The Comanche raids continued without letup from that point on. Soon larger war parties which included some New Mexicans began entering the reservation in the vicinity of the fort. The soldiers at the fort issued a few guns to Navajo men and told them to arm themselves with bows and arrows when they went out to herd the sheep. But the Navajos were no match for the well-armed, mounted raiders in the open country of the reservation and lived in constant fear of attack. They were forced to graze their herds closer to the main encampments and refused to let their women and children venture beyond the settlements. The soldiers at Fort Sumner did absolutely nothing to impede the Comanche raids except give advice until the Navajos took matters in hand. A few young Navajo men dressed as Comanches attacked the fort one night and killed five soldiers. After that the Americans were somewhat more diligent in keeping watch for Comanche raiders.

In February, 1865, General Carleton sent Navajo runners

to find Manuelito and tell him that unless he and his band came in peacefully before spring they would be hunted down and killed without quarter. Not only were the Navajos still in *Dinehtah* retarding the westward spread of ranchers and miners, but Carleton felt that as long as there was one Navajo living in freedom—and especially one as influential as Manuelito—the prisoners at Bosque Redondo would be tempted to slip away and return home. Manuelito told the runners that he would discuss surrender only with some of the headmen who had been living at Bosque Redondo—and they must come to him. A few days later six Navajo headmen from the reservation met the war chief near the Zuñi trading post. He led them west into the hills where his people were hiding. Only about a hundred men, women and children were left of Manuelito's band, but they still had horses and a few sheep. He told the men from Bosque Redondo that he would not surrender. "My God and my mother live here in the west," he said, "and I will not leave them. It is the tradition of our people that we must never cross the three rivers (to live)—the Río Grande, the San Juan and the Colorado. Nor could I go far from the Chuska mountains where I was born. I shall remain here. I have nothing to lose but my life, and that they can come and take whenever they please, but I will not go there (to Bosque Redondo)."

When Manuelito's words were repeated to General Carleton, he sent a message to the commander at Fort Wingate to "try to get Manuelito. Have him securely ironed and carefully guarded. It will be a mercy to others whom he controls to capture or kill him at once. I prefer that he should be captured. If he attempts to escape . . . he will be shot down."

The commander told some Utes where the headman and his band had been camped when he held council with the men from Bosque Redondo and sent them after him. The Utes found Manuelito's camp, attacked, and scattered the surprised Navajos. They quickly regrouped and fought off the enemy but lost most of their livestock. After the Ute attack Manuelito had only about forty horses and fifty sheep left. He quickly fled west, to the Black Mesa area, but the Utes were again sent after him. When they attacked the camp of Manuelito's band the second time, the headman and most of the warriors were away on a hunting trip. This time the Utes were successful, killing several men and taking most of the surviving men, women and children captive. Still Manuelito did not give up. In the meantime several hundred Navajos had escaped from the Bosque Redondo to return to *Dinehtah*.

Carleton, realizing that the Navajos would continue to die of exposure if something was not done about the housing situation at the reservation, conceived a plan for sheltering them in adobe apartment buildings similar to those the Pueblos lived in. Old Navajo hands were quick to point out that the Navajos detested living in close proximity. Carleton rejected this council and ordered the soldiers to supervise the Navajos in the construction of a pueblo. "The buildings," he said, "should be but one story high, and face to the placitas. By a proper arrangement—dead wall on the outside . . . a very handsome and strong place could be made (The Navajos) will spend their spare time in putting up houses, and by next winter all can be comfortably sheltered. Then to have trees planted to make shade, and I fancy there would be no Indian village in the world to compare with it in point of beauty."

Either Dr. Michael Steck or someone else in the Indian department—now completely at odds with the military—dubbed the projected Navajo pueblo "Fair Caletonia" and the Santa Fe *New Mexican* picked up the term and used it in another derisive attack on the general. But Carleton was not a man to change his mind, even under the sort of censure now leveled at his person and Indian policy, and work on the adobe apartment building in the Staked Plains commenced. It stopped suddenly when the Navajo headmen learned the intended use of the new building. The Navajos, they announced, would never live in such a place. If a death occurred inside it, as was surely to happen, all Navajos inhabiting the building would immediately abandon it. Carleton tried to use Christian logic on what he referred to as the "dark superstition of the Indians" but the Navajo headmen were adamant and the general was finally forced to compromise. The Navajos would be allowed to retain their traditional hogans; however, these would be placed in uniform rows with good intervals and wide streets between them. Then when a death occurred, a family could destroy their home and move to the end of the row, where a new dwelling would be erected.

370

Throughout the winter of 1864-65 every Navajo male who was able was put to work clearing additional land for crops of wheat, corn, pumpkins, melons, squash, beans and peas. By spring over 6,000 acres had been cleared and irrigation canals had been dug to bring water from the Río Pecos to the fields. The new post commander, General Marcellus Crocker, was so optimistic that he believed that, with the fall harvest, the Navajos at Bosque Redondo would become self-supporting. In fact he expected the crops to "subsist the Indians now at Bosque Redondo, as well as any others that may come in."

Meanwhile the Navajos and the Mescaleros who were still at Bosque Redondo were still being subsisted by issue from army commissary stores, much to the consternation of General Carleton. Now that the Navajos had been defeated, rounded up and placed on his reservation, he felt that the army's job was finished and the Indian department should take charge of caring for the Navajos—under his supervision, of course. Dr. Michael Steck would not—and could not—cooperate. He was still acting under orders received from Indian Commissioner William P. Dole almost a year before that stated the Department of the Interior was not responsible for the Indians on the reservation; they were a matter of military concern. Too, Dr. Steck's budget was not sufficient to care for the Indians that were already in his charge. The Navajos were still being given barely enough food to keep them alive and working. But a few soon found a way to get more food.

To facilitate the feeding of so many, ration tickets of cardboard were distributed to The People. They were distributed every other day by the commissary officers for food allotment. Soon, however, the Navajos were duplicating the meal tickets with such skill that they could be told from the original only by careful examination. Stamped metal discs were then substituted for the cardboard tickets. But, thanks to Henry Linn Dodge, the Navajos had been very well instructed in the art of metal working and, under instructions from General Carleton, several dozen were employed as blacksmiths at Bosque Redondo. With forged stamps and dies, the metal discs were even easier to counterfeit than had been the meal tickets. By the end of March, 1865, when 9,022 Navajos and approximately 350 Apaches were drawing supplies, almost 3,000 counterfeit metal meal discs had been counted by the commissary personnel. The army finally had to send to Washington for tickets of such intricate design that the Navajos couldn't copy them. The Navajos were soon back on half-rations. That spring a few more slipped away in hopes of making their way back to *Dinehtah*. But many of those who left, encouraged by the *Dinehanaih* who were working as spies for New Mexican slavers, were taken captive soon after leaving the reservation. Deaths continued at a steady, if alarming pace. The others worked in the fields, hating their sometimes cruel military overseers.

Again the cutworms struck the corn crop and the disaster of the year before was repeated. The total yield of grain was little over half that Commander Crocker had predicted it would be. Again the Navajos would have to be fed from army commissary supplies. The grain General Carleton sent to Bosque Redondo was full of weevils and the bacon was of such poor quality that it had been condemned as unfit for the soldiers to eat—but it was good enough for Indians.

The army continued to deny that Navajos were leaving the reservation but by May desertions had increased to the point that their concealment was impossible. Not all were returning home. Some were wandering into the settlements to find employment or beg. Others were hiring themselves out to New Mexican ranchers as peon sheepherders. But the murmurings of the old people and the Singers increased. Only by returning to *Dinehtah*—they believed—would the gods return to them and give back the *Dineh* their health.

On July 14, 1865, Barboncito and Ganado Blanco, the son of Ganado Mucho, slipped away and led their followers back to *Dinehtah*. Upon learning of the desertion of the headmen five days later, General Carleton sent a troop of soldiers, guided by Blas Lucero's Spies, after them and posted permanent guards for forty miles around Fort Sumner. In August the general ordered the post commander to kill every Navajo found off the reservation without a pass and to "let the Navajos know that large parties of citizens are in pursuit of the Navajos who would not come in from their old country. Many of the latter have already been killed. Their crops will be destroyed and they will be exterminated unless they come in. This information may put those who may have wished to leave the Bosque out of the notion."

Barboncito and Ganado Blanco, harassed by New Mexicans and the soldiers, quickly returned to Bosque Redondo. Then, late in the fall of 1865, Ganado Mucho rode into Fort Wingate and asked for a military escort for his band and his large herd of livestock, which he knew was desperately needed for food at Bosque Redondo. The women and children of his band left Fort Wingate under a military escort while Ganado Mucho and the men of his band followed with the livestock. The party with the women and children soon left the men, herding the slow-moving livestock, far behind. Not only did one of the American soldiers attempt to rape one of Ganado Mucho's daughters, but while the party was camped on the Rio Grande, a group of New Mexicans attacked and rode off with both of the young daughters of the headman. Their mother, frantic and raging, rode after them but was caught by the soldiers and taken on to Bosque Redondo. When Ganado Mucho arrived there a few days later the news that greeted him left the old headman broken in spirit. He demanded that soldiers be sent to look for his children. The girls were never found. The soldiers reported that one of them had been sold into Mexico.

In the meantime the fiasco at Bosque Redondo had come under the scrutiny of high-placed persons in Washington. In a fiery speech delivered in June, Senator Charles Sumner of Massachusetts attacked the entire system of Indian slavery in the United States and denounced General Carleton and Governor Henry Connelly especially for the situation in New Mexico. In response, President Andrew Johnson said: "It has been represented to me . . . that Indians in New Mexico have been seized and reduced into slavery; and it is recommended that the authority of the Executive branch of the Government should be exercised for the effectual suppression of a practice which is alike in violation of the rights of the Indians, and the provisions of the Organic law of said Territory.

"Concurring in this recommendation I do hereby order that the heads of the several Executive Departments do enjoin upon their subordinates, agents and employes under their respective orders, or supervision of that Territory, to discontinue the practice aforesaid, and to take all lawful means to supress the same."

In July members of a Joint Special Committee, authorized by both houses of Congress to investigate Indian problems, arrived in New Mexico. While the inspection of Bosque Redondo and the investigation in Santa Fe were cursory, it was sufficient to convince the committee, chaired by Senator James R. Doolittle of Wisconsin, that the real reason for the troubles with the Navajos had always been the slave raids of the New Mexicans. Such raids, they concluded, provoked the Navajos to retaliate as the *Dineh* were endowed, no less than other peoples, with the attributes of love and affection and when they lost their women and their children, of whom they were inordinately fond, they experienced the deepest sorrow. The committee also reported that peonage and Indian slavery were ingrained in New Mexican society and the former was authorized by a territorial statute which provided that peons receive a wage of five dollars a month on which to support themselves. The amount was insufficient, of course, and the indebtedness of the peons constantly increased, resulting in servitude from which there was no escape. As for Indian slavery, the laws against the practice were ignored by everyone from the governor to one justice of the highest court, both of whom owned Navajo slaves. Ranchers, Indian agents, military officers, civil officials and members of the legislature owned slaves, the majority of whom were women and children taken in raids. They estimated that at least five hundred Navajos were held as slaves in Santa Fe alone and the number held in other cities and on ranches throughout the territory would total several thousand. Children of the Navajo slaves, often fathered by the master of the house, were born in bondage and were sold on the market. Furthermore slave raiders still scourged the Navajo country in search of captives for the Rio Grande markets.

Word of the horrors of the Navajo defeat and imprisonment had also reached Washington and General James H. Carleton's "Indian policy" was thoroughly examined by the Congressional committee. The men from Washington were appalled at conditions at Bosque Redondo. It was apparent that if the Navajos were kept on the reservation they would eventually die off from disease and malnutrition. The hospital facilities provided for the Navajos consisted of nine small rooms, three of which were used as sleeping quarters, kitchen and mess for the medical staff. A fourth was used as a surgery and the entire building was no better than an outhouse and on the verge of collapse. The Fort Sumner medical officer reported that the Navajos often refused to enter the "hospital" as people had died inside and, too, they had not forgotten seeing sick Navajos shot to death by soldiers on the Long Walk. Senator Doolittle and his committee learned that the stock the Navajos had brought with them from *Dinehtah* as well as that provided by the quartermaster was almost all gone and most of it had been run off by the Comanches; the soil of the reservation would never support the crops needed for their survival and, for that matter, the water of the Pecos, the only water supply available to the Navajos, was so impregnated with alkali and other minerals that it was unfit for human consumption. When the Navajos watched Senator Doolittle and the men from Washington ride away from Fort Sumner that hot July day in 1865 they did not realize it, but the first step toward the return of The People to *Dinehtah* had been taken. But the wheels of bureaucracy turn slowly and it would be three long, bitter years before the realization of that dream.

FIVE

The Return to Dinetah

The findings of the Congressional committee were not immediately acted on in Washington. In fact the whole matter became so bogged down in red tape that the Department of the Interior undertook an investigation of its own and sent Julius K. Graves to New Mexico to look into the Bosque Redondo situation, now a matter of much heated debate in both Washington and Santa Fé. Graves arrived in New Mexico in December and on the last day of the year, 1865, he held council with Navajo headmen at Fort Sumner. Graves told the headmen that he had been sent to the Bosque Redondo to see that the Navajos were properly fed and cared for and asked them, one by one, to tell him of the problems impeding progress on the reservation.

The council lasted all day and the Navajo headmen, Graves reported, conducted themselves with dignity and were eloquent in expressing their complaints. This land, they said, was no good for the Navajos. The water was bitter and made them ill; the soil was poor and crops were wretched. They voiced all their complaints to the investigator, not the least of which was that the soldiers of the garrison were tempting the young women with extra rations and many of them were suffering from venereal diseases. More than anything, they concluded, the Navajos wanted to return home to *Dinehtah*.

Graves' report on conditions at Bosque Redondo and of the entire Indian slavery situation in New Mexico was even more damning than had been that of the Doolittle committee. Graves did not attack General Carleton directly but his report left little doubt as to who was responsible for the reduced circumstances of the Navajos (the Mescalero Apaches had quietly slipped away and disappeared into the mountains on the night of November 3, 1865). He was told of the weevily flour and rancid bacon that had been sent to the Navajos by Carleton after he'd rejected it as unfit for the soldiers and included an account of the matter in his report. He also reported that more than a thousand Navajos (actually the number was far greater than that) had run away from the reservation and that many of them had died of starvation while attempting to return home and pointed out that the military commander had sent troops after the runaways with orders to shoot all who refused to return. He also told of the Comanche raids and pointed out that the Navajos had no means of defending themselves from such raids; on one occasion twenty Navajos had been killed by a raiding party of Comanches and New Mexicans.

Lastly and the most damning of all as far as General James H. Carleton's place in history is concerned, Graves implied that the military commander had an ulterior motive for selecting the unsuitable Bosque Redondo for the Navajo reservation in the first place. While Graves was in no position to make what would have amounted to a most serious charge against General Carleton, he did report that the Bosque Redondo reservation was located on lands claimed by the Comanches and very near the trails that tribe had always used when raiding the ranches of southern New Mexico and northern Mexico. From the perspective of a hundred years, it becomes apparent that Carleton placed the Navajos on the Bosque Redondo to function as a buffer between the predatory Comanches and the ranches of the "civilized" New Mexicans. By locating the Navajos near the war trail of their hereditary enemies, Carleton had thrown a bone—in this case the impoverished and defenseless Navajos—in the path of the wolves with the hope that they would leave the settlers and ranchers alone. At least that phase of the general's "Indian policy" was successful.

Graves determined that the military had no acceptable excuse for failing to care properly for the Navajos and suggested that they either do so by supporting and protecting them or let the Indian department take charge of them. He also suggested that they be removed from Bosque Redondo and that their old country should be examined with a view of establishing a reservation there in an area of adequate water, fuel and arable soil.

But the citizens of New Mexico continued to ignore the congressional act that prohibited slavery. Not even the territory's congressional delegate, J. Francisco Chavez, who had been responsible for the massacre at Fort Wingate in September, 1861, freed any of his numerous Indian slaves. And General James H. Carleton ignored the reports of the investigators. Carleton still ruled New Mexico as if the entire territory was his private domain. Dr. Michael Steck had grown tired of fighting the general and resigned in May, 1865. He had been replaced by Felipe Delgado, a man more to General Carleton's liking. Delgado was replaced by a political appointee, A. Baldwin Norton, from Ohio, on February 17, 1866, and, as a result of Graves' report, Theodore H. Dodd was appointed agent to the Navajos. Dodd was the first agent since Henry Linn Dodge to become really concerned about the welfare of the Navajos. When Dodd arrived at Bosque Redondo a smallpox epidemic was threatening to carry off the entire tribe. He moved into the dilapidated agent quarters at Fort Sumner and went about his duties with tireless energy. Soon after his appointment he requested, and received permission, from the Department of the Interior to purchase a long list of agricultural tools and implements as well as much-needed clothing for his charges.

Superintendent Norton and Agent Dodd were soon at odds with General Carleton, as was just about everyone else in the territory by the spring of 1866. The territorial assembly sent a message to President Andrew Johnson, charging, ironically, that Carleton had accused New Mexicans of depredations committed by Navajos and had failed in his sworn duty to suppress Indian troubles. The assembly asked that he be replaced by a commander who would protect the territory and uphold the rights of "respectable white citizens."

In July Superintendent Norton travelled to Bosque Redondo for a council with the headmen and arrived only two days after a band of Comanches swept through the reservation, killing Navajo herders and running off 200 horses. The raid brought more sorrow to Ganado Mucho who was still grieving the loss of his daughters. One of the herders killed had been his youngest son. On the morning of July 15, the grief-stricken old man stood before Norton and made an impassioned speech that reflected the sorrow of all Navajos at Bosque Redondo: "I have lost one of my sons," he said, "and I am nearly crazy. I feel very bad. How can we protect ourselves when our enemies are much better armed than we are? We went to go back to our own country . . . we want to go back there the same as we are here. The land here will never be as good as our own country. The government does not supply us with wood here, and we had plenty there. If the government would put us on a reservation in our own country and keep us the same as here within boundaries, the government would see how we would work. We think we were born to live in our old country . . . we think we were not born to live here. . . ."

Ten days later Ganado Mucho's brother, Caballado Mucho, arrived at Fort Sumner and reported that Manuelito was still hiding but was wounded and weak and would probably surrender soon. On September 1, 1866, Manuelito and twenty-three of his followers—all that were left—rode into Fort Wingate and surrendered. They were dressed in rags and without weapons. The forty-eight-year-old war leader had held out as long as he could. A month later they arrived at Fort Sumner—ironically, only twelve days after General James H. Carleton was removed from his command. On September 19, 1866, Secretary of War Edwin M. Stanton ordered Carleton to report to duty in Louisiana. Carleton had insisted to the end that his "Indian policy" would work and refused to see that it was a miserable and tragic failure. The Santa Fé *New Mexican* heralded the commander's departure with a final stinging editorial: "It thus appears that our territory will be relieved from the presence of this man Carleton, who has so long lorded it amongst us. For five years or more he has been in supreme command of New Mexico, and during that whole time, has accomplished nothing for which he is entitled to the thanks and gratitude of our people, or the confidence of the War Department."

A. Baldwin Norton, after a thorough inspection of Bosque Redondo, said the sooner it was abondoned the better.

"The water is black and brackish," he reported, "scarcely bearable to the taste and said by the Indians to be unhealty, because one-fourth of their population has been swept off by disease . . . I have heard it suggested that there was speculation at the bottom of (establishing the reservation at Bosque Redondo). . . . Do you expect an Indian to be satisfied and contented deprived of the common comforts of life, without which a white man would not be contented anywhere? Would any sensible man select a spot for a reservation for 8,000 Indians where the water is scarcely bearable, where the soil is poor and cold, and where the muskite (mesquite) roots 12 miles distant are the only wood for the Indians to use? . . . If they remain on this reservation, they must always be held there by force and not from choice. O! let them go back, or take them where they can have good cool water to drink, wood plenty to keep them from freezing to death and where the soil will produce something for them to eat."

The statement that one-fourth of the tribe had been "swept off by disease" was not far off although later figures would be adjusted to appear otherwise. By army count there had been 9,022 Navajos on the reservation in the spring of 1865. While some had deserted the number coming in from *Dinehtah* had more than compensated for those. On June 30, 1867, Lieutenant McDowell, commander of Fort Sumner, reported that there were 7,300 Navajos living on the reservation.

After three successive crop failures, the Navajos had to be forced to work the fields at gunpoint in the spring of 1867—but to no avail. That summer a drought struck the Southwest and the Río Pecos shriveled to a mere trickle. Planting grounds parched and cracked under the intense summer sun and the corn that did come up soon withered and died. The crops that survived the heat and lack of water—pumpkins, beans and peas—were destroyed by a series of severe hailstorms in late summer. By the end of summer grazing grass was non-existent on the reservation. The small herd of Navajo stock was starving and the soldier overseers offered no solution. Finally, the Navajos saw that they had no choice but to drive their herd off the reservation, to the South in order to feed them. But the first time they attempted it they were observed by the soldiers who, without making any attempt to find out what the Navajos were doing, opened fire. The Navajos fought back, killing five soldiers and wounding four more. This unwarranted shooting of Navajos caused several families to slip away from the fort and attempt to make their way home.

Late in September Ganado Mucho, Manuelito and nine other headmen were called to Santa Fé for a council with Superintendent Norton. He told them that, finally, control of the Navajos had officially been passed from the military to the Indian department on orders from General Ulysses S. Grant, Commander in Chief of the army. But while the headmen were in Santa Fé tragedy again struck at Bosque Redondo. More than 200 Comanches stormed the Navajo camps around Fort Sumner and in the vicious battle that followed many Navajos were killed. But the Navajos fought back and repelled the attack. The commander of the fort reported: " . . . I must express my admiration of their courage and daring. From crest to crest for a distance of 16 miles they gallantly pressed the foe, many of the Navajos on foot, and unable to keep up, had dropped out, by which the Comanches became greatly superior in numbers."

The Navajos had one more problem to contend with before they could return to *Dinehtah* — their old enemy, the War Department. In spite of General Grant's orders, the military still refused to relinquish its control over the Bosque Redondo and ordered an investigation of its own into the entire situation. The War Department chose a young Lieutenant named R. McDonald of the Fifth Cavalry to conduct the investigation. The conditions Lieutenant McDonald saw at Bosque Redondo could not be denied. His report, completed on November 12, 1867, reiterated most of the findings of the investigations conducted by Julius Graves and the Doolittle Commission. He strongly recommended that the Navajos be moved as quickly as possible from Bosque Redondo to "a suitable location where wood, water and grass abound."

But the fate of the Navajos had already been determined in Washington two weeks before McDonald made his report. They would not, as General William Tecumseh Sherman had suggested, be transferred to Indian Territory. The Department of the Interior had decided the Navajos would remain in New Mexico; in fact they were to be returned to *Dinehtah*. A commission was appointed to examine their old country and select land "with water, wood, and other resources for a permanent reservation." Early in 1868 Superintendent Norton and Agent Dodge received instructions from Washington to begin preliminary steps to make the transfer. But the Navajos were not told they were going home. First another treaty had to be made.

Throughout the spring of 1868 the chaos at Bosque Redondo continued. Congress had appropriated only $100,000 for subsisting the Navajos for the fiscal year 1867-68, which, in Agent Dodd's estimation, was only one-fourth the amount needed just to keep his charges fed. The Navajos, now suffering more than ever on their wretched reservation, didn't have the heart to plant crops again. Each year the yield had been less than the year before; children had become even more emanciated. Despondent mothers now often killed their babies at birth rather than see them waste away with hunger. All spring one rumor travelled on the heels of another: the soldiers were going to come and kill everyone; they were going to be returned to *Dineh-tah* . . . no, they were going to be taken even farther away from home to a place called Indian Territory.

Then agent Dodd asked the Navajo headmen to select a spokesman for the tribe to be sent to Washington to talk to President Andrew Johnson. Barboncito was chosen and, once again, eloquently pleaded for his people and asked that they be allowed to return home.

Finally, on May 28, 1868, several army vehicles, escorted by a detachment of cavalry, arrived at Fort Sumner. The Navajo headmen were called in a council with General William T. Sherman and Colonel Samuel F. Tappan, who were there to negotiate a final peace treaty between the Navajos and the United States. Again Barboncito acted as spokesman. But the Navajos still had not been told they were returning to *Dinehtah*.

General Sherman opened the council by asking Dodd to submit a "status report" and was told that there were 7,304 Navajos on the reservation; an estimated 2,000 had died of smallpox, chicken pox, pneumonia and other causes since The People had been imprisoned at Bosque Redondo, and about 900 had escaped and never returned. Several hundred others had disappeared but it could not be determined what had happened to them. Some of those had died but their deaths had not been reported, others had slipped away to return home and still others had been taken captive by

Comanche and New Mexican raiders. Dodd reported that the Navajos' livestock consisted of 1,550 horses, a thousand of which had recently been recovered from the Comanches, 950 sheep, 1,025 goats and twenty mules.

In spite of the fact that the Department of the Interior had ordered the Navajos returned to their own country, General Sherman still advocated removing them to a reservation in Indian Territory; or perhaps he only pretended to in order to gain a better bargaining position in negotiating the treaty. Sherman, at any rate, told the Navajo headmen that he and Colonel Tappan had come to Fort Sumner "to invite some of your leading men to go and see the Cherokee country (Indian Territory) and if they like it we would give you a reservation there. . . . It will be much cheaper there than here; give you schools to educate your children in English or Spanish and take care of you until such time as you will be able to protect yourselves. We do not want you to take our word for it but send some of your wisest men to see for themselves. . . ."

Barboncito replied: ". . . When the Navajos were first created, four mountains and four rivers were pointed out to us, inside of which we should live. That was to be our country and it was given to us by the First Woman of the *Dineh*. It was told to us by our forefathers that we were never to move east of the Rio Grande or north of the San Juan rivers and I think that our coming here has been the cause of so much death among us and our animals. First Woman, when she was created, gave us this piece of land and created it especially for us and gave us the whitest of corn . . .

". . . I hope you will not ask me to go to any other country except my own. It might turn out another Hwelte. They told us this was a good place when we came, but it is not!"

News that the Navajos were going to be taken to another place that was not in their old homeland spread like wildfire through the reservation. On the second morning as General Sherman walked through the throng of Navajos outside the fort on his way to the council, women clutched at his coat and with tears in their eyes begged him to send them home. He asked the interpreter what they wanted and witnesses reported that he was visibly moved when told that they were begging to be returned to *Dinehtah*.

That morning Sherman said to Barboncito: " . . . we will discuss the other proposition of going back to your own country, and if we agree we will make a boundary line outside of which you must not go except for the purpose of trading—we must have a clearly defined boundary line and know exactly where you belong to. You must live at peace and must not fight with other Indians. If people trouble you, you must go to the nearest military post and report to the commanding officer who will punish those who trouble you. The Army will do the fighting. You must live at peace. If you go to your own country the Utes will be the nearest Indians to you. If, however, the Utes or Apaches come into your country with bows and arrows and guns, you, of course, can drive them out, but must not follow beyond the boundary line. You must not permit your young men to go to the Ute or Apache country to steal. Neither must they steal from Mexicans."

Barboncito was overjoyed. The Navajos were going home. "I am very well pleased with what you have said, and if we go back to our own country, we are willing to abide by whatever orders are issued us," he said. "We do not want to go to the right or left, but straight back to our own country."

The negotiations were concluded on the morning of June 1, 1868, and the document, prepared by the Department of State, was signed by the representatives of the United States and twenty-nine Navajo headmen including Barboncito, Armijo, Manuelito, Ganado Mucho and Delgadito. The treaty established a reservation of 3.5 million acres, "bounded on the north by the 37th degree of north latitude, south by an east and west line passing through the site of old Fort Defiance . . . east by the parallel of longitude which, if prolonged south, would pass through old Fort Lyon, or the Ojo de Oso, Bear Spring, and west by a parallel of longitude about 109°30′ west of Greenwhich, provided it embraces the outlet of Canon-de-Chilly (sic) which canon is to be all included in this reservation."

The reservation comprised only about one-tenth of the country which the Navajos had previously claimed and excluded all their fine eastern grazing lands and most of the water resources. All the Navajos, except the Enemy Navajos who were allowed to return to their home near Cebolleta, were to live within the confines of the reservation and any

Navajo "being the head of a family, shall desire to commence farming, he shall have the privilege to select . . . a tract of land within said reservation, not exceeding one hundred and sixty acres in extent. . . . Any person over eighteen years of age, not being the head of the family, may in like manner . . . select a quantity of land, not exceeding eighty acres in extent." The treaty authors had applied the principles of the Homestead Law to the Navajo treaty, either ignoring, or ignorant of, the fact that there were very few tracts of one hundred and sixty acres within the reservation that would suffice to support a family. The Law, devised for the well-watered rich soil of the East, could not be applied to that portion of *Dinehtah* given to the Navajos, much of which was desert and without water. Barboncito and the other headmen were aware of this but they did not—and could not— object. It was well enough that they were returning home.

The head of each family was to be given "seeds and agricultural implements, for the first year, not exceeding the value of one hundred dollars." For the next two years the amount was not "to exceed the value of twenty-five dollars." Clothing and raw materials to make clothing was to be furnished for the next ten years "up to the value of five dollars a year for each Navajo." Ten dollars worth of other purchases each year for ten years was promised to those Navajos engaged in farming or mechanical pursuits and "for relief of the needy during the coming winter" the Navajos were promised the "purchase of fifteen thousand sheep and goats . . . five hundred beef cattle and a million pounds of corn."

Article VI of the treaty stated: "In order to insure the civilization of the Indians entering this treaty, the necessity of education is admitted, especially of such of them as may be settled on said agricultural parts of this reservation, and they therefore pledge themselves to compel their children, male and female, between the ages of six and sixteen years to attend school; and it is hereby made the duty of the agent for said Indians to see that this stipulation is strictly complied with; and the United States agrees that, for every thirty children between said ages who can be induced or compelled to attend school, a house shall be provided, and a teacher competent to teach the elementary branches of an English education shall be furnished, who will reside among

385

said Indians, and faithfully discharge his or her duties as a teacher. The provisions of this article to continue for not less than ten years." The Navajo headmen who signed the treaty at Bosque Redondo that June day in 1868 could not realize, of course, the far-reaching implications of the wording of that section of the treaty. It would become a source of discord that would, twenty-five years hence, bring about a serious threat of renewing hostilities between the Navajos and the United States.

The Navajo headmen listened as article after article of the treaty was read, first in English, then interpreted into Spanish, and finally in Navajo. They wanted to hear what the Bilagáana were going to do about Navajo captives held as slaves by New Mexicans. When the interpreter had finished there still had been no mention of the captives. Barboncito pressed the point, as he had already tried to discuss the matter with General Sherman. Sherman replied that the United States had fought a great war on the issue of slaves and that the government had passed a law against slavery. "We do not know," he said, "that there are any Navajos held by Mexicans, but if there are you can apply to the judges of the Civil Courts and the Land Commissioners." But the matter of Navajo slaves interested Colonel Tappan. After a short, whispered conversation with General Sherman, the colonel turned to Barboncito and asked: "How many Navajos are among the Mexicans now?"

"Over half the tribe," Barboncito replied.

Again the officers engaged in a whispered conversation, after which General Sherman said: "We will do all we can to have your children returned to you. Our government is determined that the enslavement of the Navajos will cease and those who are guilty of holding them in slavery shall be punished."

It took the Navajos only two weeks to prepare for the Long Walk home. When Tsohanoai, the Sun Bearer, appeared in the eastern sky on the morning of June 18, 1868, the first of a column that would stretch out for ten miles across the New Mexico desert left Fort Sumner. Escorted by four companies of cavalry and accompanied by the agent Dodd, his wife and two children, the Navajos were dressed in the best clothing they possessed and many of them were smiling for the first time in four years. But progress was painfully slow; they moved but ten or twelve miles each day. On July 5 the Navajos passed through Albuquerque and the next day they forded the Rio Grande. When the returning exiles came into view of familiar horizons and especially sacred Tsotsil (Mount Taylor) they were so overwhelmed with joy that many of the American soldiers guarding them were moved to join their celebration. Paul A. Horgan wrote that one old man said: "When we saw the top of the mountain from Albuquerque we wondered if it was our mountain, and we felt like talking to the ground, we loved it so..." (Horgan, Holt, Rhinehart, Winston, 1954: Vol 2, 333.) Many of them fell to their knees and cried.

Now, surely, the gods would return to the *Dineh*. In this land that had been given them by Changing Woman prayersongs to the Holy Ones would be heard and the *Dineh* would again be blessed with health and goods. By the first of August the last of the long column had reached Fort Wingate. They had lost just about everything but an indomitable spirit. But they were home.

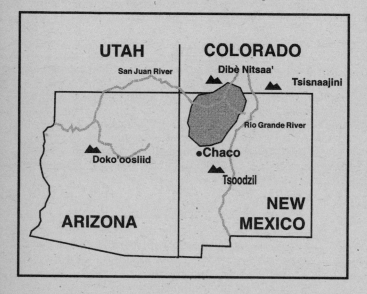

The shaded area of northwestern New Mexico is thought to be the area of the first Navajo settlements in the American Southwest at about AD 900. In recent years evidence has been found that place them as far south as Gallup, New Mexico and west to the Hopi Mesas by AD1200, or about a hundred years before the Hopi arrived in the area.

PART SIX

The Way Back

ONE

Lawbreakers and Peacemakers

The treaty of Bosque Redondo was ratified by the Senate and signed by President Andrew Johnson on August 12, 1868. It would become the most enduring and most significant agreement consummated between the United States and an aboriginal nation, in spite of the fact that the government failed to honor one article of the treaty to the letter. The Navajos waited in vain for the sheep, goats and beef cattle promised "for the relief of the needy during the coming winter."

Article VIII of the treaty, which promised the Navajos that "clothing, goods, or raw materials in lieu thereof . . . not exceeding in value five dollars per Indian" would be delivered to the Navajo agent on the first day of September of each year for ten years was so ambiguously worded that it amounted to an open invitation to Indian Bureau officials and virtually everyone connected in any way with supplying the goods to engage in the vilest practices of kickbacks and thievery. As we shall see, for the next two decades almost everyone had their hands in the Navajo pie but the Navajos.

The Navajos who had been imprisoned at Bosque Redondo returned to fields overgrown with brush that had to be cleared and cultivated again, the charred ruins of hogans and corrals that had to be rebuilt. All that was left of the once bountiful and beautiful peach orchards of Canyon de Chelly was blackened stumps. The *Dineh* sought out old homesites and, for the most part, ignored the boundary lines of the new treaty. Home was where they had lived before, where their parents and grandparents before them had lived, and there they went. They spread out over the countryside, north beyond Shiprock, northwest to Monument Valley and Navajo Mountain and to the valley of the San Juan River. Westward they pushed beyond the Hopi villages and those that had lived in the East, in Tunicha Valley and Chaco, remained there. What did lines drawn upon the paper of the Bilagáana mean to them? It was too late for crops and they knew better than to depend on American promises so they returned to that part of *Dineh-tah* where they had always lived to resettle before winter snows set in. Berries, seeds, wild tubers, rabbits and squirrels were to be had and when the winter snows came the deer would come down into the valleys to forge for food. No longer would they depend on the meager handouts of rancid bacon and weevily flour from the Bilagáana.

Manuelito led the surviving members of his family, which included his Mexican wife, Juanita, his son and a nephew, back to his old home near Tohatchi, south of Sheep Springs; Ganado Mucho, still grieving for his son and his captive daughters, led his followers back home to the Ganado Valley, which was outside the new boundary line. For the first few years after the Navajos' return home no one paid any attention to the old headman's infraction of the treaty boundary terms. Barboncito returned home to Canyon de Chelly, where everything had been destroyed.

It was just as well so many Navajos did decide to provide for themselves. At least half of those who returned from Bosque Redondo had to subsist on rations handed out to them at Fort Wingate and at Fort Defiance, where the Navajo agency had been reestablished, that first winter. By the end of the year many were on the brink of starvation. Ration day came but once a week and too often the supplies available were not sufficient to distribute food to all the Navajos. Captain F. T. Bennett, commander of the troops stationed on the reservation, was often informed that a shipment of supplies was on its way, only to wait in vain for its arrival. Somewhere between the Indian Bureau and Fort Wingate the shipments disappeared without a trace. Navajos holding ration tickets had to be turned away. On those days Big Belly, as the Navajos called the amiable Captain Bennett, could give them nothing but sympathy. The officer felt a genuine concern for the welfare of the Navajos, and the malfeasance of those in charge of supplying the treaty provisions to the Navajos were often the object of his wrath.

Once when he asked a visiting Indian Bureau official about a shipment of supplies that was long overdue at Fort Wingate and was told that the official knew nothing about it, he shouted: "Mark my words, there will be another Navajo war, and we'll have to clear. These are the best Indians on the continent, willing to work and don't want to fight. But damn it, they can't starve to death right here. We've destroyed their living, run off all the game and shut them up, and their crops failed. If we were in their place we'd fight! Ain't a man here in the government employ that's been paid a cent for twelve months. They give the Apaches sugar and coffee and flour, because they're murdering people and robbing, and won't give these men anything because they've been peaceable . . . and these fellows know it, too."

When the Navajos had been back in *Dinehtah* for a year and virtually none of the promises made by General Sherman had been kept, bands of Navajo raiders began forming—and Barboncito, as spokesman of the tribe, was soon faced with the same problems that had confronted Navajo peace leaders of the past. Both the Mormons and the Utes north and west of the reservation were soon complaining of Navajo raids as were the New Mexicans on the East. But Captain Bennett reported that in his opinion most of the complaints of the New Mexicans were "without fact or foundation."

Barboncito investigated each report of a Navajo raid and soon realized he could not solve the problem alone. Three or four thousand Navajos had never surrendered. They had retreated west, taking their herds with them, and had found refuge in the mountains north of Flagstaff, Arizona, and the area of the Coconino Plateau, while others of their number had hidden in the Navajo Mountain area and in and around the Grand Canyon where they had been befriended by the Havasupai. There people were returning home and while they were sharing their herds and food with clan relatives, they did not consider the Bosque Redondo treaty binding on their part. For the most part it was the young men of that contingent of Navajos who were raiding the Utes and the Mormons. Barboncito travelled to Fort Wingate and told Captain Bennett who the thieves were. "These go out," he said, "as if slipping between our fingers . . . giving one excuse after another to leave their homes, hunting and trading among their favorite excuses."

Agent Dodd had died five months after leaving Bosque Redondo and his duties had been turned over to Captain Bennett after J. C. French had served a short time. Barboncito, Manuelito and Ganado Mucho called on Bennett, in his new capacity, and told him that unless the government did something about the promises made the Navajos at Bosque Redondo they would not be able to keep the young men off the war trail. The young warriors were ashamed of having to stand in line to receive the small allotments of food and clothing from the military post and angry at the impoverished condition of their families. It was better to take to the raiding trail than sit by and listen to the cries of their hungry children, and when those who had never surrendered talked of stealing, they listened.

The treaty, the headmen pointed out, had promised them seed, but the amount of seed they had received that first spring was not half enough to go around to the families wanting to farm. Then, in June, unseasonable snow and, later, frost, destroyed the few crops the Navajos had been able to plant. "They were the most sorrowful, discouraged, downhearted people that could be imagined," Bennett wrote the Indian department. "Send more seeds."

But there was little Bennett could tell the headmen who called on him with pleas to help them in keeping their young men off the war trail. How could he make them understand that when he asked for seed, he received a shipment of five hundred silk hats instead? When he asked for hoes and plows he was sent fancy umbrellas; when he asked for flour, he got boxes of overcoats with velvet collars; when he asked for blankets and received, in crates marked "blankets for the Navajoe Indians," several gross of lead furniture castors; when he asked for tinned foods, he got crates of high-buttoned women's shoes? He understood what was happening, but how could he explain to the

Navajo headmen that Indian Bureau officials were giving contracts to their friends who sent their surplus products—useless to the Navajos—instead of the food, clothing, seeds and tools they were promised and so desperately needed? Barboncito could ride about the reservation and remind his people that they had lost everything once and could still be removed to the distant Indian Territory if they allowed their children to fight, but his advice would not be heeded if the government did not live up to at least some of its promises.

Then, when seven Navajos, five men, a woman and a child belonging to Delgadito's band, were shot to death by some New Mexicans near Cubero, even Manuelito had to be talked out of taking to the war trail. New Mexican ranchers still persisted in grazing their herds on the reduced Navajo lands, and when driven off by the Navajos they reported to the authorities that they had been attacked by war parties that stole their stock.

The situation was explosive when, late in 1869, the sheep promised by the government began to arrive. The Bureau of Indian Affairs informed Congress that it had purchased more than thirty-five thousand of the tough little Spanish *churros* from ranches in the vicinity of Fort Union. Perhaps so, but if they did, somewhere on the three hundred mile journey between Fort Union and Fort Wingate 20,000 animals disappeared. Captain Bennett reported that he distributed 14,000 sheep and 1,000 goats to the Navajos and wrote afterward: "I have never seen such anxiety and gratitude." Those families who were able disappeared into the mountains and valleys with their allotment of sheep to start building new herds. But more than half of that first shipment were slaughtered and eaten that winter of 1869-70.

Captain Bennett continued to defend the Navajos—a most unpopular avocation in the New Mexico of 1870—by pointing out that the few Navajo raids were actually perpetrated on New Mexicans in retaliation. "The Navajos," he said, "are obliged to fight in their own defense in many situations." His pro-Navajo stance and his constant complaints to the Indian department about sending Navajos such junk as silk hats and his pleas for the badly needed supplies they had been promised by General Sherman soon caused the powers in the Indian Bureau to decide that perhaps what the Navajos really needed was a new agent. Early in 1870 the legislators ruled that military men would no longer be eligible as Indian agents and a civilian named J. A. Manley was sent to take over that portion of Bennett's duties. Big Belly did remain at Fort Wingate as military commander, though, and never ceased aiding and defending the Navajos.

Manley was the first of nearly twenty agents who would hold that office between his appointment and 1900. Manley was just ineffectual. Others were to be thieves and scoundrels of the lowest ilk, bigots and religious fanatics. A few exceptional men would be dedicated to the task at hand. Manley served only a few months and never ventured more than a few miles from Fort Defiance. He was replaced by James A. Miller. Miller was conscientious and believed that the economic independence of the Navajos would be accomplished by rebuilding the farms that had been destroyed by Kit Carson's soldiers. His agency clerk was a young Englishman named Thomas V. Keam who would one day become the most effectual and beloved agent to serve the Navajos since Henry Linn Dodge. Soon after he took office the agent made an inspection trip to study the feasibility of building an irrigation system to bring water from the San Juan river to the adjacent farmlands, with his clerk and his interpreter, Jesus Arviso, a Mexican who had been reared by the Navajos. Miller was killed in a dawn attack by a Ute war party. Thomas Keam was appointed acting agent. Jesus Arviso remained as interpreter but was soon sharing duties with a kinsman of Zarcillos Largos, Chee Dodge, who was then about fifteen years old.

Young Thomas Keam was an able administrator. Not only was he thoroughly familiar with the problems facing the Navajos, but he had given considerable thought to their future and means of alleviating sources of conflict between them and their neighbors. He advocated extending the reservation both to the West and the South to embrace areas already occupied by Navajos such as Ganado Mucho and his band that were living outside the treaty boundary. He also realized that dividing the reservation into 160-acre family-owned parcels was not feasible and was also outside the Navajo concept of property ownership. The communal property or "squatter's rights" concept long practiced by the Navajos was, in his opinion, the only answer to the matter of property use. Keam took over the agency in the midst of the great drought of 1870. Crops were ruined and again the promised government supplies failed to materialize. The winter before Congress, preoccupied with the problems of reconstruction in the South and an exhausted treasury, had refused to pass the Indian appropriations bill. President Grant got it through only by means of a political ruse. The portion allotted the *Dineh* was far too little and once again Navajo warriors were driven in desperation to stealing.

Keam, while pleading for more sheep and other supplies for the Navajos on one hand, asked for the cooperation of Barboncito, Ganado Mucho and Manuelito on the other to stop the raids. Realizing that some machinery of organization was necessary among the Navajos themselves, Captain Bennett, with authority from Washington, had appointed these three headmen as "chiefs" of the nation. Barboncito was made head chief; Ganado Mucho was appointed subchief of the western side of the reservation and Manuelito subchief for the eastern Navajos. All three men told Keam they would cooperate to the extent of their powers in stopping the raids. Keam organized a Navajo police force and put Manuelito in charge of it. The police force proved very effective not only in stopping the raids but in returning much of the stock that had been stolen, mostly from the Mormons. Barboncito called on Mormon leader Jacob Hamblin in November, 1870, and said: "I cannot promise that no raids will take place but I will hunt down and return to you the stolen livestock. If I do not return the livestock it will be because it has been killed and eaten." The Navajo police force and the soldiers from Fort Wingate began watching the trails and the Colorado and San Juan river crossings which the young warriors used in raiding the Mormons. The raids soon ceased but the strenuous activity of policing the Navajo frontier in the middle of a bleak cold winter was too much for the aged Barboncito. He became ill and made his way home to Canyon de Chelly in December. On March 16, 1871, he died after a long illness. Ganado Mucho was appointed in his place.

Keam wrote the Indian department and related how very successful the Navajo police force had been and asked that Congress appropriate funds for wages so that it might be continued. Congress was very impressed with the success of

Manuelito's men, so impressed, in fact, that it decided that since the raids had been stopped the police force was no longer needed and ordered it disbanded. The Indian department ousted Keam and replaced him with a political appointee. But for a year or more Manuelito and his police continued to watch the war trails.

The man who succeeded Keam soon resigned and was replaced by General Carleton's old enemy, William Frederick Milton Arny, whom the Navajos called "Tarantula." Arny was, beyond a doubt, the worst agent the Navajos ever had to contend with. He was not only a religious zealot, he was also an uncompromising bigot who expected the Navajos to become second class Christians overnight. Ignoring the fact that the government had yet to honor any but a few of the commitments made in the Bosque Redondo treaty, he expected the Navajos to uphold their promises to the letter, which soon brought him in conflict with Ganado Mucho. He told the aged headman to move his livestock into the confines of the reservation and keep them there. The agent's abrupt and arrogant orders both surprised and angered Ganado Mucho. The old headman, ill with eczema, had worked hard with Manuelito and Barboncito in putting an end to the Navajo raids. Too, there was the matter of Navajo captives for which his people had never received satisfaction. Ganado Mucho could see no reason why he should vacate his traditional grazing lands and move his stock onto the already crowded reservation.

Ganado Mucho was not the only Navajo to feel the wrath of Arny's self-righteous ire. The *Dineh*, as far as he was concerned, could do only two things right: raise sheep and weave blankets. For those two products he soon located eastern markets and set himself up in business as middle man. Navajo women, as soon as they returned from Bosque Redondo, began weaving again. But, as Ruth M. Underhill wrote: ". . . not the brilliant, intricate patterns of their great period before Fort Sumner, and not their own handsome blanket dresses in red and black! These wore out gradually and were never replaced. All weaving now was for trade . . . Working against starvation, they wove what would bring quickest results. The Mormons, at Salt Lake City, would take plain saddle blankets and so would their new settlement at Tuba City, beyond the Hopis. Utes and Comanches wanted strong, rainproof camping blankets in blue and white stripes, and the Mexicans liked brighter colors. The Navajo woman put the work through her loom as fast as she could. When two or three articles were ready, her man loaded them on his scrawny horse and was off on a trip of hundreds of miles." (Underhill, Oklahoma, 1956: 156-57.)

Arny demanded that the Navajos bring their wool to the post sutler at Fort Defiance with whom the agent had made an arrangement to pay for the wool in goods. The Navajos, in spite of Arny's moralist haranguing, were charged an excessive rate of exchange by the sutler who, in turn, sold it to the agent at a considerable reduction in price. The sutler made his profit, and Arny obtained the wool below its true market value, hauled it to Albuquerque and shipped it off to eastern carpet manufacturers, making himself a tidy profit in the process. Arny also pioneered the marketing of Navajo blankets in the East. But the Navajo women could not turn out their product fast enough to satisfy the demand so Arny imported modern high-speed looms with the hope of increasing production. The Navajo women were coerced into selling their blankets to the agent but they refused to increase the output by learning to use his new looms. In his own religious fanaticism, Arny refused to realize that a religious factor was involved in Navajo weaving and that no Navajo woman could bring herself to use anything but the wooden loom she had always used.

But the Navajos did not have to stand alone against the tyrannical agent. Thomas Keam was banished from Fort Defiance because he had married a Navajo woman. According to Arny's code of religious ethics, any white man who married an Indian woman was a "lost soul" and unfit to remain in the presence of "decent white men" such as himself. Keam took his wife and moved to the canyon east of the Hopi villages that would bear his name. He secured some land, opened a trading post and fathered a brood of children. Arny crossed the military when he accused the soldiers of leading the Navajo women into prostitution and pried into the private lives of his agency employees to such an extent that almost all of his staff resigned en masse and departed without notice.

When Arny forbade the Navajos to trade with the Mormons—more "lost souls" according to him—and complained that Navajo men were leaving the reservation to purchase whiskey, Manuelito and Ganado Mucho decided that something had to be done. They made up a petition, got all the headmen to sign it, and sent it to the Commissioner of Indian Affairs requesting that Agent Arny be removed from office and from their reservation. Manuelito suggested that he be replaced with an agent "who could furnish more rations." The petition was ignored. Then, early in 1874, several Navajos were killed in southern Utah and Arny placed the blame on the Mormons. The agent used this episode to convince the Commissioner of Indian Affairs that open warfare was imminent on the northern boundary of the reservation. In August of that year the Indian Bureau authorized Arny to accompany a delegation of Navajo headmen to Washington supposedly to discuss the "Mormon problem" with President Grant. Arny's real motive was to effect a land exchange by ceding the northern portion of the reservation, bordering the San Juan River, where gold prospectors were beginning to stake claims, for a parcel of arid land to the West. Among the headmen who met with President Grant on December 10, 1874, were Manuelito, Mariano, Cayatanita and Ganado Mucho as well as Manuelito's wife, Juanita, and his son, Manuelito Segundo. Thomas Keam travelled to Washington at his own expense and it was primarily through his efforts that the land exchange fell through.

Manuelito and Ganado Mucho made up a second petition asking for the removal of Arny and sent it to President Grant. When still no action was taken, they decided to take drastic and direct action. A group of angry Navajos, led by Manuelito, stormed into the agent's office at Fort Defiance in April, 1875, and told Arny that unless he immediately left the reservation they would kill him. Agent Arny immediately left the reservation, never to return. But he had accomplished one thing: he had shown the Navajos that there was a ready market for their wool and their beautiful blankets in the distant and strange world of the Bilagáana. W. F. M. Arny had inadvertently taught the Navajos their first lesson in American economics, a lesson they would never forget.

But the Navajos still needed more land. Many, like Ganado Mucho, were living outside the boundary lines and those were increasingly coming into conflict with white settlers, especially to the East of the reservation. By the

400

middle of the 1870s Navajo agents, Department of the Interior officials and other authorities were offering proposals that would give the Navajos permission to use the public domain land that surrounded three sides of the reservation. But Congress could not be convinced that a reservation of 3.5 million acres was not sufficient to support a tribe of Indians of 11,768 people according to the "official census" of 1875. Congressmen from east of the Mississippi, where a parcel 160 acres of land was almost always sufficient to support a large family, blindly refused to become cognizant of the fact that water and soil conditions were different in the land of the Navajos. And representatives from the Southwest were elected by the very ranchers and land speculators who were waging a war to preserve public domain lands for the exclusive use of white settlers and, for that matter, advocated depriving Indians of all civil and legal rights.

To complicate the issue, Congress had awarded over 180 million acres of public domain land to railroad corporations between 1850 and 1871, and one of the most generous grants had been made to the Atchison, Topeka and Santa Fé. That railroad's projected right-of-way from Albuquerque to Los Angeles passed just north of Fort Wingate and through lands on which the Navajos had lived for centuries. The Santa Fé was granted alternate sections of land to a depth of forty and fifty miles on both sides of the right-of-way. This area contained some of the Navajos' best remaining grazing lands and water holes. The railroad insisted that the Navajos be removed from "their lands" as white people would not purchase lands from the corporation and build homes and ranches among Indians. A delegation of headmen, under the leadership of Manuelito, travelled to Washington again in 1876 to plead with President Grant to cede grazing and water rights to Navajos who were being driven from their traditional lands by the railroad, but to no avail. Grant offered, in exchange, a strip of land to the West of the reservation. At first the Navajo headmen refused, but realizing they were going to lose the southern grazing lands regardless, they relented and made the "exchange." The Executive Order of October 29, 1878, added a rectangular area of about 911,257 acres along the western boundary of the treaty reservation.

The lands acquired were virtually worthless for agricultural and grazing purposes, and by the time they were transferred to Navajo ownership, the demand for space to accommodate the spreading herds and growing population— now estimated at 16,000—had accelerated. Earlier counts and estimates did not include those Navajos who had not been imprisoned at Bosque Redondo. The Indian Bureau estimated that 8,000 Navajos were living off the reservation in the late 1870s. Bitter quarrels between the Navajos and white settlers as well as with New Mexican stockmen were increasing and several men, both whites and Navajos, had been slain in fights over grasslands and water holes. Acting on an Indian Bureau recommendation, President Rutherford B. Hayes issued an Executive Order on January 6, 1880, giving the Navajos an additional 1.2 million acres east, south and west of the reservation. Two years later President Chester A. Arthur established a rectangular reservation of 2.4 million acres just west of the Navajos for "the Moki (Hopi) and other Indians there." As many Navajos had long occupied portions of this area they considered themselves the "other Indians" referred to by the president. Additional lands were added to the Navajo reservation in 1884, 1886, 1900, 1901, 1905, 1908, 1913, 1930, 1933 and 1934, bringing the reservation to its present size of 24,000 square miles spread over New Mexico, Arizona and Utah. The reservation is roughly a third of the land area claimed by the Navajos when the Americans entered the Southwest.

Upon his return from his second visit to President Grant, Manuelito realized that the Navajos were once again in danger of losing everything. Violent attacks on the white settlers brought in by the railroad and raids on the stock of the New Mexican ranchers were increasing to alarming proportions. Too, many young Navajos hated the new way of life. Their families were still suffering from hunger and their lands, it seemed, were being constantly taken away from them. It had been ten years since the return from Hwelte and the horrors of that place had faded from the memory of many young men who had been children there. They joined with the sons of those who had remained in *Dinehtah* in organizing bands to attack the encroaching white stockmen. Manuelito was now almost sixty years of age; Ganado Mucho was ten years older and no powerful headmen had yet appeared among the young to whom they would listen. Too, the congenial agent who had replaced W. F. M. Arny, Alex G. Irvine, had in turn been replaced by Galen Eastman. The Navajos neither liked nor trusted Eastman and his influence amounted to virtually nothing among the young men who were perpetrating the raids. According to Navajo legend, a terrible sorcerer's society came into power in those first ten years after Hwelte and the practice of witchcraft seemed rife on the reservation.

Manuelito called on Ganado Mucho and they decided to take the matter of the Navajo raiders, whose actions were a threat to the welfare of all The People, in hand. Manuelito was convinced that one of the men behind the raids, a headman the Navajos called Dichin Bilqéhe, was a witch and was using sorcery to brew trouble for the more orderly portion of the tribe. They prepared a list of forty men—a list that included the name of Ganado Mucho's uncle—who were causing the trouble with the Bilagáana and, enlisting the aid of Manuelito's brother, Cayatanita, among others, they started out on a witch hunt. The ways of "witching" a person were familiar to some Navajos and the practice was sometimes used as a last resort to settle a problem, and the two shrewd old headmen decided to employ it in an effort to stop the trouble with the whites. The forty troublemakers, including Dichin Bilqéhe, who had signed the Bosque Redondo treaty as "Muerto de Hombre," were rounded up, and, after a short trial, executed. The witch hunt of the headmen was a short, violent affair and brought a stern reprimand from the American authorities, but it put an end to Navajo raiding—except for a few isolated incidents—for all time.

Navajo captives held by the New Mexicans continued to be a matter of contention for two or more decades after the return of The People from Bosque Redondo. Often Navajo headmen visited the Rio Grande settlements and attempted to appeal directly to the consciences of the New Mexicans, but their efforts were singularly unsuccessful. The slave owners almost always refused to let the Navajos see or speak to their women and children. Complaints to the Indian Bureau were to no avail and when such were made the Navajos were told that their only recourse was to resort to the courts of the land. Captain Frank Bennett, who tried to help the Navajos regain the captives, pointed out that while slavery was contrary to all existing laws in the territory, he was convinced "that any litigation would go against the Navajos, as the so-called civil authorities in all the Mexican settlements are so prejudiced against them, that justice could not be had."

Captain Bennett pleaded the cause of the Navajo captives before the Commissioner of Indian Affairs: "The Navajos believe and appreciate that their only friends are the military and other government officials. I earnestly request, that if possible, some steps be taken to do away with this system of peonage, and have the children held against their will returned to their parents—as Navajos love their children, and I think that they are entitled to them, the same as any race of people." Bennett himself visited the New Mexican settlements, often accompanying Navajo headmen in an effort to secure the release of captives. "The Mexicans," he reported, "showed not the first sign of a disposition to settle a single case, or attempt to bring to justice any of the guilty parties. They appeared to be afraid to even give evidence or assistance of any kind." But the efforts of Captain Bennett and others did not go without reward. In 1872 nearly one hundred women were returned from the New Mexican settlements to their families. The New Mexicans deliberately failed to tell their Navajo slaves that, under the laws of the land, they were free. But the news that they were legally free spread and Navajo women were soon slipping away from ranches and towns, almost always taking the children that had been born to them in captivity home with them. But as late as 1886 Navajo men were still being issued passes to go into the settlements to look for their relatives.

The New Mexicans, in turn, complained that the Navajos had never released all of their captives. Galen Eastman's successor, Denis Riordan, began a concentrated effort to find captives held by the Navajos in 1883. But, much to his bewilderment, no sooner would he free Navajo captives than they would escape from him and return to their Navajo homes. His replacement, John Bowman, was soon confronted with the same problem. He called on Manuelito and sternly ordered him to free his Mexican slaves. The Navajo headman replied, "I claim no control over them in any way. They are not slaves but members of my family, at liberty to go anywhere or do anything they wish." Confronting Manuelito's Mexican wife, the agent gave her the choice of moving to Fort Defiance and placing her children in school there or remaining with her "master." Juanita replied that she preferred to "remain in captivity" with her "master."

Agent Bowman finally understood that Navajo captives were not slaves per se but adopted members of a family. He wrote the Indian Commissioner that the slaves were "the descendants of war captives, generations back. As according to their laws, the children always take the condition of the mother. The condition of a slave here, does not seem so very hard, because there is not a very strong contract between masters and slaves." Bowman was probably not aware of it, but Ganado Mucho's father had been a Hopi captive. In his last letter to the Indian Commissioner on the subject, dated May 15, 1884, Bowman said, "(The Navajo slaves) do not want to be liberated, and I cannot see how we are able to do it. It is like guarding a jail to keep criminals from breaking in."

That ended the matter of captives held by the Navajos, but Navajos in the possession of the New Mexicans was entirely another matter. They almost always remained in a servile position throughout their life and their children often fared no better. The failure of the American government to return but a few of the Navajo captives was one of the contributing factors in causing the failure of another government project—Navajo education. Families who had lost children to slave raiders, never to see them again, refused to give up other children to be sent away to boarding schools for four, six and eight years. But that was only one of several reasons why the Navajos were extremely reluctant to "learn paper" from the Americans.

TWO

Learning Paper

A few months after the Navajos returned to *Dinehtah* from Bosque Redondo, Ulysses Simpson Grant was elected president of the United States. It has been said that Grant was the most ill-fitted man ever elected to that office. While it is true that his administrations were something of a national disgrace, characterized chiefly by bitter partisan politics and shameless corruption, Grant, personally, felt a great deal of empathy toward the Indians. But to no avail. Under Grant's administrations the Indian Bureau became a cesspool of corruption involving nepotism, kickbacks and graft. On one hand Grant instigated and approved policies that were intended to benefit the Indians and, on the other, it was during his tenure in office that the bloody Plains Indian Wars reached their zenith; hostilities were resumed with the Sioux in 1874 that culminated in the victory of the Sioux, Cheyenne and their allies over the command of General George Armstrong Custer at the Little Big Horn on July 25, 1876.

One of the plans approved by President Grant that was supposed to benefit the Indians was what he referred to as his "peace policy." Grant and his advisors were suffering from the misguided notion that the solution to the Indians' problems would be found in making Christians out of them and by giving them the benefits of the white man's education. They devised a plan whereby the "wild Indians" would be assigned to "various religious denominations on a regional basis." Each sect, after much discussion, decided on an area and the Presbyterians got the Navajos. It still cannot be determined who instigated Grant's "peace policy" (although it was suggested by well-meaning Quakers), but one must suspect that the Indian Bureau was behind it as it stands as one of the most flagrant examples of buckpassing in the annals of American history. While the army was fighting a war of extermination against the Plains Indians, on one hand, missionaries from the various Christian denominations were being sent out to "civilize" the Indians on the other.

Meanwhile the Department of the Interior, and specifically the Indian Bureau, was relieved of the burdensome chore of appropriating adequate funds to care for the Indians (funds which had, in most cases, been promised by treaty), of creating and maintaining adequate reservations and of prohibiting the theft of Indian resources. The specific duties of the Indian Bureau were passed along to the military and the churches, while that department (and, for that matter, the entire Department of the Interior) became self-serving and, for the next two decades, wallowed in a golden era of corruption.

While the Presbyterians were assigned the chore of "educating and Christianizing" the Navajos, the assignment was not made on an exclusive basis. Other denominations were also allowed to send missionaries onto the reservation if they wished and it was not long before other sectarians were competing for Navajo souls. One wonders how the Navajos ever recovered from the cultural shock. Having no interest in their souls in the first place, they were soon bombarded by white missionaries who were saying that not only was their old way an evil path but those of the other whites were also!

The Presbyterian Home Mission Board sent Miss Charity Gaston to the reservation to become the first white teacher to the Navajos. She arrived at Fort Defiance in the fall of 1871, after a six-week trip from the East, and moved into the leaky adobe house that was set aside as both living quarters for the teacher and classroom for her students—when she had any. At Bosque Redondo the Navajo headmen had pledged themselves to "compel their children, male and female, between the ages of six and sixteen to attend school." Sherman had promised that "for every thirty children between said ages who can be induced or compelled to attend school, a house shall be provided and a teacher competent to teach the elementary branches of an English education shall be furnished . . ."

Miss Gaston was a competent teacher and the house had been provided but one very important factor had been overlooked: The Navajos were scattered all over the vast, roadless reservation and there was not one place in the entire country where thirty children could be found within travelling distance of a school. Families with sheep moved from summer to winter grazing grounds. It was ten miles or more from one isolated cluster of hogans to another. Navajo families that were favorably disposed toward their children receiving an English education faced insurmountable transportation problems that would not be solved until after World War II. And very few Navajos were so disposed in the first place. They were understandably suspicious of the white man's "paper."

There was room for twenty-five students in Miss Gaston's school but there were seldom half that many present. Sometimes there would be periods of several days when no students showed up to learn paper from the white woman. Sometimes a few Navajo women brought their children to school and sat with them in the classroom while the prim, pretty Charity Gaston tackled the formidable job of "teaching paper" through an interpreter. When Miss Gaston noticed that most of the students who did attend school with some consistency were either retarded or unwell, she sought to find out why from Captain Bennett. Bennett explained that the Navajos sent their sickly children to school, knowing they would be fed. The healthy ones were kept at home to do chores. In 1872 Charity Gaston married the post physician-minister, Dr. James Menaul, and they left Fort Defiance to establish a mission at Laguna. For the next ten years the little school was home to several teachers, usually women, sent out by Presbyterian Mission Board, but the Navajo children did not learn much of the white man's paper. Chee Dodge, who often acted as interpreter for the teachers, later stated that he had actually attended school for only two months. Seven years after the departure of Charity Gaston the average attendance was only eleven.

It was not until 1879 that Congress authorized the

construction of a boarding school at Fort Defiance but failed to appropriate any funds for the project. The next year a miserly $875 was appropriated in the fiscal budget for the construction of the school. Captain Bennett, with the help of Navajo labor, installed a small sawmill, quarried stone, and began building the school. "When completed," he reported, "...it will be both spacious and admirably arranged in all its appliances . . .and will accommodate from one hundred and fifty to two hundred pupils." Before he could complete the construction of the school the Presbyterians sent J. D. Perkins to take charge of the project. Meanwhile Captain Bennett had been talking to Manuelito about education, and persuaded the headman to send his children to the East to be educated. Manuelito was so convinced of the value of a white education that he told Chee Dodge: "My grandchild, the whites have many things which we Navajos need. But we cannot get them. It is as though the whites were in a grassy canyon and there they have wagons, plows, and plenty of food. We Navajos are up on the dry mesa. We can hear them talking but we cannot get them. My grandchild, education is the ladder. Tell our people to take it."

In 1882 Manuelito sent his son and a nephew to the Indian school at Carlisle, Pennsylvania. But the son became ill there and was sent home the next year. When the boy died soon after arriving home, Manuelito became violently angry and demanded that all Navajo children be sent home to their parents. On their way to a January 19, 1883, meeting with the new Navajo agent, Denis M. Riordan, Manuelito and Ganado Mucho stopped by to admire the new school building with thick stone walls and modified mansard roof that was near completion. While Manuelito had shown the way by sending his sons to be educated, and many Navajos had followed his example, he no longer cared about the white man's paper. The headman was probably impressed with the school building squatting there where he had grazed his cattle as a young man, but others were not so impressed by the dormitory facilities that J. D. Perkins had constructed for his boarding pupils. Perkins reported that it contained bunks for sixty students. Major John G. Bourke, inspecting the Fort Defiance facilities, reported that the dormitory "consisted of one miserable, squalid, dark and musty adobe dungeon, not much more capacious than the cubbyhole of an oyster schooner; it was about 12 x 10 x 7. No light ever penetrated, but one window let darkness out from this den and one small door gave exit to some of the mustiness." The one window was covered with iron shutters to keep the boarding students from escaping.

Manuelito and Ganado Mucho found the new agent to their liking. Denis Riordan promised "to sleep on the ground, eat nothing but mutton, if necessary, in fact do whatever the occasion demands in order to make myself efficient in this position . . ." The seventy-four-year-old Ganado Mucho, particularly, approved of the new agent who promised nothing more that to do his duty. "It has been dark for so long, for so very long," he told Riordan. "Now we hope for better times."

In writing a report of the meeting, the new agent said: ". . . I am satisfied that no one with a heart in his breast could see the eager, intelligent, impassioned faces of these people and hear their expressions without being convinced that they were at least entitled to a hearing in their own way."

Riordan soon became a favorite with the Navajos; in fact within a very short time his popularity equaled that of Big Belly. But he also soon realized that the Indian Bureau did not expect much from its Navajo agent. A short time after he arrived to take up residence in the dilapidated agent quarters, he wrote: "There isn't today as much available means . . . to do this much needed work as is in the hands of a corporal of the army . . . (but) I am not just going to sit down. I am going to do what I can . . . I have made up my mind I'll just have to do it myself in the interests of humanity, and call the expenses a dead loss." It was primarily through Riordan's efforts that the Utah lands south of the San Juan River and the land north of the Hopi reservation, consisting of 2.5 million acres, were added to the reservation in 1884.

Probably no man who really took the welfare of the Navajos to heart could last long in the job as agent, and Riordan was no exception. In June, 1884, he offered his resignation. He still had not been reimbursed for expense vouchers submitted a year before. "It would require the descriptive powers of a Scott or Dickens," he wrote, "to portray the wretched conditions of this agency . . . the United States has never fulfilled its treaty promises and it is safe to assume it never will." In tendering his resignation, he took the government to task for failing to provide aid "for the sick, indigent and helpless Indians, the agent being compelled to see them suffer under his eyes and to close his ears to their requests, or else supply the much-needed articles at his own expense . . .

"The labor demanded of an agent here is such as to prevent his performing his duties in a satisfactory manner," he wrote. "The reservation embraces about 10,000 square miles of the most worthless land that ever laid out doors . . . The country is almost entirely rock. An Illinois or Iowa or Kansas farmer would laugh to scorn the assertion that you could raise anything here. However, 17,000 Indians manage to extract their living from it without government aid. If they were not the best Indians living on the continent, they would not do it."

Riordan's long report made only one reference to the deprivations he had suffered. "Knowing the failure of the government to fulfill its obligations to them," he wrote, "I for a time did my best to supply their needs. I spent some $800 in that way but the money was not repaid and the expenditure stopped. . . ." The agent gave, as a reason for his resignation, the illness of his family, brought on because of the leaky house furnished the Navajo agent. "Why doesn't the government give an agent here as good a shelter as it gives a mule at Fort Wingate?" he asked.

Ganado Mucho and Manuelito called on Riordan and offered to add $1,000 a year to his salary out of their treaty money if he would stay. But the Indian Commissioner refused to accept his resignation. He had to remain at the post until the spring of 1885. Before he left, Ganado Mucho said, "Before you came we were groping along in the bottom of a deep canyon where the sun never shone. We could see nothing but the bare rocky walls. Mr. Riordan took the lead and showed us beautiful valleys, with plenty of water and grass. He showed us how to carry out the new ideas he had been putting into our heads. He taught us how to build houses, dig ditches, and to improve ourselves in many ways." In light of Ganado Mucho's statements, the complaints of later agents that the Navajos were "sullen, uncooperative and unteachable" are suspect.

Meanwhile with the support of the Presbyterian Home Mission Board, J. D. Perkins, who was more concerned about the souls of Navajo children than their stomachs, had opened his school. Many Navajo parents came to admire the grand building but sent few of their children to learn paper. In September, 1884, several months after the school had opened, less than twenty pupils were enrolled. In October the enrollment was twenty-two. In November there were twenty-four students attending the school but that figure did not include all of those who had been enrolled in September. Agent John Bowman, who replaced Riordan, reported: "They would come and stay a day or two, get some clothes, and then run away back to their hogans, but few of them attended regularly, consequently the school done little real good."

The Navajo children, used to the warm attention of the family and clan relatives, were, of course, terrified of the cold, impersonal white teachers who shouted at them, cut their hair, and forced them to eat the strange food that made them ill, or so they thought. Actually it was measles and a variety of respiratory diseases that caused their illnesses and when several died, the children were, of course, more frightened than ever of being locked in their dank dormitory. But Agent Bowman prevented them from running away by "having one of the police in attendance" at all times. In 1885 there were only thirty-three students enrolled in the school, but with Bowman's policeman standing at the door none succeeded in running away.

In 1887 Congress passed the Compulsory Indian Education Law. Subsequently boarding schools were built at Fort Wingate, Chinle, Crown Point, Toadlena, Shiprock, Tuba City, Leupp and Tohatchi—and agents scourged the countryside for students to fill them up. The boarding schools were turned over to mission groups from the Presbyterian, Methodist, Catholic and Christian Reformed churches, among others, as Congress was of the opinion that the Christianization and acculturation of the Indians could be "promoted at minimum expense to the Government" through the religious bodies. The schools became reformatories and discipline was enforced rigidly and, often, with considerably brutality. Navajo children were kidnapped from their homes at gunpoint and sent to one of the reservation schools or to boarding schools established by the government in New Mexico, Colorado, Arizona, California and Oklahoma. Often the agents found children herding or working in fields and took them away in their buckboards, neither knowing nor caring who their parents were. Sometimes it was years before the children returned home to parents who had given them up for dead. Many of them died escaping from the schools and attempting to make their way home through the snowbound mountains.

At the boarding schools children were beaten, handcuffed, bound in leg irons, locked up in dank cellars and starved for days on end for trying to escape, infractions of rules of deportment, or, for that matter, for merely speaking Navajo. Even the Navajo agency carpenter at Fort Defiance commented on the "vile and inhumane treatment" of Navajo students. The situation at the schools was so terrible that some Navajos decided to fight rather than have their children taken from them and placed in the institutions. When Agent Dana Shipley attempted to recruit children for the schools in the Round Rock area in the fall of 1892 he was confronted with a band of angry Navajos led by a headman named Black Horse.

Black Horse and his followers had heard of the horrors of the boarding schools and they did not intend to let agent Shipley take even one of their children from them. Shipley stubbornly insisted that they give up their children and told the Navajos that failure to do so would result in police action. In a meeting at the Round Rock trading post Black Horse and Shipley got into a fight. Black Horse grabbed the agent and dragged him outside where he was attacked by several members of the angry band. Henry Chee Dodge, who had accompanied Shipley to Round Rock, managed to get the agent back inside the store. Dodge, then in his early thirties, had been appointed "head chief" of the Navajos by Denis Riordan and commanded the respect of most of his people, but Black Horse was in no mood for talk. While Dodge rode to Tsailee twenty-three miles south, for help, Black Horse and his men surrounded the store and kept watch over it for two days. Apparently he did not want to harm the agent and his aides, as has often been reported. It would have been a simple matter to burn the store and kill the whites. Black Horse was making a show of force to keep the children of his band from being sent to the dreaded boarding schools. When Dodge returned with soldiers, Black Horse and his followers retreated, but they still refused to give up their children.

Lieutenant Edwin H. Plummer was appointed Navajo agent in 1893 and soon afterwards took a party of men to visit the Chicago World's Fair. The Navajos were not very impressed with the large white city "where people lived like ants" but they were impressed with the number of whites they saw. The whites, they decided, were never going to go back where they came from as there were far too many of them. It was while visiting the fair that some Navajos encountered Athaspascans from Canada—the Live-Again *Dineh*.

The Indian schools had been placed under the control of the Civil Service in 1891 and by 1894 Agent Plummer was able to report that the teaching was "much improved." There were 206 students enrolled at Fort Defiance that year. The next year a day school was started at Tohachi and the school at Fort Defiance was repaired and improved, but Navajo parents still had not been made to understand that learning paper could be useful. As a matter of fact the agent complained that they "seemed to think they are conferring a great favor on the whites by bringing their children to school and they ought to be compensated."

In 1897 Congress, in a reversal of its earlier stand, passed a resolution stating "it be the policy of the Government hereafter to make no appropriations whatever to subsidize sectarian schools serving Indian groups." But the church missionaries were not to be dismissed so easily. The Bureau of Indian Affairs preferred that the religious groups continue operating the schools rather than resuming that responsibility itself, and made it possible for them to continue to do so by allowing the missionaries to secure treaty and tribal funds. For the next twenty years the Indians themselves subsidized the mission schools. It was not until Congress enacted a statute in 1917 providing that "no appropriation whatever out of the Treasury of the United States may be used for the education of Indian children in any sectarian school" that Indian coffers were closed to the missionaries. While they were no longer subsidized by the Navajos, the mission schools continued to operate, their numbers steadily increasing as other Christian denominations—Mormons, Pencostal, Mennonites, Seventh-Day Adventists and others—moved onto the reservation to open churches and schools. Sanctioned by the Indian Bureau, the missionaries were enabled to invade the reservation and

414

force their beliefs on the Navajos by whatever means they chose to employ. Too often their stated purpose—educating the Navajos—was secondary to "saving souls."

Even today a majority of the mission groups on the reservation are there for evangelical purposes. Some groups pursue a long-term policy of gradually superimposing Christianity on the native belief to ultimately supersede it; other groups maintain a short-term policy and strive to immediately replace the native religion with their form of Christianity. Regardless of the approach, a majority of Navajos continue to practice the native belief exclusively. Others find no inconsistency in simultaneously participating in both Christian services and Navajo ceremonies. The percentage of Navajos who are exclusively Christian, in spite of almost a hundred years of concentrated effort on the part of the missionaries, is not large.

For the most part the Navajo's attitude toward Christianity can be expressed in a shrug. There is a story that some of my Navajo friends delight in telling that graphically and humorously illustrates the collective attitude. Some years back a fundamentalist Christian missionary arrived on the reservation and went about his business of saving souls with a great deal of zeal and imagination. After several months of diligent evangelizing and only a handful of half-hearted converts to show for his efforts, the missionary decided that drastic and dramatic action was called for. As it was nearing Christmas, he decided upon a plan to bring Santa Claus to the Navajos. Announcements were sent out to the effect that on a designated day Santa Claus would come down out of the sky, land in an open area near Window Rock and distribute gifts to the children. The plan was to parachute a dummy Santa Claus out of a small plane, quickly substitute an identically dressed man on the ground, and make points with the Navajos. Never a people to pass up a free show and gifts, Navajos from miles around came to see Santa Claus. When a large crowd had assembled on the field, the plane flew over. The dummy Santa Claus with his bag of presents was thrown out but the parachute didn't open; the Santa Claus hit the ground with a thud, the Navajos shrugged and went away. As long as he remained on the reservation the missionary was called The-Man-Who-Killed-Santa-Claus by the Navajos.

But not all relationships between the Navajos and the

missionaries turned out so humorously. Efforts to weed out the native religion have been relentlessly pursued and have caused untold emotional traumas. Navajo children have been starved, beaten and suffered countless indignities in an effort to convert them to Christianity. My friend R. C. Gorman, the Navajo artist, recalls attending St. Michael's Junior High School at Fort Defiance in the late 1940s: "It was the only time in my life I remember being always hungry. The nuns gave only the larger boys who did more work milk to drink with their meals. We smaller ones made bean sandwiches and had to sneak them out to eat later. I also picked up lice and had quite a few unpleasant encounters with the nuns. Marching to mass before dawn every morning with icicles forming in my hair left me with very little enthusiasm for Catholicism."

Certainly there have been understanding men and women among the missionaries who established and have maintained schools where the first order of business was education, and several missionary groups have built and supported clinics and hospitals that have always accepted Navajo patients regardless of whether they were Christians or not. But the number of rabid evangelists waging campaigns to eradicate the native religion in the name of education has always been there too.

Beginning with that day in 1874 when J. D. Perkins opened his Fort Defiance boarding school, and until after World War II, the primary objective of Navajo schools, those operated both by Christian missionaries and the Indian Bureau, was to eradicate Navajo culture. But the Navajos quietly, stubbornly and sometimes openly resisted. As early as the mid-1880s Dr. Washington Matthews, the Fort Defiance post-surgeon, was convinced that the native culture would not survive another generation. With the aid of both Jesus Arviso and Chee Dodge, he recorded all of the ceremonies and legends he possibly could. His was a monumental work that has stood the test of time. In the late 1960s I recorded a version of a Navajo Singer's version of the Navajo legend of creation that was almost word for word the same as that recorded by Dr. Matthews eighty years prior. His fear of the eradication of Navajo culture was not unfounded—Dana Shipley reported in 1891 that "heathenish ceremonies are diminishing." However, it seems in no danger of coming to pass even today.

The efforts to destroy all vestiges of Navajo culture was brutalizing and humiliating in the boarding schools. Navajo children were taken from their homes for at least four, sometimes eight years or more, and seldom allowed to return even for a visit. Every effort was made to teach them to be white. They were forced to discard their native clothing and wear the castoffs of the dominant culture; they were told that the songs and legends taught them by their parents were the "work of the devil" and had to be erased from memory. They were not allowed to speak their own language and were, in fact, taught to forget it. Their names were changed to Charlie, Joe, Bessie, Linda or some other Christian appellation. Anything and everything that was "Indian" was forbidden—yet they were never allowed to forget that they were Indian. They were taught to be ashamed of their race, yet dressed in the style of the whites and with their hair cut to a length acceptable by the mirrionaries, they knew they were still Indians. They learned, as Oliver La Farge wrote, "to put on a mask . . . the mask of absence for protection." They learned to "act white" but remained Navajo. Very few passed through the boarding school educational system without suffering some psychological injury. Physical injury was accepted as part of the curriculum.

A Navajo woman remembers: "Once in the sixth grade we had a man who brought the food to the dining room. He was always strapping the boys and when we worked in the kitchen the cook always strapped us. Once I was hit very hard and my nose bled because I peeled the potatoes too thick. Then this man came around and he strapped (my brother) and he jumped up. He was going to fight. . . . He knocked that boy down and sat on his stomach and then he kept hitting him in the face and one of the cooks ran in and she was crying but she couldn't stop that man. (His) face was all red and swollen and (I) swore at that man and he came over to our table and said to me, 'Did you say that?' I said I didn't say anything but he made me come into the kitchen and he took some thin pieces of wood from a box and he hit my hands until he broke the wood but I wouldn't cry, so he got a piece of pinyon from the woodbox. . . . He kept on beating my hands. They got cut and swollen and I couldn't close them. . . . He said: 'Why did you say those things?' . . . I think of that man lots of times.

I hate him. Sometimes I see him even now and I get so mad I want to get even with him.

"... Then we got demerits. Most of them got them for talking Navajo. When I got a few they made me eat standing up. Sometimes they made us stand on a stool while everyone ate supper.... And after supper when we could sometimes play they made us stand in a corner. But if you had more demerits the worst thing was on Sunday afternoon, they made us stand in the sun all afternoon out by those posts ... from one o'clock to five."

After eight years or more in a boarding school with little or no contact with the family, the students were returned home. Too often homecoming was even more of a psychological shock than entering the boarding school had been. They returned, having long since forgotten Navajo, to parents and friends who spoke no English. In the 1920s Oliver La Farge wrote the poignant story of the homecoming of a girl who had, as a child, been called Running Girl by her family. The boarding school had changed her name to Lucille. When she arrived at the trading post near her home for the first reunion with her parents in eight years she didn't recognize them, nor they her, dressed as she was in tacky white clothes. "Wind Singer stopped a few yards from his daughter," La Farge wrote, "and her mother went forward alone. The girl stood still, her head hanging. The old woman moved slowly and we could see that her half-outstretched hands were trembling. Now they were close to each other, and Wind Singer's wife was touching her daughter's shoulder. There was an agony of longing on her face. She said something, and the girl's head bowed yet lower ... (she) touched the girl's face lightly, fleeting, with her hands, and the girl shrank. Then the old woman stepped back, and seemed for the first time to take in the strange clothes, the half-bare arms and neck, the short skirt ... With the same slow, gentle motions she took off her blanket,... and cast it about her daughter's shoulders.... The (school) mask on her face was so perfect that it now cried out, betraying its secret. Her mother spoke to Wind Singer; the three of them turned together and walked slowly, all with bowed heads, out the gate."

The next day Wind Singer confronted La Farge: "What is this (education)? We are men, we people. We think well of ourselves. We want our children to have what we have.

We want them to learn English and writing and those useful things, but not to forget everything white men do not know, everything that has made us strong. . . . What kind of man orders this?

"We know we are poorer than white men. We are ragged and dirty, I suppose. We live simply, a hard life. But we are not ashamed. We are strong, we are men, we have beauty. There is not one of us who would lower his face before any man. But my daughter comes back from that school, where they sent her because she was the best in school here, and she is all shame and fear. At night, when she thinks we are asleep, she cries."

And so the students returned home from the boarding schools, unprepared to take up life again as Navajos and unable to find a place in the white world. Many of them drifted into nearby towns and lived out their lives as maladjusted drunkards. Indirectly Manuelito became addicted to alcohol because of the white education system forced on the Navajos. He was the first headman to encourage Navajos to send their children away to learn paper. But when his son became ill while away at school and subsequently died, he turned away from education and to the bottle. For the last ten years of his life he sought solace in the white man's whiskey, blaming himself for the death of his son. Of the six Navajos who attended Carlisle in 1885, only one survived. And he, said the report of that year, "will be no credit to the community."

THREE

A Crowded Land

By the time Manuelito died of a combination of measles and pneumonia early in 1893—and was followed into the underworld by Ganado Mucho who died a few weeks later—the Navajos were well on their way to an amazing economic recovery, considering the circumstances. The federal government still had done very little to fulfill its treaty obligations. In 1879 it was estimated that eighty-five percent of the Navajos' subsistence came from their herds and farms, nine percent from hunting, and six percent from the government. While many families were still poor and suffered from hunger during the prolonged drought of 1878-79, the Navajos were, as one agent reported, "energetic, hardworking and industrious." Many families prospered and steadily increased their sheep herds, which were the backbone of the new Navajo economy. Agent John C. Pyle reported: "Within ten years the Navajos have grown from a band of paupers to a nation of prosperous, industrious, shrewd and—for barbarians—intelligent people. . . ."

Pyle's observations were confirmed by agent John Bowman who reported in 1886 that "the Navajo is by nature inclined to habits of industry and an independent desire to acquire property and to maintain himself . . ." and Agent Arny had already shown the Navajos a new means of acquiring property. Only five years after Arny hurriedly left the reservation under threat of death, the Navajos sold 800,000 pounds of wool to the eastern markets. Then came

the railroad snaking its way across New Mexico to Albuquerque, then to Fort Wingate and finally to Ferry—later
renamed Manuelito—just west of Gallup. The railroad took
away some of their best grazing lands and, in return, gave a
few Navajo men an opportunity to earn money as day
laborers, but it brought easy access to the wool markets. It
also brought white traders to the reservation who would act
as middlemen for Navajo wool and blankets.

The Navajos had alway been borrowers of culture, taking
that which they found useful and rejecting that which had
no appeal to them. And while they didn't give a moment's
thought to the white man's Christianity, his trade goods and
his market for Navajo wool was another matter. The railroad brought farm implements—hoes, wagons, harness, axes
and plows—calico, yarns, dyes and canned goods to the
Navajo traders who began to flock onto the reservation.
The trader swapped their merchandise for Navajo wool,
hides and, finally, blankets. The traders succeeded where
most agents had failed because their livelihood depended on
a fair trade and the ability to please their customers. And
the trader's Navajo customer was as shrewd at making a
deal as a New England Yankee. Most of the traders learned
to speak at least a few words of Navajo and thereby bridged
the communication gap that had hindered even the well-
meaning agents. Others married Navajo women and, by
custom, became a member of their families.

The traders provided the Navajos with their only real
contact with white civilization and became the interpreters
of a new economic way of life. Those that remained on the
reservation gradually found themselves functioning as doctor, dentist, lawyer and even undertaker for their Navajo
customers. Others, those that expected to make a quick
dollar, and those that treated their customers as inferior
beings, soon found they had no customers—or friends—and
left. In the early days, as Ruth Underhill wrote, " . . . the
tents and cabins of those early adventurers appeared and
disappeared like so many mushrooms as the owners moved,
changed partners, or bought each other out. By 1890, there
were nine traders on the reservation and thirty more surrounding it at different points. A ruling of 1886 had put a
ceiling on their profits, which were not to be more than 25
per cent of the cost of an article, plus freight charges. . . .
Nevertheless, Sweetland, at Tse-hili, up toward Chinle,

grossed $10,000 in one year. . . ." (Underhill, Oklahoma, 1967: 182.)

The Navajos brought in their sacks of wool and traded them for cotton cloth, canned peaches, coffee, knives, and farm tools from such traders as Thomas Keam and John Lorenzo Hubbell. Hubbell, whose father had been a Connecticut Yankee who moved to New Mexico in the late 1840s and married the daughter of a proud old New Mexican family, arrived on the reservation in the mid-1870s. Before venturing out on his own he worked for a Mr. Coddington, who operated a trading post at Fort Wingate. Hubbell bought out a trader named Leonard about 1879, established himself at Ganado near Ganado Mucho's old home and soon became a favorite of the *Dineh*. As his son, who continued the family business, later wrote, Hubbell became " . . . everything from merchant to father confessor, justice of the peace, judge, jury, court of appeals, chief medicine man and *de facto* czar of the domain. . . ."

The early trading posts were makeshift affairs. Herbert Welsh, who visited a store in Washington Pass run by Elias S. Clark and Charles Hubbell, brother of John Lorenzo, in 1884, described it: "Their impoverished store consisted of a large tent securely fastened by cords and staples, so as to be capable of resisting the violent winds to which this country is subject. The undivided compartment of the great tent served as a place of business, a kitchen, and a sleeping-room. Across the front part of the tent a rough counter had been erected, backed by a high line of shelves, on which were piled rolls of red flannel, calico, cans of preserved vegetables and fruits, bags of coffee, sugar, and all the heterogeneous collection of goods suited to attract the eye and supply the wants of a semi-savage people. In front and behind the tent, huge bags stuffed with the wool of Navajo sheep, that had been received in trade from the Indians, lay waiting departure to the east. Trotting in over the plain from various directions came, singly or in small parties, Navajo men and women carrying bags of wool behind them and ready to do business with the traders. Others within the folds of the tent leaned reflectively across the counter, meditating with the slowness characteristic of Indian deliberation upon the nature and extent of their purchases. A scene so animated and varied could not but give pleasure to one in any degree appreciative of the picturesque."

The Navajos were never a people to overlook a new—if better—way of gaining property, and by 1890 they were trading close to two million pounds of wool annually. Nine years later, with their population estimated at 20,000, their sheep herds had increased to approximately 1,000,000. They also owned 250,000 goats and over 100,000 horses. But that year—1899—they traded only about one million pounds of wool. They had discovered that more profit could be made by keeping much of the wool at home and turning it into blankets.

As we have seen, Navajo blankets had always been popular—and a means of barter—with other Indians, New Mexicans and later the Mormons of the Southwest. They were used as bed blankets, lap robes or as an extra cloak in rough weather, and cowboys preferred to use nothing but the Navajo product as saddle-blankets. Agent W.F.M. Arny had pioneered the market for the blankets in the East and had tried to increase production by importing his high-speed modern looms which the Navajo women had refused to use. The Navajo traders soon saw that the demand for the blankets far exceeded the supply. The Navajo women were weaving, besides such articles of clothing as stockings, shirts, sashes, garters and hair cords, three types of blankets: the large blankets which the whites found made lasting and beautiful rugs; the saddle blankets; and a shoulder blanket which the traders called "dougies" from the Navajo di-yu-ge which indicated a soft fluffy weave. The most popular item was the large beautiful rugs but supplying the market presented a problem. It took a Navajo woman months to save enough wool, prepare her vegetable dyes and unravel old cloth, usually of English manufacture known as baise but called "bayeta" by the Spanish traders, to obtain fine threads of red. As a result, and even with daughters and female relatives helping with the carding and spinning, a good weaver was able to complete no more than one or two blankets a year.

To solve the problem the traders entered into a loose partnership with the Navajo weavers about 1890. They began importing yarn, already spun and colored, and cotton string for warp threads. They also supplied the Navajo women with the newly invented aniline dyes in many gaudy hues and the result was disastrous. Unused to such violent color combinations, the weavers all but wrecked their trade in blankets before they learned to exercise judgment in the use of the new materials.

In 1894 John Lorenzo Hubbell's partner, C.N. Cotton, sold out to Hubbell and moved to Gallup to start what was to become a booming wholesale business in Navajo rugs. He purchased a mimeograph outfit, got hold of directories of various eastern cities and proceeded to inform "the whole country," as he phrased it, that he had Navajo rugs for sale. But such rugs they were! Ruth Underhill has said, "For the next ten years there were turned out some of the weirdest and ugliest products ever made by Indians." With the introduction of American yarns called Germantown, named for the place of their manufacture, Germantown, Pennsylvania, the Navajos set out to make bigger and brighter blankets with a vengeance. As Charles Avery Amsden wrote: "The white man wanted a large, heavy blanket, highly colored, for use on the floor of his hogan, did he? Nothing simpler; and the excited weaver set herself to piling wool into her enlarged loom without proper cleaning, spinning or dyeing. Her color combinations were as eccentric as her workmanship was sketchy; and today when you see a large, coarsely-stitched and loosely spun rug, with a pattern of diamonds or checkerboards or jagged meandered lines done in a half-dozen colors including purple, you may be fairly confident it dates from the 'boom' period of about 1890-1900, when aniline dyes were a novelty and commmercial demand an intoxicating stimulus." (Amsden, ibid. 1949: 189.) But they didn't stop with patterns of diamonds and checkerboards.. They copied patterns off linoleum, first introduced on the reservation about the same time, pictures off the canned goods purchased from the traders, the American flag and a railroad train coming down the Santa Fe tracks.

While the weavers were still adjusting their craft to the changes brought on by the boom, a new novelty was introduced on the reservation—the "store blanket." The traders swapped the store blankets for Navajo wool and sheep, and this marked the end of the Navajo blanket as such, for with no further need of laborious weaving for their own use, the Navajo women were induced to turn their skill almost exclusively to the production of the coarser, heavier type the eastern whites preferred.

But the traders, at least the more conservative faction, soon saw danger in the new innovations. John Lorenzo

Hubbell had the artist E.A. Burbank make color paintings of all the old Navajo designs and figures he could find and used them as models. "In his office at Ganado, Arizona, John Lorenzo Hubbell had scores of blanket designs, painted in oil, hung upon his walls, and they present a most surprising and wonderful combination. These are designs that have been found to be pleased to purchasers, and when a special order for a blanket of a certain design comes in, the weaver is shown the picture of the one desired. She studies it for a while, takes the wool provided, or herself prepares it, and then, with such slight variations as she is sure to introduce, goes ahead and makes her blanket," George Wharton James wrote in 1920.

In 1899 the blankets shipped to the East were worth about $50,000. The next year Fred Harvey, concessionaire of the restaurants, newsstands, and later hotels, that served Santa Fé Railroad customers, established the Indian Building at Albuquerque. Navajo women were hired to demonstrate weaving techniques on the premises and thereby, over the next several decades, aroused the interest of millions of travellers in the craft. Harvey contracted with John Lorenzo Hubbell to take his entire output of best quality blankets. They established definite prices for certain sizes coming up to their standards of weave, color and design and thereby stabilized prices—at a higher figure than those prevailing at the time. J.B. Moore, a trader at Crystal, New Mexico, also insisted on buying only quality blankets and he, Hubbell and the Fred Harvey Company were responsible for reversing the deteriorating trend in Navajo weaving. Other traders were soon forced to insist that their weavers return to the production of a quality product.

The bright dyes were discarded and Navajo weavers returned to the old soft-hued native dyes. Navajo weaving became truly an industry. In 1913 F.H. Abbott, Secretary of the Board of Indian Commissioners, estimated the total sales at one-half million dollars. Ten years later there were 5,500 weavers at work and the sales reached $750,000.

By the early 1900s the Navajos had, as Underhill has stated, reached a "new summit of prosperity" and "owned at least as much wealth as they had before Sumner days and far more than when they entered the Southwest." Of course they were not nearly as rich as they had been when the Americans entered the Southwest in 1846. But they were no longer starving and were able, finally, to turn their attention to other problems.

The most pressing problem was still land suitable for farming and grazing. The railroad brought an influx of white settlers from the East who desired land of their own and quite often it was land on which Navajos lived and considered theirs. As early as 1885 Interior Secretary Lucius Q.C. Lamar suggested closing "all entries to non—Navajos wishing to homestead on the public domain adjoining the established Navajo reservation." But his suggestion did not deter white homesteaders in the least. Conflicts between whites and Navajos continued to mount, not only in the lands opened up by the railroad but also in that section of land restored to the Navajos in 1884 lying south of the San Juan River in Utah and known as the Paiute Strip. Rumors that there were gold and silver deposits in the area had been prevalent since the time of General Carleton and, ignoring the fact that it was now part of the Navajo reservation, prospectors insisted on working the area and staking claims. At least two prospectors named Mitchell and Myerick were killed near Monument Valley in the 1880s. Then, in 1892, President Benjamin Harrison, under pressure from Southwestern congressmen, ordered the 600,000-acre section restored to the public domain. The Navajos were allowed to use the land for grazing but it was not until 1933 that an act of congress restored the land to Navajo ownership. 1893 brought conflict between the Navajos and the Mormons, who had settled on the Moencopi Wash and founded Tuba City. Navajos had lived in the area for at least fifty years before Fort Sumner and were of the opinion that the Mormons were the interlopers. An argument over water rights resulted in the death of a Mormon rancher named Lot Smith.

The situation reached a climax—and focused national attention on the Navajo need for land—when, in 1897, the Board of Supervisors of Coconino County, Arizona, ordered the eviction of sixteen Navajo families living south of the Little Colorado River in that county. W.A. Jones, Commissioner of Indian Affairs, said to be the first man to hold that office to actually visit the reservation, reported: "In January there were 16 Navajo families tending their flocks in a grazing district bounded on the west by the Colorado river . . . a tract of country which they had thus occupied for generations and which had never been surveyed. .... On January 19, the sheriff with an armed posse visited each of these 16 families and demanded that $5.00 for every 100 sheep owned by them be paid to him at once; failing to do so they were to move out immediately. The Navajo had no money; their prayer for time in which to procure money or to ascertain their rights was denied, and in default of payment of the arbitrary and unlawful sum fixed by the sheriff, the Indians were forced to gather up their belongings and move.

"Snow was falling, the weather was bitter cold, and the ewes were lambing. The Indians pleaded for a reasonable time within which to move, but were denied. Their houses and corrals were burned and they and their flocks were rounded up and pushed north toward the Little Colorado River with relentless haste, the posse keeping women, children, and animals in a fright by an intermittent fire from rifles and revolvers. When the river was reached it was found to be so deep as to require the sheep to swim. The posse surrounded the flocks and pushed them into the water, and nearly all the lambs, with many grown sheep, went down the stream or froze to death after crossing, and many died afterward from the effects of exposure."

Such incidents prompted a missionary named William R. Johnston, who had recently set up a mission at Tolcheco, Arizona, into action on behalf of the Navajos living west of the reservation. Primarily through his efforts, President William McKinley signed an Executive Order on January 8, 1900, withdrawing 1,575,369 acres of land west of the reservation—which included the Tuba City holdings of the Mormons—"from sale and allotment until further notice" although no mention was made of the possibility of the land becoming a part of the Navajo reservation. Soon after McKinley was assassinated in 1901, Johnston escorted two headmen to Washington to call on the new president, Theodore Roosevelt. Roosevelt had spent considerable time in the West and was known to be in sympathy with the Indians. The meeting between Roosevelt and the headmen resulted in the president ordering an investigation. As a result of the investigation, allotments of land were granted to some Navajo families and the Moencopi problem was solved by purchasing, for $40,000, the Mormon holdings at Tuba City. Then, on November 15, 1901, he signed an executive order granting the land to the Navajos as well as another half a million acres along the Little Colorado east of Flagstaff known as the Leupp sector. The Navajo reservation now encompassed almost 12,000,000 acres.

In 1905 President Roosevelt appointed a Washington newspaper correspondent named Francis E. Leupp as Indian Commissioner. Leupp had been, for several years, a special agent of the Indian Rights Association, and his articles on the miserable condition of Indians in the Southwest, particularly in the Navajo schools, had attracted much attention. Leupp saw that the entire Indian Bureau was in dire need of reorganization. He spent several months visiting the various agencies and optimistically announced in his first report plans for an "almost complete reorganization of the Indian Service, with the general aim of preparing the whole Indian establishment for going out of business at no distant date." He declared that "the Indian is not merely a white man in a red man's skin, but a natural warrior, a natural logician, and a natural artist. . . . He has been an economic nursling too long. He needs improvement, not transformation . . . it would be wasted effort to try to change the old. We must work on the young and their education should be chiefly vocational." Leupp thoroughly disapproved of the non-reservation boarding schools, calling them "educational almhouses," and suggested they be closed except for those offering a higher education to those Indians who desired it.

Through Leupp's efforts another 56,953 acres known as the Aneth Extension was added to the Navajo reservation in 1905. Half a century later the rich Aneth Oil Field in the Four Corners area of this section began pouring millions of dollars into the Navajo Tribal treasury. But Commissioner Leupp's plans of modernizing the Indian Bureau was hampered by the bureaucratic system and he was soon attacked on every side for what was called his "unpractical ideas." He had scarcely put his plans in action when Roosevelt's term expired and he was replaced by Robert G. Valentine. It would be twenty-five years before a new Commissioner of Indian Affairs, John Collier, again attempted to modernize the department. Leupp and Roosevelt did make one more substantial addition to the Navajo reservation. In an effort to stop conflicts between the *Dineh* and white stockmen two large tracts totaling more than three million acres were added to the reservation in 1907. About a third of this grant was land south of the reservation in Arizona. The remainder was just north and northeast of Gallup, in New Mexico, and included the Chaco Canyon area, but awarding this area to the Navajos caused what one government report termed "a growing clamor of protest brought to bear by non-Indian stockmen and politicians who were determined to force restoration to the public domain of this portion of the old Navajo Country. Since there were rumors of oil deposits in the area after 1907, the demand was especially great."

Anticipating that white politicians would be victorious in having the New Mexico lands restored to the public domain, Leupp sent allotment agents to the region and succeeded in making some two thousand allotments to Navajo residents living in the area. Leupp's fears were well founded. In January, 1911, President William Howard Taft revoked Roosevelt's order and restored all the lands in New Mexico which had been added to the Navajo reservation in 1907 to the public domain.

But white stockmen and sheepmen of New Mexico and Arizona were not satisfied with that victory. In fact it prompted them to begin relentless campaigns to retake most of the lands that had been awarded the Navajos since the Bosque Redondo treaty. New Mexico became a state on January 6, 1912, and Arizona on February 14, 1912. The first memorial of the first legislature of the state of New Mexico called upon the United States Congress to allot in severalty the Navajo reservation and to open the "surplus lands" of the reservation to white entry. The memorial also requested that Congress prohibit "further withdrawal of the lands of New Mexico for any purpose whatever." The new Commissioner of Indian Affairs, F.H. Abbott, wrote Senator Benjamin F. Shively of Indiana and pointed out there were no "surplus lands" on the Navajo reservation "owing to climatic conditions, the character of the soil, etc. . . ."

But by the next year it had become apparent that the New Mexicans had won strong support in Congress. In 1913 Senator Albert B. Fall of New Mexico proposed an amendment to the fiscal 1914 Indian appropriation bill which would have prohibited the further allotment of public domain lands in New Mexico and Arizona to Indians. According to Fall's figures, if the Navajo reservation were to be divided every Navajo would "own at least 1,100 acres" which he stated was a total amount "greatly excessive to the needs of the tribe." The Senator from New Mexico said: "They may take a thousand or five thousand or ten thousand head of sheep and run them on the range within the country adjoining my ranch, take the grass away from my cattle; occupy 160 acres each under allotment; pay no taxes; support the government not at all; and tomorrow, if they choose to do so, after having eaten off the public range, return to the Navajo Reservation and have allotted to them in severality 1100 acres. . . ."

The machinations of Senator Fall were supported wholeheartedly by Senator Henry F. Ashurst of Arizona, and also by the new Assistant Commissioner of Indian Affairs, Edgar B. Meritt. Meritt was an astute lawyer but no friend of the Indians. He took office in 1913 and held his position until 1929, serving under two commissioners, neither of whom was able to amass power equal to his. He was in charge of the Indian budget and hired the Indian superintendents and agents—and as long as he was in office nothing of consequence pertaining to health, education, irrigation or, to any extent, land extensions, was accomplished.

But the Navajos had one friend and his lone voice was more effective than the clamor set up by Fall, Ashurst, Meritt and the white stockmen. Father Anselm Weber, head missionary of the Franciscan Mission at Saint Michaels, had lived on the reservation for sixteen years and his was the voice of truth. He wrote what amounted to a diatribe which was printed in the newspapers in Washington and elsewhere under the simple heading, "A Statement of Facts."

"For several years past," Father Weber wrote, "there has been agitated the question of alloting lands in Arizona and New Mexico to the Navajos and other Indians (160 acres to each adult) and throwing open to settlement and entry under the public land laws the unallotted balance of lands now embraced in Indian reservations. The cry has been loud that these reservations are too large and are not needed by the Indians. Unfortunately some members of the delegations from these states have appeared to be influenced by exaggerated and untrue statements upon this question. . . .

"The Navajo Reservation is stocked heavier and its range is more overgrazed and run down than the range in other parts of Arizona and New Mexico. . . ." Father Weber pointed out that, in fact, the reservation was considerably more than one-third heavier stocked already than the rest of rural New Mexico and Arizona combined. "The Navajos," he wrote, "have 1,800,000 head of sheep and goats, and if other classes of livestock (horses, cattle, mules and burros) were converted to sheep units there are 2,328,000.

"As a result the soil is eroding badly in many places. Over considerable areas very little plant life is left, except sagebrush, scrub juniper and pinon. The former heavy stand of gamma grass over much of this region is nearly extinct . . . (yet) the proponents of opening the reservation point to the provision of the 1868 treaty that offered 160-acre assignments to individual Navajos. A hundred and sixty acres could not possibly sustain a Navajo or a Navajo family."

Father Weber pointed out that there was little grazing land in the western and southwestern states with "such a stock capacity that even four sections of it, 2560 acres, would maintain a family in ordinary circumstances. In face of all this, what do you think of people who urge the allotment of 160 acres of such grazing lands to the person and then opening the balance to settlement? In Arizona the State Land Commission and the cattlemen and others have insisted on the Government doing that because they want the surplus Indian lands restored to the public domain so they can use them for grazing ground."

Pointing out that the clamoring Mexicans and Americans did not and would not live on the land even if it were opened up to settlement, he added: "The clamor of these two vast, undeveloped States for the opening of the overstocked and overgrazed Navajo Reservation seems rather ludicrous. If it is absolutely necessary for the salvation of New Mexico and Arizona to open the Navajo Reservation, let it be done after adequate homestead and leasing and grazing laws have been passed . . . and after the United States has educated the Navajos to cope with their white neighbors."

While the pressure on Congress to open the "surplus lands" on the Navajo reservation subsided, it did not immediately die. Senator Ashurst, in fact, said that the whole matter of the pressure to secure more lands for the Navajos was nothing but Santa Fe Railroad propaganda! Perhaps that barb was aimed at the Fred Harvey Company which had tacitly sided with the Navajos. Under pressure Senator Fall and Assistant Commissioner Meritt announced that they had reached a "compromise." They had agreed to allot public domain lands only to those Navajos who had been residing there prior to June 30, 1913. White settlers seeking the land did not have to meet that requirement.

President Woodrow Wilson also tacitly sided with the Navajos and signed numerous executive orders which withdrew small areas of land from the public domain in regions where groups of Navajos were known to be settled. By 1916, 2,900 allotments had been made to Navajo families in the Pueblo Bonito area.

The land situation continued to worsen. Soon whites and Navajos were at each other's throats as each accused the other of trespassing on his land. Finally, in January, 1918, President Wilson gave the Navajos 94,000 acres in the Gray Mountain area. The New Mexico delegation to Congress, fearing that Wilson intended to add some portion of the disputed lands on the East to the reservation, secured the enactment of legislation to prevent further enlargement of the Navajo reservation by executive order—providing for future enlargement only by Act of Congress. In 1919 general legislation was adopted, precluding the enlargement of any Indian reservation from the public domain except by Act of Congress.

But large numbers of Navajos were still living on the public domain lands, especially that to the East of the reservation, and continued to apply for allotments. In 1930 white stockmen, aligned with mining corporations, were able to influence Congress to discontinue the allotment system. Between 1917 and 1933 almost 135,000 acres were added to the Arizona portion of the Navajo reservation. Then, on March 1, 1933, Congress restored the Paiute Strip and a small area north of the Aneth Section in Utah known as the Aneth Strip, about half a million acres in all. But the Utah congressional delegation, well aware of the oil and gas discoveries that had been made in the Four Corners country, persuaded Congress to include in the legislation a provision that that state would receive 37.5 percent of all royalties for "payment of the tuition of Indian children in white schools, and/or in the building or maintenance of roads across the lands . . . for the benefit of Indians residing therein." Also, Utah was granted the right to relinquish such school tracts as it might wish to give up within the area added to the reservation, and select like tracts of equal acreage outside the area. This, in effect, freed Utah from the responsibility of providing schools for the Indians living in the area while giving that state a percentage of Navajo oil and gas royalties for that purpose!

In 1934 the new Democratic administration sponsored bills that proposed new boundaries for the reservation on the West, South and East and provided for the relinquishment of privately owned lands within the reservation. The owners of such lands were permitted to select other public lands within the same counties. In addition, the Navajos would be permitted to buy certain privately owned lands in each state within the new boundaries. For this purpose, almost a million dollars, reimbursable from the Navajo tribal treasury, was authorized. The new Secretary of the Interior, Harold Ickes, stated that the new boundaries were "the ultimate line to which the Indians can hope to expand the reservation."

President Franklin D. Roosevelt signed the Arizona Boundary Act into law on June 14, 1934, but the bill establishing a permanent boundary in New Mexico was defeated in the House after securing Senate approval. The passage of the Arizona bill added another 1,000,000 acres to the reservation. The failure of the New Mexico bill meant continued strife and, as one government report stated, "constituted a victory and a gain in land ownership for this portion of the Old Navajo *(Dinehtah)* country, while for the Navajo population it was a serious economic blow." Using tribal funds, the Navajos purchased all the holdings of the Santa Fe Railroad within the reservation boundaries by 1935. During the decade of the 1950s the Navajo Tribal Council purchased several private ranches and other lands totalling almost 250,000 acres with revenue from the reservation oil fields in the Four Corners area bringing the Navajo reservation to its present size of approximately 16 million acres.

It took the Navajos two-thirds of a century to get back a large portion of their land—all the United States was going to let them have of it—and their economic recovery had been amazing. But the land additions to the reservation had barely kept pace with the population increase. In 1930 there were approximately 40,000 Navajos living on the reservation. The erosion and overgrazing that Father Weber had warned of in 1913 had reached such proportions that it constituted a crisis. With Edgar B. Meritt's long stranglehold on the Indian Bureau, the Indian education system, as bad as it had been to begin with, had actually deteriorated. And the *Dineh* had yet to experience more disillusionment and bitterness in their relations with the Bilagáana.

FOUR

Between Two Worlds

A survey made by a group of research experts and published in 1928 confirmed what many government authorities, and particularly Secretary of the Interior Hubert Work, had long suspected. Conditions on the Navajo reservation and, in fact, on all Indian reservations, were deplorable. Commissioner of Indian Affairs Charles H. Burke had been in office for five years, and had made several serious miscalculations in judgment, but the real power in the Indian Bureau was still in the hands of Edgar B. Meritt when Secretary Work sought outside help in June, 1926. Work, stating that a survey of conditions on the Indian reservations was needed because harmful attacks and propaganda were creating in the public mind the impression that Indian rights and welfare were being disregarded and that the Indians were not being properly dealt with, turned to the Brookings Institution, a non-profit and non-political research organization in Washington. He probably never forgave himself.

Upon being assured that all the files of the Indian Bureau would be opened to its researchers, the Brookings Institution found a sponsor for the survey—the Rockefeller

Foundation—and went to work. The resulting survey was delivered to Secretary Work on February 21, 1928. Called the Meriam report, after Lewis B. Meriam, the director of the project, it has become a classic in the field of Indian administration. The product of experts in the fields of education, health, administration, law and Indian history, the report was sober, thoughtful and highly critical of the Indian Bureau and, for that matter, the federal government. The government was faulted for its basic attitude toward the Indian. The report stated that governmental emphasis had always been on the Indian's property rather than on the Indian's welfare. To the surprise of most Indian Bureau officials, the Meriam researchers found that most Indians preferred to remain Indian and the policy of separating the individual from his family and community and placing him in a boarding school in the mistaken belief that he would become a Christian and would be assimilated into the white culture was accomplishing nothing—not even education.

And as far as the boarding students were concerned, the researchers found that "malnutrition was evident. The pupils were indolent, and when they had a chance to play, they merely sat about on the ground, showing no exuberance of healthy youth." Under the euphemism "vocational training," in nearly every school the Brookings people investigated they found "children of eleven or twelve (or younger) spending four hours a day in more or less heavy industrial work—dairying, kitchen work, laundry and shop. The work is bad for children of this age, especially children not physically well-nourished; most of it is in no sense educational . . . all the hard, menial labor required to raise food, produce milk, and butter, repair shoes, launder clothing and perform other functions necessary to the operations of the institution (is engaged in by the children).

"The laundry is an important feature of every government school. It is one of the chief sources of labor for the pupils. The superintendent of one school said he can get more work out of the children if he keeps large piles of laundry before them. An inspection of the plant verified his statement. A number of small children were literally hidden behind great piles of wet laundry in a greatly overcrowded room filled with steam. . . .

"Several dairies have milking machines, but the bulk of this work is done by hand and in some instances, the same detail of boys is kept on for the entire school year, although this work requires very early raising. Almost all dairy details include a few very small boys."

The researchers found that school employees "followed disciplinary methods which are now regarded as antiquated, even in a reform school. . . . Dressed in uniforms, the children 'stood formation' and marched from place to place. . . . They must maintain a pathetic degree of quietness. In fact, several matrons and disciplinarians said that they did not allow the children to talk in the dining rooms. Despite the fact that the children were faced with the problem of learning English, they were denied the privilege of conversation at the table as one informal opportunity to practice, and the use of their mother tongue was prohibited. . . . Nearly every boarding school visited furnished disquieting illustrations of failure to understand the underlying principles of human behavior. Punishments of the most harmful sort are bestowed in sheer ignorance."

In a majority of the boarding schools the researchers visited, the children attended school only four hours a day or even less. The rest of their time was devoted to "vocational training," as the school administrators called the heavy farm work the children were expected to perform. The researchers found dormitory living conditions abominable: "Every available space that will accommodate beds is often pressed into service. The children are frequently quartered on attic floors, in close placed beds, with the same lack of light and air. Not infrequently in these attic dormitories the fire hazard is serious." Children often slept two to a single bed "not because they preferred it to keep warm during the cold nights, but because there were no other beds for them."

The report stated that health and living standards among Indians were particularly low. The death rate of Navajo infants from gastroenteric diseases was almost twenty times that of the population as a whole. Tuberculosis and trachoma were prevalent, especially among the Indians of the Southwest. Both diseases were near epidemic proportions among the Navajos--yet Dr. Ales Hrdlicka had reported in 1909, after extensive research, that both diseases were rare among the *Dineh*. The Meriam report concluded that sweeping changes were necessary and pointed out that the majority of the Indian Service personnel were simply not qualified for the jobs which they were entrusted to perform. There had been no substantial increase in appropriations for the Indian Bureau since before World War I and the investigators found a marked tendency within the Bureau to establish a salary for a given position, not on the basis of ability or training, but solely on the wages earned by the last incumbent.

Publication of the Meriam report sent a wave of indignation sweeping across the nation. Newspaper editorials demanded that something be done about the sorry state of affairs; and a few were so bold as to demand the resignation of Commissioner Charles H. Burke. Burke resigned in 1929 and with him went Edgar B. Meritt. Meritt was the brother-in-law of the powerful Senate majority leader from Arkansas, Joe T. Robinson, and when Franklin D. Roosevelt became President of the United States on March 4, 1933, heavy political pressure was brought to bear on him to appoint Meritt Commissioner of Indian Affairs. His appointment was thwarted by Harold L. Ickes, Roosevelt's new Secretary of the Interior. Ickes told the president that Meritt was totally unqualified for the job and suggested that John Collier be appointed to the position.

John Collier had been a social reformer all his life and had, for the ten years prior to his appointment, written a periodical called *American Indian Life*. For years he had been a vociferous and unyielding critic of the Indian Bureau and advocated a complete break with the past. He charged that the allotment policy and bureaucratic control of Indian lives had proven a failure in integrating Indians into white civilization. He advocated replacing the centralized control of the Indians with self-government and economic self-sufficiency. A statement that Collier made soon after taking office is indicative of his understanding of the Indians and their society: "Modernity and white Americanism are not identical. If the Indian life is a good life, then we should be proud and glad to have this different and native culture going on by the side of ours. . . . America is coming to understand this, and to know that in helping the Indian to save himself, we are helping to save something that is precious to us as well as to him." It would be over three decades before America found the truth in Collier's words. In the meantime he was determined to see that Franklin D. Roosevelt's New Deal was also a New Deal for the Indians.

But his proposed reformation of the Indian Bureau soon came under fire.

The House Committee on Indian Affairs was his most vociferous critic and charged that his concept of Indian self-government was tinged with Communism. In April, 1935, the House Committee attempted to place Collier in an adverse position by associating him with Roger Baldwin and the American Civil Liberties Union. The implication was that by association, Collier was shielding Communism and advocating the overthrow of the government and was therefore not fit to hold the position of Commissioner of Indian Affairs.

Collier advocated neither complete separation nor complete integration, but a blending of cultures which would enable the Indian to select from the dominant culture what he believed to be helpful and good without having to sacrifice those good and desirable aspects of his native culture . . . a practice at which the Navajos were masters. As a matter of fact Collier started his program of reform with the Navajos.

To facilitate control and program direction, the Navajo reservation had been divided into separate agency jurisdictions beginning in 1910. Gradually the reservation was divided into six jurisdictions, including the Hopi, with an agent in each one. This arrangement minimized the expanse of the territory for which each agent was responsible, but it did not foster the development of tribal unity. Then, in 1921, oil was discovered within the boundaries of the original treaty reservation in the San Juan District. The Midwest Refining Company was authorized to negotiate with the Navajos of that district and a lease for oil and gas rights was secured by that company on 4800 acres of land. Shortly afterwards a council of Navajos living in the Southern District signed oil and gas leases with the company. The Department of the Interior declared that oil and gas discovered on any part of the reservation belonged to the tribe as a whole, and not to the residents of any one section.

The leases were cancelled and a "business council" was organized with Chee Dodge as chairman. The legality of this council was questioned and moves were taken to form a Navajo Tribal Council, with elected officers. In the subsequent election Chee Dodge was chosen Tribal Council Chairman.

According to his official biography, Chee Dodge was born in February, 1860, of a Navajo-Jemez mother and his father was Juan Anea, the silversmith hired by Henry Linn Dodge. There has long been speculation that Chee Dodge was actually the son of Henry Linn Dodge and the Navajo niece of Zarcillos Largos and was born three years earlier, soon after the death of the agent. Be as it may, photographs of Henry Chee Dodge bear a striking resemblance to descriptions of the beloved "Redshirt" and the reasons for the Navajos concealing the birth of his son—if that were the case—are obvious. Chee Dodge's mother disappeared during the 1863-64 campaign and the young boy was taken to Fort Sumner by a family who found him wandering alone. After Sumner he lived with an aunt who was married to a white man named Perry Williams, an issue clerk at Fort Defiance. Dodge mastered English at an early age and, as stated before, replaced Jesus Arviso as interpreter at Fort Defiance.

By the time Ganado Mucho and Manuelito died, Dodge was looked upon by most Navajos as the chief *Naataani* of the tribe. Thrifty and well-acquainted with the white man's methods of doing business, he amassed a considerable fortune. Dodge served as Tribal Council Chairman until 1928 and was re-elected to a four-year term in 1942. Actually he received very little formal education himself, but he insisted that his children attend school and urged all Navajos to see that their children got as much education as possible. His son Tom, who attended Washington University in St. Louis, was elected Tribal Council Chairman in 1932, and his daughter, Annie Dodge Wauneka, became a highly influential and respected member of the tribe. She was elected to the Tribal Council in 1951 and served five terms, constantly crusading for better health facilities and other social programs for her people. In 1963 she was honored with the Presidential Medal of Freedom Award, the highest civil honor that can be presented to an American in peacetime.

As Chairman of the Council, Chee Dodge was shrewd in his dealings with the government and frugal in money matters. During his first chairmanship over one million dollars in royalties and bonuses was deposited to the Navajos' credit with the United States Treasury.

The Tribal Council, as devised by Commissioner Charles M. Burke, was composed of one delegate and one alternate from six districts, as well as a chairman and a vice-chairman. But actually, in the early days, neither the Council nor its chairman were invested with any real power. A "Commissioner of the Navajos" was appointed by the Indian Bureau with supervisory authority over the council. The first meeting of the council was held at Toadlena on July 27, 1923. The early council membership was adversely criticized because it did not represent the true leadership of the Navajo people—most of whom did not know that it existed. Actually it was almost entirely under the domination of the Indian Bureau and possessed no real governmental powers. The council met annually, primarily to consider land leases, until it was reorganized under John Collier's directions in 1936.

In 1927 John Hunter, Superintendent of the Leupp Agency, began the development of local community organizations which came to be known as Chapters. Chapter meetings were designed to bring the Navajos together at a local level where representatives of the tribe, the Public Health Service and the Indian Bureau could discuss problems in an open meeting. The real leadership of the tribe continued to remain at the local level in the hands of headmen of families and clan groups. The Chapter idea appealed to the Navajos as it resembled the *Naachid* of the old days. They supported the program enthusiastically and willingly donated labor and materials for the construction of meeting houses.

That same year Commissioner Burke reported that "the number of livestock belonging to the Navajos is increasing considerably, and it seems to be desirable that consideration be given to plans for regulating the grazing of stock on the range in such manner as to afford protection to the individual members of the tribe in the development of their stock interests." Burke's comments were based on a recent survey that had shown that more than twenty-four percent of the Navajos owned no sheep at all; forty-two percent owned a hundred head or less; thirty-two percent owned from one hundred to twelve hundred head and only two percent owned more than twelve hundred head. "Each individual member of the tribe," Burke reasoned, "is entitled to the use of his proportionate share of lands belonging to the Reservation and no one individual is entitled to increase his livestock holdings to the exclusion of other members of the tribe."

Burke and the Indian Bureau still did not realize that the real problem was the overgrazing that Father Weber had warned of fourteen years before during the controversy over the Navajo "land surplus," and that an equal distribution of grazing lands would not solve the problem. Some Navajos, such as Chee Dodge, counted their sheep in the thousands, while others owned none or very few and worked for the *ricos* as herders. A cycle of dry weather swept over the Southwest in the 1920s, leaving the poor Navajos near destitution, while the *ricos*, who had historically claimed the right to use better lands, were not so adversely affected. The officials in Washington reasoned that because title to the reservation land was vested in the tribe, each member of the tribe possessed an equal right to its use. Under pressure from the Indian Bureau, the Navajo Tribal Council placed "The Question of Eventually Limiting the Number of Sheep, Horses, Goats and Cattle for Any One Indian, So that Benefits of the Range May Be more equitably distributed Among all Navajos" on the agenda for its November, 1928 meeting. But such a concept for land use was inconceivable to the Navajos. They had always adhered to the use pattern whereby certain lands were used by a family or a group of families and such claims were respected by members of other families and clans. Only lands that were deserted by a family or clan were open to use by others.

The Navajo Tribal Council tried to avoid the issue but Assistant Indian Commissioner Roger B. Meritt, who had travelled to Fort Defiance for the meeting, insisted they consider "the problem of land distribution."

"The grazing area of the Navajo Reservation is your greatest asset," Meritt said. "It produced an income of more than $2,500,000 in 1927, in contrast to only $70,000 from oil. Each Navajo has an equal share in that asset. Our plan is to equalize your share in the great grazing asset." Meritt pointed out that a Navajo who owned a thousand sheep that were rightly bred and fed would have an income from their sale of $3,000 to $5,000 a year and a man who owned stock in excess of that number of sheep, or the equivalent in horses and cattle, should pay fifteen cents tax per head each year. Meritt was met with about the same reaction that he would have received had he proposed the same "equalization" to a group of Iowa farmers.

Chee Dodge pointed out that there were between ten and twelve thousand Navajo families, a husband and wife being considered a family. "If we say there are ten thousand families," Dodge said, "and each family has two children, and they each can own one thousand sheep, that would be ten million sheep. Even if there were only five thousand families, that would make five million sheep, more than twice as many as the Navajos now own. How can that solve the problem of overgrazing?"

Councilman Lee Bradley pointed out that the Navajos did not own even one thousand sheep per family. "We don't have and we won't ever have, so why talk about it?" Bradley asked. In spite of the fact that Meritt and the Indian Bureau officials did not know what they were talking about and their plan, had it been put into effect, would have legally allowed a tenfold increase in the number of sheep already on the overgrazed reservation, they insisted on a "tax for excess sheep." A majority of the council voted to place an annual tax of eleven cents a head on all sheep in excess of one thousand owned by a family, knowing the council had no power to enforce such a law and that the Indian Bureau was in no position to do so. Meritt returned to Washington, satisfied that he had made progress in solving the program of overgrazing on the Navajo reservation. By the time John Collier inherited the problem in 1913, drastic measures were called for.

Collier took office in the midst of the most disastrous economic depression in the history of the United States and the Navajos were worse off than the rest of the country. In 1933 the Navajo Agency reported: "Depression for the last three years throughout the country has perhaps hit the Navajo people more severely than it has the average white person. The Navajo is almost entirely dependent upon his income from the livestock industry—principally the sale of wool and lambs. This income has greatly reduced to the vanishing point since there has been practically no market for lambs or wool. During the past winter the Navajo was forced to feed his corn, which is ordinarily sold to the trader, to his sheep. This again reduced his income."

The People could not sell their sheep and the herds quickly increased which, of course, caused the grazing problem to become acute. Collier knew that the Navajos and their land were in desperate straits and he wasted no time. In July, 1933, soon after taking office, Collier traveled to the Navajo reservation and met the headmen in council at Fort Wingate. His first step was to authorize public work projects that would provide destitute Navajos with cash wages and secure permission from the Tribal Council to construct a federal experiment station at Mexican Springs with the use of paid Navajo labor. Then he told the headmen: "The range must be saved or the Navajos must disperse into the white world. Dispersal would bring death to the Navajo spirit, the obliteration of the Navajo rainbow forever."

He returned to the reservation in November, accompanied by a staff of land and conservation specialists. He called a council at Tuba City and placed before the Navajos the plan he and his staff had devised to relieve the economic and social problems of the Navajos. Fifty new day schools would be built on the reservation, and more conservation and work programs would be launched for which federal funds would be appropriated. But to solve the problem of overgrazing there would have to be drastic reduction made in the livestock herds and a program of range control established. The huge herds of horses, the pride of their Navajo owners, would have to go because a horse consumed four times as much grass as a sheep. The reservation could support only 560,000 head of sheep and the herds would have to be reduced to that number. The Navajos were thunderstruck. Get rid of the horses? Reduce the number of sheep? *That* was going to make them rich? It was more of the white man's insanity, of course, and they had long known about that.

But Collier soon convinced the Navajo headmen that he was serious. As he later wrote, his program "launched a social, economic, and political struggle and effort well-nigh as intense and as dubious of outcome as any to be witnessed among men. It launched, also, the soil conservation movement in the United States; and that movement was to extend to every continent, in the years when there was dawning in the world's mind . . . the realization that mankind itself is faced by a silent crisis hardly less demanding than that which was facing the Navajo tribe. For the wastage of soil resource—of food potential—is going ahead on a world scale, and at an accelerating, catastrophic

444

speed." (Collier, Swallow, 1962. 64.)

The reservation was divided into districts and the number of sheep units that each district could support was determined. The Navajos were told that they would have to get rid of all sheep units above the set number for each district whether it was a horse, a cow or even the sheep. Collier was very careful to explain the reasons for the herd reduction program to the Navajo headmen but no one explained it to the women and they, by custom, owned most of the sheep. It was quite obvious to them that it was just another sinister plot of the Bilagáanas: They would get rid of the sheep, the Navajos would all starve to death and their land would be given to white settlers. Wasn't that what the whites had always wanted?

Collier understood their reaction but he also threw the burden of the sheep reduction program squarely onto the Navajo Tribal Council. While the Council accepted and affirmed the conservation program, the Council's constituency did not, but resisted it with a bitterness that, as Collier wrote, was "sometimes sad, sometimes angry and wild." Rather than get rid of the sheep, the Navajos got rid of the council—and all but killed Collier's plans for Indian self-government. Collier made arrangements through the Works Progress Administration to launch the stock reduction plan by purchasing 100,000 sheep at $1 to $1.50 per head for ewes and from $2.25 to $3 per head for wethers. Chee Dodge pointed out that at those prices the Navajo stockmen were only going to sell the government culled animals and suggested that a premium be paid for good breeding ewes, but government officials rejected the proposal. Prices, once set, could not be changed.

Through no fault of John Collier's, Washington departmental officials allowed the entire sheep reduction program to become bogged down in red tape. Conflicting orders and regulations were issued that caused even more bitterness. Each sheep owner was told that he had to sell ten percent of his stock, of which seventy-five percent had to be ewes. The two-thirds of the Navajos who owned less than one hundred sheep were, of course, hit very hard. On the other hand the large stockowners, with herds of a thousand or more, merely sold off their culls and, as a result, were enabled to maintain their herds at the highest production level.

The bitterness the Washington bureaucrats caused by bungling the sheep-reduction program was only a prologue. Turning their attention to the matter of the Navajos' goats that produced the fine Angora-like wool the woman used in their weaving, the planners decided that 150,000 would have to be disposed of at a set price of $1 per head. The goats were to be delivered in the fall of 1934 to various shipping points from which they were to be transported to packing plants in the East. But an early winter disrupted the schedule. The planners then gave the Navajos permission to slaughter as many of the goats as they could consume. Actually it was an excellent plan as the Navajos, it seemed, could consume the goats during the winter and still get paid a dollar each for them. But no, that was not what the Washington officials had in mind—the Navajos had to consume the goats immediately. In late fall, agents were sent through the country and thousands of goats were shot and left to rot. Over 3,500 goats were destroyed in Navajo Canyon in a single day. Then thousands of horses were destroyed in the same manner. This wanton distruction of the animals they had raised incensed the Navajos. Sam Ahkeah, who was elected to two terms as Chairman of the Tribal Council (1946 and 1950) later reported that he had to sell all but thirty-nine of his original 550 sheep. The senseless waste was beyond the comprehension of the Navajos and they were given opportunity to contemplate it during the long winter that followed when there was never enough food in many hogans. A Navajo woman told a newspaper correspondent: "We have thirty sheep and fourteen goats. Once we have more than one hundred sheep alone. Then policeman come from Indian agency and read law and we must sell. We hide some, they shoot others. Then policeman come, read law for grazing permits. I am frightened. All around Indians work on tree planting, but soon stop. Then we get hungry. We try to pick piñon nuts to sell, but policeman from agency come and read law and take them away.

"All around Indians are hungry and traders don't give credit anymore. They know we have few sheep, few goats, no wool. Policeman read law and they can't sell. Indian agency bring food in cans. If not Indian must beg from white man who visits. Even my children now cough too much, not enough goat milk or goat meat. Indian agency has lots of men on reservation now, but Indians have no work, no coffee, no flour, no meat. Next they will take hogans and we live under pinon tree."

John Collier's stock-reduction and grazing-restriction programs were well conceived and, in the long run, accomplished their purpose. New breeding stock was introduced on the reservation once wiser heads prevailed in Washington, and eventually wool production was increased by forty percent. But the brutal and wasteful manner in which the program was carried out caused the Navajos to look upon subsequent government programs of soil conservation, restricted grazing and stock control with a suspicion that is understandable. During this controversial period the *Dineh* decided they really had nothing much to discuss with government agents and the Chapter movement was abandoned. It was not revived until 1950.

Because of the stock-reduction controversy, the Navajo Tribal Council came into open conflict with a significant proportion of the Navajo electorate. John Collier urged a reorganization of the council along constitutional lines but that plan was thwarted when, in an 1934 election, the Navajos rejected the Indian Reorganization act—mostly because the Tribal Council urged that they vote for it. Collier continued to advocate Navajo self-government and selected Window Rock, which the Navajos called Tseghah-odzani, as the site for the new Navajo Central Agency. For centuries the great window rock there had been an important Navajo shrine and was one of the four places where Navajo Singers came with their woven water bottles to get water for the Tohee—the Water Way Ceremony. Subsequently the buildings and residences, uniform in design and constructed of russet sandstone quarried in the vicinity, were built there to house the administration offices of the Bureau of Indian Affairs as well as the Navajo tribal governmental buildings. The Navajo Tribal Council Chamber is an immense stone hogan.

In November, 1936, at the urging of Commissioner Collier, the Tribal Council appointed an Executive Committee, headed by Henry Tallman "to call a constitutional assembly for the purpose of considering adopting a constitution and bylaws for the Navajo people." The Assembly, attended by almost 250 Navajos, convened early the next year and drafted a constitution. The constitution was rejected by Secretary Ickes but he did agree to a set of regulations which included election procedures, a definition of organization of the governing body, a statement of its powers and a description of its mode of operation. Finally, in 1938, Secretary Ickes recognized the constitutional assembly as the new Tribal Council and promulgated regulations for its guidance; the new council membership was enlarged to seventy-four delegates from "election communities;" the use of the secret ballot was instigated and the minimum voting age was set at twenty-one years. The regulations issued in 1938 remain today the basis of Navajo tribal government and while they do not constitute exact self-government, *de facto* self-government has existed on the Navajo reservation since the early 1950s.

The new schools that John Collier had promised were build on the reservation and were a vast improvement over the boarding schools. Buses were provided to transport the students from hogan to schoolhouse and the day school program was enthusiastically supported by new Navajo leaders. During World War I, while Navajos were not drafted, many had volunteered and were officially thanked by President Coolidge. It was primarily these veterans, exposed to a prolonged contact with the whites in their world, who realized the advantages to be gained by an education and encouraged support of the new day schools. Too, the fact that the children were returned to the hogan each night and could report any mistreatment they received to their parents was in important factor in making the new schools a success. Unfortunately the road-building program never caught up with the construction of the schools. In the late 1930s there were only a few gravel roads on the reservation; the rest were deeply rutted wagon trails that were all but obliterated by the first rainstorm. The buses often became mired in mud and stayed there for days. The schoolhouses were often empty but at least the Navajos were willing to use them.

Then came World War II and, as had happened during the first World War, the problems of the Navajos were forgotten. The road-construction program was stopped and the buses were removed from the reservation. A few of the day schools, located where they could be reached by children on horseback or by walking, continued to operate but most of them were soon deserted. Not only the schools, but health services and other programs were allowed to deteriorate and there was nothing the Navajo leaders could do to get Washington's attention.

Man-Who-Smells-Moustache (Hitler) commanded the attention of all Americans, including that of the *Dineh*. Navajo men heard about the war on trading post radios and volunteered for the armed services even before the draft. On June 3, 1940, the Navajo Tribal Council unanimously passed a resolution stating that "the Navajo Indians stand ready as they did in 1918 to aid and defend our Government and its institutions against all subversive and armed conflict and pledge our loyalty to the system which recognizes minority rights and a way of life that has placed us among the greatest people of our race."

With the Japanese attack on Pearl Harbor, Navajos, in the tradition of a proud warrior society, flocked to recruiting stations and registration boards, even old men carrying muskets, until there were 3,600 Navajo men serving in the armed forces and a dozen women in the Women's Army Corps. Navajos fought in every theater of the war and the military commanders soon discovered that they could perform a unique service. Their complex language was completely unknown to the enemy and was ideal as a means of sending messages, in place of sending codes. A platoon of Navajo "code talkers" served throughout the Pacific campaign and the Japanese could not break the perplexing "code" that never ceased to confuse them. The Japanese were willing to pay riches to any Navajo willing to defect and teach them the language.

Hundreds of Navajos also moved off the reservation temporarily to help fill the homefront labor vacuum. They worked in the fields and orchards throughout Oregon and California and on the railroads. The military built two large ordnance depots for the manufacture of bombs and grenades near the reservation and employed Navajos both for the construction of the plants and as assembly-line workers. After four years of exposure to the world outside—to new foods, clothing, and foreign life-styles, the Navajo soldiers and workers returned to the reservation with a new appreciation of housing, possessions, money and, most of all, education. They were definitely ready to send their children to school and learn paper. But they found conditions on the reservation, after four years of government neglect, much worse than they had left. The schools were closed and in disrepair. The people who had remained on the reservation were poorer than ever. But now the Navajos, particularly the returning servicemen, knew what to do about the situation. In May, 1946, a delegation of Navajo leaders travelled to Washington to testify before congressional committees. There were, they pointed out, twenty-one thousand Navajo children of school age and less than six thousand were enrolled in all schools, federal, mission and public. In spite of a public outcry for this "group of some seventy thousand Navajos for whom not even necessary school plants existed and who, lacking an education, could not even speak, read and write the national language," Congress was slow in reacting. Several programs were quickly developed to partially satisfy the demand, including an accelerated effort to place more Navajo students in off-reservation boarding schools and to produce quonset hut and trailer schools in the remote areas, but it was only a stopgap measure. The Tribal Council stepped in and appropriated $350,000 to supply school clothing to needy children.

But the lack of schools was not the only, nor the most pressing, problem. The Navajos were starving and for once the press, at least, cared. Details of Navajo poverty were published in newspapers throughout the country. Of course all Navajos were not starving—there were still *ricos*—but many were existing on a diet of fried bread and coffee. Navajo health level lagged almost two generations behind that of the population as a whole. One person in ten had tuberculosis; treatment for trachoma had all but stopped during the war and the disease was on the increase. The hospitals on the reservation could give attention to only about half the people desiring medical aid; the blind, crippled and aged were depending entirely on handouts from relatives who often did not have enough themselves. And there was no place to turn for help. The welfare programs of New Mexico and Arizona did not apply to Indians, not even Indian war veterans. For that matter many of the benefits offered by the G.I. Bill were denied to Indian veterans.

The public responded, sending gifts of food and clothing. But such of the latter was of little use to the Navajos. Ruth Underhill said: "It was strange to see a Navajo woman in a fur coat, mounting her horse to drive a flock of sheep. It was stranger to see the boxes of evening gowns and silver slippers, whose only use was to bring a few dollars from the neighboring Mexicans. The chairman of the council was silent when a package, specially addressed to him, revealed a carefully packaged lipstick. Thus America expressed her understanding of the Indian problem." (Underhill, Oklahoma, 1967: 252.)

It would be two more long decades before America began to make an effort to understand her Indian problem. In the meantime the Navajo leaders and some government officials realized steps had to be taken to relieve the misery of the *Dineh*.

FIVE

The Navajos Help Themselves

The situation in 1947 was not unlike that of 1869 but there was one important difference: the Navajo leaders now knew how to function in a world of white bureaucracy. When Manuelito and Ganado Mucho returned from the Fort Sumner imprisonment their one wish was that The People be left alone to make their own way. But when the World War II veterans returned home they looked around the reservation and compared living conditions to those to which they had been exposed in the outside world—and turned to the federal government: "Where are those schools you promised us in 1868?" they asked. They had fought a war for the United States in which almost four hundred Navajos had died and they asked, "Who are these people in Gallup and Flagstaff who tell us they can't sell a bottle of beer to an Indian? What do these people mean, we can't vote because Indians aren't allowed to vote?"

Manuelito and Ganado Mucho had known only that Navajo children were starving, but the returning veterans knew *why* they were starving and they bombarded Washington with facts and figures. The total per capita yearly income of the Navajos was $82 as compared to the pre-World War II figure for the United States as a whole of

$579, for Arizona, $473, for New Mexico, $359, and for the state with the lowest per capita income, Mississippi, $205. The Navajos paid all federal and most state taxes except the land tax which was negligible for people of low income in Arizona and New Mexico anyway.

The Navajos called on Secretary of the Interior J.A. Krug for help. Krug called for an investigation of every phase of Navajo economics. In March, 1948, he submitted the results of his investigation to the Eightieth Congress. In all of the 25,000 square miles of the reservation, it was revealed, there were only 466 hospital beds, ninety-five miles of paved roads, three restaurants and 763 telephones (almost all of which were located in governmental offices and trading posts). Less than eight hundred Navajos had full-time jobs, while 7,841 reservation residents were on welfare, receiving an average grant of thirteen dollars per month. There were school facilities for only 7,500 students, including some buildings that were in such disrepair that they could not be used. It was determined that the land would never support more than half of the population estimated at about seventy thousand and increasing by a thousand a year. The Navajos, then, would have to be educated to new trades. Small businesses would have to be opened on the reservation—garages, shops, tourist facilities, mines to work the low-grade coal found in several localities, and roads to serve all these. Navajos would have to be encouraged to seek employment off the reservation, but that would mean dispersal. The Navajo leaders remembered John Collier's words, "Dispersal would bring death to the Navajo spirit, the obliteration of the Navajo rainbow forever."

Realizing the land would never support a pastoral economy, the Navajo leaders—people like Sam Ahkeah, Annie Dodge Wauneka, Albert George Sandoval, Paul Jones, Joe and Chabah Davis Watson, and Taylor McKenzie, the first Navajo ever to become a doctor of medicine—decided that if the Navajos were to retain their identity as a people other resources would have to be developed. It was through the efforts of such leaders that the oil and gas, mineral and lumber resources were developed over the next decade which brought wealth to the Navajos as a body corporate. And this was accomplished during a period, from 1950 onward into 1957, when there was an effort, impetuous within Congress, implacable and massive within the Administration, to obliterate John Collier's Indian New Deal and with it the Indian tribes, an effort that succeeded tragically with the Klamaths of Oregon and the Menominees of Wisconsin. But the Navajos resisted as a body; their elected leaders held the tribe intact against overwhelming government pressure to "terminate" while developing every natural resource possible and attracting outside industry to the reservation to furnish Navajos with paying jobs.

Through the concentrated efforts of both the Navajo Tribal Council and the Department of Interior, a long-range, three-purpose program was developed as a result of Secretary Krug's investigation. The program was designed to enable the Navajos to attain economic self-sufficiency through their own efforts; to assist them in becoming healthy and educated citizens, capable of enjoying the full benefits of the society as a whole; and to carry out the legal and moral obligations of the federal government to the Navajo tribe.

Two months after Secretary Krug made his report, Congress appropriated a million dollars for an emergency work relief program for the Navajos and the Hopis. Work was started at once on such projects as the construction of roads, soil conservation structures, irrigation works, and school and hospital repair. The Tribal Council set up facilities for processing employment applications for this project as well as for an off-reservation employment program initiated by the Indian Service which resulted in employment for more than 13,000 Navajos during the summer and fall of 1948 in railroad, agricultural, mining and other types of employment. While most of the work was temporary, it did result in immediate financial relief for many Navajo families.

Then, following a crisis that again brought nationwide attention to the plight of the Navajos and Hopis during the winter of 1949 when severe blizzards isolated families on the western part of the reservation, Congress was moved finally to enact on a program of long-range Navajo and Hopi economic development. On April 19, 1950, the Navajo-Hopi Long Range Rehabilitation Act was passed which called for the appropriation of ninety million dollars over a ten-year period for "a better utilization of the resources of the Navajo and Hopi reservations and for other

454

purposes." The act called for the appropriation of money for: soil and water conservation and range improvements; completion and extension of irrigation projects; surveys of timber, coal, mineral and other resources; development of business and industrial enterprises; relocation and settlement of Navajo and Hopi Indians on the Colorado River Indian Reservation; development of opportunities for off-reservation employment; construction of roads and trails, telephone and radio communication systems, hospital, school and housing facilities and the establishment of a revolving loan fund of five million dollars. It seemed, at last, that the United States was going to make an effort to fulfill its treaty obligations and correct eight years of mismanagement and neglect. While the Act authorized funds to be appropriated, none were allocated in the federal budget until 1955.

In the meantime the Navajo Tribal Council, under the chairmanship of Sam Ahkeah who was elected to that position in 1945, realizing the the *Dineh* would have to meet the government more than halfway, devised several programs to help their people and set them into motion. They hired a legal service and filed a land claim case in an effort to prove that the reservation given them by treaty, including subsequent additions, was far smaller than the lands they once occupied. Finally, after almost twenty years, the Indian Claims Commission rendered its decision on July 29, 1970, in favor of the Navajos. In its decision the Commission determined that the Navajos were entitled to compensation for over twelve million acres of *Old Dineh-tah* taken from them by the treaty of 1868. Compensation, however, was to be based on the 1868 value of the lands.

In spite of the fact that all Indians had been assured of voting privileges since 1924, neither New Mexico nor Arizona allowed the returning World War II veterans and their brethen to vote. Arizona forbade the privilege of the vote to English illiterates and both Arizona and New Mexico had laws against granting the vote to "persons under wardship," which included minors, the insane and, for all practical purposes, Indians. In 1947 the legal service retained by the Navajos launched two test cases, one in Arizona and one in New Mexico, and won them both. Off-reservation and literate Indians were assured of the right to vote in state and federal elections in both states.

In the early 1950s the Navajo Tribal Council, encouraged by its success in dealing with state government and federal bureaucracy, began to show a new spirit of independence. Much to their surprise, trading post proprietors who had been practicing a not always benevolent form of paternalism for eight decades found themselves being asked to pay rent on the land they used. Christian missionary groups, devoutly supported by funds from their home churches, were appalled when they were told the Navajos would give them no land upon which to establish missions.

Instead of waiting for help and advice from the Indian Bureau, as they had done in the past, the Navajos began turning to their own legal counsel, and rather than wait for the financial help promised them by the Long Range Rehabilitation Act, the Navajos appropriated money from Tribal funds and government loans to begin developing reservation resources. Realizing that the excellent stands of marketable timber spread over more than half a million acres in the higher altitudes of the reservation would bring a quick return, the Tribal Council appropriated funds to expand the milling facilities already existing on the reservation. By 1953 the Navajo tribal sawmill was marketing timber at a value in excess of a million dollars yearly and employing about three hundred Navajo workers in the mill and woods operations with an annual payroll of about $675,000. The tribal income and payroll remained at about the same figure for the next decade. In 1958 the Tribal Council appropriated $7.5 million of tribal funds to finance the Navajo Forest Products Industries for further commercial exploitation of Navajo timber. Forestry and lumber experts employed by the tribe now recommend an production of fifty million board feet at the large new mill at Navajo, New Mexico. The industry, wholly owned and operated by the tribe, is making a significant contribution to reservation economy, both individual and tribal, and will finance other wood product industries planned by the Tribal Council.

During World War II a small amount of uranium was mined on the reservation. The advent of the atomic age sent demands for that mineral soaring and prospectors made substantial new discoveries. Income from tribal leases to mining companies jumped from $66,000 in 1950 to $152,000 the next year. Income from mineral leases now brings an average of $1.2 million to the tribal treasury annually.

In 1950 there were only fifty-one producing oil wells on the reservation, producing royalties amounting to $42,000 yearly. The Navajo leaders encouraged the development of new oil fields, which resulted in the Texas Company bringing in a gusher in the Aneth Strip in February, 1956. Other companies rushed to obtain leases from the Tribal Council in the area now known as the Four Corners oil field. Before the end of the year the tribe had received lease-bonus, rental, and royalty payments totaling more than $35 million. Between 1957 and 1970 more than $200 million poured into tribal coffers from the new oil discoveries, and geologists predict that large new fields of gas and oil will still be discovered. In addition to the tribal income, thousands of Navajos have been, and are being, employed in drilling, constructing pipelines, booster stations, power plants, access roads, bridges, buildings and homes for oil company employees.

The income from mineral, oil and other resources enabled the tribe to develop other industries that would employ Navajos as well as bring more income to the tribe. While several of the early "pilot" enterprises were unsuccessful, others such as the Window Rock Coal Mine, the Wingate Village Housing Project, the Tribal Ram Herd, motels, cafes and other tourist facilities and the Arts and Crafts Guild which sells Navajo blankets, silverwork and other craft products, thrived and are now an important source of income.

The Tribal Council, now genuinely representative of the people, is using these scores of millions in varied enterprises toward the betterment of the Navajos as a whole. The conservation and increase of soil, herbage and waters has become a fundamental, practically unrestricted and wholly self-imposed policy. Where several other tribes distributed similar income on a per capita basis with disastrous results, the Navajos invested their revenue from oil, gas, uranium and coal deposits in banks and stocks to draw interest. All funds withdrawn from the tribal capital are earmarked to finance programs to improve the living conditions of all Navajos: for education, improved irrigation farming, toward the manufacture into finished products of the timber holdings, toward protection of the arts and crafts, and toward productive loans to tribal individuals and groups—loans that are practically a hundred percent repaid when due.

Where three decades ago the Navajos were starving, now they own industrial complexes, phone and electric systems, a shopping center, and a considerable stake in the Navajo Irrigation Project which is expected to give them an additional 110,000 acres of fertile farmland, and are in the process of creating a tribal small business administration with the aim of helping more Navajos establish their own businesses. A $10 million balanced scholarship fund was begun in the 1950s to guarantee that every Navajo who qualified for and desired a higher education could attend the college of his choice.

Primarily through their own industry, the *Dineh* have come a long way toward economic recovery. In fact, on the surface it would appear that complete recovery is just a matter of time. Unfortunately that is not the case. The Navajo per capita income in 1974 was only about $1,000, or approximately one-third of the national average, and 40,000 Navajos—a third of the entire tribe—were functional illiterates in English. To a great extent the Bureau of Indian Affairs and many boarding schools still consider Navajo pupils as "culturally deprived children" and design their curriculum with the intent of eradication of the Navajo culture. Socially the Navajos, and especially the children, are still caught between two worlds: in 1970 two Navajo boys ran away from a boarding home and froze to death in the attempt to go home.

SIX

The Navajos Today

In November, 1970, Peter MacDonald was elected Chairman of the Navajo Tribal Council over Raymond Nakai, who was seeking his third term in office. MacDonald, the first college graduate elected to lead his people, was not supported by whites living and working— mostly as government employees—on the reservation nor by politicians and civic leaders in such bordertowns as Gallup, Flagstaff, Winslow and other Anglo centers near the reservation. During his first campaign MacDonald advocated replacing non-Navajo employees of the tribe, and of the BIA, with Navajos. A few months after he took office Anthony Lincoln, himself a Navajo and formerly a BIA Associate Commissioner of Education and Programs in Washington, became the first Navajo to serve as Area Director of the Bureau of Indian Affairs. He was succeeded by Wilson Barber, also a Navajo, and Barber was replaced by James Stevens, a San Carlos Apache, who was holding the office in August, 1989, although under fire and pressure to resign from MacDonald supporters.

Upon taking office, MacDonald began encouraging Navajo college graduates to return to the reservation to teach, take social and tribal service work jobs and to assume positions of leadership that had been traditionally held by whites. An avid supporter of Navajo Community College, MacDonald headed the Office of Navajo Economic Opportunity when that office granted the Navajo Tribe funds with which to establish the college. Navajo Community College was officially founded on July 1, 1968, as the first institution of higher learning in the nation established by and run by Indians—and certainly the first such institution to employ a native "medicine man" to teach Native American traditional ceremonials.

The college opened its doors in temporary quarters at Many Farms on January 20, 1969, with an enrollment of 352 students. NCC was long a dream of a few such far-thinking Navajo leaders as Ned Hatathli and Paul Jones and of Robert A. Roessel Jr., the white educator who served as the school's president during the organizational phase. Once the college was launched, Dr. Roessel retired to become chancellor in order to devote his time raising $15 million for a permanent campus on a high plateau at Tsaile. From the beginning NCC was a project of the Dineh, designed by them to meet needs peculiarly their own.

Dr. Roessel, who arrived on the reservation to teach soon after World War II and stayed on after he married the daughter of a noted singer, has said: "Education has cheated the Navajo (in the past) and cheated them badly.

"For years, the white man's schools—and that is what the Indians called them—have educated the Indianness out of these people, taught the young people that the hogan is dirty, that their parents are ignorant. The result is a group of bleached Indian youth, who are miserable on the reservation but rarely learn to adjust when they leave for the big city. They are neither Anglo nor Indian, but just full of self-hatred." In pointing out the failure of the schools run by the bureau of Indian Affairs, Dr. Roessel said, "Every year the top students from these schools, the cream of the crop, are awarded college scholarships by the tribe and every year 90% of this 'cream of the crop' have flunked out of college. They return, directionless, unskilled, to a reservation where most jobs are held by Anglos imported by the federal government, and they end up drunk in Gallup, New Mexico."

It was precisely the failure of the schools available to

the Navajos that gave impetus to the founding of Navajo Community college. The forerunner of the college was Rough Rock Demonstration School, financed by the Navajo Office of Economic Opportunity and directed by Dr. Roessel, Rough Rock quickly became a showplace of Native American education.

Dr. Roessel brought the concepts developed at Rough Rock to Navajo Community College. The pioneering staff of the school visited the reservation chapter houses to find out what Navajos wanted taught, and as a result the experimental curriculum offers a diverse course of study, from chemistry to Navajo silver-smithing, from computer sciences to modern agricultural prac-tices. The college has become a mecca for Navajo talent. The first Navajo ever to receive a Ph.D. returned home to teach courses in agriculture and soil chemistry. The staff has included renowned Navajo silversmiths and young Navajo artists and craftsmen. Paul Jones, Navajo historian and a former tribal council chairman, held the seat of distinguished professor of Navajo Culture and History until his death. With instruction provided at various points around the reservation and a second campus at Shiprock, NCC (now Dine College) remains close to the people and emphasis is placed on what is usable—an old Navajo concept—whether it is vocational training which about two-thirds of the students choose, or solid academic subjects that will provide transfer credits toward an advanced degree. Jerold Judd, a young professor of biology who grew up on the reservation with his white trader parents, once said: "Our students demand the relevant. They want skills that will pay off, because they've seen educated Indians before who were still jobless despite their education." This is one school that is enthusiastically supported by the Navajos, even conservative "longhairs" who never received any education. The same cannot be said for Navajo—or American Indian or, for that matter, national education. The state of public education is a matter of deep concern to American educators. However, Navajo education presents a very unusual set of problems, problems that are of deep concern to Navajo elders and tribal leaders. As we have seen, and it wasn't too long ago, Navajo children were snatched up, taken away to boarding schools, forbidden to speak their language and taught that their elders were ignorant and there was something shameful about being Indian. As official policy, that no longer happens. It still happens, however. In some schools it is far more convenient to encourage the eradication of a student's Indian heritage than for school officials and teachers to learn to deal with it.

The tribal council was originally a creation of the Department of the Interior, specifically to conduct the business affairs of the tribe in, more or less, a legal manner under the direction of a "Commissioner of the Navajos" who had supervisory authority over the council. What the Commissioner actually had was virtually autocratic power over the decisions of the tribal council when it came to making leases and doing business with off reservation companies. Early leases with such companies as Gulf Oil, General Electric and DuPont were grossly unfair to the Navajo people and, as we shall see, so were leases to mine the coal that lies under Black Mesa forged between Peabody Coal Company and the Navajo and Hopi tribal councils between 1964 and 1966.

By the terms of the Treaty of 1868 "Three fourths of all adult male Indians" were required to approve leases. However, once the BIA created the "tribal business council" in 1923, that requirement was skirted and it took only a majority of council members to approve a lease. Eventually the office of "Commissioner of the Navajos" was gotten rid of. Interior, however, continued to play an important role in tribal council decisions well into the 1970s. The leases signed with Peabody Coal Company in the 1960s were for a term of thirty-five years. The catch was, Peabody agreed to pay the tribe only thirty-seven and one-half cents a ton for the coal. The value of the coal mined by Peabody at Black Mesa in 1980 was $311,300,000. Royalty paid to the tribe came to a mere $5,900,000!

The Navajos sold an unrenewable resource far too cheaply. The error was compounded when, in 1968, the Navajo and Hopi tribal councils agreed to allow the Black Mesa pipeline to mine water in order to move the coal to the power plants. Each day since then the approximately 40-50 tons of coal is ground to power, mixed with water and pumped to a power plant. The pipeline is sucking up over ten acre feet of water a day for which they pay

$7.50 an acre foot. A Los Angeles household—and much of the coal taken from Black Mesa eventually ends up as energy for Los Angeles—would pay over $500 per acre foot in 1986! So while the tribe is selling Black Mesa Pipeline Company water at $7.50 per acre foot, some Navajos are paying as much as $7,710 for the same amount of water (Source: Between Sacred Mountains, 1982, p. 237).

The lease with Peabody Coal allowed the mining company the right to build roads and buildings but required that Peabody repair the land destroyed by strip mining except for such damage done "for the normal wear, tear, and depletion incident to mining."

Peabody's interpretation—and especially in the early years before national attention was brought to the problem—was loose, to say the least. Grazing lands were dug up and piles of rock were left where grass, trees and even springs had once existed; hogans were bulldozed as part of "the normal wear, tear, and depletion incident to mining" and the people who lived in them were told to take their problems to the tribal government. These people were not paid for the land on which they'd lived for generations. Many of them had welcomed Peabody in the beginning, having been promised that the operation would bring lots of jobs to the area. Peabody did hire both Navajos and Hopis but they could not, of course, hire everyone.

Finally, in 1977 a federal law, one for which MacDonald and other tribal leaders lobbied, was passed that required the mining company to repair the land and make it useful for grazing again. However, much of the land is still in need of repair and reclamation work has been a hit and miss proposition.

In the 1950s more than 150 uranium mines were opened in four areas of Dinehtah; in the Chuska Mountains, in Monument Valley, in the Tuba City area, and near Shiprock. No safety regulations were enforced or even required. Dozens of former miners have died of a form of lung cancer that was virtually unknown among the Navajos but not uncommon to workers in European mines.

Then, in the 1960s, mines began closing, leaving behind open pits and tunnels, and milllions of tons of radioactive sand and rock. No one told the Navajos that the sand and rock were dangerous and for the next twenty years children played on and in the sand and builders mixed it in cement and used the rock for the construction of housing. Winds, especially in the Shiprock area, spread the radioactive sand over a wide area. It's still there. So are the many tunnels and pits. So is an appalling increase in cancer and birth defects.

The mining companies—at least those mining companies—are gone and with them is gone the responsibility that they denied was theirs in the first place.

The Four Corners Power Plant which, in the 1960s, was the world's largest coal-fired power plant, was built with no air pollution controls; they were not required. For years it pumped 250 tons of soot and 450 tons of smog-causing gases into the sky each and every day. Smoke from the Four Corners plant was, in fact, the last man-made thing the first astronauts were able to see from space. The smoke and smog are still visible from commerical flights flying at 35,000 feet over the area. The air pollution from the Navajo Power Plant southeast of Page, Arizona, on the reservation, is so bad that it is greatly affecting the Grand Canyon. At times the air is so laden with smog that it is impossible to see the ten miles across the canyon. Careless mining and oil exploration have brought the Navajo—and all of us—untold loss in dollars, man hours, and, most important, lives. For them, as a people, it has been tragic. In the 1970s at Church Rock, north and east of Gallup, a carelessly built dam at the United Nuclear Corporation mill broke, sending 95 million gallons of water and 1100 tons of mud, all radioactive, through the several Navajo communities that lay to the southwest of the Puerco and Little Colorado rivershed. A few years ago I wrote ''some friends of mine who live on the Puerco south of Lupton were hauling water for the sheep several years later, not trusting the flow of the river with very good reason.''

Well, two of my friends who lived there aren't living anymore. They were sisters, two young, vital, intelligent women, Ruth Morgan Green and Ninabah Morgan Cahn. Perhaps there is no connection to the Puerco spill but Ninabah certainly thought so as early as 1982 when Ruth was diagnosed with cancer. And she made her feelings known all the way from her local Chapter House to Washington, D. C. Ruth, an anthropologist and a lovely, kind woman, died of cancer two years later. Ninabah was Director, Navajo Tribal Resources, when she died in the spring of 1989. Also of cancer. They were barely past forty years of age.

Just as the Iranian hostage situation brought down President Jimmy Carter in 1980, something called "Navajo Relocation" served as the instrument of Peter MacDonald's first fall in 1982.

Public Law 93-531 was passed by Congress in 1974—a Congress that was distracted by Watergate, a resigning president and the energy crisis. This law, known as the "Relocation Act" called for the division of land that had been jointly used by the Hopi and Navajo for at least a century and there is considerable evidence to suggest that the two peoples were co-existing on the land for at least three centuries before that. The consequences of PL 93-531 was an order to remove or "Relocate" nearly 10,000 Navajos and 109 Hopis from their homes. The Hopi reservation was created in 1882 by an Executive order. It implied Hopi title to their sacred mesas and the surrounding farmlands and hunting areas they had traditionally used. Around that roughly diamond-shaped area an additional 4,000 square mile rectangle was set aside for "the use of the Hopi and...other Indians."

The Navajos already living there certainly understood that "other Indians" included them; however some whites described in the records as "troublemakers" were also living in the area. They were removed but the Navajos were left alone. Then, in 1888 and again in 1889, the military refused to carry out specific requests by the Secretary of the Interior to remove Navajos from the area. A boundary established in 1881 was worked out by an Indian agent and a trader who, with the cooperation of both Hopi and Navajo leaders from the area, walked from spot to spot, placing stone boundary markers that are still visible to this day.

The line that resulted encircled the mesas occupied by the Hopis and the surrounding farmlands, an area of approximately 600,000 acres. At that time the Hopis agreed not to cross over into the Navajo area and Navajos, in turn, promised not to build homes, graze livestock or disturb the Hopi area. The boundary, known as the Parker-Keam line, was acceptable to both Hopis and Navajos and was

465

drawn by government agents with the knowledge and consent of the Commissioner of Indian Affairs. The area reserved for the Hopis corresponds roughly to the boundaries that existed up until 1962. On at least three subsequent actions by the courts and various commissions, the Navajos' right to use the land (in one case only the land surface) was upheld.

Says Dr. Edgar S. Cahn, author of Our Brothers Keepers: The American Indian and the Law: "in the 1930s, the Secretary of the Interior and the Commissioner of Indian Affairs engaged in so many explicit actions, drawing and enforcing boundary lines that essentially followed the Parker-Keam line of 1891 that the Court (Healing v. Jones, 1962) had to admit that these actions amount to settlement by the Secretary.

"The Court got around the issue of Hopi acquiescence (over the past eighty years) to the pervasive use and occupancy by the Navajos of the remainder of the Joint Use Area (JUA) by characterizing the Navajos as bullies who intimidated the Hopis to stay within the Parker-Keam line which the two tribes had established collaboratively. Once the Court concluded that the Hopis had never abandoned claim to the land even though they had never used or occupied it, and had consistently resisted all governmental efforts to woo them off the mesas and onto the surrounding territory, then the Court reasoned that settlement of the Navajos merely gave each tribe joint use of the entire area. From there, the Court proceeded to determine that joint use necessarily meant equal use—with one exception; the area that had always been exclusively occupied by the Hopis. The Navajos never got joint rights to that area. So the Hopis got to keep 100% of what they had always occupied—and 50% of what the Navajos had always occupied."

There, in the 1962 court decision known as Healing v. Jones, you have, in a nut shell, the story of the roots of PL 93-531. Subsequently, in 1974, Congress ordered that the land be divided. Nearly 10,000 Navajos and 109 Hopis found themselves living on the wrong side of the fence.

The result has been an unmitigated disaster.

For a detailed telling of the story of the "Relocation Act" and background material, I recommend a reading of Jerry Kammer's *The Second Long Walk* (New Mexico, 1981).

In 1982, as a member of an ad hoc committee on the relocation problem, I interviewed members of an extended family who had been "relocated" from their ancestral home at Big Mountain, north of the Hopi mesas, to Winslow, Arizona, the year before. This was one of the families the relocation committee considered to be prepared for relocation off the reservation because the younger members were not "traditionalists" and they all spoke English. Too, the son-father-husband breadwinner of the family had been employed by a power company off the reservation for sixteen years prior to the removal of the family.

To begin with, the old folks refused to leave. The hogan, the homeplace, is sacred to the Navajo. It is their Holy Place. To leave the hogan and the land around it is to leave all that is sacred and true behind. "Let them fence the land, let them take away the sheep as they have done, and the goats owned by the old people," I was told. "But they cannot take away again what we are and to remove us from this land would do that. It happened once; it will not happen again."

The son, wife and grandchildren moved to Winslow and lived in a motel until a house was found for them. The two teenage daughters had always done well in reservation schools but they quickly found the "white" school in Winslow unbearable. When I interviewed the family they had lived in Winslow less than a year but the daughters—excellent students, ambitious and happy only the year before—had dropped out of school and were working as motel maids.

Others have fared worse. Many, including old people, were moved to track homes in "white" towns near the reservation and especially to Flagstaff.

These people were farmers and herders; most of the old ones and some of the younger ones did not speak English and only understood enough to get by on the reservation. They had no way of knowing how to function in such places; they didn't even know how to take care of the simple business of paying utility bills. And since the government had provided them with new housing, a sort of housing that was as foreign to most of them as a hogan would be to a family in Cleveland, Ohio, but not the means of supporting themselves, a great many soon found themselves in debt.

Burning found wood in the hogan during the winter and having the sheep to fall back on when money is scarce is one thing, but burning energy of the sort for which Black Mesa is being destoryed and having to pay utility bills and buy all foodstuff at the store is entirely another.

In short, many of these people and especially the elderly were simply dumped in nearby towns to fend for themselves. By the summer of 1986 one third of those relocated had died.

For what reason? What is this all about, one might ask. Certainly it is *hoped* one might ask that. To begin with you must go back to a Utah lawyer named John Boyden. Boyden left his job with the Department of the Interior in 1946 and sought employment with the Navajo tribe. Turned down, he next tried the Hopis and, as Edgar Cahn put it, "from that time on, things changed radically. He first became concerned about the mineral wealth which might lie under the grazing districts used by the Navajo. He sought a determination that severed the surface rights from the sub-surface mineral rights of the Navajo grazing land. Boyden was smart; he hired a Salt Lake City law firm and a public relations firm from the same city and mounted a campaign that resulted in what Peter MacDonald once referred to as 'the massive assault of Healing v. Jones.'"

The eight years that followed—1962 to 1970—were crucial. The Hopis, at least that fraction of the Hopis who had control of the tribal government, their leadership mostly Mormon converts and therefore not considered "true" or representative leaders by traditional Hopis, were organized and ready. And Boyden knew his way around Washington and the halls of Congress. Boyden also knew about the energy interests—as he was also an attorney for Peabody Coal. Certain "myths" as they were referred to later by Peter MacDonald, were circulated and made their way in print, some of which were prepared as "give away" news features prepared by the Salt Lake City public relations firm. Among those were seemingly well-researched articles that offered "proof" that the Navajos were recent arrivals in the Southwest; that this was a land battle between the Navajo and the Hopi; that the Navajo portion of the JUA being given to the Hopi was essential to the preservation of their religion and, the most telling and destructive of all, the Navajos were depicted as rich, greedy bullies picking on the poor defenseless Hopis.

Meanwhile, the Navajos did hardly anything to present their side of the story. "The eight years that followed that decision (Healing v. Jones), 1962-70, were years of paralysis, compounded by the internal division and strife between the former chairman (Raymond Nakai) and our former general counsel, Norman Littel." In that speech made before a special session of the Navajo Tribal Council on May 27, 1981, MacDonald called on "the total mobilization" of the Navajo people in seeking to reverse the Relocation Act. It was too late for MacDonald. Through no fault of his own Navajos were already being "relocated." His Hopi counterpart, Chairman Abbott Sekaquaptewa held what appeared to be a winning hand even though he stood accused by most Navajo and a fraction of traditionalist-minded Hopi as speaking for non-Indian interests rather than the Hopi people.

From the outset, the traditional leaders of the Hopi opposed the mining of Black Mesa by Peabody Coal and the legislation authorizing the relocation of the Navajos. The following is from a committee report to the Hopi Kikmongwis (traditional religious and governmental leaders who do not recognize the tribal council as a representative governmental body): "We want to meet with the Navajo Traditional and religious Headmen to work out a common stand against this bill which will again cut up our homeland and create more division. We want the Navajo Elders to sit down with us to look seriously into our Way of Life, Religion and Land in the light of our traditional and religious knowledge. We want no interference from outside people until we come up with a solution among ourselves as the First People on this land. We do not want any more cutting up of our Sacred Homeland by anyone."

The traditional Hopi also do not want anyone—anyone— digging into the earth for coal and other minerals. They look upon the Black Mesa mining operation as a profane and blasphemous piece of business. Which is probably why, as a Navajo friend put it, "No one pays any attention to them."

The report continues: "As far as the Navajo people

are concerned, it is our position that they be allowed to remain within the Hopi traditional land area as long as they do not disturb the tranquility of the Hopi people. . .the Navajo and Hopi people have lived side by side for generations and our roots are deep within the land on which we live.

"It seems to us a better solution would be for the Congress to exercise its combined wisdom and refrain from interfering into the domestic relationship of the Navajo and Hopi people.

"The day is long past, it seems to us, that the white man should try to impose its (sic) own solutions to our domestic so-called problems.

"The Hopi traditional people do not see this as a problem. It is the Hopi Council who have created this so-called problem among the Navajo and the Hopi people. It is they and their servants who have been impounding the sheep of the Navajo people. It is they who have painted such distorted pictures of the Navajo people in the press. It is they who are trying to divide the traditional Hopi land area and reduce it for their own reasons.

"We, the Hopi traditional people, do not support these unfortunate measures of the council and we wish to make it absolutely clear that we will not bear any responsibility for any consequences which may result from such ruthless behavior.

"In fact, we want to suggest to the council that they cease forthwith from their irresponsible behavior toward our Navajo neighbors."

Of course no one was "paying attention." At last count the cost of "relocation" had risen from the original estimate of $34 million to over $700 million.

To "relocate" 10,000 Navajos and 109 Hopis. . .at least half of whom are Navajo-Hopi mixed bloods by at least one educated estimate?

Two or three thousand Navajos, mostly living in the Big Moutain area north of the Hopi mesas, just refused to move. Many are still there in the summer of 1992 and the Hopi tribal council has extended the time, for that few, indefinitely.

EPILOGUE

In his initial campaign for the tribal council chairman office, Peter MacDonald promised the Navajos a "new era of self-determination." Even his most adamant detractors would have to admit, in all fairness, he proved to be an effective advocate for the Navajos. Between his first term in office, beginning in 1970, and his being ousted by Peterson Zah in 1982, he persuaded the Bureau of Indian Affairs to turn over authority of some agencies (that were being badly run and which employed far too few Navajos) to the tribe; got the federal government to build roads, sewers and housing on the reservation and fought a good uphill battle to improve the employment situation for his people. He set up a $30 million industrial development fund, persuaded General Dynamics to make electronic missile assemblies in a plant to be constructed by the tribe, and was the leader in such disparate tribal ventures as finding new markets for the tribal lumber industry, entering the computer software market, launching a Shiitake mushroom growing business, and the development of a luxury resort on the reservation. Re-elected again in 1986, he immediately launched a campaign to find new sources of income for the Navajo people.

My personal view, at the time was that MacDonald was most

effective in dealing with federal and state bureaucracy, a difficult bunch for anyone. MacDonald was just as effective in the board-rooms of the large corporations he courted for Navajo jobs. He dealt with Bilagaana politicians and company executives on their own ground and often used his "Indianness" to grab an advantage. In dealing with the outside world he was an excellent chief exec-utive for the Navajo Nation. However, he was less effective in dealing with his own people. His tendency to lose touch with the people—either through arrogance or by paying for some bad advice—cost him his office in 1982. I was there most of the sum-mer of 1982, doing field research with Navajo aides, when MacDonald was being opposed by Peterson Zah and Larry Issacs, Jr. I was in constant touch with several of MacDonald's close advisors, and also out in the field interviewing people. I heard—and overheard—people talking. There was a "dump MacDonald and his three piece suit" mood going around. I suggested to one of his attorneys they'd best get the chairman into a traditional velvet shirt and some turquoise if they wanted to beat Zah, because the people I talked to felt he'd lost touch with the electorate. Eventually MacDonald put on the velvet and turquoise but it was too late: Zah, a likable and able man but lacking in MacDonald's skills in handling the Bilagaana bureaucrats, won the election and served four capable years; only to be defeated by MacDonald in 1986..

Early in 1989 MacDonald was accused of profiting from a labyrinthine $33.4 million land deal whereby he and associates supposedly purchased the 491,000 acre Boquillas Ranch in Arizona for $26.2 million and immediately sold it to the tribe for a $7.2 million profit. When the land deal was revealed and the chairman was accused of numerous other cases of mishandling the tribe's money—including receiving payoffs from contractors—charges were filed. In the summer of 1989 the tribal council put Chairman MacDonald on paid leave. However, he refused to "go quietly" and his supporters called in members of the militant American Indian Movement (AIM, lead by Russell Means) to stage protests. Two men were killed during the protests. Means, who is not a citizen of the Navajo nation, tried to place then BIA area director, James Stevens under citizen's arrest; charges and counter charges flew back and forth.

In early 1992 MacDonald was brought to trial on the Navajo Nation counts, found guilty of several charges and sentenced to nearly seven years in jail. He was furloughed to prepare for his federal trial. On May 27 he was convicted by a federal jury of 16 counts of conspiracy, fraud and accepting bribes.

The entire MacDonald affair had a detrimental effect on the Navajo Nation. It eventually became a bone of contention that disrupted government, schools and families. The real losers were the Navajo people.

Peterson Zah again took over as tribal council chairman and, again, during a time of healing. Again, he served his people well. In all candor, I must admit that since 1992, I have been too far removed from Navajo politics to offer comment. I visit and see my friends, attended some social functions, and always leave feeling better for the experience.

While it is true that the Navajo Nation is the largest and one of the richest Native American tribes in the United States, it is also true that if all tribal income from natural resources—oil, gas, coal and so forth—credited to the Navajo account in the federal treasury was distributed on a per capita basis, each Navajo would receive less than $200 per year. Not only whites but other Indians think of the Navajos as being infinitely better off then they are. Unemployment in the Navajo Nation is over twice the national average.

Today's Navajo leaders believe that education is the answer and efforts are being made on all levels to keep Navajo children in school and in aiding them to get a higher education. A proposed alliance of educational institutions and industry would enable Navajo and Hopi students to remain in college and, hopefully, successfully graduate. "Forming an alliance such as this will not result in a hand-out but a helping hand in keeping Indian students in school," Zah said at a meeting held at Northern Arizona University in June, 1992. Officials from NAU, Navajo College, national research laboratories, and industries met to discuss competency in math and science and helping Navajo and Hopi students graduate from college. Said Zah: "The Navajo Nation invests a tremendous amount of money to send our students to school—almost $8 million a year. We need industry to meet us halfway so we can graduate more of our young people rather than having them drop out." The proposal created by the Office of Native American Programs at NAU states the need for a skilled and educated work force for the employers operating on and near the Hopi and Navajo reservations.

Similar programs have succeeded in the past. Many of the problems faced by today's Navajo people are the same as those confronting people everywhere: unemployment or under employment, drug use among both adults and young people, far too many students dropping out of school, etc. However, during recent visits, I noted a greatly improved attitude among young people. And I know teenagers and recent college graduates that I've known all of their lives. Self-image seems to have improved, along with the determination to seek a higher education, and improved living conditions among both the Navajo and the Hopi.

I cannot leave here without a salute to some of my heroes: Those 420 Navajo men who became known as "Code Talkers" during the World War 11 Pacific Campaign against Japan. Speaking Navajo, which the Japanese could not decode, Navajo soldiers were instrumental in in winning the war against Japan; the battles at Guadalcanal, Guam, and especially Iwo Jima. My favorite of the many books done on the subject is **Warriors: Navajo Code Talkers** by Kanji Kawano, Kenji Kawano and the late Carl Gorman, who became an outstanding and respected Navajo leader in the decades after the war. Most of the Code Talkers took over leadership positions upon their return home, and it was due to their influence that great social, economic and educational strides were made in the decades after the war. Ironically, the country, and the world, did not know about their heroics officially until 1969, when their work was officially declassified by the U. S. government.

The surviving Code Talkers banded themselves into a remarkable brotherhood that has, over the years, worked for the betterment of all Navajo, including offering college scholarships and travel grants to deserving young Navajos. Recently at Northern Arizona University, R. C. Gorman dedicated his life size bronze of his father, Carl, to the lasting memory of the Code Talkers.

INDEX

Hogan
  female and male, 13
  sweat hogan, 14
  as sacred place, 15
Holbrook, 289
Holt, Nicholas, 343-44
Holy People, 33-34, 46-47
Honesty, N. concept, 32
Hopi Indians
  Navajo neighbors on west, 392
  origin, 11
  peace with the N., 181-82
  raids on the N., 353
  resistance to Spaniards, 175-79
  Simonson expedition, 327
  white god legend, 139-40
Hopi Kikmongwis, 471
Horses
  on American continent, xii-xiv
  Navajo acquisition, 163
  Navajo skill with, 29, 206
House Committee on Indian
    Affairs, 439
Hozoniji (blessing rite), 23
Hubbell, Charles, 422
Hubbell, John Lorenzo, 422, 425
Herfano Mesa (Dzil'na'oodilii),
    77-78, 107-09, 113, 115,
    130-31
Huerro
  attack on hay camp, 331
  council with Simonson, 326
  Ft. Defiance blacksmith, 317
  Laguna Negra council, 328
  peace efforts, 327
  peace request, 338
  surrender, 361
de Human, Antonio Guiterrez,
    154
Humor of the N., ix, 22, 27-28
Hunter, John, 441
Ickes, Harold, 433, 438, 448
Imprisonment,
  See Fort Sumner
Incest, N. attitude, 20

Inheritance laws, 18
Intermountain Indian School, 461
Irvine, Alex G., 403
Isaacs, Lawrence Jr., *xvi*, 462
Jackson, Alexander M., 341
Jackson, Congreve, 211
James, Thomas, 189-90
Janos, 184
Jemez
  abandonment, 163
  Backus-Miles expedition, 315
  captive from, 250
  defeat by Spaniards, 178
  murder of N. emissaries, 189
  Navajo agency at, 272
  in Navajo legend, 133
  Navajo attacks, 217, 257
  Newby expedition, 218
  Pelado Peak, 8
  slave raiders from, 192
  treaty proposal, 270
  Washington expedition, 240
Jemez Indians, 163, 175, 178
Jewelry,
  See Silversmithing
Jironza Petriz de Cruzate,
    Domingo, 174
Joint Use Area (JUA), 469
Johnson, Andrew, 378
  Barboncito plea, 382
  Bosque Redondo Treaty, 391
  denunciation of slavery, 373
Johnson, Sylvester, 334
Johnson, Hezikiah, 275
Johnson, William R., 427
Jones, Paul, 453, 461, 462
Jones, Roger, 239, 253, 261, 266
Jones, W.A., 426
Jose Largo, 218, 242-43, 245
Jose Mangas, 301
Juanico, 323, 330-32
Juarz, 156
Judd, Jerold, 461
Jumano Pueblos, 158
Kammer, Jerry, 470

Navajos forbidden to trade
with, 399
Navajo raids on, 393-94, 397
source of weapons, 304, 314
Mother-in-law jokes, ix, 22
Mount Blanca (Tsisnaajini), 68,
77, 113
Mount Hesperus (Dibentsaa),
68, 78, 113
Mount Palonia, 292
Mount Taylor (Tsoodzil, Tsotsil)
Dinetah boundary, 8
first N.-Spanish contact at, 154
in N. mythology, 68, 77,
113-15
Navajo love for, 387
Spanish military site at, 185-86
Spanish missions near, 183
Mount Taylor Navajos
See Dinehanaih
Mountain Top Way, 48
Muerto de Hombre, 403
Munroe, John, 256, 259
Murder
of Brooks' slave, 306-07
of Henry Linn Dodge, 300-02
of Mangus Colorados, 349
of Mexican slave, 308-09, 312
of Narbona, 239, 243-47
of N. emissaries, 189
of Ramon Martin, 275-78, 280
Murphy, Lawrence, 355
Mythology of the N., 46-51,
55-136
See also Ceremonials

Naachid (definition), 195, 306
Naachid
at Canyon de Chelly, 306
resemblance to chapter
organization, 441
at Tsin Sikaad, 318-19, 323
Naahondzond (definition), 303
Naatani (definition), 200

Naatsis'aan, 77-78
Nadene language family, 26
Naidikisi (younger Hero Twin),
115, 123-25
Nakai, Raymond, 459,
Names
Indian names forbidden, 417
Navajo system of, 24-25
war names, 24
Narbona
Chaves massacre, 193
Doniphan treaty, 211
meeting with Reid, 205
murder of, 239, 243-47, 253
Newby treaty, 218, 237
peace desires, 238
peace efforts, 194, 203
respected headman, 186, 200
son of, 297
Washington Pass massacre, 192
wife of, 205-06
Narbona, Antonio, 186-87
Narvaez, Panfilo, 144
Naschiti Trading Post, 241
Nataallith,
See Zarcillos Largos
Nature, N. attitude toward, 31
de Nava, Pedro, 35
Navajo (New Mexico), 456
Navajo (origin of the name),
163-64
Navajo Canyon, 446
Navajo Community College, 38,
459-62, 464
Navajo Forest Products
Industries,
456
Navajo Irrigation Project, 458
Navajo Language
children forbidden to speak,
417-18
origin and characteristics,
26-27
use in World War II, 449
Navajo Mountain

Peabody Coal Company, 462 f.
Pecos pueblo, 151-52, 176, 178
Pedro Jose, 245
Pelado Peak, 8
Pelon, 304
de Penalosa, Diego, 166
Pentecostal Churches, 414
de Peralta, Don Pedro, 159-60
Peralta (New Mexico), 345
Perkins, J.D., 409, 411-12
Pheiffer, Albert W.
    Carson campaign, 356, 359,
        361
    support of Carleton, 347
    support of slavery, 305, 337
    Ute agent, 303, 324, 335
Philipp III, King of Spain, 159
Picuris, 175, 178-79
Pierce, Franklin, 275, 279
Pino, Don Pedro Bautista, 200
Pino, Nicholas, 345
Pinon, 462
Plummer, Edwin H., 10, 414
Police force, Navajo, 397-98
Polk, James Knox, 200-02
Pope, 167-68
Population of the N.
    at Bosque Redondo, 364, 366,
        371, 380, 382
    estimates of, 318, 327, 362,
        402, 458
    unemployment among, 464
Pottery, 44
Prayer of the Dawn, 50
Presbyterians, 407-09, 411-12
Property,
    See Reservation of the N.
Property ownership, xi, 5, 17-18
Public Health Service, 441
Public Law 93.531, 466 f.
Pueblo Bonito, 34, 432
    See also Chaco Canyon
Pueblo Indians (Kisani)
    attacks on the N., 304, 329,
        336, 339-40

cliff dwellings and pueblos,
9-11
    early N. relations, x, xi, 12
    early Spanish relations, 144,
        149-51
    in N. myths, 64, 66-67, 72,
        75-77, 81-82
    resistance to Spaniards, 177
    revolt against Spaniards,
        167-70, 182
    Spanish reconquest, 171-80
    slave raids by, 337, 353
    weaving skills, 12, 34
    See also Anasazi
Puerco River, 466
Pyle, John C., 420
Querechos, 144, 152, 154
Quetzalcoatl, 140-41
Rabal, Codallos y, 35
Raids,
    See Livestock raids
        Slave raiding
Railroads, 401, 421
Reed, Hiram, 258
Reid, Captain, 204-06
Religion of the N., 45-51
    See also Ceremonials
            Navajo Way
            Rites
Rencher, Abraham, 304, 333,
341
Reneros de Posada, Pedro, 174
Reservation of the N.
    boundary changes, 401-02,
410,
        426-29, 432-33
    compensation for lost lands,
        455
    establishment, 384-86
    railroads on, 401, 421
    reorganization, 439
    See Dinetah
    See Grazing lands of the N.
    See Mineral resources
    See Oil on N. lands